Northern
Plains

2007

Montana

North Dakota

South Dakota

Wyoming

ExxonMobil
Travel Publications

Acknowledgements

We gratefully acknowledge the help of our representatives for their efficient and perceptive inspections of the lodging and dining establishments listed; the establishments' proprietors for their cooperation in showing their facilities and providing information about them; and the many users of previous editions who have taken the time to share their experiences. Mobil Travel Guide is also grateful to all the talented writers who contributed entries to this book.

www.mobiltravelguide.com

Front cover photo: Mount Rushmore, Grand Tetons, Bison in Yellowstone National Park by Shutterstock

The information contained herein is derived from a variety of third-party sources. Although every effort has been made to verify the information obtained from such sources, the publisher assumes no responsibility for inconsistencies or inaccuracies in the data or liability for any damages of any type arising from errors or omissions.

Neither the editors nor the publisher assumes responsibility for the services provided by any business listed in this guide or for any loss, damage, or disruption in your travel for any reason.

ISBN: 0-7627-4262-3 or 978-0-7627-4262-2

ISSN: 1550-1930

Manufactured in the United States of America.

10 9 8 7 6 5 4 3 2 1

Contents

MAP SYMBOLS

TRANSPORTATION

CONTROLLED ACCESS HIGHWAYS

Freeway
Tollway
Under Construction
Interchange and Exit Number

OTHER HIGHWAYS

Primary Highway
Secondary Highway
Divided Highway
Other Paved Road
Unpaved Road
Check conditions locally

HIGHWAY MARKERS

Interstate Route
U.S. Route
State or Provincial Route
County or Other Route
Trans-Canada Highway
Canadian Provincial Autoroute
Mexican Federal Route

OTHER SYMBOLS

Distances along Major Highways
Miles in U.S.; kilometers in Canada and Mexico
Tunnel; Pass
Auto Ferry; Passenger Ferry

RECREATION

National Park
National Forest; National Grassland
Other Large Park or Recreation Area
Small State Park
with and without Camping
Military Lands
Indian Reservation
Trail
Ski Area
Point of Interest

CITIES AND TOWNS

National Capital
State or Provincial Capital
Cities, Towns, and Populated Places
Type size indicates relative importance
Urban Area
State and province maps only
Large Incorporated Cities
City maps only

OTHER MAP FEATURES

Time Zone Boundary
Mt. Olympus Mountain Peak; Elevation
7,965 in Feet
Perennial; Intermittent River

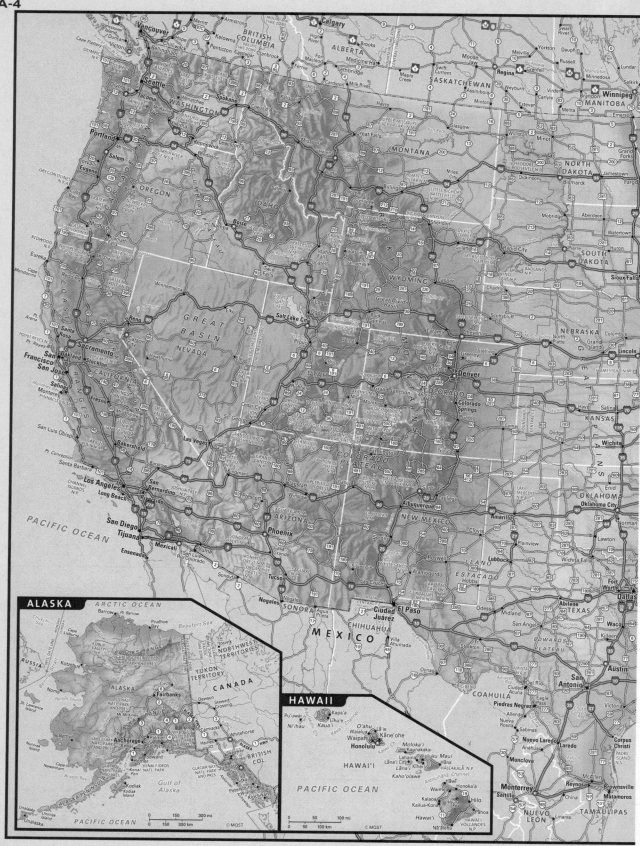

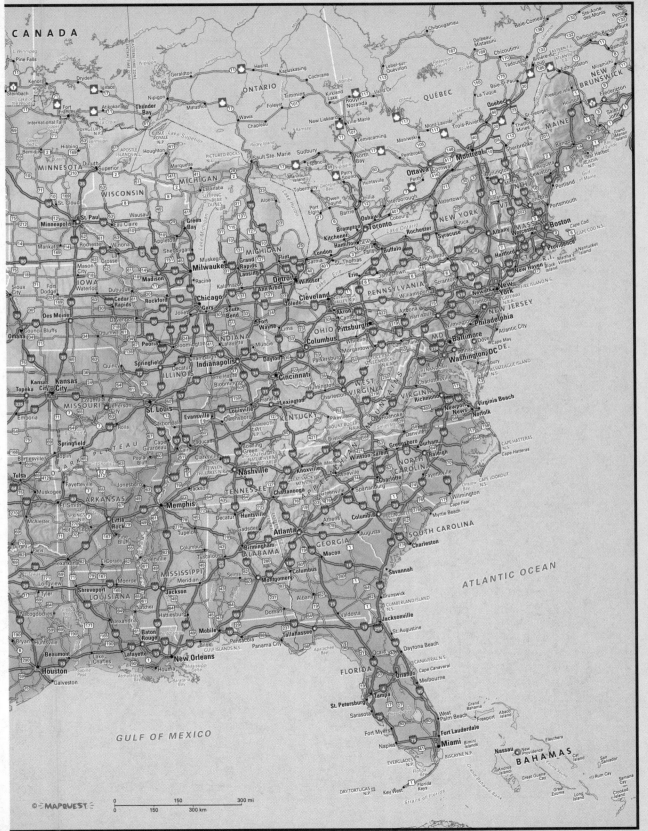

© MAPQUEST

0   150   300 mi
0   150   300 km

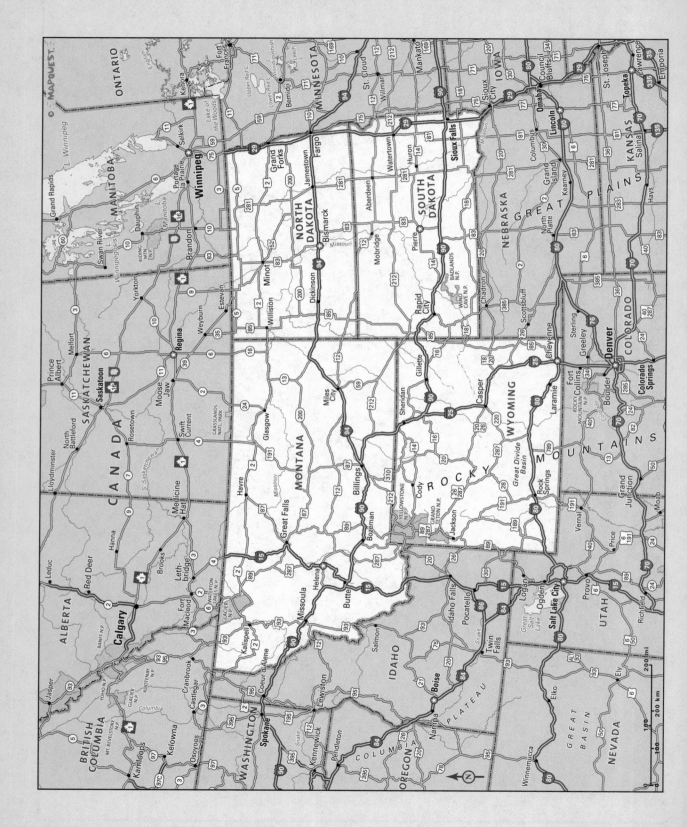

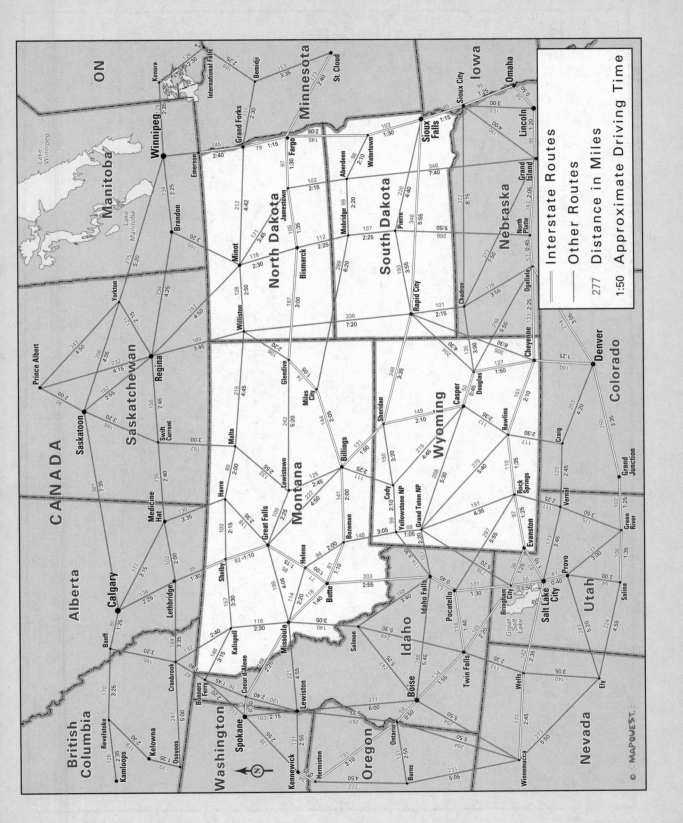

Montana

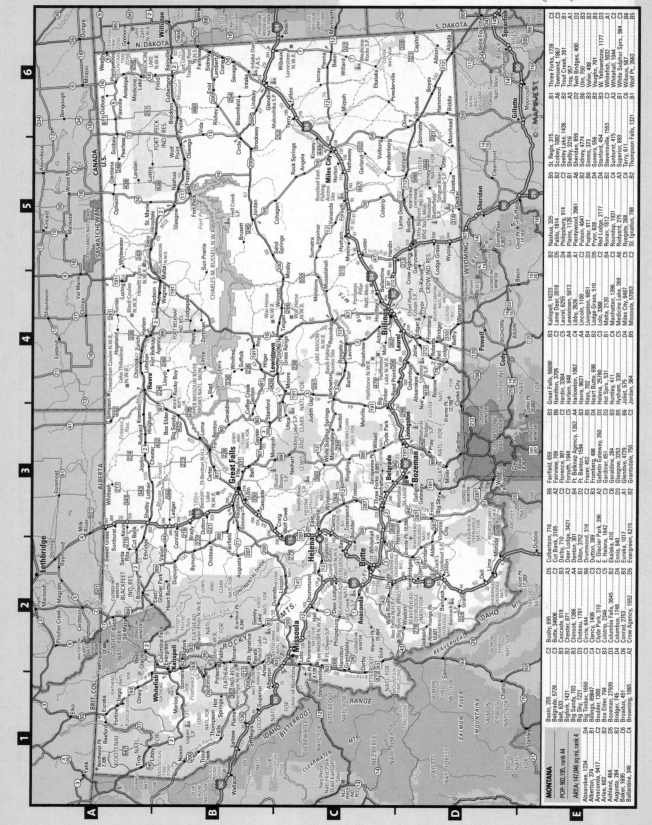

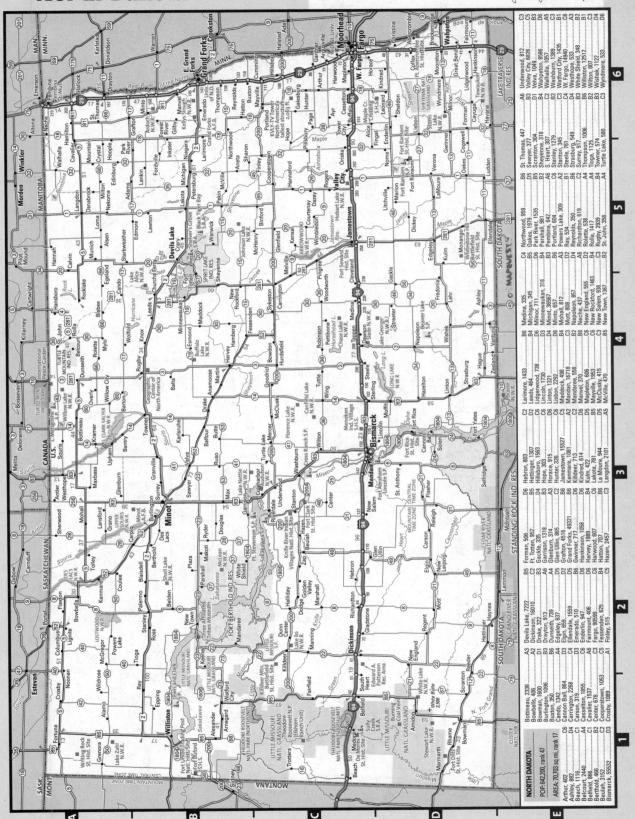

South Dakota

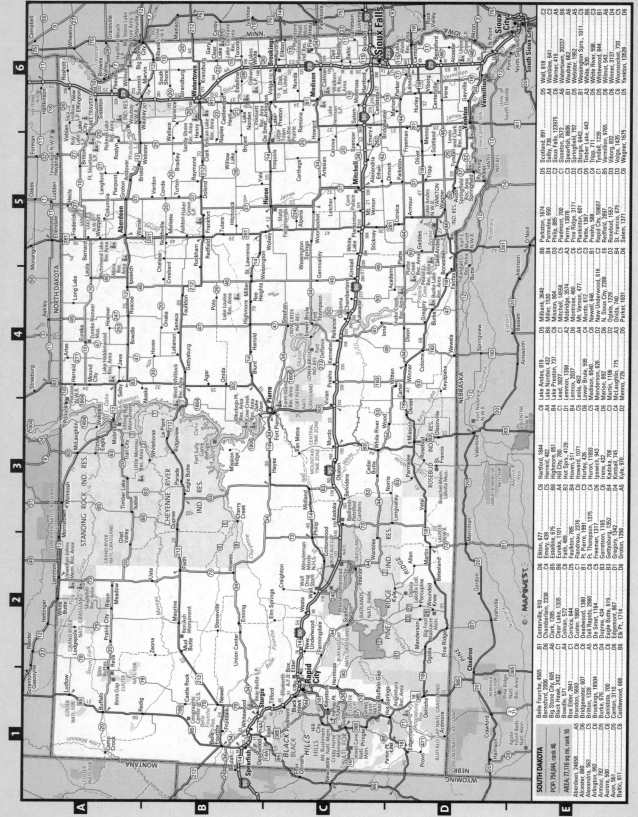

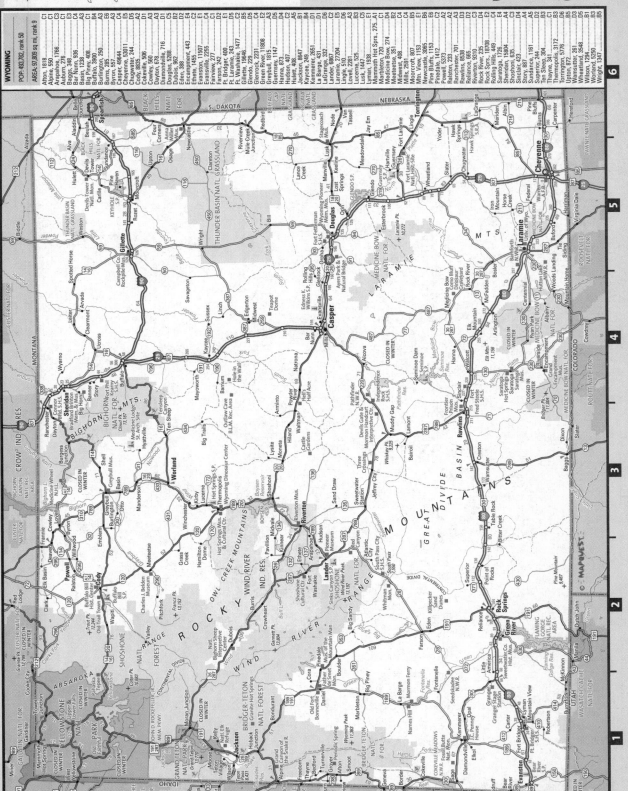

This page is a road mileage distance chart. The row labels (read on the right edge, top to bottom) and column labels (read at the bottom) are U.S./Canadian cities. Each cell gives the driving distance in miles between the row city and the column city.

Note printed at lower left:

> Distances in chart are in miles.
> To convert miles to kilometers, multiply the distance in miles by 1.609
>
> Example:
> New York, NY to Boston, MA = 215 miles or 346 kilometers (215 × 1.609)

Column headers (left to right, read from bottom of chart): ALBUQUERQUE, NM; ATLANTA, GA; BALTIMORE, MD; BILLINGS, MT; BIRMINGHAM, AL; BISMARCK, ND; BOISE, ID; BOSTON, MA; BUFFALO, NY; BURLINGTON, VT; CHARLESTON, SC; CHARLESTON, WV; CHEYENNE, WY; CHICAGO, IL; CINCINNATI, OH; CLEVELAND, OH; DALLAS, TX; DENVER, CO; DES MOINES, IA; DETROIT, MI; EL PASO, TX; HOUSTON, TX; INDIANAPOLIS, IN; JACKSON, MS; KANSAS CITY, MO; LAS VEGAS, NV; LITTLE ROCK, AR; LOS ANGELES, CA; LOUISVILLE, KY; MEMPHIS, TN; MIAMI, FL; MILWAUKEE, WI; MINNEAPOLIS, MN; MONTRÉAL, QC; NASHVILLE, TN; NEW ORLEANS, LA; NEW YORK, NY; OKLAHOMA CITY, OK; OMAHA, NE; ORLANDO, FL; PHILADELPHIA, PA; PHOENIX, AZ; PITTSBURGH, PA; PORTLAND, ME; PORTLAND, OR; RAPID CITY, SD; RENO, NV; RICHMOND, VA; ST. LOUIS, MO; SALT LAKE CITY, UT; SAN ANTONIO, TX; SAN DIEGO, CA; SAN FRANCISCO, CA; SEATTLE, WA; TAMPA, FL; TORONTO, ON; VANCOUVER, BC; WASHINGTON, DC; WICHITA, KS

A Word to Our Readers

Travelers are on the roads in great numbers these days. They're exploring the country on day trips, weekend getaways, business trips, and extended family vacations, visiting major cities and small towns along the way. Because time is precious and the travel industry is ever-changing, having accurate, reliable travel information at your fingertips is critical. Mobil Travel Guide has been providing invaluable insight to travelers for more than 45 years, and we are committed to continuing this service well into the future.

The Mobil Corporation (known as Exxon Mobil Corporation since a 1999 merger) began producing the Mobil Travel Guide books in 1958, following the introduction of the US interstate highway system in 1956. The first edition covered only five Southwestern states. Since then, our books have become the premier travel guides in North America, covering all 50 states and Canada.

Since its founding, Mobil Travel Guide has served as an advocate for travelers seeking knowledge about hotels, restaurants, and places to visit. Based on an objective process, we make recommendations to our customers that we believe will enhance the quality and value of their travel experiences. Our trusted Mobil One- to Five-Star rating system is the oldest and most respected lodging and restaurant inspection and rating program in North America. Most hoteliers, restaurateurs, and industry observers favorably regard the rigor of our inspection program and understand the prestige and benefits that come with receiving a Mobil Star rating.

The Mobil Travel Guide process of rating each establishment includes:

- Unannounced facility inspections

- Incognito service evaluations for Mobil Four-Star and Mobil Five-Star properties

- A review of unsolicited comments from the general public

- Senior management oversight

For each property, more than 450 attributes, including cleanliness, physical facilities, and employee attitude and courtesy, are measured and evaluated to produce a mathematically derived score, which is then blended with the other elements to form an overall score. These quantifiable scores allow comparative analysis among properties and form the basis that we use to assign our Mobil One- to Five-Star ratings.

This process focuses largely on guest expectations, guest experience, and consistency of service, not just physical facilities and amenities. It is fundamentally a relative rating system that rewards those properties that continually strive for and achieve excellence each year. Indeed, the very best properties are consistently raising the bar for those that wish to compete with them. These properties proactively respond to consumers' needs even in today's uncertain times.

Only facilities that meet Mobil Travel Guide's standards earn the privilege of being listed in the guide. Deteriorating, poorly managed establishments are deleted. A Mobil Travel Guide listing constitutes a positive quality recommendation; every listing is an accolade, a recognition of achievement. Our Mobil One- to Five-Star rating system highlights its level of service. Extensive in-house research is constantly underway to determine new additions to our lists.

- The Mobil Five-Star Award indicates that a property is one of the very best in the country and consistently provides gracious and courteous service, superlative quality in its facility, and a unique ambience. The lodgings and restaurants at the Mobil Five-Star level consistently and proactively respond to consumers' needs and continue their commitment to excellence, doing so with grace and perseverance.

- Also highly regarded is the Mobil Four-Star Award, which honors properties for outstanding achievement in overall facility and for providing very strong service levels in all areas. These award winners provide a distinctive experience for the ever-demanding and sophisticated consumer.

⊙ The Mobil Three-Star Award recognizes an excellent property that provides full services and amenities. This category ranges from exceptional hotels with limited services to elegant restaurants with a less-formal atmosphere.

⊙ A Mobil Two-Star property is a clean and comfortable establishment that has expanded amenities or a distinctive environment. A Mobil Two-Star property is an excellent place to stay or dine.

⊙ A Mobil One-Star property is limited in its amenities and services but focuses on providing a value experience while meeting travelers' expectations. The property can be expected to be clean, comfortable, and convenient.

Allow us to emphasize that we do not charge establishments for inclusion in our guides. We have no relationship with any of the businesses and attractions we list and act only as a consumer advocate. In essence, we do the investigative legwork so that you won't have to.

Keep in mind, too, that the hospitality business is ever-changing. Restaurants and lodgings—particularly small chains and stand-alone establishments—change management or even go out of business with surprising quickness. Although we make every effort to double-check information during our annual updates, we nevertheless recommend that you call ahead to make sure the place you've selected is still open and offers all the amenities you're looking for. We've provided phone numbers; when available, we also list fax numbers and Web site addresses.

We hope that your travels are enjoyable and relaxing and that our books help you get the most out of every trip you take. If any aspect of your accommodation, dining, or sightseeing experience motivates you to comment, please drop us a line. We depend a great deal on our readers' remarks, so you can be assured that we will read your comments and assimilate them into our research. General comments about our books are also welcome. You can write to us at Mobil Travel Guide, 7373 N Cicero Ave, Lincolnwood, IL 60712, or send an e-mail to info@ mobiltravelguide.com.

Take your Mobil Travel Guide books along on every trip you take. We're confident that you'll be pleased with their convenience, ease of use, and breadth of dependable coverage.

Happy travels!

How to Use This Book

The Mobil Travel Guide Regional Travel Planners are designed for ease of use. Each state has its own chapter, beginning with a general introduction that provides a geographical and historical orientation to the state and gives basic statewide tourist information, from climate to calendar highlights to seatbelt laws. The remainder of each chapter is devoted to travel destinations within the state—mainly cities and towns, but also national parks and tourist areas—which, like the states, are arranged in alphabetical order.

The following sections explain the wealth of information you'll find about those travel destinations: information about the area, things to see and do there, and where to stay and eat.

Maps and Map Coordinates

At the front of this book in the full-color section, we have provided state maps as well as maps of selected larger cities to help you find your way around once you leave the highway. You'll find a key to the map symbols on the Contents page at the beginning of the map section.

Next to most cities and towns throughout the book, you'll find a set of map coordinates, such as C-2. These coordinates reference the maps at the front of this book and help you find the location you're looking for quickly and easily.

Destination Information

Because many travel destinations are close to other cities and towns where travelers might find additional attractions, accommodations, and restaurants, we've included cross-references to those cities and towns when it makes sense to do so. We also list addresses, phone numbers, and Web sites for travel information resources—usually the local chamber of commerce or office of tourism—as well as pertinent statistics and, in many cases, a brief introduction to the area.

Information about airports, ground transportation, and suburbs is included for large cities.

Driving Tours and Walking Tours

The driving tours that we include for many states are usually day trips that make for interesting side excursions, although they can be longer. They offer you a way to get off the beaten path and visit an area that travelers often overlook. These trips frequently cover areas of natural beauty or historical significance.

Each walking tour focuses on a particularly interesting area of a city or town. Again, these tours can provide a break from everyday tourist attractions. The tours often include places to stop for meals or snacks.

What to See and Do

Mobil Travel Guide offers information about nearly 20,000 museums, art galleries, amusement parks, historic sites, national and state parks, ski areas, and many other types of attractions. A white star on a black background ★ signals that the attraction is a must-see—one of the best in the area. Because municipal parks, public tennis courts, swimming pools, and small educational institutions are common to most towns, they generally are not mentioned.

Following an attraction's description, you'll find the months, days, and, in some cases, hours of operation; the address/directions, telephone number, and Web site (if there is one); and the admission price category. The following are the ranges we use for admission fees, based on one adult:

- ✪ **FREE**
- ✪ **$** = Up to $5
- ✪ **$$** = $5.01-$10
- ✪ **$$$** = $10.01-$15
- ✪ **$$$$** = Over $15

Special Events

Special events are either annual events that last only a short time, such as festivals and fairs, or longer, seasonal events such as horse racing, theater, and summer concerts. Our Special Events listings also include infrequently occurring occasions that mark certain dates or events, such as a centennial or other commemorative celebration.

Listings

Lodgings, spas, and restaurants are usually listed under the city or town in which they're located. Make sure to check the related cities and towns that appear right beneath a city's heading for additional options, especially if you're traveling to a major metropolitan area that includes many suburbs. If a property is located in a town that doesn't have its own heading, the listing appears under the town nearest it, with the address and town given immediately after the establishment's name. In large cities, lodgings located within 5 miles of major commercial airports may be listed under a separate "Airport Area" heading that follows the city section.

LODGINGS

Travelers have different wants and needs when it comes to accommodations. To help you pinpoint properties that meet your particular needs, Mobil Travel Guide classifies each lodging by type according to the following characteristics.

Mobil Rated Lodgings

⊘ **Limited-Service Hotel.** A limited-service hotel is traditionally a Mobil One-Star or Mobil Two-Star property. At a Mobil One-Star hotel, guests can expect to find a clean, comfortable property that commonly serves a complimentary continental breakfast. A Mobil Two-Star hotel is also clean and comfortable but has expanded amenities, such as a full-service restaurant, business center, and fitness center. These services may have limited staffing and/or restricted hours of use.

⊘ **Full-Service Hotel.** A full-service hotel traditionally enjoys a Mobil Three-Star, Mobil Four-Star, or Mobil Five-Star rating. Guests can expect these hotels to offer at least one full-service restaurant in addition to amenities such as valet parking, luggage assistance, 24-hour room service, concierge service, laundry and/or dry-cleaning services, and turndown service.

⊘ **Full-Service Resort.** A resort is traditionally a full-service hotel that is geared toward recreation and represents a vacation and holiday destination. A resort's guest rooms are typically furnished to accommodate longer stays. The property may offer a full-service spa, golf, tennis, and fitness facilities or other leisure activities. Resorts are expected to offer a full-service restaurant and expanded amenities, such as luggage assistance, room service, meal plans, concierge service, and turndown service.

⊘ **Full-Service Inn.** An inn is traditionally a Mobil Three-Star, Mobil Four-Star, or Mobil Five-Star property. Inns are similar to bed-and-breakfasts (see below) but offer a wider range of services, most significantly a full-service restaurant that serves at least breakfast and dinner.

Specialty Lodgings

Mobil Travel Guide recognizes the unique and individualized nature of many different types of lodging establishments, including bed-and-breakfasts, limited-service inns, and guest ranches. For that reason, we have chosen to place our stamp of approval on the properties that fall into these two categories in lieu of applying our traditional Mobil Star ratings.

⊘ **B&B/Limited-Service Inn.** A bed-and-breakfast (B&B) or limited-service inn is traditionally an owner-occupied home or residence found in a residential area or vacation destination. It may be a structure of historic significance. Rooms are often individually decorated, but telephones, televisions, and private bathrooms may not be available in every room. A B&B typically serves only breakfast to its overnight guests, which is included in the room rate. Cocktails and refreshments may be served in the late afternoon or evening.

⊘ **Guest Ranch.** A guest ranch is traditionally a rustic, Western-themed property that specializes in stays of three or more days. Horseback riding is often a feature, with stables and trails found on the property. Facilities can range from clean, comfortable establishments to more luxurious facilities.

Mobil Star Rating Definitions for Lodgings

⊘ ★ ★ ★ ★ ★ : A Mobil Five-Star lodging provides consistently superlative service in an exceptionally distinctive luxury environment, with expanded services. Attention to detail is evident throughout the hotel, resort, or inn, from bed linens to staff uniforms.

○ ★ ★ ★ ★ : A Mobil Four-Star lodging provides a luxury experience with expanded amenities in a distinctive environment. Services may include, but are not limited to, automatic turndown service, 24-hour room service, and valet parking.

○ ★ ★ ★ : A Mobil Three-Star lodging is well appointed, with a full-service restaurant and expanded amenities, such as a fitness center, golf course, tennis courts, 24-hour room service, and optional turndown service.

○ ★ ★ : A Mobil Two-Star lodging is considered a clean, comfortable, and reliable establishment that has expanded amenities, such as a full-service restaurant on the premises.

○ ★ : A Mobil One-Star lodging is a limited-service hotel, motel, or inn that is considered a clean, comfortable, and reliable establishment.

Information Found in the Lodging Listings

Each lodging listing gives the name, address/location (when no street address is available), neighborhood and/or directions from downtown (in major cities), phone number(s), fax number, total number of guest rooms, and seasons open (if not year-round). Also included are details on business, luxury, recreational, and dining facilities at the property or nearby. A key to the symbols at the end of each listing can be found on the page following the "A Word to Our Readers" section.

For every property, we also provide pricing information. Because lodging rates change frequently, we list a pricing category rather than specific prices. The pricing categories break down as follows:

○ **$** = Up to $150

○ **$$** = $151-$250

○ **$$$** = $251-$350

○ **$$$$** = $351 and up

All prices quoted are in effect at the time of publication; however, prices cannot be guaranteed. In some locations, short-term price variations may exist because of special events, holidays, or seasonality. Certain resorts have complicated rate structures that vary with the time of year; always confirm rates when making your plans.

Because most lodgings offer the following features and services, information about them does not appear in the listings:

○ Year-round operation

○ Bathroom with tub and/or shower in each room

○ Cable television in each room

○ In-room telephones

○ Cots and cribs available

○ Daily maid service

○ Elevators

○ Major credit cards accepted

SPAS

Mobil Travel Guide is pleased to announce its newest category: hotel and resort spas. Until now, hotel and resort spas have not been formally rated or inspected by any organization. Every spa selected for inclusion in this book underwent a rigorous inspection process similar to the one Mobil Travel Guide has been applying to lodgings and restaurants for more than four decades. After spending a year and a half researching more than 300 spas and performing exhaustive incognito inspections of more than 200 properties, we narrowed our list to the 48 best spas in the United States and Canada.

Mobil Travel Guide's spa ratings are based on objective evaluations of more than 450 attributes. Approximately half of these criteria assess basic expectations, such as staff courtesy, the technical proficiency and skill of the employees, and whether the facility is maintained properly and hygienically. Several standards address issues that impact a guest's physical comfort and convenience, as well as the staff's ability to impart a sense of personalized service and anticipate clients' needs. Additional criteria measure the spa's ability to create a completely calming ambience.

The Mobil Star ratings focus on much more than the facilities available at a spa and the treatments it offers. Each Mobil Star rating is a cumulative score achieved from multiple inspections that reflects the spa management's attention to detail and commitment to consumers' needs.

Mobil Star Rating Definitions for Spas

⊛ ★ ★ ★ ★ ★ : A Mobil Five-Star spa provides consistently superlative service in an exceptionally distinctive luxury environment with extensive amenities. The staff at a Mobil Five-Star spa provides extraordinary service above and beyond the traditional spa experience, allowing guests to achieve the highest level of relaxation and pampering. A Mobil Five-Star spa offers an extensive array of treatments, often incorporating international themes and products. Attention to detail is evident throughout the spa, from arrival to departure.

⊛ ★ ★ ★ ★ : A Mobil Four-Star spa provides a luxurious experience with expanded amenities in an elegant and serene environment. Throughout the spa facility, guests experience personalized service. Amenities might include, but are not limited to, single-sex relaxation rooms where guests wait for their treatments, plunge pools and whirlpools in both men's and women's locker rooms, and an array of treatments, including at a minimum a selection of massages, body therapies, facials, and a variety of salon services.

⊛ ★ ★ ★ : A Mobil Three-Star spa is physically well appointed and has a full complement of staff to ensure that guests' needs are met. It has some expanded amenities, such as, but not limited to, a well-equipped fitness center, separate men's and women's locker rooms, a sauna or steam room, and a designated relaxation area. It also offers a menu of services that at a minimum includes massages, facial treatments, and at least one other type of body treatment, such as scrubs or wraps.

RESTAURANTS

All Mobil Star rated dining establishments listed in this book have a full kitchen and offer seating at tables; most offer table service.

Mobil Star Rating Definitions for Restaurants

⊛ ★ ★ ★ ★ ★ : A Mobil Five-Star restaurant offers one of few flawless dining experiences in the country. These establishments consistently provide their guests with exceptional food, superlative service, elegant décor, and exquisite presentations of each detail surrounding a meal.

⊛ ★ ★ ★ ★ : A Mobil Four-Star restaurant provides professional service, distinctive presentations, and wonderful food.

⊛ ★ ★ ★ : A Mobil Three-Star restaurant has good food, warm and skillful service, and enjoyable décor.

⊛ ★ ★ : A Mobil Two-Star restaurant serves fresh food in a clean setting with efficient service. Value is considered in this category, as is family friendliness.

⊛ ★ : A Mobil One-Star restaurant provides a distinctive experience through culinary specialty, local flair, or individual atmosphere.

Information Found in the Restaurant Listings

Each restaurant listing gives the cuisine type, street address (or directions if no address is available), phone and fax numbers, Web site (if available), meals served, days of operation (if not open daily year-round), and pricing category. Information about appropriate attire is provided, although it's always a good idea to call ahead and ask if you're unsure; the meaning of "casual" or "business casual" varies widely in different parts of the country. We also indicate whether the restaurant has a bar, whether a children's menu is offered, and whether outdoor seating is available. If reservations are recommended, we note that fact in the listing. When valet parking is available, it is noted in the description. In many cases, self-parking is available at the restaurant or nearby.

Because menu prices can fluctuate, we list a pricing category rather than specific prices. The pricing categories are defined as follows, per diner, and assume that you order an appetizer or dessert, an entrée, and one drink:

⊛ **$** = $15 and under

⊛ **$$** = $16-$35

⊛ **$$$** = $36-$85

⊛ **$$$$** = $86 and up

Again, all prices quoted are in effect at the time of publication, but prices cannot be guaranteed.

SPECIAL INFORMATION FOR TRAVELERS WITH DISABILITIES

The Mobil Travel Guide 🛈 symbol indicates that an establishment is not at least partially accessible to people with mobility problems. When the 🛈 symbol follows a listing, the establishment is not equipped with facilities to accommodate people using wheelchairs or crutches or otherwise needing easy access to doorways and rest rooms. Travelers with severe mobility problems or with hearing or visual impairments may or may not find the facilities they need. Always phone ahead to make sure hat an establishment can meet your needs.

Understanding the Symbols

What to See and Do

⊡	=	One of the top attractions in the area
$	=	Up to $5
$$	=	$5.01 to $10
$$$	=	$10.01 to $15
$$$$	=	Over $15

Lodgings

$	=	Up to $150
$$	=	$151 to $250
$$$	=	$251 to $350
$$$$	=	Over $350

Restaurants

$	=	Up to $15
$$	=	$16 to $35
$$$	=	$36 to $85
$$$$	=	Over $85

Lodging Star Definitions

★★★★★   A Mobil Five-Star lodging establishment provides consistently superlative service in an exceptionally distinctive luxury environment with expanded services. Attention to detail is evident throughout the hotel/resort/inn from the bed linens to the staff uniforms.

★★★★   A Mobil Four-Star lodging establishment is a hotel/resort/inn that provides a luxury experience with expanded amenities in a distinctive environment. Services may include, but are not limited to, automatic turndown service, 24-hour room service, and valet parking.

★★★   A Mobil Three-Star lodging establishment is a hotel/resort/inn that is well appointed, with a full-service restaurant and expanded amenities, such as, but not limited to, a fitness center, golf course, tennis courts, 24-hour room service, and optional turndown service.

★★   A Mobil Two-Star lodging establishment is a hotel/resort/inn that is considered a clean, comfortable, and reliable establishment, but also has expanded amenities, such as a full-service restaurant on the premises.

★   A Mobil One-Star lodging establishment is a limited-service hotel or inn that is considered a clean, comfortable, and reliable establishment.

Restaurant Star Definitions

★★★★★   A Mobil Five-Star restaurant is one of few flawless dining experiences in the country. These restaurants consistently provide their guests with exceptional food, superlative service, elegant décor, and exquisite presentations of each detail surrounding the meal.

★★★★   A Mobil Four-Star restaurant provides professional service, distinctive presentations, and wonderful food.

★★★   A Mobil Three-Star restaurant has good food, warm and skillful service, and enjoyable décor.

★★   A Mobil Two-Star restaurant serves fresh food in a clean setting with efficient service. Value is considered in this category, as is family friendliness.

★   A Mobil One-Star restaurant provides a distinctive experience through culinary specialty, local flair, or individual atmosphere.

Symbols at End of Listings

- Facilities for people with disabilities not available
- Pets allowed
- Ski in/ski out access
- Golf on premises
- Tennis court(s) on premises
- Indoor or outdoor pool
- Fitness room
- Major commercial airport within 5 miles
- Business center

Making the Most of Your Trip

A few hardy souls might look back with fondness on a trip during which the car broke down, leaving them stranded for three days, or a vacation that cost twice what it was supposed to. For most travelers, though, the best trips are those that are safe, smooth, and within budget. To help you make your trip the best it can be, we've assembled a few tips and resources.

Saving Money

ON LODGING

Many hotels and motels offer discounts—for senior citizens, business travelers, families, you name it. It never hurts to ask—politely, that is. Sometimes, especially in the late afternoon, desk clerks are instructed to fill beds, and you might be offered a lower rate or a nicer room to entice you to stay. Simply ask the reservation agent for the best rate available. Also, make sure to try both the toll-free number and the local number. You may be able to get a lower rate from one than from the other.

Timing your trip right can cut your lodging costs as well. Look for bargains on stays over multiple nights, in the off-season, and on weekdays or weekends, depending on the location. Many hotels in major metropolitan areas, for example, have special weekend packages that offer leisure travelers considerable savings on rooms; they may include breakfast, cocktails, and/or dinner discounts.

Another way to save money is to choose accommodations that give you more than just a standard room. Rooms with kitchen facilities enable you to cook some meals yourself, reducing your restaurant costs. A suite might save money for two couples traveling together. Even hotel luxury levels can provide good value, as many include breakfast or cocktails in the price of a room.

State and city taxes, as well as special room taxes, can increase your room rate by as much as 25 percent per day. We are unable to include information about taxes in our listings, but we strongly urge you to ask about taxes when making reservations so that you understand the total cost of your lodgings before you book them.

Watch out for telephone-usage charges that hotels frequently impose on long-distance, credit-card, and other calls. Before phoning from your room, read the information given to you at check-in, and then be sure to review your bill carefully when checking out. You won't be expected to pay for charges that the hotel didn't spell out. Consider using your cell phone if you have one; or, if public telephones are available in the hotel lobby, your cost savings may outweigh the inconvenience of using them.

Here are some additional ways to save on lodgings:

- Stay in B&B accommodations. They're generally less expensive than standard hotel rooms, and the complimentary breakfast cuts down on food costs.

- If you're traveling with children, find lodgings at which kids stay free.

- When visiting a major city, stay just outside the city limits; these rooms are usually less expensive than those in downtown locations.

- Consider visiting national parks during the low season, when prices of lodgings near the parks drop by 25 percent or more.

- When calling a hotel, ask whether it is running any special promotions or if any discounts are available; many times reservationists are told not to volunteer these deals unless they're specifically asked about them.

- Check for hotel packages; some offer nightly rates that include a rental car or discounts on major attractions.

ON DINING

There are several ways to get a less expensive meal at an expensive restaurant. Early-bird dinners are popular in many parts of the country and offer considerable savings. If you're interested in visiting a Mobil Four- or Five-Star establishment, consider going at lunchtime. Although the prices are probably still relatively high at midday, they may be half of those at dinner, and you'll experience the same ambience, service, and cuisine.

ON ENTERTAINMENT

Although many national parks, monuments, seashores, historic sites, and recreation areas may be visited free of charge, others charge an entrance fee and/or a usage fee for special services and facilities. If you plan to make several visits to national recreation areas, consider one of the following money-saving programs offered by the National Park Service:

○ **National Parks Pass.** This annual pass is good for entrance to any national park that charges an entrance fee. If the park charges a per-vehicle fee, the pass holder and any accompanying passengers in a private noncommercial vehicle may enter. If the park charges a per-person fee, the pass applies to the holder's spouse, children, and parents as well as the holder. It is valid for entrance fees only; it does not cover parking, camping, or other fees. You can purchase a National Parks Pass in person at any national park where an entrance fee is charged; by mail from the National Park Foundation, PO Box 34108, Washington, DC 20043-4108; by calling toll-free 888/467-2757; or at www.nationalparks .org. The cost is $50.

○ **Golden Eagle Sticker.** When affixed to a National Parks Pass, this hologram sticker, available to people who are between 17 and 61 years of age, extends coverage to sites managed by the US Fish and Wildlife Service, the US Forest Service, and the Bureau of Land Management. It is good until the National Parks Pass to which it is affixed expires and does not cover usage fees. You can purchase one at the National Park Service, the Fish and Wildlife Service, or the Bureau of Land Management fee stations. The cost is $15.

○ **Golden Age Passport.** Available to citizens and permanent US residents 62 and older, this passport is a lifetime entrance permit to fee-charging national recreation areas. The fee exemption extends to those accompanying the permit holder in a private noncommercial vehicle or, in the case of walk-in facilities, to the holder's spouse and children. The passport also entitles the holder to a 50 percent discount on federal usage fees charged in park areas, but not on con-

cessions. Golden Age Passports must be obtained in person and are available at most National Park Service units that charge an entrance fee. The applicant must show proof of age, such as a driver's license or birth certificate (Medicare cards are not acceptable proof). The cost is $10.

○ **Golden Access Passport.** Issued to citizens and permanent US residents who are physically disabled or visually impaired, this passport is a free lifetime entrance permit to fee-charging national recreation areas. The fee exemption extends to those accompanying the permit holder in a private noncommercial vehicle or, in the case of walk-in facilities, to the holder's spouse and children. The passport also entitles the holder to a 50 percent discount on usage fees charged in park areas, but not on concessions. Golden Access Passports must be obtained in person and are available at most National Park Service units that charge an entrance fee. Proof of eligibility to receive federal benefits (under programs such as Disability Retirement, Compensation for Military Service-Connected Disability, and the Coal Mine Safety and Health Act) is required, or an affidavit must be signed attesting to eligibility.

A money-saving move in several large cities is to purchase a **CityPass.** If you plan to visit several museums and other major attractions, CityPass is a terrific option because it gets you into several sites for one substantially reduced price. Currently, CityPass is available in Boston, Chicago, Hollywood, New York, Philadelphia, San Francisco, Seattle, southern California (which includes Disneyland, SeaWorld, and the San Diego Zoo), and Toronto. For more information or to buy one, call toll-free 888/330-5008 or visit www. citypass.net. You can also buy a CityPass from any participating CityPass attraction.

Here are some additional ways to save on entertainment and shopping:

○ Check with your hotel's concierge for various coupons and special offers; they often have two-for-one tickets for area attractions and coupons for discounts at area stores and restaurants.

○ Purchase same-day concert or theater tickets for half-price through the local cheap-tickets outlet, such as TKTS in New York or Hot Tix in Chicago.

- Visit museums on their free or "by donation" days, when you can pay what you wish rather than a specific admission fee.

- Save receipts from purchases in Canada; visitors to Canada can get a rebate on federal taxes and some provincial sales taxes.

ON TRANSPORTATION

Transportation is a big part of any vacation budget. Here are some ways to reduce your costs:

- If you're renting a car, shop early over the Internet; you can book a car during the low season for less, even if you'll be using it in the high season.

- Rental car discounts are often available if you rent for one week or longer and reserve in advance.

- Get the best gas mileage out of your vehicle by making sure that it's properly tuned up and keeping your tires properly inflated.

- Travel at moderate speeds on the open road; higher speeds require more gasoline.

- Fill the tank before you return your rental car; rental companies charge to refill the tank and do so at prices of up to 50 percent more than at local gas stations.

- Make a checklist of travel essentials and purchase them before you leave; don't get stuck buying expensive sunscreen at your hotel or overpriced film at the airport.

FOR SENIOR CITIZENS

Always call ahead to ask if a discount is being offered, and be sure to carry proof of age. Additional information for mature travelers is available from the American Association of Retired Persons (AARP), 601 E St NW, Washington, DC 20049; phone 202/434-2277; www.aarp.org.

Tipping

Tips are expressions of appreciation for good service. However, you are never obligated to tip if you receive poor service.

IN HOTELS

- Door attendants usually get $1 for hailing a cab.

- Bell staff expect $2 per bag.

- Concierges are tipped according to the service they perform. Tipping is not mandatory when you've asked for suggestions on sightseeing or restaurants or for help in making dining reservations. However, a tip of $5 is appropriate when a concierge books you a table at a restaurant known to be difficult to get into. For obtaining theater or sporting event tickets, $5 to $10 is expected.

- Maids should be tipped $1 to $2 per day. Hand your tip directly to the maid, or leave it with a note saying that the money has been left expressly for the maid.

IN RESTAURANTS

Before tipping, carefully review your check for any gratuity or service charge that is already included in your bill. If you're in doubt, ask your server.

- Coffee shop and counter service waitstaff usually receive 15 percent of the bill, before sales tax.

- In full-service restaurants, tip 18 percent of the bill, before sales tax.

- In fine restaurants, where gratuities are shared among a larger staff, 18 to 20 percent is appropriate.

- In most cases, the maitre d' is tipped only if the service has been extraordinary, and only on the way out. At upscale properties in major metropolitan areas, $20 is the minimum.

- If there is a wine steward, tip $20 for exemplary service and beyond, or more if the wine was decanted or the bottle was very expensive.

- Tip $1 to $2 per coat at the coat check.

AT AIRPORTS

Curbside luggage handlers expect $1 per bag. Car-rental shuttle drivers who help with your luggage appreciate a $1 or $2 tip.

Staying Safe

The best way to deal with emergencies is to avoid them in the first place. However, unforeseen situations do happen, so you should be prepared for them.

IN YOUR CAR

Before you head out on a road trip, make sure that your car has been serviced and is in good working order. Change the oil, check the battery and belts, make sure that your windshield washer fluid is full and your tires are properly inflated (which can also improve your gas mileage). Other inspections recommended by the vehicle's manufacturer should also be made.

Next, be sure you have the tools and equipment needed to deal with a routine breakdown:

- Jack
- Spare tire
- Lug wrench
- Repair kit
- Emergency tools
- Jumper cables
- Spare fan belt
- Fuses
- Flares and/or reflectors
- Flashlight
- First-aid kit
- In winter, a windshield scraper and snow shovel

Many emergency supplies are sold in special packages that include the essentials you need to stay safe in the event of a breakdown.

Also bring all appropriate and up-to-date documentation—licenses, registration, and insurance cards—and know what your insurance covers. Bring an extra set of keys, too, just in case.

En route, always buckle up! In most states, wearing a seatbelt is required by law.

If your car does break down, do the following:

- Get out of traffic as soon as possible—pull well off the road.
- Raise the hood and turn on your emergency flashers or tie a white cloth to the roadside door handle or antenna.
- Stay in your car.
- Use flares or reflectors to keep your vehicle from being hit.

IN YOUR HOTEL

Chances are slim that you will encounter a hotel or motel fire, but you can protect yourself by doing the following:

- Once you've checked in, make sure that the smoke detector in your room is working properly.
- Find the property's fire safety instructions, usually posted on the inside of the room door.
- Locate the fire extinguishers and at least two fire exits.
- Never use an elevator in a fire.

For personal security, use the peephole in your room door and make sure that anyone claiming to be a hotel employee can show proper identification. Call the front desk if you feel threatened at any time.

PROTECTING AGAINST THEFT

To guard against theft wherever you go:

- Don't bring anything of more value than you need.
- If you do bring valuables, leave them at your hotel rather than in your car.
- If you bring something very expensive, lock it in a safe. Many hotels put one in each room; others will store your valuables in the hotel's safe.
- Don't carry more money than you need. Use traveler's checks and credit cards or visit cash machines to withdraw more cash when you run out.

For Travelers with Disabilities

To get the kind of service you need and have a right to expect, don't hesitate when making a reservation to question the management about the availability of accessible rooms, parking, entrances, restaurants, lounges, or any other facilities that are important to you, and confirm what is meant by "accessible."

The Mobil Travel Guide 🔣 symbol indicates establishments that are not at least partially accessible to people with special mobility needs (people using wheelchairs or crutches or otherwise needing easy access to buildings and rooms). Further information about these criteria can be found in the earlier section "How to Use This Book."

A thorough listing of published material for travelers with disabilities is available from the Disability Bookshop, Twin Peaks Press, Box 129, Vancouver, WA 98666; phone 360/694-2462; disabilitybookshop.virtualave.net. Another reliable organization is the Society for Accessible Travel & Hospitality (SATH), 347 Fifth Ave, Suite 610, New York, NY 10016; phone 212/447-7284; www.sath.org.

Border-Crossing Regulations

A passport is required for travel into Canada for US citizens.

Each traveler may bring up to $800 worth of goods purchased in Canada back into the United States duty free. In addition, federal regulations permit each US citizen 21 years of age or older to bring back 1 liter of alcoholic beverage duty free in a 30-day period. Travelers are not permitted to bring in plants, fruits, or vegetables. State regulations vary, so check locally before entering Canada. New regulations may be issued at any time.

For more information about traveling to Canada, including safety information, look for the US State Department's Consular Information Sheet at travel.state.gov/canada.html, or request it by fax by calling 202/647-3000.

Important Toll-Free Numbers and Online Information

Hotels

Adams Mark...............................800/444-2326
www.adamsmark.com

America's Best Value Inn...................888/315-2378
www.americasbestvalueinn.com

AmericInn...............................800/634-3444
www.americinn.com

AmeriHost Inn...........................800/434-5800
www.amerihostinn.com

Amerisuites.............................800/833-1516
www.amerisuites.com

Baymont Inns...........................800/621-1429
www.baymontinns.com

Best Inns & Suites......................800/237-8466
www.bestinn.com

Best Western...........................800/780-7234
www.bestwestern.com

Budget Host Inn........................800/283-4678
www.budgethost.com

Candlewood Suites 888/226-3539
www.candlewoodsuites.com

Clarion Hotels 800/252-7466
www.choicehotels.com

Comfort Inns and Suites 800/252-7466
www.comfortinn.com

Country Hearth Inns 800/848-5767
www.countryhearth.com

Country Inns & Suites...................800/456-4000
www.countryinns.com

Courtyard by Marriott 800/321-2211
www.courtyard.com

Crowne Plaza Hotels and Resorts...........800/227-6963
www.crowneplaza.com

Days Inn................................800/544-8313
www.daysinn.com

Delta Hotels 800/268-1133
www.deltahotels.com

Destination Hotels & Resorts 800/434-7347
www.destinationhotels.com

Doubletree Hotels.......................800/222-8733
www.doubletree.com

Drury Inn 800/378-7946
www.druryhotels.com

Econolodge 800/553-2666
www.econolodge.com

Embassy Suites..........................800/362-2779
www.embassysuites.com

ExelInns of America......................800/367-3935
www.exelinns.com

Extended StayAmerica 800/398-7829
www.extendedstayhotels.com

Fairfield Inn by Marriott 800/228-2800
www.fairfieldinn.com

Fairmont Hotels.........................800/441-1414
www.fairmont.com

Four Points by Sheraton.................888/625-5144
www.fourpoints.com

Four Seasons 800/819-5053
www.fourseasons.com

Hampton Inn............................800/426-7866
www.hamptoninn.com

Hard Rock Hotels, Resorts, and Casinos 800/473-7625
www.hardrockhotel.com

Harrah's Entertainment 800/427-7247
www.harrahs.com

Hawthorn Suites........................800/527-1133
www.hawthorn.com

Hilton Hotels and Resorts (US) 800/774-1500
www.hilton.com

Holiday Inn Express......................800/465-4329
www.hiexpress.com

Holiday Inn Hotels and Resorts...........800/465-4329
www.holiday-inn.com

Homestead Studio Suites...............888/782-9473
www.extendedstayhotels.com

Homewood Suites.......................800/225-5466
www.homewoodsuites.com

Howard Johnson........................800/406-1411
www.hojo.com

Hyatt..................................800/633-7313
www.hyatt.com

Inns of America.........................800/826-0778
www.innsofamerica.com

InterContinental........................888/424-6835
www.intercontinental.com

Joie de Vivre...........................800/738-7477
www.jdvhospitality.com

Kimpton Hotels 888/546-7866
www.kimptonhotels.com

Knights Inn.............................800/843-5644
www.knightsinn.com

La Quinta...............................800/531-5900
www.lq.com

Le Meridien.................................800/543-4300	**Ritz-Carlton**................................800/241-3333
www.lemeridien.com	www.ritzcarlton.com
Leading Hotels of the World.................800/223-6800	**RockResorts**........................... 888/367-7625
www.lhw.com	www.rockresorts.com
Loews Hotels 800/235-6397	**Rodeway Inn**................................800/228-2000
www.loewshotels.com	www.rodeway.com
MainStay Suites 800/660-6246	**Rosewood Hotels & Resorts**............. 888/767-3966
www.mainstaysuites.com	www.rosewoodhotels.com
Mandarin Oriental 800/526-6566	**Select Inn** 800/641-1000
www.mandarinoriental.com	www.selectinn.com
Marriott Hotels, Resorts, and Suites 800/228-9290	**Sheraton** 888/625-5144
www.marriott.com	www.sheraton.com
Microtel Inns & Suites 800/771-7171	**Shilo Inns** 800/222-2244
www.microtelinn.com	www.shiloinns.com
Millennium & Copthorne Hotels 866/866-8086	**Shoney's Inn**................................800/552-4667
www.millenniumhotels.com	www.shoneysinn.com
Motel 6....................................800/466-8356	**Signature/Jameson Inns**.....................800/822-5252
www.motel6.com	www.jamesoninns.com
Omni Hotels 800/843-6664	**Sleep Inn** 877/424-6423
www.omnihotels.com	www.sleepinn.com
Pan Pacific Hotels and Resorts.............800/327-8585	**Small Luxury Hotels of the World**...........800/525-4800
www.panpacific.com	www.slh.com
Park Inn & Park Plaza 888/201-1801	**Sofitel** 800/763-4835
www.parkinn.com	www.sofitel.com
The Peninsula Group .... Contact individual hotel	**SpringHill Suites** 888/236-2427
www.peninsula.com	www.springhillsuites.com
Preferred Hotels & Resorts Worldwide.......800/323-7500	**St. Regis Luxury Collection**.............. 888/625-5144
www.preferredhotels.com	www.stregis.com
Quality Inn................................800/228-5151	**Staybridge Suites**...........................800/238-8000
www.qualityinn.com	www.staybridge.com
Radisson Hotels 800/333-3333	**Summit International** 800/457-4000
www.radisson.com	www.summithotelsandresorts.com
Raffles International Hotels and Resorts.....800/637-9477	**Super 8 Motels** 800/800-8000
www.raffles.com	www.super8.com
Ramada Plazas, Limiteds, and Inns..........800/272-6232	**The Sutton Place Hotels**................ 866/378-8866
www.ramada.com	www.suttonplace.com
Red Lion Inns...............................800/733-5466	**Swissôtel**..................................800/637-9477
www.redlion.com	www.swissotels.com
Red Roof Inns..............................800/733-7663	**TownePlace Suites**..................... 888/236-2427
www.redroof.com	www.towneplace.com
Regent International 800/545-4000	**Travelodge** 800/578-7878
www.regenthotels.com	www.travelodge.com
Relais & Chateaux 800/735-2478	**Vagabond Inns**...............................800/522-1555
www.relaischateaux.com	www.vagabondinn.com
Renaissance Hotels 888/236-2427	**W Hotels** 888/625-5144
www.renaissancehotels.com	www.whotels.com
Residence Inn 800/331-3131	**Wellesley Inn and Suites**....................800/444-8888
www.residenceinn.com	www.wellesleyinnandsuites.com

WestCoast Hotels 800/325-4000
www.westcoasthotels.com
Westin Hotels & Resorts .800/937-8461
www.westinhotels.com
Wingate Inns 800/228-1000
www.thewingateinns.com
Woodfin Suite Hotels 800/966-3346
www.woodfinsuitehotels.com
WorldHotels 800/223-5652
www.worldhotels.com
Wyndham Hotels & Resorts 800/996-3426
www.wyndham.com

Airlines

Air Canada 888/247-2262
www.aircanada.com
AirTran 800/247-8726
www.airtran.com
Alaska Airlines 800/252-7522
www.alaskaair.com
American Airlines 800/433-7300
www.aa.com
ATA 800/435-9282
www.ata.com
Continental Airlines 800/523-3273
www.continental.com
Delta Air Lines 800/221-1212
www.delta.com
Frontier Airlines 800/432-1359
www.frontierairlines.com
Hawaiian Airlines 800/367-5320
www.hawaiianairlines.com
Jet Blue Airlines 800/538-2583
www.jetblue.com

Midwest Airlines 800/452-2022
www.midwestairlines.com
Northwest Airlines 800/225-2525
www.nwa.com
Southwest Airlines 800/435-9792
www.southwest.com
Spirit Airlines 800/772-7117
www.spiritair.com
United Airlines 800/241-6522
www.united.com
US Airways 800/428-4322
www.usairways.com

Car Rentals

Advantage 800/777-5500
www.arac.com
Alamo 800/327-9633
www.alamo.com
Avis 800/831-2847
www.avis.com
Budget 800/527-0700
www.budget.com
Dollar 800/800-4000
www.dollar.com
Enterprise 800/325-8007
www.enterprise.com
Hertz 800/654-3131
www.hertz.com
National 800/227-7368
www.nationalcar.com
Payless 800/729-5377
www.paylesscarrental.com
Rent-A-Wreck.com 800/535-1391
www.rentawreck.com
Thrifty 800/847-4389
www.thrifty.com

Meet The Stars

Mobil Travel Guide 2007 *Five-Star* Award Winners

CALIFORNIA
Lodgings
The Beverly Hills Hotel, *Beverly Hills*
Chateau du Sureau, *Oakhurst*
Four Seasons Hotel San Francisco, *San Francisco*
Hotel Bel-Air, *Los Angeles*
The Peninsula Beverly Hills, *Beverly Hills*
Raffles L'Ermitage Beverly Hills, *Beverly Hills*
St. Regis Monarch Beach Resort & Spa, *Dana Point*
St. Regis San Francisco, *San Francisco*
The Ritz-Carlton, San Francisco, *San Francisco*

Restaurants
The Dining Room, *San Francisco*
The French Laundry, *Yountville*

COLORADO
Lodgings
The Broadmoor, *Colorado Springs*
The Little Nell, *Aspen*

CONNECTICUT
Lodging
The Mayflower Inn, *Washington*

DISTRICT OF COLUMBIA
Lodging
Four Seasons Hotel Washington, DC *Washington*

FLORIDA
Lodgings
Four Seasons Resort Palm Beach, *Palm Beach*
The Ritz-Carlton Naples, *Naples*
The Ritz-Carlton, Palm Beach, *Manalapan*

GEORGIA
Lodgings
Four Seasons Hotel Atlanta, *Atlanta*

The Lodge at Sea Island Golf Club, *St. Simons Island*

Restaurants
The Dining Room, *Atlanta*
Seeger's, *Atlanta*

HAWAII
Lodging
Four Seasons Resort Maui, *Wailea, Maui*

ILLINOIS
Lodgings
Four Seasons Hotel Chicago, *Chicago*
The Peninsula Chicago, *Chicago*
The Ritz-Carlton, A Four Seasons Hotel, *Chicago*

Restaurants
Alinea, *Chicago*
Charlie Trotter's, *Chicago*

MAINE
Restaurant
The White Barn Inn, *Kennebunkport*

MASSACHUSETTS
Lodgings
Blantyre, *Lenox*
Four Seasons Hotel Boston, *Boston*

NEVADA
Lodging
Tower Suites at Wynn, *Las Vegas*

Restaurants
Alex, *Las Vegas*
Joel Robuchon at the Mansion, *Las Vegas*

NEW YORK
Lodgings
Four Seasons, Hotel New York, *New York*
Mandarin Oriental, *New York*
The Point, *Saranac Lake*

The Ritz-Carlton New York, Central Park, *New York*
The St. Regis, *New York*

Restaurants
Alain Ducasse, *New York*
Jean Georges, *New York*
Masa, *New York*
per se, *New York*

NORTH CAROLINA
Lodging
The Fearrington House Country Inn, *Pittsboro*

PENNSYLVANIA
Restaurant
Le Bec-Fin, *Philadelphia*

SOUTH CAROLINA
Lodging
Woodlands Resort & Inn, *Summerville*

Restaurant
Dining Room at the Woodlands, *Summerville*

TENNESSEE
Lodging
The Hermitage, *Nashville*

TEXAS
Lodging
The Mansion on Turtle Creek, *Dallas*

VERMONT
Lodging
Twin Farms, *Barnard*

VIRGINIA
Lodgings
The Inn at Little Washington, *Washington*
The Jefferson Hotel, *Richmond*

Restaurant
The Inn at Little Washington, *Washington*

Mobil Travel Guide has been rating establishments with its Mobil One- to Five-Star system since 1958. Each establishment awarded the Mobil Five-Star rating is one of the best in the country. Detailed information on each award winner can be found in the corresponding regional edition listed on the back cover of this book.

Four-Star Establishments in Northern Plains

Wyoming

★★★★ Lodgings
Amangani, *Jackson Hole*
Four Seasons Resort Jackson Hole, *Jackson Hole*

★★★★ Spa
The Spa at the Four Seasons Resort Jackson Hole, *Jackson Hole*

Montana

This magnificent state took its name from the Spanish *montaña*--meaning mountainous. The altitude of about half the state is more than 5,000 feet, and the sprawling ranges of the Continental Divide rise more than 2 miles into air so clear, photographers must use filters to avoid overexposure. The names of many towns, though, indicate that Montana has more than mountains. Grassrange, Roundup, and Buffalo tell of vast prairie regions, where tawny oceans of wheat stretch to the horizon and a cattle ranch may be 30 miles from front gate to front porch. Big Timber and Highwood suggest Montana's 22 million acres of forests; Goldcreek and Silver Gate speak of the roaring mining days (the roaring is mostly over, but you can still pan for gold in almost any stream); and Jim Bridger reminds us of the greatest mountain man of them all. Of special interest to vacationing visitors are Antelope, Lame Deer, and Trout creeks, which indicate hunting and fishing *par excellence*.

First glimpsed by French traders Louis and François Verendrye in 1743, Montana remained unexplored and largely unknown until Lewis and Clark crossed the region in 1805. Two years later, Manuel Lisa's trading post at the mouth of the Big Horn ushered in a half-century of hunting and trapping.

The Treasure State's natural resources are enormous. Its hydroelectric potential is the greatest in the world--annual flow of the four major rivers is enough to cover the whole state with 6 inches of water. The 25 major dams include Fort Peck, one of the world's largest hydraulic earthfill dams. Near Great Falls, one of the world's largest freshwater springs, pours out nearly 400 million gallons of wa-

Population: 902,195
Area: 145,392 square miles
Elevation: 1,800-12,799 feet
Peak: Granite Peak (Park County)
Entered Union: November 8, 1889 (41st state)
Capital: Helena
Motto: Oro y Plata (Gold and silver)
Nickname: Treasure State, Big Sky Country
Flower: Bitterroot
Bird: Western Meadowlark
Tree: Ponderosa Pine
Fair: July-August in Great Falls
Time Zone: Mountain
Web Site: www.visitmt.com
Fun Facts:
• Montana has the largest grizzly bear population in the lower 48 states.
• In Montana, the elk, deer, and antelope populations outnumber humans.

ter every day. In more than 1,500 lakes and 16,000 miles of fishing streams, the water is so clear you may wonder if it's there at all.

For a hundred years the state has produced gold and silver, with Virginia City (complete with Robbers' Roost situated within convenient raiding distance) probably the most famous mining town. Montana produces about $1 billion worth of minerals a year. Leading resources are coal, copper, natural gas, silver, platinum, and palladium. Montana also produces more gem sapphires than any other state. Farms and ranches totaling 67 million acres add $2 billion a year to the state's economy.

Along with the bounty of its resources, Montana's history has given us Custer's Last Stand (June 25, 1876), the last spike in the Northern Pacific Railroad (September 8, 1883), the country's first Congress-

Calendar Highlights

JANUARY

Montana Pro Rodeo Circuit Finals *(Great Falls)*. *Montana Expo Park, Four Seasons Arena. Phone 406/727-8900.* www.montanaprorodeo.com. The best riders in the state compete for a chance to reach the nationals.

FEBRUARY

Chocolate Festival *(Anaconda)*. *Phone 406/563-2422.* Chocolate baking contest with winning creations sold at a charity bake sale. Free chocolates at local merchants. Various "sweetheart" activities are held throughout town.

JULY

State Fair *(Great Falls)*. *Montana Expo Park. Phone 406/727-8900.* www.montanastatefair.com. Rodeo, livestock exhibits, horse racing, petting zoo, commercial exhibits, entertainment, carnival.

Wild Horse Stampede *(Wolf Point)*. Chamber of Commerce and Agriculture, phone 406/653-2220. One of Montana's best and oldest rodeos.

AUGUST

Montana Cowboy Poetry Gathering *(Lewistown)*. *Phone 406/538-5436.* Modern-day cowboys and admirers of Western folklore relate life "down on the range" through original poetry.

Western Montana Fair and Rodeo *(Missoula)*. *Fairgrounds. Phone 406/721-3247.* Live horse racing, three-night rodeo, nightly fireworks. Carnival, livestock, commercial exhibits. Musical performances, demolition derby, blacksmith competition.

OCTOBER

Bridger Raptor Festival *(Bozeman)*. *Bridger Bowl Ridge area. Phone 406/585-1211.* View birds of prey, including the largest concentration of migrating Golden Eagles in the contiguous 48 states, on their trip south.

---

woman (Jeannette Rankin of Missoula, in 1916), the Dempsey-Gibbons fight (July 4, 1923) and a state constitution originally prefaced by the Magna Carta, the Declaration of Independence, the Articles of Confederation, and the United States Constitution.

When to Go/Climate

Montana's weather is changeable, and temperatures are cold for much longer than they are warm. To the east of the divide, weather is more extreme than to the west, due to winds blowing unhindered across the plains. There is heavy snowfall in the mountains, and summer doesn't really begin until July. Summer is tourist season; early fall is less crowded, and temperatures are still good for outdoor adventures.

AVERAGE HIGH/LOW TEMPERATURES (°F)

Billings

Jan 32/14	**May** 67/43	**Sep** 72/47
Feb 39/19	**Jun** 78/58	**Oct** 61/38
Mar 46/25	**Jul** 87/58	**Nov** 45/26
Apr 57/34	**Aug** 85/57	**Dec** 34/17

Missoula

Jan 30/15	**May** 66/38	**Sep** 71/40
Feb 37/21	**Jun** 74/50	**Oct** 57/31
Mar 47/25	**Jul** 83/50	**Nov** 41/24
Apr 58/31	**Aug** 82/50	**Dec** 30/16

If you come in winter, bring your mittens. Temperatures can drop below zero, but the climate is milder than perceived because of the state's location in the interior of the continent. Snowmobiling, downhill skiing, and cross-country skiing are popular sports here. Summer days are warm, dry, and sunny.

Parks and Recreation

Water-related activities, hiking, riding, various other sports, picnicking, and visitor centers, as well as camping, are available in many of Montana's parks. Parks are open approximately May-September. Day-use fee, $5 per vehicle. Park Passport $24 per year. Camping (limited to 14 days), $10-$15/ site per night. Additional fees may be charged at some areas for other activities. Pets on leash only. For information on state parks, write to the Parks Division, Montana Department of Fish, Wildlife, and Parks, 1420 E Sixth Avenue, Helena 59620. Phone 406/444-3750.

FISHING AND HUNTING

Game fish include all species of trout as well as salmon, whitefish, grayling, sauger, walleye, paddlefish, sturgeon, pike, burbot, channel catfish, and bass. Nonresident fishing license: annual, $50; two-day consecutive license, $25; nonfee permit needed in Glacier and Yellowstone national parks.

Big game include moose, elk, deer, antelope, bighorn sheep, mountain goat, mountain lion, and black bear; game birds include both mountain and prairie species. Nonresident hunting license: game birds, $125; various types of elk and deer combination licenses are available. Licenses for moose, sheep, goat, and antelope are awarded through special drawings. Licenses for mountain lion must be purchased by August 31.

A $7 conservation license is a prerequisite to a hunting or fishing license. For detailed information, write to Montana Fish, Wildlife, and Parks, PO Box 200701, Helena 59620-0701. Phone 406/444-2535 (general information) or 406/444-2950 (special licensing).

Driving Information

Safety belts are mandatory for all persons anywhere in a vehicle. Children under 6 years or under 60 pounds in weight must be in an approved safety seat anywhere in a vehicle. For more information, phone 406/444-3412.

INTERSTATE HIGHWAY SYSTEM

The following alphabetical listing of Montana towns in this book shows that these cities are within 10 miles of the indicated interstate highways. Check a highway map for the nearest exit.

Highway Number	Cities/Towns within 10 Miles
Interstate 15	Butte, Dillon, Great Falls, Helena.
Interstate 90	Anaconda, Big Timber, Billings, Bozeman, Butte, Deer Lodge, Hardin, Livingston, Missoula, Three Forks.
Interstate 94	Billings, Glendive, Miles City.

Additional Visitor Information

Several pamphlets and brochures, which comprise a "Vacation Planning Guide," list points of interest, motels, campgrounds, museums, events, and attractions. They may be obtained from Travel Montana, 1424 Ninth Avenue, PO Box 200533, Helena, 59620-0533. Phone toll-free 800/847-4868.

Three periodicals are recommended to Montana visitors. They are *Montana: Magazine of Western History,* quarterly, Montana Historical Society, 225 North Roberts Street, Helena 59601; *Montana Magazine Inc,* bimonthly, 3020 Bozeman, Helena 59624; and *Montana Outdoors,* bimonthly, Department of Fish, Wildlife, and Parks, 1420 East Sixth

BOB MARSHALL WILDERNESS COMPLEX

Bob Marshall (1901-1939) was many things: a hiker who would cover 40 miles in a day, a scientist who studied forest ecology, and a visionary thinker who was among the founders of the Wilderness Society. The concept of a roadless wilderness untouched by man is beloved and fiercely defended today, but it was a virtually unknown philosophy in Marshall's time. Because his ideas helped spur the eventual establishment of the US Forest Service's concept of wilderness areas, it's fitting that the largest tract of official USFS wilderness bears his name.

Affectionately known as The Bob, the Bob Marshall Wilderness Complex consists of three separate wilderness areasBob Marshall, Great Bear, and Scapegoatthat total more than 1.5 million acres in all. It was among the first parcels of land protected by the Wilderness Act of 1964, and today it is the largest single chunk of undeveloped wildland in the lower 48. The reason is clear: places like this define what is meant by terms like nature and wilderness, a rugged, mountainous landscape teeming with alpine lakes, crystalline waterfalls, dense green forests, and wildlife running the gamut from gray wolves, grizzly bears, and Canadian lynx to owls and bald eagles.

The Continental Divide runs through the complex for roughly 60 miles, including an especially impressive (and massive) escarpment named the Chinese Wall, 22 miles long, 1,000 feet high, and a favorite nesting spot of eagles. As the primary access trails traverse the valley carved by the South Fork of the Flathead

River, another popular destination is the valley's Salmon Lake, the largest lake in the entire wilderness complex. There are also numerous peaks that top out over 9,000 feet, including craggy Scapegoat Mountain in the complex's southern reaches, a haven for elk, deer, bears, and mountain goats.The Bob's big recreational draws are backpacking and horse-packing. Numerous outfitters take groups on guided horse-packing trips, but there is only one licensed backpacking guide service (High Country Adventures, out of Choteau; phone 406/466-5699; www.high-country-adventures.bigstep.com). These multiday trips often include meals, transportation, and gear, as well as a week, give or take, of guided backcountry exploration, covering 5 to 10 miles of trail in an average day. Backpacking without a guide is also quite popular, but a good deal of preparation is essentialand it's critical to remember that this is bear country.

For those with less time (and those who don't fancy sleeping outdoors), the complex is full of great day hikes. The best jumping-off points are Seeley Lake, Augusta, and West Glacier. Out of Augusta, a good day hike is up Elk Creek Pass, a moderate 6-mile jaunt; overnighters and more experienced hikers can continue another 6 steep miles up to the summit of Steamboat Mountain. Northeast of Seeley Lake, Pyramid Pass is another good day-hiking area (especially for those who want to stop for a little creek-fishing as well), but the ascent is more difficult, climbing more than 1,600 feet in 4 miles.

EXPLORING MONTANA'S BITTERROOT RIVER VALLEY

Take this scenic alternative to freeway driving along I-15 and I-90. From Missoula, follow Highway 93 south along the Bitterroot River. At first, the valley is wide and filled with farms, but then the mountains close in: the jagged Bitterroot Range rears to the west and the gentle Sapphire Range rises to the east. This is one of Montana's most scenic valleys and holds some of its best fishing. Near Florence, visit the Daly Mansion, which was home to one of the super-rich Copper Kings in the 1880s. Just below the Continental Divide, stop at Lost Trail Hot Springs. After climbing up to Lost Trail Pass, turn

back toward Montana on Highway 43 and drop by Big Hole National Battlefield, where the Battle of the Big Hole, one of the West's most dramatic Army/Indian battles, was fought. Paths lead to the battle site, where Chief Joseph and the Nez Perce defeated the US Army; there's also a good interpretive center. The little ranch town of Wisdom, with its excellent fine-art gallery, is the fishing capital of Big Hole (the Big Hole River is a blue ribbon fishing river), a broad, prairielike valley filled with historic cattle ranches flanked by towering mountain ranges. Continue along Highway 278 through lovely high prairies, stopping by Bannack, the territorial capital of Montana and one of the best-preserved ghost towns in the West (also a state park). Join I-15 at Dillon, a handsome Victorian town that is home to Montana's oldest college and considerable historic architecture. **(Approximately 207 miles)**

MONTANA'S UNIQUE LANDMARKS

Stanford is in the center of the Judith Basin, an area of high prairie ringed by low-slung mountain ranges. This was one of the centers of the old open-range cattle ranches, and cowboy artist Charlie Russell painted many of the unique, monumental buttes and mountains in the area. From the farm and ranch lands around Stanford, leave Highway 200 and cut north on Highway 80. The horizon is filled with odd blocklike buttes rising directly out of the plains. The largest is Square Butte, which from a distance looks like a completely square block of rock towering thousands of feet above the range. These odd formations are lava batholiths, which formed as subterranean lakes of molten rock that cooled and were later exposed by erosion. Square Butte is protected by the Bureau of Land Management, but anyone with a high-clearance vehicle can climb up the side to a plateau 1,000 feet above the prairie for views that stretch hundreds of miles. The prairie ecosystem on the butte is considered pristine, an example of the flora that once greeted Lewis and Clark. Past Square Butte, the road dips into a vast abandoned river channel that once carried the Ice-Age Missouri River. As the route approaches the present-day river, you can see glimpses of the famed White Cliffs of the Missouri, which so impressed Lewis and Clark. (This section of the Missouri is protected as a Wild and Scenic River and is otherwise essentially roadless.) The route drops onto the Missouri at Fort Benton, the upper terminus of the Missouri riverboat trade of the 1850s. Fort Benton is one of the oldest towns in the state and has several good museums and historic buildings. Here the route joins Highway 87. **(Approximately 48 miles)**

Anaconda (C-2)

See also Butte, Deer Lodge

Founded 1883
Population 10,278
Elevation 5,265 ft
Area Code 406
Zip 59711
Information Chamber of Commerce, 306 E Park St; phone 406/563-2400
Web Site www.anacondamontana.org

Chosen by Marcus Daly, a copper king, as the site for a copper smelter, the city was first dubbed with the tongue-twisting name of Copperopolis, but was later renamed. In 1894, the "war of the copper kings" was waged between Daly and W. A. Clark over the location of the state capital. Clark's Helena won by a small margin. After his rival's death, the world's largest copper smelter was built, standing 585 feet, 1 1/2 inches.

What to See and Do

Big Hole Basin. *Anaconda. 25 miles SW on Hwy 274.* Fishing, hunting; raft races; lodge, skiing.

Copper Village Museum and Arts Center. *401 E Commercial St, Anaconda (59711). Phone 406/563-2422.* Located in the Anaconda City Hall Cultural Center, this museum and arts center features local and traveling art exhibitions; theater, music, and films; and a museum of local pioneer and industrial history. The building is on the National Register of Historic Places. (Tues-Sat 10 am-4 pm; closed holidays) **FREE**

Discovery Ski Area. *505 Hickory St, Anaconda (59711). 18 miles NW on Hwy 1. Phone 406/563-2184. www.skidiscovery.com.* This 548-acre ski area with 55 trails has two triple lifts, three double chairlifts, two beginner lifts; snowmaking; patrol, school, rentals; restaurant, bar. Longest run 1 1/2 miles; vertical drop 1,670 feet. Cross-country trails. (Thanksgiving-early Apr, daily) **$$$$**

Georgetown Lake. *Anaconda. 15 miles W on Pintler Scenic Rte (Hwy 1).* Water-skiing, boating, fishing, swimming, camping, picnicking, wilderness area; in winter, skiing and snowmobiling.

Ghost towns and sapphire mines. *Anaconda. Near Georgetown Lake on Pintler Scenic Rte (Hwy 1).* Inquire at local chambers of commerce or visitor centers.

Lost Creek State Park. *3201 Spurgin Rd, Missoula (59804). 1 1/2 miles E on Hwy 1, then 2 miles N on Hwy 273, then 6 miles W on an unnumbered road. Phone 406/542-5500.* The highlights of this 25-acre park are the gray limestone cliffs and the pink-and-white granite formations that rise 1,200 feet above the canyon floor. Mountain goats, bighorn sheep, and other wildlife are often seen on the clifftops. A short hiking trail leads to the 50-foot-high Lost Creek Falls. Twenty-five sites provide opportunities for tent and trailer camping. Pets are allowed on leash only. (May-Nov) **FREE**

Old Works. *1205 Pizzini Way, Anaconda (59711). Phone 406/563-5827. www.oldworks.org.* This 18-hole Jack Nicklaus signature golf course is located on the developed grounds of a former copper smelter. The site also features a fully accessible trail that skirts the foundations of the old works and allows interpretation of the town's smelting heritage (free). Dining room. (Late May-Oct, daily, weather permitting) **$$$$**

⭐ Visitor center. *306 E Park St, Anaconda (59711). Phone 406/563-2400. www.anacondamt.org.* Housed in a replica turn-of-the-century railroad station, Anaconda's visitor center has a display of smelter works photographs, an outdoor railroad exhibit, and a video presentation highlighting area attractions. Self-guided walking tours; historic bus tours (Memorial Day-Labor Day, daily); tourist information for both city and state. (Mid-May-mid-Sept: Mon-Sat 9 am-5 pm; rest of year: Mon-Fri 9 am-5 pm) **FREE**

Special Events

Chocolate Festival. *Downtown, Anaconda (59711). Phone 406/563-2422.* Chocolate baking contest with winning creations sold at a charity bake sale. Free chocolates at local merchants. Various "sweetheart" activities are held throughout town.

Wayne Estes Memorial Tournament. *Anaconda. Phone 406/563-2400.* One of the largest basketball tournaments in the Northwest. Slam dunk, three-point contest. Last weekend in Mar.

Full-Service Resort

⭐ ⭐ ⭐ FAIRMONT HOT SPRINGS RESORT. *1500 Fairmont Rd, Anaconda (59711). Phone 406/797-3241; toll-free 800/332-3272; fax 406/797-3337. www.fairmontmontana.com.* The four hot springs swimming and soaking pools are the pride of this resort. Fed by 155-degree natural hot springs water and cooled to various comfortable temperatures, the pools (open 24 hours to guests and until 9:30 pm to the general public for a fee) also include a 350-foot enclosed water slide. A great place for family fun, the resort has a children's playground, wildlife zoo, sand volleyball and basketball courts, and offers hayrides and dogsledding in season. Winter brings opportunities for downhill and cross-country skiing, ice skating, ice fishing, and snowmobiling. Watch out for the "mile high, mile long" fifth hole and the 10,000-square foot green on the 6,471-yard golf course. Conference and convention facilities accommodate groups of up to 500; family reunions are popular here as well. 152 rooms, 3 story. Check-in 3 pm, check-out 11 am. Restaurant, bar. Fitness room. Two indoor pools, two outdoor pools, whirlpool. Golf, 18 holes. Tennis. **$**
🚶 🏊 🍴 ⛷

Restaurant

⭐ ⭐ BARCLAY II SUPPER CLUB. *1300 E Commerical Ave, Anaconda (59711). Phone 406/563-5541.* Menu highlights include steaks, seafood, and lobster. American menu. Dinner. Closed Mon. Bar. Children's menu. Casual attire. Reservations recommended. **$$**

Big Hole National Battlefield

Web Site www.nps.gov/biho

10 miles W of Wisdom on Hwy 43 or 16 miles E of Lost Trail Pass on Hwy 43, off Hwy 93, near the Idaho border.

A memorial to those who died in a battle between the US Army and the Nez Perce tribe, Big Hole National Battlefield is part of a larger system of parklands known as the Nez Perce National Historic Park. The Nez Perce, or Nimiipuu, people lived in their traditional homeland, a large, untamed swath stretching from Washington to Idaho, for generations before the westward expansion of the United States set the stage for conflict. The federal policy as of 1877 was to force tribes onto reservations to clear the way for white settlers, but a contingent of 750 Nez Perce resisted and escaped into what is now Montana, stopping in the Big Hole to rest and possibly settle. Six weeks later, however, on August 9, 1877, US soldiers ambushed the camp; casualties were high. The surviving Nez Perce fled east, and most surrendered two months later. More than 655 acres of the battlefield are preserved today. Facilities here include two visitor centers with exhibits and hiking trails.

Three self-guided trails lead through the Siege Area, the Nez Perce Camp, and the Howitzer Capture Site. Wildlife roams the area; fishing is permitted with a license. The Visitor Center Museum exhibits firearms and relics of the period (summer, daily 8:30 am-6 pm; winter, daily 9 am-5 pm; closed Jan 1, Thanksgiving, Dec 25). Interpretive walks are presented daily in summer. Fees are collected from late May to late September; some access roads are closed in winter.

Big Sky (D-3)

See also Bozeman

Population 450
Elevation 5,934 ft
Area Code 406
Zip 59716
Information Sky of Montana Resort, 1 Lone Mountain Trail; phone 406/995-5000 or toll-free 800/548-4486
Web Site www.bigskyresort.com

Located 45 miles southwest of Bozeman in Gallatin National Forest (see), Big Sky is a resort community developed by the late newscaster and commentator Chet Huntley. Golf, tennis, skiing, fishing, whitewater rafting, and horseback riding are among the many activities available in the area.

What to See and Do

Big Sky Resort. *1 Lone Mountain Trail, Big Sky (59716). Phone 406/995-5000; toll-free 800/548-4486. www.bigskyresort.com.* Quad, three high-speed quads, four triple, five double chairlifts, four surface tows; patrol, school, rentals; bar, concession area, cafeteria; nursery. Longest run 6 miles; vertical drop 4,350 feet. (Mid-Nov-mid-Apr, daily) Fifty miles of cross-country trails. Gondola.

Tram. Also summer activities. **$$$$**

River trips. Yellowstone Raft Company. *Big Sky. Phone 406/995-4613; toll-free 800/348-4376. www.yellowstoneraft.com.* Half- and full-day whitewater raft trips on Gallatin and Madison rivers. No experience necessary. Paddle or oar powered rafts. Also departs from Gardiner (see). **$$$$**

Limited-Service Hotels

★ ★ **BEST WESTERN BUCK'S T-4 LODGE.** *46625 Gallatin Rd (Hwy 191), Big Sky (59716). Phone 406/995-4111; toll-free 800/822-4484; fax 406/995-2191. www.buckst4.com.* 74 rooms, 2 story. Closed early-mid-May. Pets accepted; fee. Complimentary continental breakfast. Check-in 4 pm, check-out 11 am. Restaurant. Whirlpool.**$**

★ ★ **RAINBOW RANCH LODGE.** *42950 Gallatin Rd (Hwy 191), Big Sky (59716). Phone 406/995-4132; toll-free 800/937-4132; fax 406/995-2861. www.rainbowranch.com.* 16 rooms. Closed mid-Dec-Apr. Pets accepted. Complimentary continental breakfast. Check-in 3 pm, check-out 11 am. Restaurant. Whirlpool.**$$**

Full-Service Resort

★ ★ ★ **BIG SKY RESORT.** *1 Lone Mountain Trail, Big Sky (59716). Phone 406/995-5000; toll-free 800/548-4486; fax 406/995-5001. www.bigskyresort.com.* This resort, established by famed newscaster Chet Huntley, features condos of various layouts and themes for picking the type perfect for your needs. Daily programs for kids in addition to plenty of seasonal recreational offerings are available.666 rooms. Closed mid-Apr-May and mid-Oct-late Nov. Check-in 5 pm, check-out 10 am. Two restaurants, two bars. Children's activity center. Fitness room, spa. Outdoor pool, children's pool, two whirlpools. Golf. Tennis. Airport transportation available.**$$**

Full-Service Inn

★ ★ ★ **BIG EZ LODGE.** *7000 Beaver Creek Rd, Big Sky (59716). Phone 406/995-7000; toll-free 877/244-3299; fax 406/995-7007. www.bigezlodge.com.* 3 rooms. Closed mid-Oct-mid-Nov and mid-Apr-mid-May. Complimentary full breakfast. Check-in 4 pm, check-out 11 am. Restaurant, bar. Fitness room. Whirl-pool.**$$$**

Specialty Lodging

LONE MOUNTAIN RANCH. *750 Lone Mountain Ranch Rd, Big Sky (59716). Phone 406/995-4644; toll-free 800/514-4644; fax 406/995-4670. www.lmranch. com.* Discover nature and yourself all over again, here at the Lone Mountain. The log cabins provide a rustic sense, with modern touches. Great fishing, water sports, and nature activities are available, or just relax with a therapeutic massage. 30 rooms. Closed mid-Apr-May and mid-Oct-Nov. Check-in 3 pm, check-out 10 am. Restaurant, bar. Children's activity center. Whirlpool. Airport transportation available.**$$$**

Restaurant

★ ★ ★ **LONE MOUNTAIN RANCH DINING ROOM.** *160069 Big Sky, Big Sky (59716). Phone 406/995-2782; fax 406/995-4670. www.lmranch.com.* Visitors can enjoy dining in a spacious log cabin, complete with elk antler chandeliers, a large stone fireplace, and spectacular views. Elk, bison, and pheasant are featured weekly alongside traditional entres of pasta, beef, and fish. American menu. Breakfast, lunch, dinner. Closed Apr-May and Oct-Nov. Bar. Children's menu. Casual attire. Reservations recommended. **$$$**

Big Timber (C-3)

See also Bozeman, Livingston

Population 1,557
Elevation 4,081 ft
Area Code 406
Zip 59011
Web Site www.bigtimber.com

Some of the tall cottonwoods that gave this settlement its name and the grasses that endowed the county with the name "Sweet Grass" remain. Livestock ranches make Big Timber their selling and shopping center. It is also a popular dude ranch area, with good hunting and fishing facilities. The Yellowstone and Boulder rivers provide good trout fishing. The first dude ranch in the state was started here around 1911. Natural bridge and falls area is located approximately 25 miles south of town.

A Ranger District office of the Gallatin National Forest (see BOZEMAN) is located here.

Special Event

NRA/MRA Rodeo. *112 S 18th St, Big Timber (59011). Phone 406/252-1122.* Mid-May-mid-Sept.

Limited-Service Hotel

★ **SUPER 8.** *2080 Big Timber Loop, Big Timber (59011). Phone 406/932-8888; toll-free 800/800-8000; fax 406/932-4103. www.super8.com.* 41 rooms, 2 story. Pets accepted; fee. Complimentary continental breakfast. Check-in 2 pm, check-out 11 am.**$**

Restaurant

★ ★ **THE GRAND.** *139 McLeod St, Big Timber (59011). Phone 406/932-4459; fax 406/932-4248. www. thegrand-hotel.com.* This 1890 hotel dining room features vintage photos and many original furnishings. Located just off Interstate 90, it is situated between the Beartooth and Crazy mountains. The menu selections, salads, and homemade desserts are all well prepared and presented. American menu. Dinner. Bar. Children's menu. Casual attire. Reservations recommended. **$$**

Bigfork (B-2)

See also Kalispell, Polson

Population 1,080
Elevation 2,968 ft
Area Code 406
Zip 59911
Information Chamber of Commerce, Old Towne Center, PO Box 237; phone 406/837-5888
Web Site www.bigfork.org

Surrounded by lakes, a river, and a dam, Bigfork's businesses are electric power and catering to tourists who visit the east shore of Flathead Lake (see POLSON), the largest freshwater lake west of the Mississippi. The quaint downtown area offers art galleries, specialty shops, and an array of restaurants; lodging options range from small inns to high-end resorts. The Bob Marshall and Swan wilderness areas lie in the town's backyard, with a host of recreational opportunities to choose from. A Ranger District office of the Flathead National Forest (see KALISPELL) is located here.

What to See and Do

Bigfork Art and Cultural Center. *525 Electric Ave, Bigfork (59911). Phone 406/837-6927.* Exhibits by artists and crafters of northwestern Montana; gift shop. (Spring and fall, Wed-Sat; summer, Tues-Sat; closed Jan) **FREE**

Flathead Lake State Park-Wayfarers Unit. *490 N Meridian Rd, Kalispell (59901). 14 miles N of Polson on Hwy 93. Phone 406/837-4196. fwp.state.mt.us/parks.* At 28 miles long and 15 miles wide, Flathead Lake is the largest freshwater lake west of the Mississippi. There are six state park units surrounding the lake (also see POLSON), the nearest to Bigfork being the Wayfarers unit. It's renowned for its fishing, especially for lake trout. At this easily accessible unit on the northeastern shore, you can swim, launch a boat, hike to the cliffs over the shoreline, picnic, and camp (May-Sept; no hookups). Pets are allowed, and entry is free for Montana residents. **$**

Wayfarers Unit. *Bigfork. Off Hwy 35. Phone 406/837-4196.* Hiking trails. Camping (dump station, patrons only).

Yellow Bay Unit. *Bigfork. 10 miles S on Hwy 35. Phone 406/752-5501.* Joint state/tribal fishing license required. No RVs or trailers permitted.

Swan Lake. *200 Ranger Station Rd, 1935 3rd Ave E, Bigfork (59911). 14 miles SE of Big Fork on Hwy 83. Phone 406/837-5081.* A slender finger of water 20 miles long and a mere mile wide, Swan Lake is one of a chain of lakes on the Clearwater River. It's known first and foremost as a fishing destination: in the spring, northern pike are the prime catch; in the summer and fall, it's Kokanee salmon and bull trout. Swan Lake is also popular with boaters, and there are campsites and hiking trails near its shores, as well as the village of the same name on its southern tip.

Special Events

Bigfork Summer Playhouse. *526 Electric Ave, Bigfork (59911). Phone 406/837-4886. www.bigforksummerplayhouse.com.* One of Montana's most acclaimed summer stock theaters, the Bigfork Summer Playhouse, originated in the 1960s and today is a popular cultural draw in the Flathead Valley. It stages a number of Broadway musicals every summer, with recent productions of *Always...Patsy Cline* and *Carousel* under its belt. In the off-season, a children's theater company performs regularly. Mid-May-mid-Sept:

Mon-Sat 8 pm.

Wild West Day. *Bigfork. Phone 406/837-5888.* Sept.

Limited-Service Hotel

★ ★ **MARINA CAY RESORT & CONFERENCE CENTER.** *180 Vista Ln, Bigfork (59911). Phone 406/837-5861; toll-free 800/433-6516; fax 406/837-1118. www.marinacay.com.* 180 rooms, 3 story. Check-in 3 pm, check-out 11 am. Restaurant, bar. Outdoor pool, whirlpool. Airport transportation available. Business center. On Bigfork Bay of Flathead Lake.**$**
🏊 🚶

Specialty Lodgings

AVERILL'S FLATHEAD LAKE LODGE. *150 Flathead Lake Lodge Rd, Bigfork (59911). Phone 406/837-4391; fax 406/837-6977. www.flatheadlakelodge.com.* Averill's Flathead Lake Lodge offers visitors an once-in-a-lifetime vacation experience. Resting on 2,000 acres on the eastern shores of Montana's largest freshwater lake, this lodge is a paradise for outdoor enthusiasts. Anglers delight in fly fishing here, the placid waters are perfect for sailing and canoeing, and the state's best golf course is down the road, but horses are the focus at this authentic dude ranch. From riding instruction and horse competition to team roping and guest rodeos, this resort gives city slickers a taste of cowboy culture. Younger guests create long-lasting memories while learning about horse care and barn duties as part of the Junior Wranglers program. The log lodges capture the essence of the Old West with buffalo-hide couches and river-rock fireplaces, and the family-style meals remind diners of traditional cookouts with roasted meats and other classic Western dishes.38 rooms, 2 story. Closed early Sept-early June. Complimentary full breakfast. Check-in 3 pm, check-out 11 am. High-speed Internet access, wireless Internet access. Bar. Children's activity center. Beach. Outdoor pool. Tennis. Airport transportation available.**$$$$**
🏊 🎿

O'DUACHAIN COUNTRY INN. *675 Ferndale Dr, Bigfork (59911). Phone 406/837-6851; toll-free 800/837-7460; fax 406/837-0778. www.montanainn.com.* 5 rooms, 3 story. Pets accepted, some restrictions; fee. Complimentary full breakfast. Check-in 3 pm, check-out 11 am. Whirlpool. Authentic log home.**$**

Restaurants

★ ★ **BIGFORK INN.** *604 Electric Ave, Bigfork (59911). Phone 406/837-6680.* International menu. Dinner. Bar. Children's menu. Casual attire. Outdoor seating. **$$**
🖪

★ ★ ★ **COYOTE ROADHOUSE.** *600 Three Eagle Ln, Bigfork (59911). Phone 406/837-1233; fax 406/837-4250. www.coyoteroadhouse.com.* International menu. Dinner. Closed Mon-Tues. Children's menu. Casual attire. Outdoor seating. **$$**

★ ★ ★ **SHOWTHYME.** *548 Electric Ave, Bigfork (59911). Phone 406/837-0707; fax 406/837-3176. www.showthyme.com.* Located in an old bank building (1910), this restaurant features original brick walls and engraved tin ceilings. Menu selections include steak, fresh seafood, and chicken, and the desserts are homemade. American menu. Dinner. Closed Jan. Bar. Children's menu. Casual attire. Reservations recommended. Outdoor seating. **$$$**
🖪

Billings (C-4)

See also Hardin

Founded 1882
Population 81,151
Elevation 3,124 ft
Area Code 406
Information Billings Area Chamber of Commerce, 815 S 27th St, PO Box 31177, 59107; phone 406/252-4016 or toll-free 800/735-2635
Web Site www.billingscvb.visitmt.com

On the west bank of the Yellowstone River, Billings, seat of Yellowstone County, was built by the Northern Pacific Railway and took the name of railroad President Frederick K. Billings. Today, it is the center of a vast trade region. Billings is a major distribution point for Montana's and Wyoming's vast strip-mining operations. Industries include agriculture, tourism, and oil trade. Billings offers excellent medical facilities and is a regional convention center. It is also the headquarters of the Custer National Forest (see HARDIN).

What to See and Do

Boothill Cemetery. *Billings. E end of Chief Black Otter Trail.* Final resting place of Billings' gunmen and law-men who died with their boots on.

Chief Black Otter Trail. *Billings. Starts at E end of city.* Drive above city, past Boothill Cemetery, up Kelly Mountain and down along edge of sheer cliff. Excellent view of Billings.

Geyser Park. *4910 Southgate Dr, Billings (59101). Phone 406/254-2510.* Includes 18-hole miniature golf course; water bumper boats, Lazer-Tag, Go-Karts and track; concessions. (May-Oct, daily; closed holidays) **$$$**

Moss Mansion. *914 Division St, Billings (59101). Phone 406/256-5100. www.mossmansion.com.* In 1901, architect H. J. Hardenbergh created the three-story estate. Original furnishings. (Daily) **$$**

Peter Yegen, Jr.--Yellowstone County Museum. *1950 Terminal Cir, Billings (59102). At Logan Field Airport, on Hwy 3. Phone 406/256-6811.* Native American artifacts, antique steam locomotive, horse-drawn vehicles; dioramas depict homesteading days and Native American sacrificial ceremony; vast display of valuable guns, saddles, precious stones. Breathtaking view of Yellowstone Valley and the mountains. (Mon-Sat; closed holidays) **DONATION**

Pictograph Cave State Park. *Billings. I-90 at Lockwood exit, 6 miles S on county road. Phone 406/245-0227.* Inhabited 4,500 years ago; pictographs on walls. Picnicking. (Mid-Apr-mid-Oct) **$$**

Range Rider of the Yellowstone. *Billings. Near the airport, off Chief Black Otter Trail.* Life-size bronze statue of a cowboy and his mount; posed for by William S. Hart, an early silent film cowboy star.

Rocky Mountain College. *1511 Poly Dr, Billings (59101). Phone 406/657-1026. www.rocky.edu.* (1878) (850 students) The first college in Montana. The campus's sandstone buildings are some of Billings' oldest permanent structures.

Western Heritage Center. *2822 Montana Ave, Billings (59101). Phone 406/256-6809. www.ywhc.org.* Featuring rotating exhibits relating to the history of the Yellowstone Valley from prehistoric to modern times. (Tues-Sat; closed holidays) **DONATION**

Yellowstone Art Museum. *401 N 27th St, Billings (59101). Phone 406/256-6804. yellowstone.artmuseum .org.* The standout attraction in Billings, the onetime Yellowstone County Jail was renovated in the 1960s into this excellent facility. After a significant expansion in the late 1990s, it emerged as the top art museum in Montana and is among the best in the entire Rocky Mountain region.

The focus is squarely on works by Montana artists, and there is an especially strong emphasis on contemporary art. The permanent Montana Collection includes more than 3,000 pieces in all; living practitioners are represented alongside such historic luminaries as Charles Russell and cowboy illustrator Will James. Temporary exhibitions tend toward the edgy and modern, but not exclusively: a recent exhibition showcased art depicting Montana as seen by Lewis and Clark. The auditorium hosts lectures, films, and classes, and a nice museum store is on-site. (Tues-Sun; closed Jan) **$$**

ZooMontana. *2100 S Shiloh Rd, Billings (59106). Phone 406/652-8100. www.zoomontana.org.* The state's only wildlife park features homestead petting zoo. (Mid-Apr-mid-Oct, daily; rest of year, weekends, weather permitting)**$$**

Special Events

Montana Fair. *Metra Park, 308 6th Ave N, Billings (59101). Phone 406/256-2400. www.montanafair.com.* Attractions at this fair include 4-H exhibits, music, various shows, a carnival, and rodeo. Mid-Aug.

Northern International Livestock Exposition. *Metra Park, 308 6th Ave N, Billings (59101). Phone 406/256-2400. www.thenile.org.* Trade shows, horse shows and sales, and a professional rodeo are some of the features here; it is one of the top livestock shows and rodeos in the region. Oct.

Limited-Service Hotels

★ **BEST WESTERN PONDEROSA INN.** *2511 1st Ave N, Billings (59101). Phone 406/259-5511; toll-free 800/628-9081; fax 406/245-8004. www.bestwestern.com.* A great choice for families traveling to Billings, the Best Western Ponderosa Inn offers clean facilities, a friendly staff, and a downtown location near many restaurants and shops. 131 rooms, 2 story. Pets accepted, some restrictions. Complimentary continental breakfast. Check-in 2 pm, check-out 11 am. Fitness room. Outdoor pool. Airport transportation available.**$**

★ **BOOTHILL INN AND SUITES.** *242 E Airport Rd, Billings (59105). Phone 406/245-2000; toll-free 866/266-8445; fax 406/245-8591. www.boothillinn .com.* 69 rooms. Complimentary continental breakfast. Check-in 3 pm, check-out 11 am. Fitness room. Indoor pool, whirlpool.**$**

★ ★ **CLARION HOTEL THE HISTORIC NORTHERN HOTEL.** *19 N Broadway St, Billings (59101). Phone 406/245-5121; fax 406/245-1067. www .northernhotel.net.* In the heart of downtown Billings, just steps away from local shopping and arts venues, this historic hotel provides a warm, friendly place to stay. Originally built in 1906, the building was rebuilt in 1940 after a fire. 160 rooms, 10 story. Pets accepted. Check-in 4 pm, check-out 11 am. Restaurant, bar. Fitness room. Airport transportation available. Business center.**$**

★ **COUNTRY INN & SUITES - BILLINGS.** *231 Main St, Billings (59105). Phone 406/245-9995; toll-free 800/456-4000; fax 406/294-9999. www.countryinns .com.* The staff is welcoming and the atmosphere cozy at this Country Inn & Suites, located near Metra Park, home of the Montana Fair. 67 rooms. Complimentary continental breakfast. Check-in 3 pm, check-out noon. High-speed Internet access. Fitness room. Indoor pool, whirlpool.**$**

★ **FAIRFIELD INN.** *2026 Overland Ave, Billings (59102). Phone 406/652-5330; toll-free 800/228-2800; fax 406/652-5330. www.fairfieldinn.com.* Budget-minded travelers will find this Fairfield Inn to be a great choice for its well-kept rooms and convenient location off of Interstate 90. 63 rooms, 3 story. Pets accepted, some restrictions. Complimentary continental breakfast. Check-in 3 pm, check-out noon. High-speed Internet access, wireless Internet access. Indoor pool, whirlpool.**$**

★ **HOLIDAY INN EXPRESS.** *430 Cole St, Billings (59102). Phone 406/259-8600; toll-free 800/465-4329; fax 406/259-8601. www.hiexpress.com.* Guests stopping by this Holiday Inn Express off of Interstate 90 can count on a good night's rest in the clean and comfortable rooms.66 rooms. Complimentary continental breakfast. Check-in 1 pm, check-out 11 am. High-speed Internet access. Fitness room. Indoor pool, whirlpool. Business center.**$**

★ **QUALITY INN.***2036 Overland Ave, Billings (59102). Phone 406/652-1320; toll-free 800/228-5151; fax 406/652-1320. www.qualityinn.com.* Located off of Interstate 90, the Quality Inn Homestead Park is a convenient and comfortable place to stay in Billings.119 rooms, 2 story. Pets accepted. Complimentary full breakfast. Check-in 3 pm, check-out noon.

High-speed Internet access, wireless Internet access. Indoor pool, whirlpool. Airport transportation available. Business center. **$**

Full-Service Hotel

★ ★ ★ **SHERATON BILLINGS HOTEL.** *27 N 27th St, Billings (59101). Phone 406/252-7400; toll-free 800/588-7666; fax 406/252-2401. www.sheraton.com.* From families to business travelers, everyone will feel welcomed at the Sheraton Billings hotel. Rooms here are modern with brick and dark wood accents and offer great views of the city and mountains. 282 rooms, 23 story. Pets accepted. Check-in 3 pm, check-out noon. High-speed Internet access. Restaurant, bar. Fitness room. Indoor pool, children's pool, whirlpool. Airport transportation available. Business center. **$**

Restaurants

★ ★ **GEORGE HENRY'S.** *404 N 30th St, Billings (59101). Phone 406/245-4570; fax 406/245-3745.* Built in 1882, this former boardinghouse and tearoom still retains much of the ambience of an earlier day. It is conveniently located downtown, near hotels and shopping areas. American menu. Lunch, dinner. Closed Sun; holidays. Children's menu. Business casual attire. Outdoor seating. **$$**

★ ★ ★ **JULIANO'S.** *2912 N 7th Ave, Billings (59101). Phone 406/248-6400.* Chef/owner Carl Shunzo Kurokawa creates "fusion" cuisine in an inventive, artful manner. The specialties include exotic meats. Try the ostrich and shrimp napoleon or the roasted ostrich. This converted Victorian home (1902) features turn-of-the-century decor. International menu. Lunch, dinner. Closed Sun; holidays; late Dec-early Jan. Children's menu. Business casual attire. Reservations recommended. Outdoor seating. **$$**

★ ★ **REX.** *2401 Montana Ave, Billings (59101). Phone 406/245-7477; fax 406/248-6469.* Specializing in beef and seafood, this family-friendly restaurant prides itself on its food, service, and location. Situated in the historic district, the building dates to 1910 but has an up-to-date feel. The decor features exposed brick walls, pressed tin ceilings, and wood and tile flooring. Live piano music is provided on Friday and Saturday nights. American menu. Lunch, dinner. Closed Thanksgiving, Dec 25. Bar. Casual attire. Reservations recommended. Outdoor seating. **$$**

★ ★ ★ **WALKER'S GRILL.** *2700 1st Ave N, Billings (59101). Phone 406/245-9291; fax 406/248-7607. www.walkersgrill.com.* This is the place to go for both locals and visitors. The menu changes seasonally and features a variety of meat, seafood, and pasta dishes. The Southwest tapas tables are popular with lots to choose from, and an extensive wine list is offered. American menu. Dinner. Bar. Children's menu. Casual attire. Reservations recommended. **$$**

Bozeman (D-3)

See also Big Sky, Big Timber, Livingston, Three Forks, White Sulphur Springs

Settled 1864
Population 22,660
Elevation 4,810 ft
Area Code 406
Information Chamber of Commerce, 2000 Commerce Way, 59718; phone 406/586-5421 or toll-free 800/228-4224
Web Site www.bozemanchamber.com

Blazing a trail from Wyoming, John M. Bozeman led a train of immigrants who settled here and named the town for their leader. The first settlements in the Gallatin Valley were agricultural, but were economically surpassed by the mines nearby. Today, small grain farming, livestock, dairying, tourism, and the state university are important sources of income. The city is the marketplace for the cattle-producing Gallatin Valley.

What to See and Do

Bridger Bowl Ski Area. *15795 Bridger Canyon Rd, Bozeman (59715). 16 miles NE via Hwy 86, in Gallatin National Forest. Phone 406/587-2111; toll-free 800/223-9609. www.bridgerbowl.com.* Founded in the 1950s, Bridger Bowl is the perfect low-key antidote to today's typical overcrowded, overdeveloped ski resort. It's the locals' favorite and a nonprofit enterprise, which translates to an emphasis on good skiing over the almighty dollar. There are no on-mountain accommodations, but the lift tickets are inexpensive, the lift lines are short, and the snow is so dry it's called "powder smoke." On the 2,200 acres of terrain, there are 69 trails (25 percent beginner, 35 percent intermediate, 30 percent expert, and 10 percent extreme) spread over 2,600 vertical feet and served by seven lifts (one quad, two triples, and four doubles). Perched 400 feet above the top of the lifts, "The Ridge" is known as some of the steepest, most extreme terrain within the boundaries of any resort in the West. On-site are a ski school, a ski shop, and a daycare facility; a shuttle service connects the slopes with hotels in Bozeman. (Mid-Dec-Apr, daily) **$$$$**

Gallatin National Forest. *10 E Babcock St, Bozeman (59715). N and S of town. Phone 406/587-6701. www. fs.fed.us/r1/gallatin.* One of the crown jewels of the National Forest system, the 1.8-million-acre Gallatin National Forest is part of the Greater Yellowstone Ecosystem and is home to endangered grizzly bears, bald eagles, and gray wolves. There are six majestic mountain ranges, countless trout streams, and two wilderness areas--the Lee Metcalf and the Absaroka-Beartooth--within Gallatin's boundaries. Recreational pursuits are myriad, with fishing, hiking, climbing, cross-country skiing, and snowshoeing among the most popular. One of the best hiking areas is the Hyalite Drainage, south of Bozeman, with trails for every level of ability. Right outside West Yellowstone are the Rendezvous Ski Trails, a 20-mile groomed cross-country ski trail system; Bridger Bowl (see) and Lone Mountain Ranch are ski resorts that have leases on forest land. There are also nearly 40 developed campgrounds as well as two dozen bare-bones rental cabins (with stoves but, alas, no running water) once occupied by rangers. The forest headquarters is in Bozeman, with additional ranger offices in Big Timber, Livingston, Gardiner, and West Yellowstone. Forest rangers provide interpretive programs in summer at the Madison River Canyon Earthquake Area (see WEST YELLOWSTONE).

Montana State University. *1711 W College St, Bozeman (59715). 11th Ave, College St, 7th Ave, and Lincoln St, at S edge of town. Phone 406/994-0211.www.montana. edu.* (1893) (11,000 students) On campus is

> **Museum of the Rockies**. *600 W Kagy Blvd, Bozeman (59715). Phone 406/994-3466.* Montana's foremost natural history museum is a product of Montana State University, and it's located on campus in south Bozeman. While the exhibits cover Montana's native cultures and the state's recent history, the centerpiece is the largest dinosaur collection in the United States. The paleontology curator, MSU professor Jack Horner, is renowned, having served as a dinosaur consultant on the *Jurassic Park* films. There are both robotic re-creations and the fossils on which they were based (including a T. rex specimen and a Triceratops skull). Many of

the dinosaur fossils were found at Egg Mountain, a dino hotspot across the state near Choteau. Also on-site is a seasonal living history farm populated by costumed interpreters who show visitors what Montana pioneer life was all about. The Taylor Planetarium has both astronomy-oriented presentations and nighttime laser shows accompanied by loud rock and roll. (Mon-Sat 9 am-5 pm, Sun 12:30-5 pm; closed holidays) **$$**

Special Events

Bridger Raptor Festival. *Bozeman Ranger District, 3710 Fallon, Bozeman (59718). Bridger Bowl ridge area. Phone 406/585-1211.* View birds of prey, including the largest concentration of migrating Golden Eagles in the contiguous 48 states, on their trip south. Usually late Sept or early Oct.

Gallatin County Fair. *Gallatin County Fairgrounds, 901 N Black Ave, Bozeman (59715). Phone 406/582-3270.* This traditional county fair includes carnival rides, music, food, arts and crafts, livestock shows, rodeo events, and more. Third weekend in July.

Montana Winter Fair. *Bozeman (59715). Fergus County Fairgrounds. Phone 406/538-8841; toll-free 800/406-8841.* Enjoy the Montana scenery while at this state winter fair. Attractions include a livestock show, horse show and sale, fiddlers contest, art swap and shop, death by chocolate competition, quilts and leather working divisions, and farm equipment displays. Late Jan or early Feb.

Sweet Pea Festival. *Buffalo Exchange, 1005 W Main, Bozeman (59715). Phone 406/586-4003. www.sweetpeafestival.org.* This festival of the arts features a juried art show, music, a flower show, food concessions, and a parade. First full weekend in Aug.

Limited-Service Hotels

★ ★ **BEST WESTERN GRANTREE INN.***1325 N 7th Ave, Bozeman (59715). Phone 406/587-5261; toll-free 800/624-5865; fax 406/587-9437. www.bestwestern .com.* 119 rooms, 2 story. Pets accepted. Check-in 3 pm, check-out noon. High-speed Internet access, wireless Internet access. Restaurant, bar. Fitness room. Indoor pool, whirlpool. Airport transportation available. Business center.**$**

⬛🏋🏊🚶

★ **HAMPTON INN.** *75 Baxter Ln, Bozeman (59715). Phone 406/522-8000; toll-free 800/426-7866; fax*

406/522-7446. *www.hamptoninn.com.* 70 rooms, 2 story. Complimentary continental breakfast. Check-in 3 pm, check-out 11 am. High-speed Internet access, wireless Internet access. Fitness room. Indoor pool, whirlpool. Airport transportation available. Business center.**$**

★ ★ **HOLIDAY INN.** *5 E Baxter Ln, Bozeman (59715). Phone 406/587-4561; toll-free 800/366-5101; fax 406/587-4413. www.holiday-inn.com.* 179 rooms, 2 story. Pets accepted, some restrictions. Check-in 4 pm, check-out noon. High-speed Internet access, wireless Internet access. Restaurant, bar. Fitness room. Indoor pool, whirlpool. Airport transportation available. Business center.**$**

★ **LA QUINTA INN.** *6445 Jackrabbit Ln, Belgrade (59714). Phone 406/388-2222; toll-free 800/531-5900; fax 406/388-7501. www.lq.com.* 65 rooms. Pets accepted. Complimentary continental breakfast. Check-in 3 pm, check-out 1 pm. Fitness room. Indoor pool, whirlpool.**$**

★ **MICROTEL.** *612 Nikles Dr, Bozeman (59715). Phone 406/586-3797; toll-free 800/597-3797; fax 406/586-4247. www.microtelinn.com.* 61 rooms. Pets accepted; fee. Complimentary continental breakfast. Check-in 3 pm, check-out noon. Indoor pool, whirlpool.**$**

Full-Service Inn

★★**GALLATIN GATEWAY INN.***76405 Gallatin Rd (Hwy 191), Bozeman (59718). Phone 406/763-4672; toll-free 800/676-3522; fax 406/763-4777. www.gallatingatewayinn.com.* This historic (1927), restored railroad hotel is located in the heart of Yellowstone Country and close to all the outdoor activities offered there. Guest rooms are individually decorated in a Western theme. 33 rooms, 2 story. Pets accepted. Complimentary continental breakfast. Check-in 3 pm, check-out 11 am. Restaurant, bar. Outdoor pool, whirlpool. Tennis. Airport transportation available.**$$**

Specialty Lodging

GALLATIN RIVER LODGE. *9105 Thorpe Rd, Bozeman (59718). Phone 406/388-0148; toll-free 888/387-0148; fax 406/388-6766. www.grlodge.com.* 6 rooms. Pets accepted; fee. Complimentary full breakfast.

Check-in 2 pm, check-out 11 am. Restaurant, bar. Whirlpool.**$$**

Restaurants

★★**BOODLES.** *215 E Main St, Bozeman (59715). Phone 406/587-2901; fax 406/586-6623.* Located in an 1880s saloon building, this restaurant features an Old English club decor. Continental menu. Lunch, dinner. Closed Sun; Jan 1, Thanksgiving, Dec 25. Bar. Casual attire. **$$**

★ ★ ★ **GALLATIN GATEWAY INN.** *76405 Gallatin Rd, Bozeman (59718). Phone 406/763-4672; fax 406/763-4117. www.gallatingatewayinn.com.* Impeccable service and an outstanding wine list are some of the features in this facility, located in a restored, historic railroad hotel. American menu. Dinner. Bar. Children's menu. Reservations recommended. **$$**

★ ★ **JOHN BOZEMAN'S BISTRO.** *125 W Main St, Bozeman (59715). Phone 406/587-4100; fax 406/587-0875. www.johnbozemansbistro.com.* International menu. Lunch, dinner. Closed Sun-Mon; holidays. Children's menu. Casual attire. Reservations recommended. **$$**

Browning (A-2)

See also Glacier National Park

Population 1,170
Elevation 4,362 ft
Area Code 406
Zip 59417

The eastern gateway to Glacier National Park (see), Browning is the capital of the Blackfeet Nation. The town was named for a US Commissioner of Indian Affairs. The reservation itself covers 2,348,000 acres.

What to See and Do

Museum of the Plains Indian. *Hwy 2 W and 89, Browning (59417). 13 miles from Glacier National Park. Phone 406/338-2230.* A collection of Blackfeet and Northern Plains Native American tribal artifacts, plus the history of the tribes of the northern Great Plains. Administered by the Department of the Interior, Indian Arts and Crafts Board. (June-Sept: daily 9 am-4:45 pm; rest of year: Mon-Fri 10 am-4:30 pm; closed Jan 1, Thanksgiving, Dec 25)**$**

Special Event

North American Native American Days Powwow. *Blackfeet Reservation, Bozeman Ranger District, 3710 Fallon, Bozeman (59718). Phone 406/338-7276.* Mid-July.

Butte (C-2)

See also Anaconda, Three Forks

Settled 1864
Population 33,336
Elevation 5,549 ft
Area Code 406
Zip 59701
Information Butte-Silver Bow Chamber of Commerce, 1000 George St; toll-free 800/735-6814
Web Site www.buttecvb.com

Settled more than 100 years ago, Butte, atop the "richest hill on earth," harvests treasures of copper along with by-product gold, silver, and other metals from 1,000 acres of mines. Although mined for more than a century, this treasure chest seems to be inexhaustible. Butte's famous old properties continue to produce high-grade ores. Modern mining techniques have exposed vast new low-grade mineral resources.

Butte was born as a bonanza silver camp. When the silver ores became lower grade at comparatively shallow depths, copper ores were discovered. Although development of the copper mines was a slow process, culminating in the "war of the copper kings," fortunes were made and lost and battles were fought in court for control of ore on surface and underground.

The brawny, colorful mining-camp days of Butte are over. Although copper mining still plays an important role in the Butte economy, it is also a retailing, distribution, and diversified industrial center. A Ranger District office of the Deerlodge National Forest is located here.

What to See and Do

Arts Chateau. *321 W Broadway, Butte (59701). Phone 406/723-7600. www.artschateau.org.* (1898). Originally the home of Charles Clark, now a heritage museum and arts center. A stairway leads from the first-floor galleries to the fourth-floor ballroom. Stained-glass windows, intricate moldings. (Mon-Sat noon-5 pm) **$$**

Berkeley Pit. *200 Shields St, Butte (59701). Phone 406/723-3177.* A mile-long man-made gash that's allegedly visible from the moon, the Berkeley Pit is a reminder of the world's richest hill, a former mountain of copper adjacent to downtown Butte. An estimated 290 million tons of copper ore were pulled from the ground here, leaving the 1,780-foot deep pit and thousands of miles of underground tunnels. Unfortunately, groundwater has been seeping into the pit since mining operations ended in 1983, made toxic by tailings left over from the mining days. (Entire flocks of birds have met their fates by merely landing in the acidic water.) Thankfully, a water treatment plant went into operation in 2003 to combat the pit's pollution. Just east of downtown, there is a tunnel leading to an observation platform that's open from March to November; the spot is Butte's most-visited tourist attraction.

Copper King Mansion. *219 W Granite St, Butte (59701). Phone 406/782-7580.* (Circa 1888) The restored 32-room home of Senator W. A. Clark, a prominent political figure of Montana's early mining days; of particular interest are the frescoed ceilings and walls, stained-glass windows, nine hand-carved fireplaces, antique pipe organ, and silver and crystal collections. (May-Sept, daily) **$$**

Dumas Brothel Museum. *45 E Mercury St, Butte (59701). Phone 406/494-6908. www.thedumasbrothel.com.* Listed on the National Register of Historic Places, this museum is one of the few remaining buildings in the West purposely built as a brothel. Various brothel-related exhibits. Gift shop. Not recommended for children. Tours (Memorial Day-Labor Day, daily; rest of year by appointment) **$$**

Montana Tech of the University of Montana. *1300 W Park St, Butte (59701). Phone 406/496-4266. www.mtech.edu.* (1893) (1,900 students) A mineral energy-oriented college near mining operations. On campus is

Mineral Museum. *1300 W Park St, Butte (59701). Phone 406/496-4414.* Mineral display; some fossils; specimens from collection of 15,100 rotate periodically; special fluorescent and Montana minerals. Guided tours. (Mon-Fri; also by appointment; closed holidays) **FREE**

Old No. 1. *1000 George St, Butte (59701). Phone toll-free 800/735-6814.* Tour of city aboard replica of early-day streetcar departs from the Chamber of Commerce office. (Memorial Day-Labor Day, daily) **$$**

Our Lady of the Rockies. *3100 Harrison Ave, Butte (59701). Phone 406/782-1221. www.ourladyoftherockies.org.* This 90-foot likeness of Mary, the mother of

The Richest Hill on Earth

Butte, the quintessential Old West mining town, was the nation's largest single source of silver in the late 19th century and the largest source of copper until the 1930s. Butte's magnificent homes and commercial and civic buildings attest to its early wealth and importance. Its massive smokestacks, soot-grimed trick buildings, and the yawning Berkeley Pit mine also serve as historic reminders of the environmental damage of rabid, unregulated mining.

Butte contains the nation's second-largest National Historic Landmark District, with over 4,500 historic structures within 2,700 acresfrom elegant mansions of Copper Kings to humble miner's cottages, boarding houses, and hotels that once housed an estimated 100,000 people.

Begin a tour of Butte at the Copper King Mansion (219 W Granite St). This private home was built in 1888 by William Clark, one of the three Copper Kings of Butte, at a time when he was one of the world's richest men. This three-story brick High Victorian mansion contains 30 rooms, many with frescoed ceilings, carved staircases, inlaid floors, and Tiffany windows. Clark spent $300,000 on the building and imported many craftsmen from Europe. The third floor boasts a 60-foot-long ballroom and a chapel. The mansion is open for tours daily.

Walk one block south on Washington Street. Clark's son Charles was so taken by a chateau he visited in France that he procured the plans and had it reconstructed in Butte. Now known as the Arts Chateau (321 W Broadway St), the building serves as Butte's community arts center.

Continue one block south on Washington, and turn west on Park Street. Another gem of old Butte architecture is the Mother Lode Theater (316 W Park St). This magnificent old vaudeville theater has been refurbished and serves as Butte's performing arts center. The theater is home to the Butte Symphony and a regional theater troupe.

Walk east on Park Street toward the core of downtown, which is found along Park and Broadway streets. Be sure to stop at Butte Hill Bakery (7 S Montana) to order a pasty, a form of meat pie that was a lunchtime staple for miners.

The showpiece of Butte civic architecture is the Butte-Silver Bow Courthouse (155 West Granite Street), built in 1910. A lovely stained-glass dome tops the four-story rotunda, murals decorate the ceilings, and oak fixtures predominate throughout. Butte leaders spent almost twice as much on this courthouse as the state spent on the Montana Capitol.

Continue along Park or Broadway to Main Street, and turn south. The Dumas Brothel (45 E Mercury St) was Butte's longest-lived house of ill repute, in operation from 1890 until 1982. Now a museum, the two-story brick building still has quite a few architectural features distinctive to a house of prostitution, such as windows onto the corridors and bedrooms that the miners more appropriately called cribs. This is the only surviving building from Butte's once thriving red-light district.

Also unusual is Mai Wah (17 W Mercury St), a museum dedicated to telling the story of Chinese miners and workers who pioneered in Butte. The Mai Wah building once housed a number of Chinese-owned businesses; Butte's China Alley, the heart of the old Chinatown, is adjacent.

Jesus, sits atop the Continental Divide overlooking town. Trips to the mountaintop are available in summer. **$$**

World Museum of Mining and 1899 Mining Camp. *W Park St, Butte (59701). At Granite. Phone 406/723-7211.* Outdoor and indoor displays of mining mementos; turn-of-the-century mining camp, Hell Roarin' Gulch. Picnic area. (Memorial Day-Labor Day, daily; rest of year, daily except Mon) **$**

Special Events

Butte Vigilante Rodeo. *6400 Albany, Butte (59701). Phone 406/494-3002.* Professional riders compete in rodeo events including bronco, bull, and bareback riding; barrel racing; and calf roping. July.

Evel Knievel Days. *3336 Harrison Ave, #218, Butte (59701). Phone 406/494-2825. www.knievelweek.com.* Legendary daredevil Evel Knievel was born and raised in Butte, but in his youth he was known more for getting in trouble with the law than for death-defying stunts. Locals resisted honoring him until 2003, when the town put on the inaugural Evel Knievel Days festival. Now an annual summer event, the schedule includes a weekend of stunt shows, parades, and children's activities. Late July.

St. Patrick's Day Festival. *Butte.* A raucous street party that's rooted in Butte's deep Irish heritage (many of the area's miners were immigrants), Butte's St. Patrick's Day is one of the wildest annual events in the West. The festivities include a kickoff parade, bagpipers playing around every bend, corned beef and cabbage galore, and keg after keg of green beer. The action is centered around Butte's historic Uptown neighborhood.

Limited-Service Hotels

★**COMFORT INN.** *2777 Harrison Ave, Butte (59701). Phone 406/494-8850; toll-free 800/228-5150; fax 406/494-2801. www.comfortinn.com.* 145 rooms, 3 story. Pets accepted; fee. Complimentary continental breakfast. Check-in 2 pm, check-out 11 am. Fitness room. Indoor pool, two whirlpools. Airport transportation available.**$**

★ **HOLIDAY INN EXPRESS.** *One Holiday Park Dr, Butte (59701). Phone 406/494-6999; toll-free 800/465-4329; fax 406/494-1300. www.hiexpress.com.* 83 rooms, 5 story. Complimentary continental breakfast. Check-in 3 pm, check-out noon. High-speed Internet access, wireless Internet access. Fitness room. Airport transportation available. Business center.**$**

Restaurants

★ ★ ★ **LYDIA'S.** *4915 Harrison Ave, Butte (59701). Phone 406/494-2000; fax 406/494-3332.* This local favorite's Victorian decor features many antique stained-glass windows. Menu selections include steak and Italian dishes, which are presented by an attentive staff. Italian, American menu. Dinner. Closed holidays. Bar. Children's menu. Casual attire. Reservations recommended. **$$**

★ ★ ★ **UPTOWN CAFE.** *47 E Broadway, Butte (59701). Phone 406/723-4735. www.uptowncafe.com.* Paintings by local artists adorn the walls at this new American bistro in the heart of the historic Uptown district. Wonderfully fresh seafood, steaks, pasta, and poultry are all creatively prepared with home-style

flair and served by a knowledgeable and attentive staff. American menu. Lunch, dinner. Closed holidays. Casual attire. Reservations recommended. **$$**

Chinook (A-4)

See also Havre

Population 1,512
Elevation 2,438 ft
Area Code 406
Zip 59523
Information Chamber of Commerce, PO Box 744; phone 406/357-2100
Web Site www.chinookmontana.com

Gas wells, farming, and grazing are the main concerns of this town, which takes its name from the much-desired January and February winds that melt the snow, exposing grass for cattle.

What to See and Do

Bear's Paw Battleground. *Chinook. 16 miles S on Hwy Sec 240.* Scene of final battle and surrender of Chief Joseph of the Nez Perce following the trek north from the Big Hole River, ending Montana's Native American wars in 1877. It was here that Chief Joseph spoke the eloquent words "From where the sun now stands, I will fight no more forever." This is the newest addition to the Nez Perce National Historic Park system. Picnicking.

Blaine County Museum. *501 Indiana St, Chinook (59523). Phone 406/357-2590.* Local historical exhibits. (Memorial Day-Labor Day, daily; rest of year, Mon-Fri) **FREE**

Special Event

Blaine County Fair. *B. C. Fairgrounds, Dike Rd, Chinook (59523). Phone 406/357-3205.* July.

Columbia Falls (B-2)

See also Kalispell, Whitefish

Population 2,942
Elevation 3,087 ft
Area Code 406
Zip 59912
Information Flathead Convention & Visitor Bureau, 15 Depot Park, Kalispell, 55901; phone 406/756-9091 or toll-free 800/543-3105

Web Site www.columbiafallschamber.com

A gateway to Glacier National Park (see), and the north fork of the Flathead River, this is an area of superb hunting and fishing. Here also is the *Hungry Horse News,* Montana's only Pulitzer Prize-winning newspaper.

What to See and Do

Big Sky Water Slide. *Hwy 2 and Hwy 206, Columbia Falls. Jct Hwy 2, Hwy 206; 1 mile SE via Hwy 2. Phone 406/892-5025.* Ten waterslides, inner tube river run, hot tubs. Picnicking, concessions. (Memorial Day-Labor Day, daily) **$$$$**

Glacier Maze. *Hwy 2 E, Coram (59901). 10 miles NE on Hwy 2 E. Phone 406/387-5902.* A two-level, three-dimensional maze with passages more than 1 mile long; also 18-hole miniature golf course. Picnicking, concessions. (May-Labor Day, daily) **$$**

Hungry Horse Dam and Power Plant. *Columbia Falls. Hwy 2 E 6 miles. Phone 406/387-5241.* One of world's largest concrete dams (564 feet), set in a wooded canyon near Glacier National Park. The reservoir is approximately 34 miles long and 3 1/2 miles at its widest point. Pictorial and interactive displays; video (mid-May-late Sept, daily). Several recreation and camping sites of the Flathead National Forest (see KALISPELL) are on the reservoir. **FREE**

Special Event

Heritage Days. *233 13th St E, Columbia Falls (59912). Downtown. Phone 406/751-4756.* This annual celebration features a rodeo, Saturday parade, street dance, craft fair, car show, and more. Late July.

Full-Service Resort

★ ★ **MEADOW LAKE GOLF AND SKI RESORT.** *100 St. Andrews Dr, Columbia Falls (59912). Phone 406/892-0330.* This resort provides year-round fun for the entire family. Enjoy golf, tennis, and volleyball in the summer, or ice skating and other indoor recreation in the recreation center for kids. Large, comfortable rooms, each with private veranda area, are available. 24 rooms, 3 story. Pets accepted; fee. Check-in 4 pm, check-out 11 am. Restaurant, two bars. Children's activity center. Fitness room. Indoor pool, outdoor pool, children's pool, whirlpool. Golf, 18 holes. Tennis. Airport transportation available. Business center. **$$**

Cooke City (D-4)

See also Red Lodge, Cody, WY

Settled 1873
Population 100
Elevation 7,651 ft
Area Code 406
Zip 59020
Information Chamber of Commerce, PO Box 1071; phone 406/838-2272
Web Site www.cookecitychamber.com

Once the center of a gold rush area in which $1 million was panned from the rushing streams, Cooke City today is busy serving tourists on their way to Yellowstone National Park (see WYOMING). Available locally are Jeep, horse, and snowmobile trips.

What to See and Do

Grasshopper Glacier. *Cooke City. 14 miles NE on mountain trail in the Absaroka-Beartooth Wilderness, Custer National Forest (see HARDIN).* One of the largest icefields in the United States; so named because of the millions of grasshoppers frozen in its 80-foot ice cliff. Accessible only by trail, the last 2 miles reached only by foot; be prepared for adverse weather. Grasshoppers are visible only during brief periods; glacial ice must be exposed by snow melt, which generally does not occur until mid-August, while new snow begins to accumulate in late August.

Restaurant

★ **LOG CABIN CAFE.** *Hwy 212, Silver Gate (59081). Phone 406/838-2367.* American menu. Dinner. Closed mid-Sept-mid-May. Children's menu. Casual attire. Outdoor seating. **$$**

Deer Lodge (C-2)

See also Anaconda, Helena

Settled 1862
Population 3,378
Elevation 4,521 ft
Area Code 406
Zip 59722
Information Powell County Chamber of Commerce, 1171 S Main St; phone 406/846-2094

Web Site www.powellcountymontana.com

Near Montana's first important gold discovery at Gold Creek, this town was first a trapping and trading center, later an important stage and travel station between the early gold camps. Remnants of old mining camps are a few miles from town.

What to See and Do

Frontier Montana. *1106 Main St, Deer Lodge (59722). Phone 406/846-3111.* Museum houses Western memorabilia including weapons, clothing, bar. (Memorial Day-Labor Day) **$$$**

Grant-Kohrs Ranch National Historic Site. *210 Missouri, Deer Lodge (59722). North edge of town. Phone 406/846-2070.* Preserved in its pioneer state, this was once headquarters for more than a million acres of ranchland. The house was called the "finest home in Montana Territory." Original furniture, horse-drawn vehicles, and buildings provide an authentic look into history. Visitors may tour the house, barns, and bunkhouse. In season, see blacksmith and ranch hands at work, 19th-century style. (Daily; closed Jan 1, Thanksgiving, Dec 25) **FREE**

Montana Territorial Prison. *1106 Main St, Deer Lodge (59722). Phone 406/846-3111.* Montana prison from 1871 to 1979. A sandstone wall, built in 1893, surrounds the 5-acre complex. The 1912 castlelike cell block remains intact and offers the visiting public a rare view of early prison life. Montana Law Enforcement Museum on grounds. (Daily)

Powell County Museum. *1103 Main St, Deer Lodge (59722). Phone 406/846-3111.* Displays reflect the history of Powell County and southwest Montana. (June-Labor Day, daily) **$$**

Towe Ford Museum. *1106 Main St, Deer Lodge (59722). Phone 406/846-3111.* Collection of antique Ford cars. There are 100 on display, dating from 1903. Picnic area. (Daily)

Yesterday's Playthings. *1017 Main St, Deer Lodge (59722). Phone 406/846-1480.* Extensive doll collection from different periods and cultures. Antique toys. (Mid-May-mid-Sept, daily)

Special Events

Powell County Territorial Days. *Main St, Deer Lodge. Phone 406/846-2094.* Activities at this community celebration include a parade, car show, foot race event, craft vendors, and children's games. Third weekend in June.

Tri-County Fair. *Deer Lodge (59722). Tri-County Fairgrounds, off I-90, Deer Lodge exit. Phone 406/846-3627.* Encompassing Deer Lodge, Powell, and Granite counties, this annual fair features 4-H exhibits, a rodeo, and carnival. Third weekend in Aug.

Limited-Service Hotels

★ **SUPER 8.** *1150 N Main, Deer Lodge (59722). Phone 406/846-2370; toll-free 800/800-8000; fax 406/846-2373. www.super8.com.* 57 rooms, 2 story. Pets accepted; fee. Complimentary continental breakfast. Check-in 2 pm, check-out 11 am. **$**

Dillon (D-2)

Founded 1880
Population 3,991
Elevation 5,096 ft
Area Code 406
Zip 59725
Information Tourist Information Center & Chamber of Commerce, 125 S Montana, PO Box 425; phone 406/683-5511
Web Site www.beaverheadchamber.com

Named after a president of the Union Pacific Railroad, Dillon is in a ranching community. Its farms and ranches produce more than 200,000 tons of hay each year. Livestock raising is also important.

What to See and Do

Bannack State Park. *4200 Bannack Rd, Dillon (59725). 5 miles S on I-15, then 21 miles W on Hwy 278, then 4 miles S on county road. Phone 406/834-3413.* Bannack was a bustling frontier town after John White discovered gold here in 1862. It even served as Montana's first territorial capital for a short stint later in the decade. The population peaked at about 3,000 residents, but the mining economy proved boom or bust, and it fluctuated wildly until the bottom dropped out in the 1930s. At that time, Bannack was essentially abandoned and became a ghost town. However, the state of Montana took over in the 1950s and preserved about 60 structures as a state park, including cabins, a courthouse, a church, and an old Masonic lodge. An annual living history festival, Bannack Days, is held in July, and visitors can also pan for gold during the summer months. There are two campgrounds in the vicinity, one of which rents teepees to overnight guests.

Beaverhead County Museum. *15 S Montana St, Dillon (59725). Phone 406/683-5027.* Geological displays, mining, livestock and commercial artifacts, pioneer housewares, outdoor interpretive area. (Apr-early Nov, daily; closed holidays and rest of year) **FREE**

Beaverhead-Deerlodge National Forest. *420 Barrett St, Dillon (57925). E and W off Hwy 91, I-15. Phone 406/683-3900. www.fs.fed.us/r1/b-d.* The largest of Montana's national forests at 3.3 million acres, Beaverhead-Deerlodge is a top recreational destination in both winter and summer. Cross-country skiing, snowmobiling, and snowshoeing are all popular pursuits when there is snow on the ground; scenic drives, hikes, and fishing trips are the top warm-weather pursuits. There are numerous alpine lakes, campgrounds, and rental cabins, as well as a few ghost towns and two wilderness areas--Lee Metcalf and Anaconda-Pintler-- within its boundaries. The largest body of water in the Beaverhead-Deerlodge is Georgetown Lake, about 23 miles west of Anaconda, with a surface area of 1,466 acres, ringed by cross-country skiing and snowmobile trails. Canyon Ferry Lake is a top destination for iceboating--by which specialized vessels skate around a frozen lake powered by the wind in their sails. Offices administering the forest are in Butte, Dillon, and several other area towns.

Maverick Mountain Ski Area. *475 Maverick Mountain Rd, Dillon (59725). 40 miles NW on Hwy 278. Phone 406/834-3454. www.skimaverick.com.* A small but steep resort in southwestern Montana, Maverick Mountain is unique in that it actually guarantees great snow--disappointed skiers can get their money back after the first half-hour. It is known for its racing runs and difficult terrain (20 percent beginner, 35 percent intermediate, 35 percent expert, and 10 percent extreme), with a 2,020-foot vertical drop on 170 acres. You'll also find cross-country trails. (Dec-Apr, Thurs-Sun; closed Dec 25) **$$$$**

Special Events

Bannack Days. *Bannack State Park, 4200 Bannack Rd, Dillon (59725). Phone 406/834-3413.* Reliving of gold rush days in Bannack. Gold panning; demonstrations. Third weekend in July.

Beaverhead County Fair & Jaycee Rodeo. *15 S Montana, Dillon (59725). Phone 406/683-5511.* Festivities at this annual fair include a rodeo, carnival, livestock show, concert, and juried arts and crafts show. Five days before Labor Day.

Limited-Service Hotels

★ **COMFORT INN.** *450 N Interchange, Dillon (59725). Phone 406/683-6831; toll-free 800/228-5150; fax 406/683-2021. www.comfortinn.com.* 48 rooms, 2 story. Pets accepted, some restrictions; fee. Complimentary continental breakfast. Check-in 2 pm, check-out 11 am. Indoor pool.**$**

★ **GUESTHOUSE INN & SUITES.** *580 Sinclair St, Dillon (59725). Phone 406/683-3636; toll-free 800/241-8378; fax 406/683-3637. www.guesthouseintl .com.* Located just off I-15, with mountain views all around, this newer motel has quiet, spacious rooms.58 rooms. Pets accepted; fee. Complimentary full breakfast. Check-in 2 pm, check-out noon. Fitness room. Indoor pool, whirlpool.**$**

Ennis (D-3)

See also Three Forks, Virginia City

Settled 1864
Population 773
Elevation 4,939 ft
Area Code 406
Zip 59729
Web Site www.ennischamber.com

Surrounded by three Rocky Mountain ranges in the Madison River Valley and encircled by cattle ranches, Ennis has good trout fishing and big-game hunting. Beartrap Canyon offers whitewater floats. Swimming, boating, snowmobiling, and Nordic skiing are popular. A Ranger District office of the Beaverhead-Deerlodge National Forest (see DILLON) is located here.

What to See and Do

National Fish Hatchery. *180 Fish Hatchery Rd, Ennis (59729). 12 miles S off Hwy 287. Phone 406/682-4847.* Raises rainbow trout. (Daily) **FREE**

Fort Benton (B-3)

See also Great Falls

Founded 1846
Population 1,660
Elevation 2,632 ft
Area Code 406
Zip 59442
Information City Clerk, PO Box 8; phone 406/622-5494
Web Site www.fortbenton.com

Established as a fur-trading post and named in honor of Senator Thomas Hart Benton of Missouri, this famous frontier outpost at the head of navigation on the Missouri River became a strategic commercial stronghold. Supplies were received here and shipped overland to trappers and miners throughout Montana. The seat of Chouteau County and one of the oldest communities in the state, it continues as a trading center. The Lewis and Clark State Memorial in Fort Benton Park honors the surveyors who opened the area for trade and commerce.

What to See and Do

Museum of the Northern Great Plains. *1205 20th St*, Fort Benton (59442). *Phone 406/622-5316. www.fortbenton .com/museums.* Agricultural and homestead history displays. (Early May-Labor Day, daily 10 am-5 pm) **$$**

Museum of the Upper Missouri River. *1204 Front St, Fort Benton (59442). 18th and Front sts. Phone 406/622-5494. www.fortbenton.com/museums.* Displays of steamboats, freighting, stagecoaches, fur and Canadian trade. (Early May-Sept, daily 10 am-5 pm) **$$**

Ruins of Old Fort Benton. *Old Fort Park, Front and Main sts, Fort Benton (59442). On riverfront.* (1847) One building and parts of another remain of old trading post and blockhouse.

Special Events

Chouteau County Fair. *Fort Benton (59442). Chouteau County Fairgrounds. Phone 406/622-5505.* The activities at this county fair include a rodeo, concert, demolition derby, arts and crafts, 4-H exhibits, and more. A canoe launch and campground are also available. Early July.

Summer Celebration. *Old Fort Park, Front and Main sts, Fort Benton (59442). Phone 406/622-5728.* Activities at this annual celebration include a parade, arts and crafts, historical tours, entertainment, a fishing derby, and a fireworks display. Overnight camping is also available. Mid-June.

Gardiner (D-3)

Founded 1883
Population 600
Elevation 5,314 ft
Area Code 406
Zip 59030
Web Site www.gardinerchamber.com

Gardiner was established as the original entrance to Yellowstone Park. Named for a trapper who worked this area, Gardiner is the only gateway open throughout the year to Yellowstone National Park (see WYOMING). A Ranger District office of the Gallatin National Forest (see BOZEMAN) is located here.

What to See and Do

River trips. Yellowstone Raft Company. *Gardiner. Phone 406/848-7777; toll-free 800/858-7781.* Half- and full-day whitewater raft trips on the Yellowstone, Gallatin, and Madison rivers. Departures from Gardiner and Big Sky (see). Reservations recommended. **$$$$**

Special Event

Gardiner Summer Series Rodeo. *222 Park St, Gardiner (59030). Phone 406/848-7971.* NRA-sanctioned rodeo. June.

Limited-Service Hotels

★ ★ **BEST WESTERN MAMMOTH HOT SPRINGS.** *Hwy 89 W, Gardiner (59030). Phone 406/848-7311; toll-free 800/828-9080; fax 406/848-7120. www.bestwestern.com/mammothhotsprings.* 85 rooms, 2 story. Pets accepted; fee. Check-in 4 pm, check-out 11 am. Restaurant, bar. Indoor pool, whirlpool. On the Yellowstone River.**$**

★ ★ **COMFORT INN.** *107 Hellroaring St, Gardiner (59030). Phone 406/848-7536; toll-free 800/228-5150; fax 406/848-7062. www.yellowstonecomfortinn.com.* 77 rooms, 3 story. Complimentary continental breakfast. Check-in 4 pm, check-out 10 am. Restaurant, bar. Whirlpool.**$**

★ **YELLOWSTONE VILLAGE INN.**
*Yellostone Park North Entrance, Gardiner (59030).
Phone 406/848-7417; toll-free 800/228-8158; fax
406/848-7418. www.yellowstonevinn.com.* 43 rooms, 2
story. Complimentary continental breakfast. Check-
in 3:30 pm, check-out 11 am. Indoor pool. **$**

Specialty Lodging

YELLOWSTONE SUITES B&B. *506 Fourth St,
Gardiner (59030). Phone 406/848-7937; toll-free
800/948-7937. www.wolftracker.com/ys.* 4 rooms.
Complimentary full breakfast. Check-in 4 pm, check-
out 11 am. **$**

Restaurant

★ ★ **YELLOWSTONE MINE.** *Hwy 89, Gardiner
(59030). Phone 406/848-7336; fax 406/848-7120.* Steak
menu. Breakfast, dinner. Bar. Children's menu.
Casual attire. **$$**

Glacier National Park

See also Three Forks, Virginia City

Web Site www.nps.gov/glac

Big, rugged, and primitive, Glacier National Park is
nature's unspoiled domain. Human civilization is
reduced to insignificance by the wild grandeur of
these million acres. It's the place for a snowball fight in
midsummer, for glacial solitude, for fishing, for alpine
flowers, and for lonely and remote campgrounds
along fir-fringed lakes. The park is also a living text-
book in geology.

Declared a national park on May 11, 1910, these
1,013,595 acres of spectacular scenery are preserved
year after year much as they were when Meriwether
Lewis saw them in the distance in 1806. The United
States and Canada share these treasures of nature; the
204 square miles of Canada that are linked to Glacier
are known as the Waterton-Glacier International
Peace Park. Glacier National Park contains 50 glaciers,
among the few in the United States, some of which
are relatively accessible. There are more than 200 lakes
and 1,400 varieties of plants, 63 species of animals—
from mice to moose—and 272 varieties of birds.

Visitors here can choose from a variety of activities
during their stay; you can enjoy the scenery from the
shadow of a hotel or chalet, share the camaraderie of
a community campground, or seek solitude in the
wilderness. The delights of Glacier, however, should be
savored cautiously. Rangers recommend that visitors
stay on the trails and never hike alone. The behavior
of wild animals can be unpredictable.

This is a land where winter does not beat a full retreat
until mid-June and sometimes returns in mid-
September. The summer season extends between
those periods, but until July, high snowbanks line the
roads and the mountains are capped with snow. Late
June is a time of cascading waterfalls and profuse
wildflowers. In the fall, the dense forests are a blaze of
color set against a background of snow-covered peaks.
Winter brings deep-snow peace that only the hardiest
souls invade for cross-country skiing or photography.

Spectacular views of the park may be seen from
your car, particularly when crossing the Continental
Divide on Going-to-the-Sun Road; it is 50 miles long
and one of the most magnificent drives in the world
(approximately mid-June-mid-Oct). As of January
1994, vehicles in excess of 21 feet in length (including
combinations of units) and 8 feet in width (including
mirrors) are prohibited from Going-to-the-Sun Road
between Avalanche and Sun Point. Vehicles exceeding
these restrictions may use Highway 2 or can be parked
at the Avalanche or Sun Point parking areas. The road
continuously winds up and down in tight curves and
requires caution. This unforgettable ride links the
east and west sides of the park, passing over Logan
Pass (a visitor center with exhibits is here; June-Sept,
daily; closed rest of year) for a 100-mile view from an
elevation of 6,646 feet. It connects with Highway 89
at St. Mary (here is a visitor center with exhibits and
programs; May-Sept, daily) and with Highway 2 at
West Glacier. Highway 89 on the east side of the park
is the Blackfeet Highway, extending from Browning
to Canada. The road to Many Glacier Valley branches
from Highway 89, 9 miles north of St. Mary. The road
to Two Medicine Lake leaves Highway 49, 4 miles
north of East Glacier Park. Chief Mountain Inter-
national Highway (Hwy 17) leads to Waterton Lakes
National Park in Canada.

Most of the park, however, including the glaciers, is accessible only by trail. There are 732 miles of maintained trails penetrating to remote wilderness areas. Whether you're going by foot or on horseback, magnificent and isolated parts of Glacier await discovery.

There are eight major and five semiprimitive campgrounds. The camping limit is seven days. Most campgrounds are available on a first-come, first-served basis. Fish Creek and St. Mary campgrounds (fee) may be reserved ahead of time through the National Park Reservation System by calling toll-free 800/365-2267. Visitors planning to camp overnight in Glacier's backcountry must obtain a Backcountry User Permit and camp in designated sites.

Place-name signs and roadside exhibits mark the major roads from late May to mid-September. Also, ranger-naturalists conduct daily walks and campfire programs that are both rewarding and scenic. Parkwide guided hikes for day and overnight trips are available through Glacier Wilderness Guides, PO Box 535, West Glacier 59936. Guided bus tours are available through Glacier Park, Inc, Dial Tower, Dial Corporate Center, Phoenix, AZ 85077 (Oct-mid-May) or East Glacier Park 59434 (rest of year). Saddle horses are available through Mule Shoe Outfitters, LLC, PO Box 322, Kila 59920, and at Many Glacier, Lake McDonald Lodge, and Apgar Village Lodge. Launch service operates on Two Medicine, Swiftcurrent, Josephine, St. Mary, and McDonald lakes through Glacier Park Boat Co, PO Box 5262, Kalispell 59903, and between the townsite in Waterton Lakes National Park, Canada, and the head of Waterton Lake in Glacier National Park through Waterton Shoreline Cruises, PO Box 126, Waterton, Alberta, Canada T0K 2M0 (June-Aug).

For detailed information, contact the Superintendent, Glacier National Park, West Glacier 59936. Golden Eagle Passports are accepted (see MAKING THE MOST OF YOUR TRIP). Seven-day pass: per vehicle $20, per person $5.

What to See and Do

Avalanche Creek. Flows through deep gorge filled with spray. Two-mile hike to Avalanche Lake Basin with waterfalls, 2,000-foot-high cliffs. Camping; picnicking.

Belly River Country. Trails, lake fishing, backcountry camping, glacial valleys.

Cut Bank. A primitive, densely wooded valley. At head of valley is 8,011-foot Triple Divide Peak. Hiking, camping.

Flattop Mountain. Between the Lewis Range and the Livingston Range; meadows and groves of trees contrast with dense forest growth elsewhere.

St. Mary Lake. Emerald green, with peaks on three sides. Fishing, boating, hiking. The 1 1/2-hour boat tours leave from Rising Sun Boat Landing (mid-June-mid-Sept, daily). Self-guided trail from Sun Point.

East Glacier Area (A-2)

Web Site www.eastglacierpark.org

Limited-Service Hotels

★ **GLACIER PARK LODGE.** *Midville Dr, East Glacier (59912). Phone 406/892-2525; fax 406/892-1375. www.bigtreehotel.com.* 161 rooms. Closed Oct-mid-May. Check-in 3 pm, check-out noon. Two restaurants, two bars. Outdoor pool. Golf, 9 holes. **$$** ⌷ 🛝

★ ★ **THE RESORT AT GLACIER, SAINT MARY LODGE.** *Hwy 89 and Going-to-the-Sun Rd, St. Mary (59417). Phone 406/732-4431; toll-free 800/368-3689; fax 406/732-9265. www.glcpark.com.* 123 rooms, 3 story. Closed mid-Oct-Apr. Pets accepted, some restrictions; fee. Check-in 4 pm, check-out 11 am. Restaurant, two bars. **$**

Restaurants

★ ★ **GLACIER VILLAGE.** *304-308 Hwy 2 E, East Glacier (59434). Phone 406/226-4464.* American menu. Dinner. Closed late Sept-early May. **$$**

★ ★ **SNOW GOOSE GRILLE.** *Hwy 89, St. Mary (59417). Phone 406/732-4431. www.glcpark.com.* American menu. Breakfast, lunch, dinner. Closed Oct-mid-May. Bar. Children's menu. **$$**

West Glacier Area

See also Bozeman, Butte, Ennis

What to See and Do

Granite Park. *Going-to-the-Sun Rd and Highland Trail, West Glacier (59936). Phone toll-free 800/521-7238.*

Trails, glacial valleys, alpine flowers. Accessible only by foot. Reservations required.

⭐ **Lake McDonald.** *Going-to-the-Sun Rd and Mt Brown Trail, West Glacier (59936). Phone toll-free 800/521-7238.* The largest lake in the park at 10 miles long and 1 mile wide; heavily forested shores with peaks rising 6,000 feet above the lake. Trail to Sperry Glacier. One-hour boat tours and horseback riding trips leave from Lake McDonald Lodge (see) (mid-June-mid-Sept, daily).

Many Glacier Area. *Hwy 89 to Babb, West Glacier (59936). Phone 602/207-2600.* Fishing, boating (trips), camping, hiking, riding; trails to Morning Eagle Falls, Cracker Lake, Grinnell Glacier and Lake, Iceberg Lake. Footpaths go around Swiftcurrent and Josephine lakes and to Appekunny Falls and Cirque. Self-guided trail from hotel.

Red Eagle Lake. *Hwy 89 and Going-to-the-Sun Rd, West Glacier (59936). Phone 406/888-7800.* Located in a glacially carved basin with dramatic falls and gorge. Backcountry camping.

River rafting. *Hwy 2 and Hwy 89, West Glacier (59936). Phone 406/888-7800.* Four companies offer several 1/2- to 6-day trips on the Middle and North forks of the Flathead River. Guided fishing trips, combination trips. For information and reservations contact

Glacier Raft Co. *11957 Hwy 2 E, West Glacier (59936). Phone 406/888-5454; toll-free 800/332-9995.*

Great Northern Whitewater. *12127 Hwy 2 E, West Glacier (59936). Phone 406/387-5340; toll-free 800/735-7897.* **$$$$**

Montana Raft Company & Glacier Wilderness Guides. *11970 Hwy 2 E, West Glacier (59936). Phone 406/387-5555; toll-free 800/521-7238.* **$$$$**

Wild River Adventures. *11900 Hwy 2 E, West Glacier (59936). Phone 406/387-9453; toll-free 800/826-2724.* **$$$$**

Sperry and Grinnell glaciers. *Going-to-the-Sun Rd and Highland Trail, West Glacier (59936). Phone 406/888-7800.* Largest in the park. Inquire about trips to Grinnell.

Two Medicine Valley. *Hwy 49 to Two Medicine Valley Rd, West Glacier (59936). Phone 406/888-7800.* Deep valleys and towering peaks surround the mountain lake. Brook, rainbow trout; trails for hiking; boating; camping.

Limited-Service Hotels

⭐ ⭐ **IZAAK WALTON INN.** *290 Izaak Walton Inn Rd (Hwy 2), Essex (59916). Phone 406/888-5700; fax 403/888-5200. www.izaakwaltoninn.com.* Old railroad hotel (1939); restored sleeper cars available for rental (three-day minimum). 33 rooms, 3 story. Complimentary continental breakfast. Check-in 3 pm, check-out 11 am. Restaurant, bar. **$**

⭐ ⭐ **LAKE MCDONALD LODGE.** *Going-to-the-Sun Rd, West Glacier (59434). Phone 406/892-2525; fax 406/892-1375. www.glacierparkinc.com.* Rustic hunting lodge amid giant cedars. 100 rooms, 2 story. Check-in 3 pm, check-out 11 am. Two restaurants, bar. **$**

⭐ **VILLAGE INN.** *Going-to-the-Sun Rd, Apgar (59434). Phone 406/756-2444. www.glacierparkinc.com.* On the shore of Lake McDonald. 36 rooms, 5 story. Check-in 3 pm, check-out 11 am. **$**

Glasgow (B-5)

Founded 1887
Population 3,572
Elevation 2,090 ft
Area Code 406
Zip 59230
Information Glasgow Area Chamber of Commerce & Agriculture, 740 Hwy 2 E, PO Box 832; phone 406/228-2222
Web Site www.glasgowmt.net

Glasgow has had four booms in its history. The first was opening of land to white settlement in 1888, the second when another 18 million acres were opened around 1910. In the 1930s, Glasgow was headquarters for the 10,000 construction workers on Fort Peck Dam. Glasgow AFB made its home 18 miles northeast of town from 1954 to 1968; the flight facilities are now owned by Boeing and the residential area is being developed into a military retirement community. Wheat and livestock are raised in Valley County.

What to See and Do

Fort Peck Dam and Lake. *Fort Peck. 20 miles SE on Hwy 24.* Built by Army Corps of Engineers. Largest hydraulic earthfill dam in the world, forming huge reservoir with 1,600-mile lakeshore. Dam rises 280 1/2 feet above Missouri River; total length 21,026 feet; road follows crest of the dam, leading to mile-long concrete spillway.

Information center; museum. Guided tours of power plant (Memorial Day-Labor Day, daily; rest of year, by appointment). Self-guided nature trail. There are several recreation areas with fishing, camping (fee), trailer sites, boating (ramps), concession.

Hell Creek State Park. *Glasgow. 50 miles S on Hwy 24, then 6 miles W on county road. Phone 406/232-4365.* Swimming; fishing; boating (ramp, rentals). Picnicking. Camping (no hookups).

Valley County Pioneer Museum. *816 Hwy 2 W, Glasgow (59230). 1/2 mile W on Hwy 2. Phone 406/228-8692.* Displays of Native American artifacts; photos of pioneers and events of their time; pioneer farm machinery. Also fossils and aviation display. (Memorial Day-Labor Day, daily) **FREE**

Special Events

Fort Peck Summer Theater. *Fort Peck. 17 miles SE on Hwy 24. Phone 406/228-9219.* Professional cast performs musicals, comedies. Historical landmark. Late June-Labor Day.

Highland Games Festival. *Glasgow. Phone 406/228-2222.* Scottish games and music. Mid-Sept.

Longest Dam Run. *Kiwanis Park, 740 Hwy 2 E, Glasgow (59230). Phone 406/228-2222.* Foot of Fort Peck Dam. 5K and 10K run/walk crosses 1.8 miles of dam. Refreshments, prizes. Third week in June.

Montana Governor's Cup Walleye Tournament. *Fort Peck Lake, 740 Hwy 2 E, Glasgow (59230). Phone 406/228-2222.* Anglers from 18 states, Canada, and all over Montana come to Fort Peck Lake attempting to win the first place prize at this fishing tournament. Other events include a Gals and Guys Tournament; Youth Derby; barbecue for the fisherman and families; and a fish fry, which is open to the public. Early July.

Northeast Montana Fair and Rodeo. *Glasgow (59230). Fairgrounds at W edge of city. Phone 406/228-8221.* Exhibits, midway, rodeo, nightly shows. Three days in late July or early Aug.

Glendive (B-6)

Settled 1864
Population 4,802
Elevation 2,078 ft
Area Code 406
Zip 59330

Information Chamber of Commerce & Agriculture, 313 S Merrill Ave; phone 406/365-5601
Web Site www.glendivechamber.com

Glendive is the shipping center for the crops of Dawson County. It also serves the oil wells, railroad yards, and natural gas fields that ring the city.

What to See and Do

Fishing. *Glendive.* The unusual spatula-nosed paddlefish (*Polyodon spathula*) is found here in the Yellowstone River. Fishing for this rare, prehistoric species is permitted mid-May-June only.

Frontier Gateway Museum. *Belle Prairie Rd, Glendive (59330). 1 mile E off I-94, exit 215. Phone 406/377-8168.* Collection depicts Glendive and early Dawson County; "Main Street 1881" exhibit in basement; one-room schoolhouse, blacksmith shop, display of early farm machinery on grounds and five other buildings in complex. (June-Aug, daily) **FREE**

Hunt moss agates. *Along Yellowstone River.*

Makoshika State Park. *1301 Snyder Ave, Glendive (59330). 1/4 mile SE on Snyder Ave. Phone 406/377-6256.* A rugged chunk of badlands--Makoshika is the Lakota word for bad earth--this park stands out in the surrounding sea of prairie. Beyond the craggy sandstone formations, there is a diverse wildlife population residing on the park's 11,531 acres, including turkey vultures, bobcats, and golden eagles. The visitor center displays a triceratops skull that was unearthed on-site, and there is also a campground (no hookups), a pair of hiking trails, and a Frisbee golf course.

Special Events

Buzzard Day. *Makoshika State Park, 1301 Snyder Ave, Glendive (59330). Phone 406/377-6256.* Day-long activities; softball tournaments, concerts, BBQ. Early June.

Dawson County Fair and Rodeo. *2200 N Merrill Ave, Glendive (59330). Phone 406/377-6781.* Four days in mid-Aug.

Great Falls (B-3)

See also Fort Benton

Founded 1884
Population 55,097
Elevation 3,333 ft

Area Code 406
Information Chamber of Commerce, 710 1st Ave N, PO Box 2127, 59403; phone 406/761-4434
Web Site www.greatfallschamber.org

Great Falls's growth has been powered by thriving diversified industry, agriculture and livestock, construction, and activity at nearby Malmstrom AFB. The city takes its name from the falls of the Missouri River, a source of electric power.

What to See and Do

⭐**C. M. Russell Museum Complex and Original Log Cabin Studio.** *400 13th St N, Great Falls (59401). Phone 406/727-8787. www.cmrussell.org.* Born in St. Louis, Charles Marion Russell (1864-1926) worked as a wrangler in Montana's Judith Basin before he found his true calling: painting the inhabitants and landscapes of the West. He was the first well-known Western artist who also lived in the West, and his life's work includes more than 4,000 pieces. On the site of Russell's former home (and adjacent log studio), there also stands an impressive museum that houses 2,000 of Russell's artworks, personal possessions, and other relevant artifacts. His vivid style depicts cowboys, Native Americans, buffalo, and other symbols of the Old West, capturing humanity and menace; the museum's collection includes his paintings, sketches, and bronzes. There is also an excellent collection of work by other Western artists, past and present, and Russell's old log studio and home are also open to visitors. (May-Sept: Mon-Sat 9 am-6 pm, Sun noon-t pm; rest of year: Tues-Sat 10 am-5 pm, 1-5 pm) **$$**

Giant Springs State Park and State Trout Hatchery. *4600 Giant Springs Rd, Great Falls (59405). 4 miles NE on River Dr. Phone 406/454-5840.* One of the largest freshwater springs in the world produces nearly 390 million gallons of water every 24 hours. The hatchery next to the springs raises trout. Picnic grounds. (Daily)**$**

Lewis and Clark National Forest. *1101 15th St N, Great Falls (59401). E on Hwy 87, 89, 200. Phone 406/791-7700.* More than 1.8 million acres of canyons, mountains, meadows, and wilderness. Parts of the Scapegoat Wilderness and the Bob Marshall Wilderness (384,407 acres), with the 15-mile-long, 1,000-foot-high Chinese Wall are here. Activities include scenic drives, stream and lake fishing, big-game hunting, hiking, camping (fee), picnicking, winter sports.

Lewis and Clark National Historical Trail Interpretive Center. *4201 Giant Springs Rd, Great Falls (59403). 3 miles NW on Giant Springs Rd. Phone 406/727-8733. www.fs.fed.us/r1/lewisclark/lcic.* No facility better tells the story of Meriwether Lewis and William Clark's legendary journey than this attractive structure on a bluff above the banks of the Missouri River. What is now Great Falls was in 1805 the site of the most arduous leg of the expedition, where the waterfalls (which have since been dampened by hydroelectric projects) forced the Corps of Discovery to portage their riverboats and other supplies across 18 miles of often-rugged terrain. A variety of interactive exhibits tell this story and others, tracing the fascinating history of Lewis and Clark, chronologically and from both the explorers' perspectives and that of the Native Americans they encountered. Throughout the day, interpreters lecture on topics ranging from the medical techniques used on the expedition to the ecology of the land in the early 19th century. There are also costumed actors demonstrating skills of the era and a theater with regular screenings of an excellent documentary. (Memorial Day wknd-Sept: daily 9 am-6 pm; rest of year: Tues-Sat 9 am-5 pm, Sun noon-5 pm) **$**

Malmstrom AFB. *228 75th St N, Great Falls (59405). 1 mile E of 2nd Ave N and Bypass Rd. Phone 406/731-4046. www.malmstrom.af.mil.* Home of the 341st Space Wing and center of one of the largest intercontinental ballistic missile complexes in the world. Museum featuring historical military displays. Tours by appointment. **FREE**

Paris Gibson Square Museum of Art. *1400 1st Ave N, Great Falls (59401). Phone 406/727-8255.www.the-square.org.* Historical school building contains a gallery with changing displays of contemporary regional art. Gift shop; lunchtime café. (Memorial Day-Labor Day, Tues-Sun, rest of year, Mon-Sat) **FREE**

University of Great Falls. *1301 20th St S, Great Falls (59405). Phone 406/761-8210.* (1932) (1,000 students) A 40-acre campus. Chapel sculpture and stained-glass windows designed and produced at the college. The pool in McLaughlin Memorial Center is open to the public (inquire for days, hours, fees).

Special Events

Montana Pro Rodeo Circuit Finals. *Montana Expo-Park, 400 3rd St NW, Great Falls (59401). Four Seasons Arena. Phone 406/727-8900. www.montanaprorodeo. com.* Mid-Jan.

Montana State Fair. *Montana ExpoPark, 400 3rd St NW, Great Falls (59401). Phone 406/727-8900. www.*

montanastatefair.com. Rodeo, livestock exhibits, horse racing, petting zoo, commercial exhibits, entertainment, carnival. Late July-early Aug.

Limited-Service Hotels

★★BEST WESTERN HERITAGE INN. *1700 Fox Farm Rd, Great Falls (59404). Phone 406/761-1900; toll-free 800/548-8256; fax 406/761-0136. www.bestwestern .com.* 234 rooms, 2 story. Pets accepted. Check-in 3 pm, check-out noon. High-speed Internet access. Restaurant, bar. Fitness room. Indoor pool, whirlpool. Airport transportation available. Business center.**$**

★ DAYS INN. *101 14th Ave NW, Great Falls (59404). Phone 406/727-6565; toll-free 800/329-7466; fax 406/727-6308. www.daysinngreatfalls.com.* 61 rooms, 2 story. Pets accepted; fee. Complimentary continental breakfast. Check-in 3 pm, check-out 11 am.**$**

★ FAIRFIELD INN. *1000 9th Ave S, Great Falls (59405). Phone 406/454-3000; toll-free 800/228-9290; fax 406/454-3000. www.fairfieldinn.com.* 63 rooms, 3 story. Complimentary continental breakfast. Check-in 2 pm, check-out noon. Indoor pool, whirlpool. Business center.**$**

★ ★ HOLIDAY INN. *400 10th Ave S, Great Falls (59405). Phone 406/727-7200; toll-free 800/257-1998; fax 406/268-0472. www.holiday-inn.com/greatfallsmt* . 168 rooms, 7 story. Pets accepted; fee. Check-in 2 pm, check-out noon. High-speed Internet access. Restaurant, bar. Fitness room. Indoor pool, whirlpool. Airport transportation available. Business center.**$**

★ ★ TOWNHOUSE INNS. *1411 S 10th Ave, Great Falls (59405). Phone 406/761-4600; toll-free 800/442-4667; fax 406/761-7603. www.montana-motels.com.* 109 rooms, 2 story. Pets accepted; fee. Check-in 3 pm, check-out 11 am. Restaurant, bar. Indoor pool, whirlpool. Airport transportation available.**$**

Restaurant

★ ★ JAKER'S STEAK, RIBS & FISH HOUSE. *1500 10th Ave S, Great Falls (59405). Phone 406/727-1033; fax 406/727-9977. www.jakers.com.* American

menu. Lunch, dinner. Closed Thanksgiving, Dec 25. Bar. Children's menu. Casual attire. **$$**

Hamilton (C-2)

See also Missoula

Population 2,737
Elevation 3,572 ft
Area Code 406
Zip 59840
Information Bitterroot Valley Chamber of Commerce, 105 E Main; phone 406/363-2400
Web Site www.bvchamber.com

Hamilton is the county seat and main shopping center for Ravalli County and headquarters for the Bitterroot National Forest.

What to See and Do

Bitterroot National Forest. *1801 N First St, Hamilton (59840). Surrounding Hamilton with access by Hwys 93 and 38. Phone 406/363-7161. www.fs.fed.us/r1/bitterroot.* 1,579,533 acres. Lake and stream fishing, big game hunting; Anaconda-Pintler Wilderness, Selway-Bitterroot Wilderness, and River of No Return Wilderness. Mountain lakes, hot springs. Scenic drives in Bitterroot Valley; Skalkaho Falls. Hiking and riding trails, winter sports, camp and picnic sites. Inquire locally for wilderness pack trips. Fees may be charged at recreation sites.

Daly Mansion. *251 Eastside Hwy, Hamilton (59840). 2 miles NE on Hwy 269. Phone 406/363-6004. www.dalymansion.org.* (Circa 1890). This 42-room mansion was the home of Marcus Daly, an Irish immigrant who became one of Montana's "copper kings" through the copper mines near Butte. Seven Italian marble fireplaces, original furniture, transplanted exotic trees, "dollhouse" built for Daly children. Tours (Apr-Oct, daily 10 am-5 pm; rest of year, by appointment). **$$**

Fort Owen State Park. *Stevensville. 20 miles N, off Hwy 93 to Stevensville, then 5 miles E on Hwy 269.* A restoration of Montana's first white settlement, more a trading post than a fort. Day use only.

Lost Trail Powder Mountain. *7674 Hwy 93 S, Sula (59827). 50 miles S. Phone 406/821-3211. www.losttrail .com.* Three chairlifts, three rope tows; patrol, ski school, rentals, concession area. Vertical drop 1,200 feet. (Dec-Apr: Thurs-Sun, holidays) Cross-country trails.

Painted Rocks State Park. *Conner. 20 miles S on Hwy 93, then 23 miles SW on Hwy 473, in the Bitterroot Mountains. Phone 406/542-5500.* Swimming; fishing; boating (ramp). Picnicking. Camping (no hookups). **$$**

St. Mary's Mission. *Stevensville. 20 miles N off Hwy 93; W end of 4th St. Phone 406/777-5734. www. saintmarysmission.org.* (1841). Picturesque log church and residence; one of the oldest churches in Northwest (present structure built in 1866); also old pharmacy (1868). Restored and furnished to period. Pioneer relics, Chief Victor's house and cemetery. Site is first in religion, education, agriculture, music in Montana. Gift shop. Guided tours. Park, picnicking. (Mid-Apr-mid-Oct, daily) **$$**

Special Events

Chief Victor Days. *Victor Park, Hamilton (59840). Phone 406/363-2400.* July.

McIntosh Apple Days. *Ravalli County Museum, 205 Bedford St, Hamilton (59840). Phone 406/363-3338.* Oct.

Ravalli County Fair. *Fairgrounds, Hamilton (59840). Fairgrounds Rd and Hwy 93. Phone 406/363-3411.* Late Aug.

Full-Service Resort

★ ★ ★ **TRIPLE CREEK RANCH.** *5551 W Fork Rd, Darby (59829). Phone 406/821-4600; toll-free 800/654-2943; fax 406/821-4666. www.triplecreekranch.com.* With the mountains of Montana as your backdrop, this ranch allows guests to experience the wilderness in its natural setting. Log cabins, trout-filled lakes, horseback riding, and hiking trails will keep guests coming back for the fresh mountain air and relaxing atmosphere. 19 rooms. Pets accepted, some restrictions. Children over 16 years only. Complimentary full breakfast. Check-in 3 pm, check-out noon. Restaurant, bar. Fitness room. Outdoor pool, whirlpool. Tennis. Business center. **$$$$**

🐾 🏃 🛥 🏃

Hardin (C-5)

See also Billings

Population 2,940
Elevation 2,902 ft
Area Code 406
Zip 59034

Information Chamber of Commerce, 21 E 4th St; phone 406/665-1672
Web Site www.custerslaststand.org

Hardin became the seat of Big Horn County after the area was opened to white settlers in 1906. It is the trading center for ranchers, farmers, and Native Americans from the Crow Reservation.

What to See and Do

Bighorn Canyon National Recreation Area. *Fort Smith (59035). 43 miles S on Hwy 313.* (See LOVELL, WY)

Custer National Forest. *Hardin. E via Hwy 212; includes Beartooth Hwy, a National Forest Scenic Byway. Phone 406/657-6361. www.fs.fed.us/r1/custer.com.* (see RED LODGE) Approximately 1.2 million acres in Montana and South Dakota; Little Missouri Grasslands, an additional 1.2 million acres in North Dakota, is also included. Rolling pine hills and grasslands; picnicking; saddle and pack trips; big game hunting; camping.

Little Bighorn Battlefield National Monument. *I-90 and 3rd St, Hardin (59022). 2 miles SE of the Crow Agency. The entrance is 1 mile E of I-90 on Hwy 212. Phone 406/638-3204 (visitor information). www.nps.gov/libi.* As the US government looked westward after the Civil War, the construction of roads and forts threatened the traditional way of life of the Cheyenne and Sioux tribes, among others. In the late 1860s and early 1870s, a series of skirmishes between Native warriors and US soldiers escalated, and Lieutenant Colonel George Custer was dispatched to lead 12 companies of the Seventh Cavalry against the uprising. At a ridge above the Little Bighorn River, Custer's party was surprised and overwhelmed by a far larger contingent of Sioux and Cheyenne warriors, and 220 men were killed on June 25 and 26, 1876. The battlefield became a memorial for the fallen US soldiers soon thereafter; an Indian Memorial was dedicated in 2003. The visitor center includes historical displays; there are walking trails, self-guided auto routes, and guided bus tours. National Park Service personnel provide interpretive programs (Memorial Day-Labor Day) and guided tours of Custer National Cemetery. Also located here are a national cemetery, established in 1879, and the Reno-Benteen Battlefield, 5 miles southeast, where the remainder of the Seventh Cavalry withstood until late on June 26. Headstones show where the soldiers' fell, and a large obelisk marks the mass grave of the Seventh Cavalry. **$$**

Special Events

Crow Fair. *Crow Reservation, Hardin (59034). S on Hwy 313.* Features largest all-Native American rodeo in the country. Aug.

Little Bighorn Days. *Held throughout town, Hardin. Phone 406/665-1672.* Custer's last stand reenactment. Military Ball, rodeo, street dance, bed races, children's games. Third weekend in June.

Harlowton (C-4)

Population 1,049
Elevation 4,167 ft
Area Code 406
Zip 59036
Information Chamber of Commerce, PO Box 694; phone 406/632-4694

A Ranger District office of the Lewis and Clark National Forest (see GREAT FALLS) is located here.

What to See and Do

Deadman's Basin Fishing Access Site. *Harlowton. 23 miles E on Hwy 12 to milepost 120, then 1 mile N on county road. Phone 406/247-2940.* Swimming; fishing; boating. Picnicking.

Fishing, camping. Martinsdale, Harris and North Fork lakes. *Harlowton. W on Hwy 12.* **Lebo Lake.** 9 miles W on Hwy 12 to Twodot, then 7 miles S on Hwy 296.

Special Event

Harlowton Rodeo. *Chief Joseph Park, Harlowton (59036). Phone 406/632-4694.* Chief Joseph Park. NRA approved; parade, concessions, campgrounds. Early July.

Havre (A-4)

See also Chinook

Founded 1887
Population 10,201
Elevation 2,494 ft
Area Code 406
Zip 59501
Information Chamber of Commerce, 518 1st St, PO Box 308; phone 406/265-4383
Web Site www.havremt.com

Center of a cattle and wheat-producing area, Havre (HAVE-er) is an important retail and wholesale distribution point for northern Montana. It is one of the oldest and largest division points on the Burlington Northern Santa Fe (formerly Great Northern) Railway.

What to See and Do

Beaver Creek Park. *Havre. About 10 miles S, in Bear Paw Mountains. Phone 406/395-4565.* 10,000 acres. Swimming; fishing; boating. Skiing, cross-country skiing, snowmobiling. Camping (fee). **Fresno Lake.** Water-skiing, boating, camping. 15 miles NW. **FREE**

Fort Assinniboine. *Havre. 6 miles SW on Hwy 87. Phone 406/265-4383.* Built in 1879-1883 and used as a military fort until 1911. In 1913, it became an agricultural experiment station. Some original buildings still stand. Tours (June-Sept). **$$**

H. Earl Clack Memorial Museum. *Havre Heritage Center, 306 3rd Ave, Havre (59501). Phone 406/265-4000.* Regional history. (Apr-Oct, Wed-Sun; rest of year, by appointment) **FREE** Museum manages

Wahkpa Chu'gn. *14 Meadowlakes Estates, Havre (59501). 1/2 mile W on Hwy 2. Phone 406/265-6417.* Archaeological excavation of prehistoric bison jump site. Also campground (fee). Tours (Memorial Day-Labor Day, Tues-Sun). **$$**

Havre Beneath the Streets. *100 3rd Ave, Havre (59501). Phone 406/265-8888.* Tour an "underground mall" where many of the first businesses in the town were established. Includes turn-of-the-century Sporting Eagle Saloon; Holland and Son Mercantile; Wah Sing Laundry; even an opium den. Tours take approximately one hour. Reservations required. (Daily) **$$**

Special Events

Great Northern Fair. *1676 Hwy 2 W, Havre (59501). Phone 406/265-7121.* Second week in Aug.

Rocky Boy Powwow. *Rocky Boy Indian Reservation, Havre (59501). Phone 406/395-4282.* First weekend in Aug.

Limited-Service Hotel

★ **BEST WESTERN GREAT NORTHERN INN.** *1345 First St, Havre (59501). Phone 406/265-4200; toll-free 888/530-4100; fax 406/265-3656. www.bestwestern.com.* A convenient stop for travel across northern Montana, this motel has quiet, spacious rooms and a nice pool and fitness center. It's located on Highway 2 near shopping and dining areas.75 rooms. Complimentary continental breakfast. Check-in 2 pm, check-out 11 am. Fitness room. Outdoor pool, whirlpool.**$**

🧍 🏊

Helena (C-3)

See also Deer Lodge, White Sulphur Springs

Settled 1864
Population 24,569
Elevation 4,157 ft
Area Code 406
Zip 59601
Information Helena Area Chamber of Commerce, 225 Cruse Ave, Suite A; phone 406/442-4120 or toll-free 800/743-5362 (outside MT)
Web Site www.helenachamber.com

Montana's state capital and fourth-largest city, Helena was the site of one of the state's largest gold rushes. In 1864, a party of discouraged prospectors decided to explore a gulch--now Helena's Main Street--as their "last chance." This gulch and the area surrounding it produced more than $20 million in gold. A hundred cabins soon appeared. The mining camp, known as "Last Chance," was renamed Helena, after a town in Minnesota. Besides being the governmental center for Montana, today's Helena hosts agricultural and industrial business, including an important smelting and ore refining plant in East Helena.

What to See and Do

Archie Bray Foundation. *2915 Country Club Ave, Helena (59601).* Phone 406/443-3502. Internationally recognized resident program, workshop, gallery, and classroom.

Canyon Ferry State Park. *7667 Canyon Ferry Rd, Helena (59601). 10 miles E on Hwy 12/287, then 6 miles N on Hwy 284.* Phone 406/475-3319. (Chinamans Unit) There are numerous recreation sites around this reservoir, which was created in 1954 by the construction of the Canyon Ferry Dam. Swimming, water-skiing; fishing; boating. Picnicking. Camping (no hookups).

Cathedral of St. Helena. *530 N Ewing St, Helena (59601).* Gothic cathedral with 230-foot spires and 68 stained-glass windows made in Germany. Modeled after a cathedral in Vienna, Austria. (Daily)

Frontier Town. *Helena. 15 miles W on Hwy 12, atop MacDonald Pass.* Phone 406/442-4560. Rustic pioneer village shaped with solid rock and built with giant logs. 75-mile view of the Continental Divide. Restaurant, bar. (Mother's Day-early Oct, daily) **FREE**

Gates of the Mountains. *Helena. 16 miles N, off Hwy 15.* Phone 406/458-5241. This 12-mile, two-hour Missouri River cruise explores the deep gorge in Helena National Forest, discovered and named by Lewis and Clark. Views of cliffs, canyons, wildlife, and wilderness. (Memorial Day weekend-mid-Sept, daily) Launching facilities (Apr-Nov). **$$$**

Gold Collection. *350 N Last Chance Gulch, Helena (59601).* Phone 406/447-2000. Collection includes nuggets, wire and leaf gold, gold dust and coins. (Mon-Fri; closed holidays) **FREE**

Helena National Forest. *2880 Skyway Dr, Helena (59601). Adjacent to Helena, accessible from Hwys 12, 91, and 287; I-15; and Hwy 200.* Phone 406/449-5201. *www .fs.fed.us/r1/helena.* Surrounding Montana's capital city, Helena National Forest is rife with recreational opportunities and lures anglers, mountain bikers, hikers, and other outdoor buffs every weekend. Two prime attractions are the Scapegoat Wilderness Area, a great area for day hiking, and the Gates of the Mountains Wilderness Area, where the Missouri River flows out of a seemingly impassable rock wall. (Boat tours are a great way to explore the latter.) There are Ranger District offices in Helena, Lincoln, and Townsend.

Holter Museum of Art. *12 E Lawrence, Helena (59601).* Phone 406/442-6400. *www.holtermuseum.org.* Changing exhibits featuring paintings, sculpture, photography, ceramics, weaving. (June-Sept: Mon-Sat 10 am-5 pm, Sun noon-5 pm; Oct-May: Tues-Fri 10:30 am-5 pm, Sat-Sun noon-5 pm) **DONATION**

⭐ **Last Chance Tour Train.** *6th and Roberts sts, Helena (59601).* Phone toll-free 188/842-3102. *www.lctours .com.* Departs from historical museum. Covered trains tour the city's major points of interest, including Last Chance Gulch. (Mid-May-Sept, Mon-Sat) **$$**

Marysville Ghost Town. *Helena. 7 miles N, off Hwy 279.* A ghost town with abandoned saloons, churches, and buildings, complete with a fully-functioning restaurant Marysville House amidst the ruins. Restaurant (Wed-Sat; summer, Tues-Sat).

⭐ **Montana Historical Society Museum.** *225 N Roberts St, Helena (59601).* Phone 406/444-2694. *www.his.state. mt.us/museum.* Adjacent to the Montana State Capitol,

Last Chance Gulch

Montana's capital city straddles one of history's richest gold strikes Last Chance Gulch and consequently the city has a rich legacy of monuments and architecture.

Begin at the Montana Historical Society (225 N Roberts St), across from the state capitol. Montana's premier museum, this captivating complex mixes fine art and exhibits charting the state's history. Of special interest is the MacKay Gallery of Charles M. Russell Art, one of the nation's largest public collections of Russell's painting and sculpture.

Walk west on 6th Street to the Montana State Capitol at 1301 6th Avenue. This imposing structure, domed with a cupola of Butte copper, was built in 1899 and enlarged in 1912 by the extensions containing the present legislative wings. Significant paintings and murals decorate the interior. In the House Chambers hangs *Lewis and Clark Meeting the Flathead Indians at Ross' Hole* by Charley Russell, one of his largest and most acclaimed works. In the lobby of the House of Representatives are six paintings by E. S. Paxson, which detail the state's history. Tours of the capitol are given daily on the hour, 9 am-5 pm.

Continue walking down 6th Street to the Old Governor's Mansion (304 N Ewing). Built in 1883 by a local entrepreneur, the 20-room residence served as the governor's home from 1913 to 1959. The building is now owned by the Montana Historical Society, which has restored the ornate building to its historic splendor. Free tours are offered.

Continue down Ewing Street to Lawrence Street, and turn west. The Cathedral of St. Helena (530 N Ewing St) was begun in 1908 but wasn't finished until 1924. Modeled after a cathedral in Vienna, Austria, Helena's largest church dominates the skyline with its 230-foot twin spires. Its stained glass was fashioned in Germany.

Continue west on Lawrence Street to Last Chance Gulch, the site of Helena's gold rush. In the 1860s, Prickly Pear Creek snaked down from the mountains through a thicket of mining claims called Last Chance Gulch. As mining gave way to commerce, the gulch remained the main street; its winding path, and especially the one-claim-sized business buildings, still reflect its mining past. The old business district of Helena is still impressive, even after a 1933 earthquake destroyed some of its buildings.

The Power Block (58-62 N Last Chance Gulch) was built in 1889; note that on the southeast corner, each of the five floors has windows grouped in corresponding numbers of panes. The Securities Building (101 N Last Chance Gulch), built in 1886, is a Romanesque former bank with curious carved thumbprints between the first-floor arches. The Montana Club (24 W 6th St) was Montana's most prestigious private club: membership was open only to millionaires. The club's present building was designed by Cass Gilbert, the designer of the US Supreme Court Building.

Be certain to stop in at The Parrot (42 N Last Chance Gulch), an old-fashioned ice-cream parlor and chocolate confectioner that's one of Helena's longest operating business. The Atlas Building (7-9 N Last Chance Gulch) is one of Helena's most fanciful; on a cornice upheld by Atlas, a salamander and lizards in symbolic battle.

this museum has as its main exhibition Montana Homeland, covering the last 12,000 years of the state's history. On display are artifacts relating to everything from agriculture to transportation, as well as a collection of artworks by Montana's own Charles Russell and a special display about Big Medicine, a rare albino buffalo who called the National Bison Range in northwest Montana home. His mounted hide is the centerpiece of the exhibit. (Memorial Day-Labor Day, daily; rest of year, Tues-Sat; closed Jan 1, Thanksgiving, Dec 25) **$**

Mount Helena City Park. *225 Cruse Ave, Helena (59601). Phone 406/447-8463.* Perched 1,300 feet above downtown Helena, this 800-acre mountain park offers excellent hiking and mountain biking along the southwest edge of town. There are six trails, including the 1906 Trail up to the summit (5,468 feet above sea level). They connect to even longer trails in the adjacent Helena National Forest (see).

Original Governor's Mansion. *304 N Ewing St, Helena (59601). Phone 406/444-4789.* (1888) Restored 22-room brick house used as governor's residence from 1913 to 1959.

Pioneer Cabin. *212 S Park Ave, Helena (59601). Phone 406/443-7641.* (1864). Depicts frontier life (1864-1884); many authentic furnishings. (Memorial Day-Labor Day, Mon-Fri; rest of year, by appointment) **$**

Reeder's Alley. *S Park Ave, Helena (59601). Near S end of Last Chance Gulch. Phone 406/442-3222.* This area, which previously housed miners, muleskinners, and Chinese laundry workers, now houses specialty shops and a restaurant.

State Capitol. *1301 6th Ave, Helena (59620). Bounded by Lockey and Roberts sts, 6th and Montana aves. Phone 406/444-2511.* Neoclassic structure faced with Montana granite and sandstone, topped with a copper dome. Murals by Charles M. Russell, E. S. Paxson, and other artists on display inside. (Daily; guided tours mid-June-Labor Day) **FREE**

Special Events

Eagle Watch. *Helena. Phone 406/442-4120.* Bald eagles migrate to nearby Missouri River to feed on salmon. Mid-Nov-mid-Dec.

Governor's Cup Marathon. *Various locations, Helena (59601).* Early June.

Last Chance Stampede and Fair. *Lewis and Clark County Fairgrounds, Custer Ave and Henderson St, Helena (59601). Phone 406/442-1098.* Rodeo. July.

Montana Traditional Dixieland Jazz Festival. *Various downtown locations, Helena (59601). Phone 406/442-4120.* Mid-June.

Race to the Sky Dog Sled Races. *Various starting points, Helena (59601). Phone 406/442-4008.* Feb.

Western Rendezvous of Art. *Neill and Benton aves, Helena (59601). Phone 406/442-4263.* Mid-Aug.

Limited-Service Hotels

★ ★ **JORGENSON'S INN AND SUITES.** *1714 11th Ave, Helena (59601). Phone 406/442-1770; toll-free 800/272-1770; fax 406/449-0155. www.jorgensons-inn.com.* 116 rooms, 3 story. Check-in 3 pm, check-out noon. Restaurant, bar. Indoor pool. Airport transportation available. Business center. **$**

★ ★ **RED LION COLONIAL HOTEL.** *2301 Colonial Dr, Helena (59601). Phone 406/443-2100; toll-free 800/325-4000; fax 406/442-0301. www.redlion.com.* 149 rooms, 2 story. Pets accepted, some restrictions; fee. Check-in 3 pm, check-out noon. High-speed Internet access, wireless Internet access. Restaurant, bar. Fitness room. Indoor pool, outdoor pool, whirlpool. Airport transportation available. **$**

Specialty Lodging

THE SANDERS - HELENA'S BED & BREAKFAST. *328 N Ewing, Helena (59601). Phone 406/442-3309; fax 406/443-2361. www.sandersbb.com.* This bed-and-breakfast was built in 1875 by Senator Wilbur Fisk Sanders but renovated in 1987 with much of the original woodworking preserved. The guest rooms feature elegant furnishings and offer a feel of warmth and welcome. Guests can pass the day by exploring Mount Helena by bike or by trail. 7 rooms, 2 story. Complimentary full breakfast. Check-in 4 pm, check-out 11 am. High-speed Internet access. **$**

Restaurants

★ **JADE GARDEN.** *3128 N Montana Ave, Helena (59602). Phone 406/443-8899; fax 406/443-8390.* Chinese menu. Lunch, dinner. Closed Thanksgiving, Dec 25. Bar. Children's menu. Casual attire. **$**

★ ★ **ON BROADWAY.** *106 Broadway, Helena (59601). Phone 406/443-1929; fax 406/443-1929. www.onbroadwayhelena.com.* This former 1889 grocery store is located in the original old downtown area of Helena--Last Chance Gulch. Some of the original brick walls still stand along with newer walls of pine. Seafood and Italian dishes are among the favorites, and the desserts are homemade.

International, Italian menu. Dinner. Closed Sun; holidays. Bar. Casual attire. **$$**

★ ★ **STONEHOUSE.** *120 Reeder's Alley, Helena (59601). Phone 406/449-2552; fax 406/447-2558.* Located close to downtown, this 1880s stonehouse features great views of the surrounding hills and mountains. The steaks, prime rib, and seafood dishes are among the specialties. American menu. Dinner. Closed Sun;

holidays. Bar. Children's menu. Casual attire. Reservations recommended. Outdoor seating. **$$**

★ **WINDBAG SALOON.** *19 S Last Chance Gulch, Helena (59601). Phone 406/443-9669.* This restored historic building features original stone walls and tin ceilings. Old photos of early settlers are on the walls, and there are views of the nearby mountains.

American menu. Lunch, dinner. Closed Sun; holidays. Bar. Children's menu. Casual attire. **$$**

Kalispell (B-2)

See also Bigfork, Columbia Falls, Libby, Whitefish

Founded 1891
Population 11,917
Elevation 2,955 ft
Area Code 406
Zip 59901
Information Flathead Convention & Visitor Bureau, 15 Depot Park; phone 406/756-9091 or toll-free 800/543-3105
Web Site www.kalispellchamber.com

Center of a mountain vacationland, Kalispell is the convention center of the Flathead Valley. Seed potatoes and sweet cherries are grown and processed in great quantities. Recreational activities abound in the area.

What to See and Do

Conrad Mansion. *Woodland Ave E, Kalispell (59901). Six blocks E of Main St on 4th St E. Phone 406/755-2166. www.conradmansion.com.* (1895) A 23-room Norman-style mansion, authentically furnished and restored. Tours (Mid-May-mid-Oct: Tues-Sun 10 am-5 pm).

Flathead Lake. *490 N Meridian Rd, Kalispell (59901). 9 miles S on Hwy 93. Phone 406/837-4196.* (See POLSON)

Flathead National Forest. *1935 3rd Ave E, Kalispell (59901). Near Hwy 2, 93, adjacent to W and S sides of Glacier National Park. Phone 406/755-5401.* A 2.3 million-acre forest; including part of 1,009,356-acre Bob Marshall Wilderness; 286,700-acre Great Bear Wilderness, and the 73,573-acre Mission Mountains Wilderness; 15,368-acre Jewel Basin hiking area and the 219-mile Flathead National Wild and Scenic river system. Spectacular geological formations; glaciers, wild areas. Swimming, fishing, boating, canoeing; riding, picnicking, camping (June-Sept; fee), hunting, outfitters and guides, winter sports; recreation resorts, scenic drives.

Hockaday Center for the Arts. *2nd Ave E and 3rd St E, Kalispell (59901). Phone 406/755-5268.* Changing exhibits; sales gallery. (Tues, Thurs-Sat 10 am-6 pm, Wed 10 am-8 pm; closed holidays) **$$**

Lawrence Park. *E off N Main St, Kalispell (59901). Phone 406/758-7700.* Preserved in natural state. Picnic, playground facilities. **FREE**

Woodland Park. *705 2nd St E, Kalispell (59901). 8 blocks E of Main St on 2nd St E. Phone 406/758-7700.* 37 acres. Flower and rock gardens; mile-long lagoon; skating rink (winter); picnicking, kitchen; playground; pool, wading pool (fees). (Daily) **FREE**

Special Events

Agriculture-Farm Show. *20 N Main St, Kalispell (59901). Phone 406/758-4423.* Two days in mid-Feb.

Flathead Music Festival. *Kalispell. Phone 406/758-2800.* July.

Glacier Jazz Stampede. *Westcoast Outlaw Hotel, 1701 Hwy 93 S, Kalispell (59901). Phone 406/862-3814.* Oct.

Northwest Montana Fair and Rodeo. *Flathead County Fairgrounds, 265 N Meridian Rd, Kalispell (59901). Phone 406/758-5810.* Mid-Aug.

Quarter Horse Show. *Flathead County Fairgrounds, 265 N Meridian, Kalispell (59901). Phone 406/758-2800.* July.

Youth Horse Show. *Flathead County Fairgrounds, 265 N Meridian, Kalispell (59901). Phone 406/758-2800.* May.

Limited-Service Hotels

★ **BEST WESTERN WHITE OAK GRAND.** *4824 Hwy 93 S, Kalispell (59901). Phone 406/857-2400; toll-free 888/226-1003; fax 406/857-2401. www.bestwestern .com.* 60 rooms. Complimentary continental breakfast. Check-in 3 pm, check-out 11 am. High-speed Internet access, wireless Internet access. Fitness room. Indoor pool, whirlpool. Airport transportation available. Business center. **$**

⊁ ⇌ ⊀

★ **DAYS INN.** *1550 Hwy 93 N, Kalispell (59901). Phone 406/756-3222; toll-free 800/329-7466; fax 406/756-3277. www.daysinn.com.* 53 rooms, 2 story. Pets accepted, some restrictions; fee. Complimentary continental breakfast. Check-in 1 pm, check-out 11 am. **$**

Flathead Lake

The largest natural freshwater lake west of the Mississippi River, Flathead Lake is 28 miles long, 15 miles across, and surrounded by evergreen-clad mountains. The center of a valley of the same name, the lake is ringed with resorts and camp-grounds and is a top recreation destination in the summertime. Many choose to stay in Polson, Bigfork, or one of the other communities near the water's edge, but much of the land here is owned by the state, making the lake a camping hotspot.

On Flathead Lake's shores are five units of Montana's state park system. Another unit is in the lake itself: Wild Horse Island, at 2,163 acres, is one of the largest inland islands in the United States. These lakeside parks include Big Arm, a popular south-lake departure point for tours of the island and home to a pebble beach; Finley Point, also on the south side of the lake, with boat slips and RV campsites for rent; Wayfarers, in the forests on the northeast shore, with nice trails and great sunsets; West Shore, which sees less traffic and is popular among anglers; and Yellow Bay, amidst the cherry orchards on the south side of the lake. Rife with such wildlife as bighorn sheep, black bears, and bald eagles, Wild Horse Island is a popular destination for day trips, but unlike the parks on the shore camping is not allowed.

Whether you're roughing it or not, a great way to explore Flathead Lake is to tour it by boat: take a scheduled tour, charter a boat for a custom expedition, or rent a watercraft and navigate the lake on your own. The Flathead Convention and Visitors Bureau (phone 406/756-9091; www.fcvb.org) is the best source of up-to-date information about boating and tours.

Many outfitters specialize in fishing trips on the lake, with trophy trout being the prime catch; you'll also find yellow perch and whitefish. (If you fish in the southern half of the lake part of the Flathead Indian Reservations you must have a tribal permit in addition to a Montana state fishing license; both are available at local sporting goods stores.) Beyond the lake, there are a number of excellent golf courses. In winter, downhill skiing at Blacktail Mountain near Lakeside threatens to make the lake a four-season destination.

There are plenty of chances to get civilized, too, from theater and dining in Bigfork to the Mission Mountain Winery on the southwestern shore. All in all, the west side of the lake is less developed than the east side.

Some say that the lake is the domain of a North American counterpart to Scotland's Loch Ness Monster. Since the first sighting in 1889, reports of a mysterious whale-like creature, measuring somewhere between 10 and 20 feet from tip to tail, pop up every few years. Some argue that folks are merely seeing an overgrown sturgeon, and not Montana's Nessie. At its deepest point, however, Flathead Lake is 386 feet to the bottom, giving the mythical beast plenty of room to hide.

★★**WESTCOAST OUTLAW HOTEL.** *1701 Hwy 93 S, Kalispell (59901). Phone 406/755-6100; toll-free 800/325-4000; fax 406/756-8994. www.westcoasthotels .com.* 220 rooms, 3 story. Pets accepted; fee. Check-in 3 pm, check-out noon. High-speed Internet access, wireless Internet access. Restaurant, bar. Fitness room. Two indoor pools, whirlpool. Tennis. Casino. **$**

Specialty Lodging

FLATHEAD LAKE SUITES. *829 Angel Point Rd, Lakeside (59922). Phone 409/844-2204; toll-free 800/214-2204. www.angelpoint.com.* On Flathead Lake near Glacier National Park, this hotel offers spectacular views of the Rockies from private balconies in the suites. Along with 300 feet of private beach for swimming and canoeing, it is also close to many ski areas. 3 rooms, all suites. Check-in 3 pm, check-out 11 am. Beach. No credit cards accepted. **$**

Lewistown (B-4)

See also Bigfork, Columbia Falls, Libby, Whitefish

Founded 1881

Population 6,051
Elevation 3,963 ft
Area Code 406
Zip 59457
Information Chamber of Commerce, PO Box 818;
phone 406/538-5436
Web Site www.lewistownchamber.com

At the geographic center of the state, amid some of Montana's finest farming and ranching country, Lewistown is a farm trade community. The area is famous for hard, premium wheat and high-grade registered cattle. Originally a small trading post on the Carroll Trail, it was first called "Reed's Fort," and later renamed to honor a Major Lewis who established a fort 2 miles south in 1876.

What to See and Do

Big Spring Creek. *Lewistown. Runs north and south.* One of the top rainbow trout streams in the country. Picnic grounds.

Charles M. Russell National Wildlife Refuge. *Airport Rd, Lewistown (59457). 70 miles NE via Hwy 191 or Hwy 200.* Phone 406/538-8706. cmr.fws.gov. Missouri River "Breaks" and prairie lands; wildlife including pronghorn, elk, mule and whitetail deer; bighorn sheep, sage and sharptail grouse. Refuge (daily, 24 hours). Lewistown headquarters (Mon-Fri; closed holidays). **FREE**

Fort Maginnis. *Lewistown. 15 miles E on Hwy 87, then 10 miles N.* Ruins of 1880 frontier post.

Historical points of 19th-century gold mining. *Lewistown.* **Maiden.** 10 miles N on Hwy 191, then 6 miles E. **Kendall.** 16 miles N on Hwy 191, then 6 miles W on gravel road. **Giltedge.** 14 miles E on Hwy 87, then 6 miles NW.

Special Events

Central Montana Horse Show, Fair, Rodeo. *Fergus County Fairgrounds, 100 Fairgrounds Rd, Lewistown (59457).* Phone 406/538-8841. Last full week in July.

Charlie Russell Chew-Choo. *Lewistown.* Phone 406/538-5436. The 3 1/2-hour dinner train runs through the rugged beauty of central Montana. Sat in June-Sept.

Drag Races. *Cottonwood Creek Rd, Lewistown (59457).* Phone 406/453-7555. Quarter-mile races. NHRA sanctioned. May-late Sept.

Montana Cowboy Poetry Gathering. *211 E Main, Lewistown (59457).* Phone 406/538-5436. Modern-day cowboys and admirers of Western folklore relate life "down on the range" through original poetry. Third weekend in Aug. **$$$$**

Limited-Service Hotel

★ **SUPER 8.** *102 Wendell Ave, Lewistown (59457). Phone 406/538-2581; toll-free 800/800-8000; fax 406/538-2702. www.super8.com.* 44 rooms, 2 story. Check-in 1 pm, check-out 11 am.**$**

Libby (A-1)

See also Bonners Ferry, Kalispell, also Sandpoint, ID

Settled 1863
Population 2,532
Elevation 2,086 ft
Area Code 406
Zip 59923
Information Chamber of Commerce, 905 W 9th St, PO Box 704; phone 406/293-4167
Web Site www.libby.org

Nestled in the Cabinet Mountains, Libby, formerly a gold town, is now busy processing logs. It is headquarters for Kootenai National Forest which has three Ranger District offices.

What to See and Do

Camping. Libby Ranger District. *12557 Hwy 37, Libby (59923).* Phone 406/293-7773. Includes three campgrounds: **Howard Lake Campground;** 26 miles S on Hwy 2, 5 miles on W Fisher Rd. **McGillvray Campground;** 13 miles NE, near Lake Koocanusa. **McGregor Lake;** 53 miles SE on Hwy 2.

Heritage Museum. *1367 Hwy 2 S, Libby (59923). 1 1/4 miles S via Hwy 2.* Phone 406/293-7521. Located in 12-sided log building and features various exhibits on area pioneers; animal exhibits; art gallery; exhibits by the Forest Service, mining interests, the lumber industry. (June-Aug, Mon-Sat, also Sun afternoons) **DONATION**

Kootenai National Forest. *1101 W Hwy 2, Libby (59923). Surrounds Libby, accessible on Hwys 2, 37, and 56.* Phone 406/293-6211. www.fs.fed.us/r1/kootenai. More than 2.2 million acres. Includes 94,360-acre Cabinet Mountains Wilderness. Scenic drives along the Yaak River, Lake Koocanusa Reservoir, Fisher River, and Bull River;

Giant Cedars Nature Trail. Ross Creek Cedars. Fishing. Boating, canoeing. Hiking trails. Cross-country skiing. Picnicking. Camping. In the forest is

Turner Mountain Ski Area. *Libby (59932). 23 miles NW on Pipe Creek Rd. Phone 406/293-4317.* T-bar, rope tow; patrol, school, rentals; snack bar. (Dec-Apr: Fri-Sun 9:30 am-4 pm) **$$$$**

Libby Dam. *17115 Hwy 37, Libby (59923). 17 miles NE on Hwy 37. Phone 406/293-5577.* Lake Koocanusa extends 90 miles upstream. A US Army Corps of Engineers project. Fishing; boating (dock). Picnicking. (Daily) Visitor center and gift shop; tours of dam and powerhouse; viewpoints (Memorial Day-Labor Day, daily). **FREE**

Special Events

Logger Days. *905 W 9th St, Libby (59923). Phone 406/293-4167.* Adult and child logging contests. Carnival, parade, karaoke contest. Vendors, food. Early July.

Nordicfest. *320 Mineral Ave, Libby (59923). Phone 406/293-4167.* Scandinavian festival, parade, dances, food, melodrama. Third weekend in Sept.

Livingston (D-3)

See also Big Timber, Bozeman

Settled 1882
Population 6,701
Elevation 4,503 ft
Area Code 406
Zip 59047
Information Chamber of Commerce, 208 W Park; phone 406/222-0850
Web Site www.yellowstone-chamber.com

Railroading has been a key to the town's history and economy since railroad surveyors first named it Clark City; later the present name was adopted to honor a director of the Northern Pacific Railway. Today agriculture, ranching, and tourism are the chief industries. Farm products from Paradise and Shields valleys also pass through the town. Trout fishing is excellent in the Yellowstone River. A Ranger District office of the Gallatin National Forest (see BOZEMAN) is located here.

What to See and Do

Depot Center. *200 W Park, Livingston (59047). Park and 2nd sts. Phone 406/222-2300.* Changing exhibits and cultural art shows. Gift shop. (Mid-May-mid-Oct, Mon-Sat, also Sun afternoons) **$$**

Emigrant Gulch. *Livingston. 37 miles S, off Hwy 89.* Gold was discovered here in 1862. Chico and Yellowstone City boomed busily but briefly--the gold supply was limited and the Crow were aggressive. Both are ghost towns now.

Park County Museum. *118 W Chinook,* Livingston (59047). *Phone 406/222-4184.* "House of Memories;" pioneer tools, library, old newspapers, sheep wagon, stagecoach, Native American and archaeological exhibits. Northern Pacific Railroad Room. (Memorial Day-Labor Day, afternoons; rest of year, by appointment) **$$**

Special Event

Rodeo Days. *Fairgrounds, Livingston (59047). Phone 406/222-0850.* Early July.

Limited-Service Hotels

★ ★ **BEST WESTERN YELLOWSTONE INN.** *1515 W Park St, Livingston (59047). Phone 406/222-6110; toll-free 800/770-1874; fax 406/222-3357. www. theyellowstoneinn.com.* 98 rooms, 3 story. Pets accepted; fee. Complimentary continental breakfast. Check-in 3 pm, check-out 11 am. Restaurant, bar. Indoor pool. **$**

★ ★ **CHICO HOT SPRINGS RESORT.** *1 Chico Rd, Pray (59065). Phone 406/333-4933; toll-free 800/468-9232; fax 406/333-4694. www.chicohotsprings. com.* 102 rooms, 7 story. Pets accepted, some restrictions; fee. Check-in 3 pm, check-out 11 am. Restaurant, bar. Children's activity center. Fitness room, spa. Outdoor pool, whirlpool. **$**

Specialty Lodging

MOUNTAIN SKY GUEST RANCH. *Big Creek Rd, Emigrant (59027). Phone 406/333-4911; toll-free 800/548-3392; fax 406/587-3397. www.mtnsky.com.* Mountain Sky is a family-friendly ranch offering a variety of activities. Enjoy the beautiful countryside horseback riding, or reflect on it by the pool. 30 rooms. Closed mid-Oct-Apr. Complimentary full breakfast. Check-in 2 pm, check-out 10 am. Children's activity center. Outdoor pool, whirlpool. Tennis. Airport transportation available. **$$$$**

Restaurant

★ ★ ★ **CHATHAMS LIVINGSTON BAR AND GRILL.** *130 N Main St, Livingston (59047). Phone 406/222-7909.* A known hangout for Hollywood types, this restaurant is located in downtown Livingston. The Western decor features an 1880s mahogany bar, and there is plenty of artwork on display. Owner Russell Chatham ensures quality food and excellent service. An excellent and affordable wine list is available as well. American menu. Lunch, dinner. Closed Thanksgiving, Dec 25. Bar. Casual attire. Reservations recommended. **$$**

Malta (B-4)

Population 2,340
Elevation 2,255 ft
Area Code 406
Zip 59538
Information Malta Area Chamber of Commerce, PO Box 1420; phone 406/654-1776 or toll-free 800/704-1776
Web Site www.maltachamber.com

What to See and Do

Bowdoin National Wildlife Refuge. *Malta (59538). 7 miles E via Old Hwy 2. Phone 406/654-2863.* Approximately 15,500 acres provide excellent nesting, resting; and feeding grounds for migratory waterfowl. The refuge also supports whitetailed deer and pronghorns. Use of the self-guided drive-through trail is recommended. (Daily; weather permitting) **FREE**

Phillips County Museum. *431 Hwy 2 E, Malta (59538). Phone 406/654-1037.* Features Native American, homestead, and dinosaur exhibits. (Mid-May-Labor Day, daily) **DONATION**

Miles City (C-5)

Population 8,461
Elevation 2,358 ft
Area Code 406
Zip 59301
Information Chamber of Commerce, 901 Main St; phone 406/232-2890
Web Site www.mcchamber.com

This trade, industrial, and energy-concerned city is also a livestock and agricultural center. Seat of Custer County, the city is named for a US infantry general. Here are the Livestock Auction Saleyards where about 25 percent of Montana's livestock is processed.

What to See and Do

Custer County Art Center. *Water Plant Rd, Miles City (59301). W via Hwy 10, 12. Phone 406/234-0635.* Housed in the former holding tanks of old Miles City Water Works, overlooking the Yellowstone River. Contemporary art exhibits. Gift shop. (Tues-Sun afternoons; closed holidays) **FREE**

Range Riders Museum and Pioneer Memorial Hall. *Main St, Miles City (59301). Phone 406/232-6146.* Exhibits and memorabilia of the days of the open range. The Bert Clark gun collection is one of the largest in the Northwest. (Apr-Oct) **$$**

Special Events

Ballon Roundup. *Fairgrounds, I-94 and exit 135, Miles City (59301). Phone 406/232-2890.* Fourth weekend in June.

Bucking Horse Sale. *Fairgrounds, I-94 and exit 135, Miles City (59301). Phone 406/234-2890.* Born in 1951, it grew out of the Miles City Roundup. Features Wild Horse Stampede, bronco and bull riding, and the sale of both bucking horses and bulls. Third weekend in May.

Eastern Montana Fair. *Fairgrounds, I-94 and exit 135, Miles City (59301). Phone 406/234-2890.* Four days in late Aug.

Limited-Service Hotels

★ **BEST WESTERN WAR BONNET INN.** *1015 S Haynes Ave, Miles City (59301). Phone 406/234-4560; toll-free 800/780-7234; fax 406/234-0363. www.bestwestern.com.* 54 rooms, 2 story. Pets accepted; fee. Complimentary continental breakfast. Check-in 2 pm, check-out noon. Indoor pool, whirlpool. Business center. **$**

★ **HOLIDAY INN EXPRESS.** *1720 S Haynes Ave, Miles City (59301). Phone 406/234-1000; toll-free 888/700-0402; fax 406/234-1365. www.hiexpress.com.* 52 rooms, 2 story. Complimentary continental breakfast. Check-in 2 pm, check-out 11 am. Indoor pool, whirlpool. **$**

Missoula

See also Hamilton

Settled 1860
Population 42,918
Elevation 3,200 ft
Area Code 406
Information Chamber of Commerce, 825 E Front, PO Box 7577, 59807; phone 406/543-6623
Web Site www.exploremissoula.com

Since the days of the Lewis and Clark Expedition, Missoula has been a trading and transportation crossroads. It is a lumber and paper manufacturing center, the hub of large reserves of timber, and the regional headquarters of the US Forest Service and Montana State Forest Service.

What to See and Do

★**Aerial Fire Depot.** *5765 W Broadway, Missoula (59808). 7 miles W on Hwy 10, I-90, 1/2 mile W of Johnson Bell Airport. Phone 406/329-4900.* Forest Service headquarters for aerial attack on forest fires in western United States. Smokejumpers trained and based here during summer.

Rocky Mountain Research Station Fire Sciences Laboratory. *Missoula. Phone 406/329-4934.* Conducts research in fire prevention and control and the beneficial uses of fire in forest management. Tours by appointment.

Smokejumper Center. *Missoula. Phone 406/329-4934.* Training and dispatching center for airborne fire crews; parachute and fire training. **FREE**

Visitor center. *Hwy 10 W, Missoula (59808). Phone 406/329-4934.* Fire management exhibits, guided tour of parachute loft and training facilities; films, information on recreational facilities in 13 national forests in region. (Memorial Day-Labor Day: daily 8:30 am-5 pm; rest of year: by appointment)

Art Museum of Missoula. *335 N Pattee, Missoula (59808). Phone 406/728-0447.* Art of the Western states. Changing exhibits. Educational programs. **FREE**

Historical Museum at Fort Missoula. *Bldg 322, Fort Missoula, Missoula (59804). 5 miles S from I-90 via Reserve St to South Ave, then 1 mile W. Phone 406/728-3476.* Established to interpret the history of Missoula County and the forest management and timber production in western Montana. The museum features indoor galleries with permanent and changing exhibits; outdoor area includes ten historic structures, four are restored. Located in the core of what was originally Fort Missoula (1877-1947). Several original buildings remain. Other areas include railroad and military history. (Summer, daily; winter, Tues-Sun)

Lolo National Forest. *Missoula. Surrounds Missoula, accessible on Hwys 10, 12, 93; Hwys 200 and 83; and I-90. Phone 406/329-3750. www.fs.fed.us/r1/lolo.* Located in west-central Montana, Lolo National Forest is a popular recreation destination in both summer and winter, with hiking and cross-country skiing being the prime activities. Foot trails to 100 lakes and peaks in the more than 2 million acres of forest, which include the Welcome Creek Wilderness and Rattlesnake National Recreation Area and Wilderness, part of Scapegoat Wilderness, and Selway-Bitterroot Wilderness. Fishing is another big draw here, with four excellent rivers and their myriad tributaries running through the Lolo. The historic Lolo Trail and Lewis and Clark Highway (Hwy 12) over the Bitterroot Mountains takes visitors along the route of famed exploration. The forest is also home to more than 25 campgrounds and several fire lookouts and cabins available for rental (mid-May-Sept, full-service campgrounds, some free); of special note is the popular Hogback Homestead Cabin, a rustic two-story cabin that accommodates eight guests and has a wood stove, a water pump, and propane lighting. In the town of Huson, the Forest Service operates the unique Ninemile Wildlands Training Center, where visitors can enroll in classes covering such skills as horsemanship, backcountry survival, and historic preservation. There are Ranger District offices in Missoula, Huson, Plains, Seeley Lake, and Superior.

Marshall Mountain Ski Area. *Milltown (59802). 7 miles NE via I-90, E Missoula exit. Phone 406/258-6000. www .marshallmtn.com.* Triple chairlift, T-bar, rope tow; school, patrol, rentals, snowmaking; half-day rates; cafeteria, bar, snack bar. Longest run 2 1/2 miles; vertical drop 1,500 feet. Night skiing. (Dec-Mar, Tues-Sun)

Missoula Carousel. *Caras Park, 1 Caras Park, Missoula (59802). Just W of the Higgins Bridge. Phone 406/549-8382.* Carousel features hand-carved horses--the first such carousel in the United States to do so in over 60 years. Gift shop. (Daily)

Missoula Public Library. *301 E Main St, Missoula (59802). Phone 406/721-2665.* Outstanding collection of historical works on Montana and the Northwest and genealogical materials.

Montana Snowbowl. *Missoula (59807). 3 miles NW on I-90 (Reserve St exit), then 9 miles N on Grant Creek Rd to Snow Bowl Rd. Phone 406/549-9777. www.montana snowbowl.com.* Spread over two mountains linked by a skiable saddle, Montana Snowbowl is an underrated resort with an impressive 2,600-foot vertical drop. There are plenty of close-in runs for experienced skiers on Snowbowl's 950 acres (20 percent beginner, 40 percent intermediate, and 40 percent expert), and the backside Lavelle Creek Area is ideal for families, with runs for all ski levels in close proximity. There is a restaurant and a ski school, and in-mountain accommodations are available at a European-style lodge. (Late Nov-Apr, Mon, Wed-Sun) In summer, visitors enjoy the area's hiking trails and mountain biking opportunities. **$$$$**

Paxson Paintings. *County Courthouse, 200 W Broadway, Missoula (59801). Broadway between Orange and Higgins sts. Phone 406/721-5700.* Eight murals depicting Montana's history by one of the West's outstanding artists. (Mon-Fri 8 am-5 pm; closed holidays) **FREE**

St. Francis Xavier Church. *420 W Pine St, Missoula (59802). Phone 406/542-0321.* (1889). Steeple highlights this structure built the same year Montana became a state. (Daily)

University of Montana. *32 Campus Dr, Missoula (59812). University and Arthur aves. Phone 406/243-0211. www.umt.edu.* (1893) (10,000 students) At the foot of Mount Sentinel. University Center Gallery and Gallery of Visual Arts. Campus tours.

Special Events

International Wildlife Film Festival. *Missoula (59801). Downtown. Phone 406/728-9380. www.wildlifefilms.org.* The biggest event of its kind, this weeklong film fest in May showcases the best wildlife films the world has to offer, with a strong emphasis on conservation of wildlife and its habitat. Held at several downtown venues, it kicks off with a parade and an outdoor community festival and continues with numerous public screenings, as well as workshops and lectures. May.

Western Montana Fair and Rodeo. *Fairgrounds, 1101 South Ave, Missoula (59801). Phone 406/721-3247.* Mid-Aug.

Western Montana Quarter Horse Show. *Fairgrounds, 1101 South Ave W, Missoula (59801). Phone 406/543-6623.* Late June.

Limited-Service Hotels

★ **BEST WESTERN GRANT CREEK INN.** *5280 Grant Creek Rd, Missoula (59808). Phone 406/543-0700; toll-free 888/543-0700; fax 406/543-0777. www .bestwestern.com/grantcreekinn.* Courteous employees, a convenient location near Interstate 90, and comfortable facilities make the Best Western Grant Creek Inn a popular choice for lodging in Missoula. 126 rooms, 4 story. Pets accepted; fee. Complimentary continental breakfast. Check-in 3 pm, check-out noon. High-speed Internet access, wireless Internet access. Fitness room. Indoor pool, whirlpool. Airport transportation available. Business center. **$**

★ ★ **DOUBLETREE HOTEL.** *100 Madison, Missoula (59802). Phone 406/728-3100; toll-free 800/222-8733; fax 406/728-2530. www.doubletree.com.* Located on the scenic Clark Fork River, the Doubletree Hotel features a cheery staff that welcomes guests upon arrival with warm cookies. 172 rooms, 3 story. Pets accepted, some restrictions; fee. Check-in 3 pm, check-out noon. High-speed Internet access, wireless Internet access. Restaurant, bar. Fitness room. Outdoor pool, whirlpool. Business center. **$**

★ **HAMPTON INN.** *4805 N Reserve St, Missoula (59802). Phone 406/549-1800; toll-free 800/426-7866; fax 406/549-1737. www.hamptoninn.com.* Ideal for both business and leisure travelers, the Hampton Inn features clean and comfortable accommodations and great basic amenities. 61 rooms, 4 story. Pets accepted; fee. Complimentary continental breakfast. Check-in 2 pm, check-out noon. High-speed Internet access, wireless Internet access. Fitness room. Indoor pool, whirlpool. Airport transportation available. Business center. **$**

★ ★ **HOLIDAY INN.** *200 S Pattee St, Missoula (59802). Phone 406/721-8550; toll-free 800/399-0408; fax 406/721-7427. www.himissoula.com.* A stay at the Holiday Inn affords guests a great location in downtown Missoula within walking distance to shops, restaurants, and bars. Beds are turned down upon arrival, and a selection of pillows is available. 200 rooms, 4 story. Pets accepted; fee. Check-in 4 pm, check-out noon. High-speed Internet access, wireless Internet access. Restaurant, bar. Fitness room. Indoor pool, whirlpool. Airport transportation available. Business center. **$**

★ **QUALITY INN.** *3803 Brooks St, Missoula (59804). Phone 406/251-2665; fax 406/251-5733. www. qualityinn.com.* 81 rooms, 3 story. Pets accepted; fee.

Complimentary continental breakfast. Check-in 2 pm, check-out noon. Whirlpool. Airport transportation available.**$**

★ **RED LION.** *700 W Broadway, Missoula (59802). Phone 406/728-3300; toll-free 800/733-5466; fax 406/728-4441. www.redlion.com.* Budget travelers will find standard, reliable accommodations at the Red Lion Inn Missoula. 76 rooms, 2 story. Pets accepted; fee. Complimentary continental breakfast. Check-in 3 pm, check-out noon. High-speed Internet access, wireless Internet access. Fitness room. Outdoor pool, whirlpool. Airport transportation available.**$**

Specialty Lodging

THE EMILY A. BED & BREAKFAST. *Hwy 83 N, mile marker 20, Seeley Lake (59868). Phone 406/677-3474; toll-free 800/977-4639; fax 406/677-3474. www.theemilya .com.* Guests can choose between a relaxing vacation or one filled with adventure. Total relaxation can be found on one of the porches while you watch nature at its best, or for the adventurous, go horseback riding, fishing, or even take a dogsled ride. 5 rooms, 2 story. Complimentary full breakfast. Check-in 2 pm, check-out 11 am.**$**

Restaurant

★★**DEPOT.** *201 W Railroad St, Missoula (59801). Phone 406/728-7007.* Unique paintings, exposed brick walls, wood tables, and a relaxed atmosphere set the tone for the evening at this casual eatery. The paintings--all Montana related--add a creative dimension to the room. Extensive beer and wine selections are offered in addition to mixed drinks. Situated on the corner of Ryman and Railroad streets, it is north of downtown. American menu. Dinner. Closed holidays. Bar. Casual attire. Reservations recommended. Outdoor seating. **$$**

Polson (B-2)

See also Bigfork

Population 3,283
Elevation 2,931 ft
Area Code 406
Zip 59860
Information Chamber of Commerce, 7 Third Ave W, PO Box 667; phone 406/883-5969
Web Site www.polsonchamber.com

At the south edge of Flathead Lake, Polson is the trade center for a productive farming area and a provisioning point for mountain trips. According to legend, Paul Bunyan dug the channel from Flathead Lake to Flathead River.

What to See and Do

Flathead Lake Biological Station. *311 Bio Station Ln, Polson (59860). Hwy 35, Mile Marker 17 1/2, midway between Bigfork and Polson. Phone 406/982-3301. www.umt.edu/biology/flbs/home.htm.* Run by the University of Montana, this state-of-the-art ecological research and education center established in 1899 attracts scholars and casual visitors alike. Free public seminars for adults and children are somewhat technical but meant for a general audience. Natural laboratories for teaching and research; museum; self-guided nature trips. (Mon-Fri; closed holidays) **FREE**

Flathead Lake Cruise. *303 Hwy 93 E, Polson (59860). Phone 406/883-3636.* Port Polson Princess departs from Kwataqnuk Resort for sightseeing around Flathead Lake. View the Narrows, Bird Island and Wildhorse Island. (June-Sept, daily) Reservations recommended. **$$$$**

Flathead Lake State Park. *490 N Meridian Rd, Kalispell (59901). Phone 406/837-4196. fwp.state.mt.us/parks.* At 28 miles long and 15 miles wide, with an average depth of 220 feet, Flathead Lake is the largest freshwater lake west of the Mississippi. It was formed by glacial action. There are six state park units surrounding the lake (see also BIGFORK), the nearest to Polson being the Big Arm Unit. Fishing, especially for lake trout, is best in early spring and late fall. The lake also offers opportunities for swimming, boating (ramp), and water-skiing. Around the lake, visitors enjoy bird-watching (including bald eagles), wildlife-viewing, and tent and trailer camping. Pets are allowed on leash only, and entrance is free for Montana residents. By boat, you can reach the day-use-only Wild Horse Island, at 2,000 acres the largest island in the lake. **$**

Big Arm Unit. *Polson. 13 miles N, along W shore on Hwy 93.* Also fishing (joint state/tribal license required). Camping (no hookups, dump station).

Elmo Unit. *Polson. 16 miles N on Hwy 93.*

Finley Point Unit. *Polson. 12 miles N off Hwy 35.*

National Bison Range. *132 Bison Range Rd, Moiese (59824). 32 miles S on Hwy 93, then 13 miles SW on Hwy 212 to main entrance. Phone 406/644-2211.* Visitor center, exhibits, nature trails; picnic grounds near headquarters. Bison, antelope, bighorn sheep, deer, elk, and other big game species roam over 18,500 acres of fenced-in range. A 19-mile self-guided tour route rises 2,000 feet over Mission Valley (mid-May-mid-Oct, daily). Motorcycles and bicycles are not permitted on the drives. **$$**

Ninepipe and Pablo National Wildlife Refuges. *132 Bison Range, Moiese (59824). Pablo is 7 miles S on Hwy 93; Ninepipe is 18 miles S on Hwy 93. Phone 406/644-2211.* More than 180 species of birds have been observed on these waterfowl refuges, including ducks, geese, grebes, great blue herons, and cormorants. Fishing permitted at certain times and areas in accordance with tribal and state regulations. Joint state/tribal recreation permit and fishing stamp required. Portions of (or all) refuges may be closed during waterfowl season and nesting period. Visitors may obtain more information, including regulations, from Refuge Manager at National Bison Range, 132 Bison Range Rd, Moiese 59824.

Polson-Flathead Historical Museum. *708 Main St, Polson (59860). 8th Ave and Main St. Phone 406/883-3049.* Native American artifacts and farm and household items from the opening of the Flathead Reservation in 1910; home of Rudolph, a Scotch-Highland steer, who appeared in over 136 parades in five states and Canada; wildlife display and old stagecoach. (Summer, daily)

River rafting. Flathead Raft Company. *1501 Hwy 93, Polson (59860). Phone 406/883-5838; toll-free 800/654-4359. www.flatheadraftco.com.* Offers half-day whitewater trips on Lower Flathead River, leaving from Port Polson, at south end of Flathead Lake. **$$$$**

Limited-Service Hotel

★ ★ **BEST WESTERN KWATAQNUK RESORT.** *303 Hwy 93 E, Polson (59860). Phone 406/883-3636; toll-free 800/882-6363; fax 406/883-5392. www.kwataqnuk .com.* 112 rooms, 3 story. Pets accepted; fee. Check-in 3 pm, check-out 11 am. Restaurant, bar. Indoor pool, outdoor pool, whirlpool. **$**

Red Lodge (D-4)

See also Cooke City, Cody, WY

Population 1,958
Elevation 5,553 ft
Area Code 406
Zip 59068
Information Chamber of Commerce, PO Box 988; phone 406/446-1718
Web Site www.redlodge.com

The seat of Carbon County and a busy resort town, Red Lodge was, according to legend, named for a Native American band whose tepees were painted red. It is a most magnificent approach to Yellowstone National Park (see WYOMING) and gateway to the half-million-acre Beartooth-Absaroka Wilderness Area. A Ranger District office of the Custer National Forest (see HARDIN) is located here.

What to See and Do

Beartooth Highway (National Forest Scenic Byway). *Red Lodge.* Highway 212 travels 64 miles over an 11,000-foot pass in the Beartooth Mountains to the northeast entrance of Yellowstone National Park. Includes Rock Creek Vista Point; Granite Peak, highest point in Montana (12,799 feet); a 345,000-acre portion of the Absaroka-Beartooth Wilderness; Grasshoper Glacier (see COOKE CITY). The area is characterized by alpine plateaus, rugged peaks, and hundreds of lakes. Offers winter sports and trout fishing. Views of glaciers, lakes, fields of alpine flowers, peaks and canyons. There are no service areas or gas stations on the 64-mile (2 1/2-hour) stretch between Red Lodge and Cooke City. Beartooth Highway is closed each winter between Red Lodge and Cooke City (closing dates depend on snow conditions) and is open approximately June-September.

Red Lodge Mountain Ski Area. *Red Lodge (59068). 6 miles W off Hwy 212, in Custer National Forest. Phone 406/446-2610; toll-free 800/444-8977. www.redlodge mountain.com.* Triple, two high-speed detachable quads, four double chairlifts, mitey-mite; patrol, school, rentals; snowmaking; restaurant, cafeteria, bar, daycare. Longest run 2 1/2 miles; vertical drop 2,400 feet. (Thanksgiving-Apr, daily)

Special Events

Festival of Nations. *Red Lodge Civic Center, Red Lodge*

(59068). Phone 406/446-1718. Exhibits, nightly entertainment reflecting several European cultures. Art demonstrations and displays. Early-mid-Aug.

Music Festival. *Red Lodge Civic Center, Red Lodge (59068). Phone 406/446-1718.* Features performances by faculty members from schools throughout the country. June.

Top of the World Bar. *Red Lodge. 30 miles SW via Hwy 212.* Citizens of Red Lodge welcome travelers with free beverages served from a bar carved from a snow bank atop 11,000-foot Beartooth Pass. July.

Winter Carnival. *Red Lodge Mountain Resort, Red Lodge (59068). 6 miles W off Hwy 212, in Custer National Forest. Phone 406/446-1718.* Ski races, snow sculpting, entertainment. Mar.

Limited-Service Hotels

★ **COMFORT INN.** *612 N Broadway, Red Lodge (59068). Phone 406/446-4469; toll-free 800/228-5150; fax 406/446-4669. www.comfortinn.com.* 53 rooms, 2 story. Pets accepted; fee. Complimentary continental breakfast. Check-in 2 pm, check-out 11 am. Fitness room. Indoor pool, whirlpool.**$**

★ ★ **POLLARD HOTEL.** *2 N Broadway, Red Lodge (59068). Phone 406/446-0001; toll-free 800/765-5273; fax 406/446-0002. www.pollardhotel.com.* 39 rooms, 3 story. Complimentary continental breakfast. Check-in 4 pm, check-out 11 am. Restaurant, bar. Fitness room. Restored hotel built in 1893.**$**

★ ★ **ROCK CREEK RESORT.** *Hwy 212, Red Lodge (59068). Phone 406/446-1111; toll-free 800/667-1119; fax 406/446-3688. www.rockcreekresort.com.* Situated below Beartooth Pass and beside Rock Creek, this resort features such adventurous activities as snowmobiling, skiing, kayaking, and golfing. Guests can take a day trip to Yellowstone National Park (see WYOMING) located just two hours away or Cody, Wyoming (see), which is just 67 miles from the lodge. 87 rooms, 3 story. Check-in 3 pm, check-out 11 am. Two restaurants, two bars. Fitness room. Indoor pool, whirlpool. Tennis.**$**

Restaurants

★ ★ **ARTHUR'S GRILL.** *2 N Broadway, Red Lodge (59068). Phone 406/446-0001; toll-free 800/765-5273; fax*

406/446-0002. www.pollardhotel.com. American menu. Breakfast, lunch, dinner. Bar. Children's menu. Casual attire. Reservations recommended. Outdoor seating. **$$**

★ ★ **OLD PINEY DELL.** *Hwy 212, Red Lodge (59068). Phone 406/446-1196; toll-free 800/667-1119; fax 406/446-3688. www.rockcreekresorts.com.* American menu. Dinner, Sun brunch. Bar. Children's menu. Casual attire. Reservations recommended. **$$**

Sidney (B-6)

Population 5,217
Elevation 1,931 ft
Area Code 406
Zip 59270
Information Chamber of Commerce, 909 S Central; phone 406/482-1916
Web Site www.sidneymt.com

Irrigation in Richland County produces bountiful crops of sugar beets and wheat, which are marketed at Sidney, the county seat. Oil fields, open-pit coal mining, and livestock feeding contribute to the town's economy.

What to See and Do

MonDak Heritage Center. *120 3rd Ave SE, Sidney (59270). Phone 406/433-3500.* Seventeen-unit street scene displaying historical artifacts of the area; changing art exhibits; historical and art library, gift shop. (Tues-Sun afternoons; summer daily; closed holidays) **$$**

Special Events

Peter Paddlefish Day. *909 S Central Ave, Sidney (59270). Phone 406/482-1916.* The sighting of Peter on his spawning run up the Yellowstone River indicates a normal run-off on the Yellowstone and a normal season. Last Sat in Apr.

Richland County Fair and Rodeo. *1400 S 19th Ave, Sidney (59270). Phone 406/433-2801.* Exhibits, livestock shows, petting zoo, carnival, PRCA rodeos, country western show. Early Aug.

Sunrise Festival of the Arts. *Central Park, Sidney (59270). Phone 406/433-1916.* Central Park. Second Sat in July.

Three Forks (C-3)

See also Bozeman, Butte, Ennis

Population 1,203
Elevation 4,080 ft
Area Code 406
Zip 59752
Web Site www.threeforksmontana.com

In 1805, Lewis and Clark discovered the source of the Missouri River, beginning of the world's largest river chain, at the confluence of the Jefferson, Madison, and Gallatin rivers here. Native Americans resisted settlement of the valley, a favorite bison hunting ground, but before long it became a trading post headquarters for hunters and trappers.

What to See and Do

Lewis and Clark Caverns State Park. *Whitehall (59752). E of Whitehall. 19 miles W of Three Forks on Hwy 2, Mile Marker 271. Phone 406/287-3541. www.fwp.state.mt.us.* These caverns on the Jefferson River were discovered not by Lewis and Clark, but rather by local ranchers in the late 1800s. The surrounding 3,000plus acres became Montana's first state park in 1937. The park's centerpiece is the limestone cave system, one of the largest in the region and accessible only by two-hour, 2-mile guided tours from May through September. Year-round facilities include a campground with shower facilities and RV dump station, rental cabins, and an aboveground nature trail. **$$**

Madison Buffalo Jump State Monument. *Three Forks. E on I-90, then 7 miles S on Buffalo Jump Rd. Phone 406/285-4880.* Native American hunting technique of herding charging buffalo over cliffs is illustrated. Hiking. Picnicking. Day use only. **$$**

Missouri Headwaters State Park. *1400 S 19th Ave, Bozeman (59718). 3 miles E on I-90, then E on Secondary Hwy 205, then 3 miles N on Secondary Hwy 286. Phone 406/994-4042.* Where Lewis and Clark discovered the source of the Missouri River. Fishing; boating (ramp). Picnicking. Camping (no hookups, dump station).

Virginia City (D-3)

See also Ennis

Settled 1863
Population 142
Elevation 5,822 ft
Area Code 406
Zip 59755
Information Bovey Restoration, PO Box 338; phone 406/843-5377 or toll-free 800/648-7588. Chamber of Commerce; toll-free 800/829-2969
Web Site www.virginiacitychamber.com

On May 26, 1863, gold was found in Alder Gulch. The old days of the rough 'n' tough West are rekindled in this restored gold boomtown, once the capital of the territory. Alder Gulch (Virginia and Nevada cities) sprouted when six men who had escaped from Native Americans discovered history's richest placer deposit. Ten thousand gold miners arrived within a month, followed by bands of desperadoes; 190 murders were committed in seven months. Vigilantes hunted down 21 road agents and discovered that the sheriff was the leader of the criminals. Nearly $300 million in gold was washed from Alder Gulch, but the area faded as the diggings became less productive and Nevada City became a ghost town. In 1946, a restoration program began, which has brought back much of the early mining-town atmosphere.

What to See and Do

Boot Hill. *Virginia City.* Graves of five criminals hanged by the vigilantes.

Restored buildings. *305 W Wallace, Virginia City (59755). Phone 406/843-5377; toll-free 800/648-7588.* Includes the offices of the *Montana Post*, first newspaper in the state; the Gilbert Brewery, dressmaker's shop, Wells Fargo Express office, livery stable, barbershop, blacksmith shop, general store, many others. Includes

Gilbert's Brewery. *305 W Wallace, Virginia City (59755). E Cover St. Phone 406/843-5377.* Virginia City's first brewery was built in 1864. The main building has been restored and the original brewery is still inside. Musical variety shows (mid-June-mid-Sept: Mon, Wed-Sun). **$$$**

Nevada City. *Virginia City. 1 1/2 miles W on Hwy 287.* Authentic buildings include early mining camp stores, homes, school, offices. Music Hall has large collection of mechanical musical machines. (Memorial Day-mid-Sept, daily) **FREE**

Nevada City Depot. *Virginia City.* Houses steam railroad museum (fee) of early-day engines and cars. Train ride to Virginia City. (Early June-Labor Day, daily)

Robbers' Roost. *Virginia City. 15 miles W on Hwy 287.* Old-time stage station often used by outlaws.

St. Paul's Episcopal Church. *Virginia City (59755). Idaho St.* (Elling Memorial) (1902) Built on the site of a 1867 building; oldest Protestant congregation in state. Tiffany windows.

Thompson-Hickman Memorial Museum. *224 E Wallace St, Virginia City (59755).* Phone 406/843-5238. Relics of the gold camps. (May-Sept, daily) **DONATION**

Virginia City-Madison County Historical Museum. *Wallace St, Virginia City (59755).* Phone 406/843-5500. Traces western Montana history. (Early June-Labor Day, daily) **$**

Special Event

Classic melodramas. *Old Opera House, 305 W Wallace, Virginia City (59755).* Phone 406/843-5314; toll-free 800/829-2969. Virginia City Players present 19th-century entertainment. Tues-Sun. Reservations required. Early June-Labor Day.

West Yellowstone (D-3)

Population 913
Elevation 6,666 ft
Area Code 406
Zip 59758
Information Chamber of Commerce, 30 Yellowstone Ave, PO Box 458; phone 406/646-7701
Web Site www.westyellowstonechamber.com

At the west entrance to Yellowstone National Park (see WYOMING), this town serves as a hub for incoming tourists. Not too long ago, West Yellowstone was abandoned and snowbound in the winter; today winter sports and attractions allow the town to serve visitors all year. A Ranger District office of the Gallatin National Forest (see BOZEMAN) is located here.

What to See and Do

Buffalo Bus Lines. *429 Yellowstone Ave, West Yellowstone (59758).* Phone 406/646-9564; toll-free 800/426-7669.

Gray Line bus tours. *555 Yellowstone Ave, West Yellowstone (59758).* Phone toll-free 800/523-3102.

Grizzly & Wolf Discovery Center. *201 S Canyon St, West Yellowstone (59758).* Phone 406/646-7001; toll-free 800/257-2570. www.grizzlydiscoveryctr.com. Bear and wolf preserve and educational facility. Interactive exhibits, films, presentations. Wildlife-themed gift shop. (Daily; closed holidays) **$$$**

Interagency Aerial Fire Control Center. *West Yellowstone. 2 miles N on Hwy 191.* Phone 406/646-7691. A US Forest Service facility. Guided tour by smokejumpers who explain firefighting techniques. (Late June-Labor Day, daily) **FREE**

Madison River Canyon Earthquake Area. *Hwy 191 N, West Yellowstone. 8 miles N on Hwy 191, then 17 miles W on Hwy 287, in Gallatin National Forest.* Phone 406/646-7369. Includes Quake Lake, formed by an earthquake on August 17, 1959. This area, with its slides and faults, is a graphic demonstration of earthquake damage. Camping (mid-June-mid-Sept; Beaver Creek Campground, fee/night). Visitor Center (on Hwy 287, 22 miles W of Hwy 191) with talks, exhibits; list of self-guided tours (Memorial Day-Labor Day, daily). Road through area (all year). For details inquire at the Chamber of Commerce or at the US Forest Service Office on Highway 191/287 north of town; or contact PO Box 520. **$$**

Xanterra Parks & Resorts. *West Yellowstone.* Phone 307/344-7311. www.xanterra.com. Offers guided snowcoach tours and cross-country ski trips through Yellowstone National Park (see WYOMING) departing from West Yellowstone and other locations surrounding the park (mid-Dec-early Mar). Summer season offers full-day bus tours, boat tours, and horseback rides in the park (June-Aug). Reservations recommended.

Yellowstone IMAX Theatre. *101 S Canyon St, West Yellowstone (59758).* Phone 406/646-4100; toll-free 888/854-5862. Six-story-high screen shows *Yellowstone*, a film interpreting the history, wildlife, geothermal activity, and grandeur of America's first national park. Exhibits include wildlife photography, props used in film, and "Effects of the Yellowstone Hot Spot." (Daily, shows hourly) **$$$**

Special Events

Playmill Theater. *29 Madison Ave, West Yellowstone (59758).* Phone 406/646-7757. Musical comedies and melodramas. Daily except Sun. Memorial Day-Labor Day.

World Snowmobile Expo. *West Yellowstone. Phone 406/646-7701.* Third weekend in Mar.

Yellowstone Rendezvous Marathon Ski Race. *Rendezvous Ski Trails, West Yellowstone (59758). Phone 406/646-7701.* Mar.

Limited-Service Hotels

★ **BEST WESTERN DESERT INN.** *133 Canyon St, West Yellowstone (59758). Phone 406/646-7376; toll-free 800/780-7234; fax 406/646-7759. www.bestwestern. com.* 78 rooms. Complimentary continental breakfast. Check-in 3 pm, check-out noon.**$**

★ **CLUBHOUSE INN & SUITES.** *105 S Electric St, West Yellowstone (59758). Phone 406/646-4892; fax 406/646-4893.* 77 rooms, 3 story. Closed mid-Mar-mid-Apr and late Oct-mid-Dec. Pets accepted. Check-in 3 pm, check-out noon. Fitness room. Indoor pool, whirlpool. Business center.**$**

★ **GRAY WOLF INN & SUITES.** *250 S Canyon St, West Yellowstone (59758). Phone 406/646-0000; toll-free 800/852-8602; fax 406/646-4232. www.graywolf-inn. com.* 102 rooms, 3 story. Pets accepted, some restrictions. Complimentary continental breakfast. Check-in 3 pm, check-out 11 am. Indoor pool, whirlpool. Airport transportation available.**$**

★ ★ **HOLIDAY INN SUNSPREE RESORT WEST YELLOWSTONE.** *315 Yellowstone Ave, West Yellowstone (59758). Phone 406/646-7365; toll-free 800/646-7365; fax 406/646-4433. www.doyellowstone .com.* 123 rooms, 3 story. Check-in 4 pm, check-out 11 am. Restaurant, bar. Fitness room. Indoor pool, whirlpool. Airport transportation available.**$$**

★ ★ **STAGE COACH INN.** *209 Madison Ave, West Yellowstone (59758). Phone 406/646-7381; toll-free 800/842-2882; fax 406/646-9575. www.yellowstoneinn .com.* 83 rooms, 2 story. Pets accepted, some restrictions. Check-in 3 pm, check-out 11 am. Restaurant, bar. Whirlpool.**$**

Restaurant

★ ★ **THREE BEAR.** *205 Yellowstone Ave, West Yellowstone (59758). Phone 406/646-7811. www.threebearlodge*

.com. American menu. Breakfast, dinner. Closed Dec 25; late Mar-early May, late Oct-mid-Dec. Bar. Children's menu. Casual attire. **$$**

White Sulphur Springs (C-3)

See also Bozeman, Helena

Population 963
Elevation 5,100 ft
Area Code 406
Zip 59645
Web Site www.meagherchamber.com

Mineral springs, as well as fine hunting and fishing, make this a popular summer and fall resort town. It lies in a mile-high valley ringed by mountains--the Castles, Crazies, and Big and Little Belts. Agates may still be found in the area. A Ranger District office of the Lewis and Clark National Forest (see GREAT FALLS) is located here.

What to See and Do

Showdown Ski Area. *9 miles S on Hwy 89, Neihart (59465). 29 miles N on Hwy 89, in Lewis and Clark National Forest. Phone 406/236-5522; toll-free 800/433-0022. www.show downmontana.com.* Triple, double chairlift, Pomalift, free beginners tow; patrol, school, rentals; cafeteria, bar; day care. Longest run 2 miles; vertical drop 1,400 feet. (Late Nov-mid-Apr: Wed-Sun 9:30 am-4 pm) **$$$$**

Whitefish (A-1)

See also Columbia Falls, Kalispell

Population 4,368
Elevation 3,036 ft
Area Code 406
Zip 59937
Information Flathead Convention & Visitor Bureau, 15 Depot Park, Kalispell, 59901; phone 406/756-9091 or toll-free 800/543-3105
Web Site www.fcvb.org

On the shore of Whitefish Lake, this community prospers from tourism and railroading. The town is headquarters for a four-state summer vacation area and is a winter ski center. A growing forest products industry and the railroad constitute the other side of Whitefish's economy. A Ranger District office of the Flathead National Forest (see KALISPELL) is located here.

What to See and Do

Big Mountain Ski and Summer Resort. *Whitefish. 8 miles N on County 487 in Flathead National Forest; shuttle bus trips daily in winter. Phone toll-free 800/858-5439. www.skiwhitefish.com.* Double , four triple, two high-speed quad chairlifts, T-bar, platter lift, patrol; school, rentals; hotels, restaurants, bars, cafeteria, concession area; sleigh rides; nursery. Longest run 3 1/2 miles; vertical drop 2,500 feet. (Late Nov-mid-Apr, daily) Cross-country trails. Gondola (also operates in summer) provides views of Rockies, Flathead Valley; travels 6,800 feet to summit of Big Mountain Summer activities (June-early Oct): gondola rides overlooking Glacier National Park (see), hiking, mountain biking, tennis; outdoor theater, events.

⭐ **Whitefish Lake.** This lake is 7 miles long, 2 miles wide. Studded with resorts, particularly on the east shore; swimming, water-skiing; fishing; sailing; picnicking. On lake is

Whitefish State Park. *State Park Rd, Whitefish (59937). 1/2 mile W on Hwy 93, Mile Marker 129, then 1 mile N. Phone 406/862-3991.* Swimming; fishing; boating (ramp). Picnicking. Camping (no hookups). Standard fees.

Special Event

Winter Carnival. *Whitefish. Phone 406/862-3501.* First weekend in Feb.

Limited-Service Hotels

⭐⭐ **GROUSE MOUNTAIN LODGE.** *2 Fairway Dr, Whitefish (59937). Phone 406/862-3000; toll-free 800/321-8822; fax 406/862-0306. www.grmtlodge.com.* 145 rooms. Check-in 4 pm, check-out 11 am. Restaurant, bar. Fitness room. Indoor pool, two whirlpools. Airport transportation available. Business center.**$$**

🕈 ⛳ 🚶

⭐⭐ **KANDAHAR THE LODGE AT BIG MOUNTAIN.** *3824 Big Mountain Rd, Whitefish (59937). Phone 406/862-6098; toll-free 800/862-6094; fax 406/862-6095. www.kandaharlodge.com.* 50 rooms, 4 story. Closed mid-Apr-May and Oct-late Nov. Complimentary full breakfast. Check-in 3 pm, check-out 11 am. High-speed Internet access, wireless Internet access. Restaurant, bar. Fitness room. Whirlpool. Business center.**$$**

🔲 🕈 🚶

⭐ **PINE LODGE.** *920 Spokane Ave, Whitefish (59937). Phone 406/862-7600; toll-free 800/305-7463; fax 406/862-7616. www.thepinelodge.com.* 76 rooms, 4 story. Pets accepted, some restrictions. Complimentary continental breakfast. Check-in 4 pm, check-out 11 am. Fitness room. Indoor pool, outdoor pool, whirlpool. Airport transportation available. Business center.**$**

🐾 🕈 ⛳ 🚶

Specialty Lodging

GOOD MEDICINE LODGE. *537 Wisconsin Ave, Whitefish (59937). Phone 406/862-5488; toll-free 800/860-5488; fax 406/862-5489. www.goodmedicine lodge.com.* 9 rooms, 2 story. Complimentary full breakfast. Check-in 3 pm, check-out 11 am. High-speed Internet access, wireless Internet access. Whirlpool.**$**

Wolf Point (B-5)

Population 2,880
Elevation 1,997 ft
Area Code 406
Zip 59201
Information Chamber of Commerce & Agriculture, 218 3rd Ave S, Suite B; phone 406/653-2012
Web Site www.wolfpoint.com

During the winters of the 1870s, trappers poisoned wolves and hauled the frozen carcasses to this point on the Missouri River for spring shipment to St. Louis. Wolf Point is the seat of Roosevelt County and a trading point for oil, wheat, and cattle. Hunting for antelope, deer, and sharp-tailed and sage grouse is popular here.

Special Events

Wadopana Powwow. *Phone 406/653-3476.* First weekend in Aug.

Wild Horse Stampede. *Phone 406/653-2200.* One of Montana's best and oldest rodeos. Contact Chamber of Commerce and Agriculture for information. Second weekend in July.

North Dakota

In Bismarck stands a heroic statuary group, *Pioneer Family,* by Avard Fairbanks; behind it, gleaming white against the sky, towers the famous skyscraper capitol. One symbolizes the North Dakota of wagon trains and General Custer. The other symbolizes the North Dakota that has emerged in recent years--a land where a thousand oil wells have sprouted, dams have harnessed erratic rivers, vast lignite resources have been developed, and industry is absorbing surplus farm labor created by mechanization.

At various times, Spain, France, and England claimed what is now North Dakota as part of their empires. French Canadian fur trappers were the first Europeans to explore the land. With the Louisiana Purchase, Lewis and Clark crossed Dakota, establishing Fort Mandan. The earliest permanent European settlement was at Pembina with the establishment of Alexander Henry's trading post in 1801. Settlers from the Earl of Selkirk's colony in Manitoba arrived in 1812. The first military post at Fort Abercrombie served as a gateway into the area for settlers. The Dakota Territory was organized on March 2, 1861, but major settlement of what later became North Dakota followed after the entry of the Northern Pacific Railroad in the early 1870s.

This is a fascinating land of prairies, rich river valleys, small cities, huge ranches, and vast stretches of wheat. Bordering Canada for 320 miles to the north, it shares straight-line borders with Montana to the west and South Dakota to the south. The Red River of the North forms its eastern boundary with Minnesota. The Garrison Dam (see) has changed much of the internal geography of the state's western areas, converting the Missouri River, known as "Big Muddy," into a broad waterway with splendid recreation areas bordering the reservoir, Lake Sakajawea. In addition, the Oahe Dam

Population: 638,800

Area: 70,665 square miles

Elevation: 3,506 feet

Peak: White Butte (Slope County)

Entered Union: November 2, 1889 (39th state, same day as South Dakota)

Capital: Bismarck

Motto: Liberty and union, now and forever, one and inseparable

Nickname: Flickertail State, Sioux State, Peace Garden State

Flower: Wild Prairie Rose

Bird: Western Meadowlark

Tree: American Elm

Fair: July in Minot

Time Zone: Central and Mountain

Web Site: www.ndtourism.com

Fun Fact:
- North Dakota grows more sunflowers than any other state.

in South Dakota impounds Lake Oahe, which stretches north almost to Bismarck. To the southwest stretch the Badlands in all their natural grandeur, amid the open range about which Theodore Roosevelt wrote so eloquently in his *Ranch Life and the Hunting Trail.*

North Dakota's wealth is still in its soil--agriculture, crude oil, and lignite (a brown variety of very soft coal). It is estimated that one-third of the state is under oil and gas lease, and it ranks high in the nation for the production of oil; the largest deposits of lignite coal in the world are here. The same land through which Custer's men rode with range grass growing up to their stirrups now makes North Dakota the nation's number one cash grain state. North Dakota leads the nation in the production of barley, durum, spring wheat, pinto beans, oats, and flaxseed. Nearly 2,000,000 head of cattle and more than

Calendar Highlights

JUNE

Buffalo Trails Day (*Williston*). Parade, chuck wagon breakfast, old-time music, contests, games. *Phone 701/859-4361.*

Fort Seward Wagon Train (*Jamestown*). A week-long wagon train experience. Wagons are pulled by draft horses or mules; train stops along the way at historical sites. Participants dress and camp in the manner of the pioneers. *Phone 701/252-6844.*

Medora Musical (*Medora*). Outdoor musical extravaganza; Western songs, dance. *Phone 401/623-4444 or toll-free 800/633-6721.*

JULY

Grand Forks County Fair (*Grand Forks*). County Fairgrounds. *Phone 701/772-3421 or 701/746-0444.*

North Dakota State Fair (*Minot*). State Fairgrounds. 4-H, livestock, commercial exhibits; horse and tractor pulls, carnival, machinery show, concerts, auto races, demolition derby. *Phone 701/857-7620. www.ndstatefair.com.*

AUGUST

Pioneer Days (*Fargo*). Bonanzaville, USA. Celebration of area pioneer heritage. People in period costume, parades, arts and crafts. *Phone 701/282-2822.*

SEPTEMBER

United Tribes Powwow (*Bismarck*). One of the largest in the nation, featuring Native American dancing and singing, events, food, games, crafts, and contests. *Phone 701/255-3825. www.united-tribespowwow.com.*

165,000 sheep are produced on North Dakota grass.

While the rural areas comprise the economic backbone of North Dakota, attractions attributed to a "big city" can be found. In July 1981, blackjack became a legal form of gambling, causing a number of casinos to open statewide. High-stakes games and slot machines can be found in casinos operated by Native Americans on four reservations. Pari-mutuel horseracing was legalized in 1987. All gambling profits, above expenses, go to non-profit and charitable organizations.

This is the state in which to trace 19th-century frontier history, to explore the International Peace Garden (see BOTTINEAU), to stand at the center of the continent, to watch Native American dances and outdoor dramas, to fish in the 180-mile-long Lake Sakajawea, or to watch the 10 million migratory waterfowl that soar across the sky each spring and fall.

When to Go/Climate

North Dakota winters are long and merciless, with bitter cold temperatures and insistent winds. Spring is cool and rainy; summers are hot and sunny. Summer hailstorms and thunderstorms are not uncommon in the Badlands.

AVERAGE HIGH/LOW TEMPERATURES (°F)

Bismarck

Jan 20/-2	May 68/42	Sep 71/43
Feb 26/5	Jun 77/56	Oct 59/33
Mar 39/18	Jul 84/56	Nov 39/18
Apr 55/31	Aug 83/54	Dec 25/3

Fargo

Jan 15/-4	May 69/44	Sep 69/46
Feb 21/3	Jun 77/59	Oct 57/35
Mar 35/17	Jul 83/59	Nov 37/19
Apr 54/32	Aug 81/57	Dec 20/3

Parks and Recreation

Water-related activities, hiking, riding, various other sports, picnicking and visitor centers, as well as camping, are available in many state parks. Camping facilities ($3-$14/night with electricity; $5-$8/night, no electricity; $4 less with annual permit) at state parks. All motor vehicles entering a state park must obtain a motor vehicle permit: annual $25; daily $5. Pets on leash only. The North Dakota Tourism Department, 604 East Boulevard Avenue, Bismarck 58505, offers information on facilities at national, state, and local parks and recreation areas. Phone toll-free 800/435-5663.

EXPLORING THE SHEYENNE RIVER VALLEY

The wide, forested valley of the Sheyenne River is a green and shady oasis in the prairies of North Dakota. This peaceful country road is a nice break both from the prairies and from freeway driving. Highway 21 follows the Sheyenne River closely, winding through fields and into basswood, oak, and elm forests, past historic frontier forts and pioneer settlements.

From Valley City, follow Highway 21 south. The route passes the old Ellis-Nelson one room school, built in 1883, and then winds through the Daily Historical Site. When James Daily built the first bridge across the Sheyenne River here in 1878, he established the settlement that became the social and economic center of the entire region. However, when the Northern Pacific Railroad built its own bridge across the river and founded Kathryn just a few miles south in 1900, the old town drifted into ghost town status. Kathryn was founded by the Northern Pacific Railroad, and built in a boom that lasted about five years. Today, the slumbering little village retains a pleasant turn-of-the-century main street with historic churches and school buildings

.South of Kathryn is the Standing Rock State Historic Site. Called Inyan Bosendata by Sioux Indians who consider it sacred, the rock, which is four feet tall and shaped like an inverted cone, stands above a complex of prehistoric burial mounds dating from the Woodland Period, 1 to 1400 AD. Across the highway is Little Yellowstone Park, which provides picnic and camping facilities.

The town of Fort Ransom, established in 1878, boasts a number of compelling sites in a small area. The town is located at the base of Pyramid Hill, which is a man-made mound nearly 100 feet high and 600 feet on each side. Although the mound was built an estimated 5,000 to 9,000 years ago, recent Scandinavian residents have built a Viking memorial on the hillock. Fort Ransom has a national historic district, which contains the county historical museum, a water-powered mill, and a general store. The Standing Rock Church dates from the 1880s. At Fort Ransom State Park, explore the hiking trails that lead through the woods, or rent a canoe and paddle along the slow-moving river. Of the original Fort Ransom, which was built as a deterrent to the Sioux during the 1860s, an original gun turret remains, and the wooden stockade has been rebuilt. Just across a ravine from the old fort site is Writing Rock, a monolith with peculiar inscriptions and figures carved into it. The site is mentioned in the legends of local Native Americans. East from Fort Ransom toward Lisbon, the route passes through the Sheyenne State Forest, with 508 acres of prairie and woodlands, and a network of hiking and mountain biking trails. **(Approximately 55 miles)**

THE FREE-FLOWING MISSOURI RIVER

There's very little of the free-flowing Missouri River left in North Dakota; only one portion, from Garrison Dam to Bismarck, resembles the broad prairie river as seen by Lewis and Clark. This route explores a section of Missouri River wetlands, allowing modern-day explorers the chance to see the cottonwood forests and wetlands that once stretched along the Missouri, before hydroelectric dams tamed the river.

From Mandan, travel north on Highway 25, which follows the Missouri's western banks. The route passes through farmland and then drops onto a broad, arid basin, with the green, cottonwood-fringed Missouri in the distance. If you don't mind traveling a few miles on gravel roads, turn off Highway 25 east toward the community of Price. Follow the road north along the banks of the river. A number of wildlife refuges string along the river; you may see wild turkeys, deer, or bald eagles. Stop at the Cross Ranch State Park, a wetlands preserve with summer canoe rentals.

At Hensler, turn west on Highway 200A to visit Fort Clark State Historic Site. Fort Clark was built between 1830-1831 by the American Fur Company as a trading post near a Mandan Indian earthlodge village. A second fort, Primeau's Post, was built on the site in the early 1850s and operated in competition with Fort Clark for much of that decade. Artists Karl Bodmer and George Catlin visited the site, as did German Prince Maximilian, John James Audubon, and more than 50 steamboats per year. Many of Bodmer's paintings were of the people and village of Fort Clark. Fort Clark was the scene of small pox and cholera epidemics that decimated the Mandan and Arikara Indian villages located here. The site contains foundations of both fort structures, the remains of the earthlodge village, and a large native burial ground

.Continue west along Highway 200A. At Stanton, follow County Highway 37 north to the Knife River Indian Village National Historic Site. One of the largest Hidatsa villages was located at the confluence of the Missouri and the Knife rivers, where this new interpretive center and earthlodge reconstruction are now found. Displays in the interpretive center are excellent and explain the culture and lifestyle of the Hidatsa. Trails lead out to a reconstructed earthlodge; in summer, docents demonstrate traditional Hidatsa crafts and activities. Other trails lead to actual village sites. More than 50 earthlodge remains suggest that Native Americans lived in this location for nearly 8,000 years, ending with five centuries of Hidatsa earthlodge village occupation. The circular depressions at the three village sites are up to 40 feet in diameter and are a silent testimony to the people that lived here

.Continue north to join Highway 200 and follow it across the Garrison Dam, the third-largest earth-filled dam in the United States. The dam backs up the Missouri River 175 miles to the west in 378,000-acre Lake Sakakawea. Continue to Highway 83, then head south, zipping past the coal strip mines at Underwood. At Washburn, leave the freeway and follow signs to the Fort Mandan Historic Site, where volunteers have reconstructed Lewis and Clark's log fort. The Lewis and Clark Expedition spent the winter of 1804-1805 here in a cottonwood blockade above the Missouri River. It was here that they met French-Canadian Toussaint Charbonneau, who would serve as their interpreter, and his young Shoshone wife, Sacajawea. This reconstruction of Fort Mandan is downstream from the original site, which has been eaten away by the river. The triangular fort is quite modest and small, considering that there were 40-odd members of the expedition living here. Also at the park are a visitor center, gift shop, and picnic area along the river.

Return to Highway 83 and travel south for 7 miles, then exit at Highway 1804 and follow this scenic route south along the free-flowing Missouri's eastern banks to Bismarck. **(Approximately 162 miles)**

FISHING AND HUNTING

Species found in the state are trout, pike, sauger, walleye, bass, salmon, panfish, catfish, and muskie. Fishing season is year-round in many waters. Obtain state's fishing regulations for details. Nonresident license, $35. There is a $2 certificate fee for each license.

The pothole and slough regions of central North Dakota annually harbor up to 4 million ducks; waterfowl hunting is tops. Pheasants, sharptails, Hungarian partridge, and deer are also found here. Nonresident small game license $85; with waterfowl 895. There is a $2 certificate fee for each license.

For further information, contact the State Game and Fish Department, 100 North Bismarck Expressway, Bismarck 58501-5095; phone 701/406-6409.

Driving Information

Children 10 years and under must be in an approved passenger restraint anywhere in a vehicle: children ages 3-10 must be properly secured in approved safety seats or buckled in safety belts; children under age 3 must be properly secured in approved safety seats. Phone 701/328-2455.

INTERSTATE HIGHWAY SYSTEM

The following alphabetical listing of North Dakota towns in this book shows that these cities are within 10 miles of the indicated interstate highways. Check a highway map for the nearest exit.

Highway Number	Cities/Towns within 10 Miles
Interstate 29	Fargo, Grafton, Grand Forks, Wahpeton.
Interstate 94	Bismarck, Dickinson, Fargo, Jamestown, Mandan, Medora, Valley City.

Additional Visitor Information

North Dakota Tourism Department, 604 East Boulevard Avenue, Bismarck 58505; phone toll-free 800/435-5663; has helpful travel information. *North Dakota Horizons,* published quarterly, is available from the Greater North Dakota Association, PO Box 2639, Bismarck 58502.

Three tourist information centers are open year-round. These centers are Fargo Information Center, located at I-94, 45th Street exit; Grand Forks Travel Center, located on I-29, exit 141; and Pembina

Travel Center, located in the tower building with observation deck, on Hwy 59, adjacent to I-29.

Five tourist information centers are open Memorial Day-Labor Day. These centers are Beach Tourist Information Center, located at the North Dakota-Montana border on I-94; Bowman Information Center, located on Hwy 12 W; Lake Agassiz Travel Center, located on I-29, exit 2; Oriska Information Center, located at Oriska Rest area, 12 miles E of Valley City on I-94; and Williston Information Center, located at Hwy 2 and 6th Avenue W.

Bismarck (D-3)

Settled 1873
Population 49,256
Elevation 1,680 ft
Area Code 701
Information Bismarck-Mandan Convention & Visitors Bureau, 1600 Burnt Boat Dr, 58503; phone 701/222-4308 or 800/767-3555
Web Site www.bismarckmandancvb.com

Lewis and Clark camped near here in 1804 and Jim Bridger, Prince Maximilian of Wied, Sitting Bull, General Sully, General Sibley, Theodore Roosevelt, and the Marquis de Mores all figured in Bismarck's history. On the east bank of the Missouri, near the geographic center of the state and within 150 miles of the geographic center of the continent, the city flourished as a steamboat port called "the crossing." As the terminus of the Northern Pacific Railway, it gained new importance and was named for the Chancellor of Germany to attract German capital to invest in building transcontinental railroads. General Custer came to Bismarck to take command of the newly constructed Fort Abraham Lincoln nearby and in 1876 rode out to his fatal rendezvous with Sitting Bull. In 1883, Bismarck became the capital of the Dakota Territory, and in 1889, the seat of the new state.

What to See and Do

Camp Hancock State Historic Site. *Main and 1st sts, Bismarck (58505). Phone 701/328-2666.* This site preserves part of a military camp established in 1872 to provide protection for workers then building the Northern Pacific Railroad. Site includes the headquarters building, now wood sheathed; an early Northern Pacific Railroad locomotive; and one of Bismarck's oldest churches, which was moved to the site and restored. (Mid-May-mid-Sept, Wed-Sun) **FREE**

Double Ditch Indian Village. *Bismarck. 9 1/2 miles NW via Hwy 1804. Phone 701/328-2666.* State historic site contains the ruins of large Mandan Native American earthlodge village inhabited from 1675-1780; earthlodge and two surrounding fortifications are clearly discernible. (Daily) **FREE**

Lewis & Clark Riverboat. *Bismarck. North River Rd at Riverboat Jct. Phone 701/255-4233. www.lewisanclarkriverboat.com.* Daily cruises to Fort Abraham Lincoln State Park; also dinner, family, pizza, and moonlight cruises. (Memorial Day-Labor Day, daily)

McDowell Dam Recreation Area. *1953 93rd St, Bismarck (58501). 6 miles E on Hwy 10. Phone 701/255-7385.* Swimming beach, boating (no motors; ramp, dock; canoe, paddle, and kayak rentals; Memorial Day-Labor Day); walking trails, picnicking (shelters by reservation), playground. Alcoholic beverage permit required. (Daily) **FREE**

⭐ **North Dakota State Capitol.** *600 E Boulevard Ave, Bismarck (58505). Phone 701/328-2480.* Constructed in 1933 on a $2 million budget after the original building burned in 1930, this state capitol building stands out from its traditionally domed peers. The 19-story Art Deco limestone tower is one of only four vertically oriented capitols in the United States (along with those in Nebraska, Louisiana, and Florida). Beyond its distinctive exterior, the Skyscraper of the Prairies, capped with an observation deck, features lavish interiors fashioned from wood, stone, and metal from all over the globe and the cavernous Great Hall running to the legislative quarters. Tours are available on weekdays in the summer. Also on the grounds are the **former Governors' Mansion,** now restored and featuring historic displays, and the **North Dakota Heritage Center,** a regional history museum with an impressive collection of Plains Indians artifacts. Outdoors are two notable sculptures, one of Lewis and Clark guides, Sakajawea, and another dubbed *The Pioneer Family (By Avard Fairbanks).* **FREE** Also on the grounds are

Former Governors' Mansion State Historic Site. *320 East Ave B, Bismarck (58501). 4th St and Ave B. Phone 701/328-2666.* This restored three-story Victorian mansion, built in 1884, was occupied from 1893 to 1960. Interpretive exhibits; governors' portraits. (Mid-May-mid-Sept, Wed-Sun afternoons, also by appointment)

North Dakota Heritage Center. *612 Boulevard Ave, Bismarck (58501). Phone 701/328-2666.* Permanent and changing exhibits on history and settlement of northern Great Plains. State archives and research library. Gift shop. (Daily, limited hours Sun; closed holidays) **FREE**

Riverside-Sertoma Park. *Bismarck. Along the Missouri River at W Bowen Ave and Riverside Park Rd. Phone 701/255-1107.* Playground; amusement park with miniature golf, children's rides. (Late Apr-Labor Day wkend, daily; some fees). **$$** Adjacent is

Dakota Zoo. *602 Riverside Park Rd, Bismarck (58502). Phone 701/223-7543.* More than 600 mammals, birds, and reptiles on 80 acres. Miniature train ride (fee); concessions. (Apr-Sept: daily 10 am-7 pm; Oct-Mar: Fri-Sun 1-5 pm) **$$**

Ward Earthlodge Village Historic Site. *4480 Fort Lincoln Rd, Bismarck (58554). Near Burnt Boat Dr at Grandview Ln. Phone 701/222-6455.www.bisparks.org.* Mandan Indians once occupied this bluff above the Missouri River, living in dome-shaped homes built of logs and earth. By the time Lewis and Clark passed through the region, the village was deserted; however, depressions remain where the houses once stood, and the site is now part of the city park system. Interpretive signs explain how the village was constructed and elements of Mandan cultural life. Spectacular views from the bluff. For more information, contact Bismarck Parks and Recreation. (Daily dawn-dusk) **FREE**

Special Events

Folkfest. *Bismarck. Phone 701/222-4308.* Downtown. Mid-Sept.

United Tribes Powwow. *3315 University Dr, Bismarck (58504). Phone 701/255-3285. www.unitedtribes powwow.com.* Among the most attended powwows in the United States, this annual event is one of the top cultural happenings in North Dakota. Some 1,500 Native American dancers and drummers, representing more than 70 tribes and clothed in traditional garb, perform at the Lone Star Arena at United Tribes Technical College. You'll find singing, dancing, and drumming competitions, as well as a softball tournament, a parade, an intertribal summit, a pageant, and plenty of food. Early Sept.

Limited-Service Hotels

★★BEST WESTERN RAMKOTA HOTEL. *800 S 3rd St, Bismarck (58504). Phone 701/258-7700; toll-free 800/780-7234; fax 701/224-8212. www.bestwestern.com.* 306 rooms, 3 story. Pets accepted, some restrictions; fee. Check-in 3 pm, check-out noon. High-speed Internet access. Restaurant, bar. Fitness room. Indoor pool, children's pool, whirlpool. Airport transportation available.**$**
🐾 🕍 ⇌

★EXPRESSWAY INN.*200 E Bismarck Expy, Bismarck (58504). Phone 701/222-2900; toll-free 800/456-6388; fax 701/222-2900.* 163 rooms, 5 story. Pets accepted; fee. Complimentary continental breakfast. Check-in 2 pm, check-out 11:30 am. High-speed Internet access, wireless Internet access. Fitness room. Outdoor pool, whirlpool. Airport transportation available.**$**
🐾 🕍 ⇌

★ FAIRFIELD INN. *135 Ivy Ave, Bismarck (58504). Phone 701/223-9293; toll-free 800/228-2800. www.fairfieldinn.com.* 63 rooms, 3 story. Complimentary continental breakfast. Check-in 3 pm, check-out noon. High-speed Internet access, wireless Internet access. Indoor pool, whirlpool.**$**
⇌

★ ★ KELLY INN - BISMARCK.*1800 N 12th St, Bismarck (58501). Phone 701/223-8001; toll-free 800/635-3559; fax 701/221-2685.www.kellyinns.com.* 101 rooms, 2 story. Pets accepted, some restrictions. Check-in 2 pm, check-out 11 am. High-speed Internet access. Restaurant, bar. Fitness room. Indoor pool, whirlpool. Airport transportation available.**$**
🐾 🕍 ⇌

★★RADISSON HOTEL BISMARCK. *605 E Broadway Ave, Bismarck (58501). Phone 701/255-6000; toll-free 800/333-3333; fax 701/223-0400. www.radisson.com.* 215 rooms, 9 story. Pets accepted. Check-in 4 pm, check-out noon. High-speed Internet access. Restaurant, bar. Fitness room. Indoor pool, whirlpool. Airport transportation available. Business center.**$**
🐾 🕍 ⇌ 🕍

★RAMADA LIMITED SUITES. *3808 E Divide Ave, Bismarck (58501). Phone 701/221-3030; toll-free 800/295-3895; fax 701/221-3030. www.ramada.com.* 66 rooms, 3 story. Pets accepted; fee. Complimentary continental breakfast. Check-in 3 pm, check-out 11 am. Wireless Internet access. Fitness room. Indoor pool, whirlpool.**$**
🐾 🕍 ⇌

Restaurants

★ **MERIWETHER'S.** *1700 River Rd, Bismarck (58501). Phone 701/258-0666.* Located on the Missouri River, this restaurant features a "Lewis and Clark" theme with lots of Old West artifacts and photos. American menu. Lunch, dinner, Sun brunch. Closed Thanksgiving, Dec 25. Bar. Children's menu. Casual attire. Outdoor seating. **$$**

★ ★ **PEACOCK ALLEY.** *422 E Main St, Bismarck (58501). Phone 701/255-7917; fax 701/255-7231.www. peacockalley.com.* Located in the downtown area of Bismarck, this former 1880s hotel features turn-of-the-century Victorian decor. American, seafood menu. Lunch, dinner, brunch. Closed Thanksgiving, Dec 25. Bar. Children's menu. Casual attire. **$$**

Bottineau (A-3)

Founded 1883
Population 2,598
Elevation 1,635 ft
Area Code 701
Zip 58318
Information Greater Bottineau Area Chamber of Commerce, 519 Main St; phone 701/228-3849 or toll-free 800/735-6932
Web Site www.bottineau.com

What to See and Do

Bottineau Winter Park Ski Area. *1 Winter Park Rd, Bottineau (58318). 11 miles NW via county roads in the Turtle Mountains. Phone 701/263-4556. www.skibwp. com.* Two T-bars, hand tow; patrol, triple chairlift, school, rentals, snowmaking; snack bar. Longest run 1,200 feet; vertical drop 200 feet. (Mid-Nov-mid-Mar, Thurs-Sun) **$$$$**

⭐ **International Peace Garden.** *Hwy 281, Dunseith (58329). Astride the Canadian border, 18 miles E on Hwy 5 to Dunseith, then 13 miles N on Hwy 281, Hwy 3. Phone 701/263-4390. www.peacegarden.com.* Straddling the United States-Canada border where North Dakota becomes Manitoba, this 2,339-acre park is dedicated to international peace, with its home nations' longtime friendship as the focal point. Officials dedicated the garden in 1932 after selecting the location based on aesthetic appeal: the spot is nestled in the midst of the gentle green undulation of the Turtle Mountains, a sea of wheat fields, and dense forests to the north. While the periphery is relatively wild, the 150,000 flowers planted here annually are the center of attention, sculpted into a multitude of designs and landscapes that also include trees and fountains. Beyond the gardens, there is a chapel--its limestone walls are engraved with hundreds of messages of peace--and a bell tower housing 14 chimes that weigh more than a ton each. There are also two restaurants and a campground with RV hookups (May-mid-Oct). (Front gate 8 am-10 pm) **$$**

J. Clark Salyer National Wildlife Refuge. *RR, Upham (58789). 12 miles W on Hwy 5, then 14 miles S on Hwy 14. Phone 701/768-2548. www.fws.gov/jclarksalyer.* Long, narrow, irregularly shaped 58,693-acre refuge stretching from Canadian border to point about 25 miles south of Bottineau. Fishing; hunting, picnicking, birdwatching, photography permitted on some parts of refuge during specified periods. Self-guided auto tour (May-Oct); also canoe trail on Souris River. Details at headquarters, 2 miles north of Upham (daily; office closed weekends, holidays). Contact Refuge for road conditions. **FREE**

Lake Metigoshe State Park. *2 Lake Metigoshe State Park, Bottineau (58318). 12 miles N on Lake Rd, 2 miles E of Bottineau Fairgrounds. Phone 701/263-4651. www. ndparks.com/parks/lmsp.htm.* This park is one of the top year-round recreation destinations in North Dakota, located just south of the United States-Canada border. Metigoshe Washegum, or clear water lake surrounded by oaks, is the Chippewa name for the beautiful lake here, an angling hotspot tucked in the rolling greenery of the Turtle Mountains. Summer activities include boating, swimming, and hiking (guides available); cross-country skiing and snowmobiling take precedence in winter, with 250 miles of groomed trails devoted to the latter. There are campsites and rental cabins. **$**

Special Event

International Music Camp. *International Peace Garden, Hwy 281, Dunseith, Bottineau (58329). Phone 701/263-4390.* Music, dance, drama, art; Saturday concerts with guest conductors; old-time fiddlers' contest. Seven weeks in early June-July.

Bowman (D-1)

Population 1,741
Elevation 2,960 ft
Area Code 701
Zip 58623
Information Chamber of Commerce, PO Box 1143;

phone 701/523-5880
Web Site www.bowmannd.com

What to See and Do

Bowman-Haley Lake. *Bowman. 21 miles SE via Hwy 12 or Hwy 85.* Phone 701/252-7666. Rolled earth-fill dam 74 feet high, 5,730 feet long. Two-mile-long reservoir, fishing for panfish, boating (ramp); rental cabins, picnicking, concession. **FREE**

Butte View State Park. *Bowman. 1 mile E on Hwy 12.* Phone 701/859-3071. Picnicking, camping (electric hookups, dump station). (Mid-May-mid-Sept, daily)

Carrington (C-4)

See also Jamestown

Founded 1882
Population 2,267
Elevation 1,587 ft
Area Code 701
Zip 58421
Information Chamber of Commerce, 871 Main St, PO Box 439; phone 701/652-2524 or toll-free 800/641-9668
Web Site www.cgtn-nd.com

What to See and Do

Arrowwood Lake Area. *Carrington. 14 miles S on Hwy 281, then 6 miles E on gravel road.* The James River flows through Arrowwood Lake, Mud Lake, and Jim Lake in a 30-mile interconnecting chain of waterways to Jamestown. Along eastern and western shores is

> **Arrowwood National Wildlife Refuge.** *7745 11th St SE, Pingree (58476). Headquarters are 6 miles E of Edmunds on gravel road.* Phone 701/285-3341. Hunting, picnicking. Self-guided auto tour, wildlife observation. (Daily) **FREE**

Garrison Diversion Conservancy District. *401 Hwy 281 NE, Carrington (58421). 1 mile N on Hwy 281.* Phone 701/652-3194. "Nerve center" for the multipurpose 130,000-acre irrigation Garrison Diversion Unit. Project tours with advance notice. (Mon-Fri)

Devils Lake (B-5)

Settled 1882
Population 7,782

Elevation 1,473 ft
Area Code 701
Zip 58301
Information Devils Lake Area Chamber of Commerce, Hwy 2 E, PO Box 879; phone 701/662-4903 or toll-free 800/233-8048
Web Site www.devilslakend.com

Located near the shore of Devils Lake, the city is in the heart of some of the best fishing in the North. The opening of the federal land office here in 1883 sparked growth of the city.

What to See and Do

Devils Lake. *Devils Lake. 6 miles S.* Gets its name from the Indian name Miniwaukan which means "bad water." Bolstered by legends of drowned warriors, the name evolved into Devils Lake. Fishing, boating; hunting, golfing, biking, snowmobiling, picnicking, camping (fee).

Devils Lake Area Welcome Center. *Hwy 2 E, Devils Lake. 1 1/2 miles E on Hwy 2.* Phone 701/662-4903; toll-free 800/233-8048. Tourist information. (Daily) **FREE**

⭐ **Fort Totten State Historic Site.** *Devils Lake. 18 miles SW on Hwy 20.* Phone 701/766-4441. (1867) Built to protect the overland route to Montana; it was the last outpost before 300 miles of wilderness. One of the best-preserved military forts west of the Mississippi; 16 original buildings. Pioneer Daughters Museum; interpretive center, commissary display; videotape program of the site's history. Summer dinner theater (see SPECIAL EVENT). Self-guided tours. (Memorial Day-Labor Day, daily; rest of year, by appointment) **$**

Sullys Hill National Game Preserve. *Devils Lake. 18 miles SW on Hwy 20, on Devils Lake, 1 mile E of Fort Totten.* Phone 701/766-4272. More than 1,600 scenic acres of which 700 acres are a big game enclosure populated by bison, deer, elk, prairie dogs, and turkeys; 4-mile self-guided auto tour. (May-Oct, daily) Nature trail. Observation towers. **FREE**

Special Event

Fort Totten Little Theater. *Fort Totten Historic Site, Devils Lake. 18 miles SW on Hwy 20.* Phone 701/766-4441. Adaptive use of historic auditorium (1904). Broadway musical productions. Wed-Thurs, Sat-Sun in July.

Limited-Service Hotel

★ **COMFORT INN.** *215 Hwy 2 E, Devils Lake (58301). Phone 701/662-6760; toll-free 888/266-3948; fax 701/662-8440. www.comfortinn.com.* 87 rooms, 2 story. Pets accepted; fee. Complimentary continental breakfast. Check-in 2 pm, check-out 11 am. Indoor pool, whirlpool. Business center.**$**

Full-Service Inn

★ ★ **TOTTEN TRAIL HISTORIC INN.** *Phone 701/766-4787; fax 701/662-5334. www.tottentrailinn. com.* 10 rooms. Closed Oct-Apr. Complimentary full breakfast. Check-in 3 pm, check-out noon.**$**

Dickinson (C-2)

See also Medora

Settled 1880
Population 16,097
Elevation 2,420 ft
Area Code 701
Zip 58601
Information Chamber of Commerce, 314 Third Ave W, PO Box C; phone 701/225-5115
Web Site www.dickinsonchamber.org

What to See and Do

Joachim Regional Museum. *1266 Museum Dr. Dickinson (58602). Phone 701/456-6225. www.joachi museum.org.* Art gallery; dinosaur exhibit; doll house; cowboy memorabilia. (May-Sept, daily) **$$**

Patterson Reservoir. *Dickinson. 3 miles W on Hwy 10, then 1 mile S.* Part of Missouri River Valley reclamation project. Swimming (June-Aug, daily), fishing, boating; volleyball, horseshoes, picnicking, camping (Memorial Day weekend-Labor Day weekend; fee). Park (Apr-Sept, daily).

Special Event

Roughrider Days Celebration. *Dickinson. Phone 701/225-5115. www.roughriderdaysfair.com.* Rodeo, parade, tractor pulls, street dance, demolition derby, races, carnival. July 4 weekend.

Limited-Service Hotels

★ **AMERICINN.** *229 15th St W, Dickinson (58601).*

Phone 701/225-1400; toll-free 800/634-3444; fax 701/483-9682. www.americinn.com. 46 rooms, 2 story. Pets accepted, some restrictions. Complimentary continental breakfast. Check-in 3 pm, check-out noon. Indoor pool, whirlpool. Airport transportation available.**$**

★ **COMFORT INN.** *493 Elk Dr, Dickinson (58601). Phone 701/264-7300; toll-free 877/424-4777; fax 701/264-7300. www.comfortinn.com.* 116 rooms, 2 story. Pets accepted. Complimentary continental breakfast. Check-in 3 pm, check-out 11 am. High-speed Internet access. Fitness room. Indoor pool, children's pool, whirlpool.**$**

Fargo (C-6)

See also Moorhead, Wahpeton

Founded 1872
Population 74,111
Elevation 900 ft
Area Code 701
Information Fargo-Moorhead Convention & Visitors Bureau, 2001 44th St SW, 58103; phone 701/282-3653 or toll-free 800/235-7654
Web Site www.fargomoorhead.org

Fargo, the largest city in North Dakota, is the leading retail and wholesale center of the rich Red River Valley and one of the leading commercial centers in the Northwest. Farm products and byproducts keep many factories busy. The city is named for William G. Fargo of the Wells-Fargo Express Company. It is also the hometown of baseball great Roger Maris; a display museum filled with his personal memorabilia is located in West Acres Mall.

With blackjack legal in North Dakota, Fargo has taken the lead in promoting its gaming tables. There are approximately 30 casinos in the city, making it a major tourist attraction for the three-state region including Minnesota and South Dakota. Charities and nonprofit organizations run the casinos and collect all profits above expenses.

What to See and Do

 Bonanzaville, USA. *1351 W Main Ave, West Fargo (58078). 4 1/2 miles W of Hwy 29 on Main Ave or via I-94, exit 343 (Hwy 10 W). Phone 701/282-2822. www. bonanzaville.com.* More than 45 buildings reconstruct the 19th-century farm era. Hemp Antique Vehicle Museum, 1884 locomotive, train depot, model RR, pioneer farm homes, church, school, log cabins, sod house, home of roll-film camera inventor, general stores, farm machinery buildings, operating farmsteads, doll house, Plains Indian Museum, and more. (See SPECIAL EVENTS) Village and museums (May-late Oct, daily; rest of year, Mon-Fri). **$$**

Children's Museum at Yunker Farm. *1201 28th Ave N, Fargo (58102). Phone 701/232-6102. www. childrensmuseumyunker.org.* Hands-on exhibits include Legoland, infant-toddler play center, puppet theater. Also outdoor playground; picnic shelters. (Summer, daily; rest of year, Tues-Sun) **$**

Fargo Theatre. *314 Broadway, Fargo (58102). Phone 701/235-4152.* (1937) Classic and first-run films; stage productions; Wurlitzer organ concerts (weekends) in streamlined *modern* theater.

Fargo-Moorhead Community Theatre. *333 4th St S, Fargo (58103). Phone 701/235-6778.* Units for the hearing impaired available.

North Dakota State University. *1301 N 12th Ave N, Fargo (58102). Phone 701/231-8643.* (1890) (Over 10,000 students) Herbarium and wildlife museum in Stevens Hall; North Dakota Institute for Regional Studies at NDSU Library (Mon-Fri; closed holidays). Campus tours.

Special Events

Pioneer Days. *Bonanzaville, USA, 1351 W Main Ave, Fargo (58078). Phone 701/282-2822. www.bonanzaville.com.* Celebration of area pioneer heritage. People in period costume, parades, and arts and crafts. Third weekend in Aug.

Red River Valley Fair. *West Fargo (58078). Fairgrounds, 5 miles W on I-94, exit 85, in West Fargo. Phone 701/282-3653.* Pioneer village, livestock exhibits. Mid-June.

Limited-Service Hotels

★ **AMERICINN.** *1423 35th St SW, Fargo (58103). Phone 701/234-9946; toll-free 800/634-3444; fax 701/234-9946. www.americinnfargo.com.* This is the perfect property for a traveler who wants amenities but is on a budget. The hotel is located just off Interstate 29 on the south side of Fargo with a mixed residential/commercial area nearby. 61 rooms, 2 story. Pets accepted; fee. Complimentary continental breakfast. Check-in 3 pm, check-out 11 am. High-speed Internet access, wireless Internet access. Fitness room. Indoor pool, whirlpool. Business center. **$**

★ ★ **BEST WESTERN FARGO DOUBLE-WOOD INN.** *3333 13th Ave S, Fargo (58103). Phone 701/235-3333; toll-free 800/433-3235; fax 701/280-9482. www.bestwestern.com.* This family-friendly hotel is located in a busy commercial area on the south side of Fargo. Both business and leisure travelers will appreciate the many services and amenities offered--Internet access, meeting rooms, passes to a nearby fitness center, in-room refrigerators and microwaves, and a casino (sans slots). 172 rooms, 3 story. Pets accepted, some restrictions; fee. Check-in 3 pm, check-out noon. High-speed Internet access, wireless Internet access. Restaurant, bar. Indoor pool, whirlpool. Airport transportation available. Business center. Casino. **$**

★ ★ **BEST WESTERN KELLY INN.** *3800 Main Ave, Fargo (58103). Phone 701/282-2143; toll-free 800/580-1234; fax 701/281-0243. www.bestwestern.com.* Centrally located off Interstate 29, this hotel is near many attractions including the Fargo Dome, NDSU, Hector International Airport, and West Acres shopping mall. The grounds are attractive with the hotel surrounding the pool area, which includes a children's pool, and a gazebo. There is an on-site casino, but it doesn't include any one-armed bandits. 133 rooms, 2 story. Complimentary continental breakfast. Check-in, check-out 11 am. High-speed Internet access. Restaurant, bar. Fitness room. Indoor pool, outdoor pool, children's pool, whirlpool. Business center. Casino. **$**

★ **COMFORT SUITES.** *1415 35th St S, Fargo (58103). Phone 701/237-5911; toll-free 800/228-5150; fax 701/237-5911. www.choicehotels.com.* This all-suite property is located off Interstate 29 on the south side of the city. The spacious guest suites offer refrigerators, microwaves, and sleeper sofas--perfect for families. A complimentary continental breakfast is offered, and the indoor pool and whirlpool are great places to relax. 66 rooms, 2 story, all suites. Pets accepted. Complimentary continental breakfast. Check-in 2 pm, check-out 11 am. High-speed Internet access, wireless Internet access. Indoor pool, whirlpool. Business center. **$**

★ **COUNTRY INN & SUITES BY CARSON.** *3316 13th Ave, Fargo (58102). Phone 701/234-0565; toll-free 888/201-1746; fax 701/478-0320. www.countryinns. com.* When you pull up to this property, you'll see why it's called "Country" Inn & Suites--shutters and lattice work decorate the outside. The guest rooms continue the country theme with warm colors, comfy furnishings, and dried flower wreaths hung above the beds. For a meal or a quick bite, the Green Mill restaurant next door provides room service. Families will enjoy the short drive to Red River Zoo (2 miles). 99 rooms, 3 story. Pets accepted, some restrictions; fee. Complimentary continental breakfast. Check-in 3 pm, check-out noon. Wireless Internet access. Fitness room. Indoor pool, whirlpool. Airport transportation available. Business center.**$**

★ **FAIRFIELD INN.** *3902 9th Ave SW, Fargo (58103). Phone 701/281-0494; toll-free 800/228-2800; fax 701/281-0494. www.fairfieldinn.com.* This affordable limited-service hotel is located just off Interstate 29 on the west side of Fargo. Retail shops and restaurants are nearby. All rooms have interior entrances and some rooms include refrigerators and microwaves. 63 rooms, 3 story. Complimentary continental breakfast. Check-in 3 pm, check-out noon. High-speed Internet access, wireless Internet access. Indoor pool, whirlpool.**$**

★ **HAMPTON INN.** *3431 14th Ave SW, Fargo (58103). Phone 701/235-5566; toll-free 800/426-7866; fax 701/235-7382. www.hamptoninn.com.* This limited-service property is located in a mixed residential/commercial area with restaurants nearby. The complimentary continental breakfast will get your day off to a good start, and the indoor pool and whirlpool will help you unwind after a busy day.75 rooms, 2 story. Complimentary continental breakfast. Check-in 3 pm, check-out 11 am. High-speed Internet access. Indoor pool, whirlpool. Business center.**$**

★ ★ **HOLIDAY INN.** *3803 13th Ave S, Fargo (58103). Phone 701/282-2700; toll-free 877/282-2700; fax 701/281-1240. www.holiday-inn.com.* Families will love this property. It's located off Interstate 29 at Interstate 94 and is across the street from a shopping mall and restaurants. The furnishings are standard for the chain, but the amenities are a plus. There is a pirate ship in the pool area. The property also features a restaurant, which is very popular with the locals. 308 rooms, 7 story. Pets accepted, some restrictions. Check-in 4 pm, check-out noon. Two restaurants, bar. Fitness room. Indoor pool, children's pool, whirlpool. Airport transportation available. Business center.**$**

★ **HOLIDAY INN EXPRESS.** *1040 40th St S, Fargo (58103). Phone 701/282-2000; toll-free 800/465-4329; fax*

701/282-4721. www.hiexpress.com. This is a convenient hotel for business or leisure travelers--some of its amenities include an indoor pool, business services, high-speed Internet access, airport transportation, and complimentary continental breakfast. It's located off the Interstate and is near restaurants, shops, and businesses. 77 rooms, 4 story. Pets accepted; fee. Complimentary continental breakfast. Check-in 3 pm, check-out noon. High-speed Internet access. Indoor pool, whirlpool. Airport transportation available.**$**

★ **KELLY INN - FARGO.** *4207 13th Ave SW, Fargo (58103). Phone 701/277-8821; toll-free 800/635-3559; fax 701/277-0208. www.kellyinnfargo.com.* Budget-minded travelers will enjoy staying at this friendly property located just off the Interstate. Rooms are clean and comfortable, there's an indoor pool, whirlpool, business center, and a complimentary continental breakfast is offered. Don't overpack though--this hotel doesn't have an elevator. 59 rooms, 2 story. Pets accepted, some restrictions. Complimentary continental breakfast. Check-in 2 pm, check-out 11 am. Wireless Internet access. Indoor pool, whirlpool. Business center.**$**

★ ★ **RADISSON HOTEL FARGO.** *201 5th St N, Fargo (58102). Phone 701/232-7363; toll-free 800/333-3333; fax 701/298-9134. www.radisson.com/fargond.* The second-tallest building in the state of North Dakota, this downtown hotel occupies thirteen of the eighteen floors of the building. The hotel is connected to Fargo's climate-controlled skywalk system so guests can get around town comfortably during winter. Guest rooms feature Sleep Number beds, Internet access, and beautiful city views. The hotel has a lap pool, whirlpool, fitness room, and a business center. This is a great hotel for business or leisure travelers. 151 rooms, 18 story. Pets accepted, some restrictions; fee. Check-in 3 pm, check-out noon. High-speed Internet access. Restaurant, bar. Fitness room. Indoor pool, whirlpool. Airport transportation available. Business center.**$**

★ **SLEEP INN.** *1921 44th St SW, Fargo (58103). Phone 701/281-8240; toll-free 800/424-6423; fax 701/281-2041. www.sleepinnfargo.com.* Connected to the MainStay Suites, this Sleep Inn is located off Interstate 94 in a business park on the west side of Fargo. The Fargodome arena, West Acres Mall, North Dakota State University, and Minnesota State University Moorhead are all nearby. 61 rooms, 2 story. Pets accepted, some restrictions. Complimentary continental breakfast. Check-in 2 pm, check-out 11 am. High-speed Internet access, wireless Internet access. Fitness room. Indoor pool, children's pool, whirlpool. Airport transportation available. Business center.**$**

Restaurant

★ ★ **MEXICAN VILLAGE.** *814 Main Ave, Fargo (58103). Phone 701/293-0120; fax 701/298-2911.* www. *mexicanvillagefm.com.* Mexican menu. Lunch, dinner. Closed Thanksgiving, Dec 25. Children's menu. Casual attire. **$**

Garrison Dam (B-3)

Area Code 701

58 miles N of Bismarck on Hwy 83, then 11 miles W on Hwy 200.

The Garrison Project represents one of the key projects of the Missouri River Basin constructed by the US Army Corps of Engineers. The project cost nearly $300 million. Flood control, power generation, irrigation, navigation, recreation, and fish and wildlife are the project purposes. Garrison Dam is one of the largest rolled earthfill dams in the world. It cuts more than 2 miles across the Missouri River and rises 210 feet above the river channel with Hwy 200 carried on its crest. Behind the dam, Lake Sakakawea stretches approximately 180 miles. Beaches, fishing, and boating (ramps) are available on the 1,300-mile shoreline. There are also picnic areas and camping facilities (early May-mid-Oct; fee) and resorts. Displays in powerhouse lobby. (Memorial Day-Labor Day, daily; rest of year, Mon-Fri) Guided tours (Memorial Day-Labor Day, daily; rest of year, by appointment).

What to See and Do

Audubon National Wildlife Refuge. *3275 11th St NW, Coleharbor (58531). 16 miles SE of Garrison via Hwy 37 to I-83. Phone 701/442-5474.* www.audubon.fws. *gov.* Wildlife observation and 8-mile auto trail. (Daily; closed holidays) **FREE**

Garrison Dam National Fish Hatchery. *Phone 701/654-7451.* Produces northern pike, paddlefish, walleye, rainbow trout, and Chinook salmon for waters in northern Great Plains; visitor center and aquarium. (Memorial Day-Labor Day, daily 8 am-3:30 pm) **FREE**

Knife River Indian Villages National Historic Site. *Stanton. National Historic Site, 19 miles S of Garrison Dam via Hwy 200, 1/4 mile N of Stanton via Hwy 37. Phone 701/745-3300.* Three visible Hidatsa earthlodge village sites. Ranger-guided tours to reconstructed earthlodge, self-guided trails, cross-country ski trails. Visitor Center; museum exhibits, demonstrations, orientation film. (Daily; closed Jan 1, Thanksgiving, Dec 25) **FREE**

Lake Sakakawea State Park. *On the south shore of a 180-mile long lake. Phone 701/487-3315.* Swimming (beach); fishing for pike, salmon, walleye, sauger, trout, and catfish; boating (ramp, rentals, marina); hiking, cross-country skiing, snowmobiling, ice fishing, picnicking, playground, concession, tent and trailer facilities. Summer interpretive programs, sailing regattas. **$**

Grafton (B-6)

See also Grand Forks

Population 4,840
Elevation 825 ft
Area Code 701
Zip 58237
Information Chamber of Commerce, 432 Hill Ave, PO Box 632; phone 701/352-0781
Web Site www.graftonchamber.org

The seat of Walsh County and a transportation and farming junction, Grafton bears the name of the New Hampshire county where the pioneer settlers of this area began their westward trek.

What to See and Do

Heritage Village. *Grafton. Just W of downtown on Hwy 17. Phone 701/352-3280.* Includes furnished farmhouse; country church; depot with caboose; taxidermy shop and working carousel. (May-Sept, Sun; also by appointment)

Homme Dam Recreation Area. *Park River. 19 miles W on Hwy 17. Phone 701/284-7841.* In wooded valley of Park River, well stocked for fishing. Boating (docks, ramps); winter sports, picnicking, camping (fee). (Apr-Nov, daily) **$**

Grand Forks (B-6)

See also Grafton

Settled 1871
Population 49,425

Elevation 834 ft
Area Code 701
Information Convention & Visitors Bureau, 4251 Gateway Dr, 58203; phone 701/746-0444 or toll-free 800/866-4566
Web Site www.visitgrandforks.com

Grand Forks stands at the point where the Red River of the North and Red Lake River form a fork. Socially, culturally, and commercially the town is closely allied with its cousin city across the river, East Grand Forks, Minnesota. First a French fur trading post, Grand Forks later developed as a frontier river town. The arrival of the railroad and cultivation of nearby farmland brought about another change in its personality. The University of North Dakota plays a dominant role in the city's culture and economy. Grand Forks AFB is 14 miles west on Hwy 2.

What to See and Do

Grand Forks County Historical Society. *2405 Belmont Rd, Grand Forks (58201). Phone 701/775-2216. www.grandforkshistory.com.* Society maintains **Campbell House,** historic pioneer cabin of agricultural innovator Tom Campbell. Original log cabin portion dates from 1879. Also on grounds are log post office (1870), one-room schoolhouse, and Myra Carriage Museum. **Myra Carriage Museum** houses collection of late 19th- and early 20th-century artifacts from surrounding area. (May-Oct: daily 1-5 pm) **$**

Turtle River State Park. *3084 Park Ave, Arvilla (58214). 22 miles W on Hwy 2. Phone 701/594-4445. www.ndparks. com/parks/trsp.htm.* Situated in a green valley carved out by the gently winding Turtle River, this 784-acre park (named for Bell's Terrapins, which are mud turtles) is a big recreational draw in the Grand Forks area. Because the river is stocked with rainbow trout, angling is probably the most popular pursuit, but there are a myriad of hiking and biking trails, as well as cross-country ski routes and a sledding hill that see a good deal of use in the winter. For overnighters, a dozen duplex rental cabins, with running water but without kitchens, and 125 campsites are available. **$**

University of North Dakota. *Grand Forks. W end of University Ave. Phone 701/777-3304; toll-free 800/225-5863. www.und.edu.* (1883) (12,430 students) The *Eternal Flame of Knowledge,* an immense steel-girded sphere, commemorates Old Main and past presidents. J. Lloyd Stone Alumni Center, historic turn-of-the-century mansion; Center for Aerospace Sciences Atmospherium; North Dakota Museum of Art; Chester Fritz Library houses artwork. Tours.

Special Events

Grand Forks County Fair. *County Fairgrounds, Grand Forks (58201). Phone 701/772-3421.* July.

Native American Annual Time Out and Wacipi. *Grand Forks. Phone 701/777-4291.* University of North Dakota Indian Association. Early Apr.

Potato Bowl Week. *Grand Forks. Phone 701/777-3304.* Queen pageant, parade, football game, other events. Early Sept.

State Hockey Tournament. *Engelstad Arena, University of North Dakota, Grand Forks (58202). Phone 701/772-3304.* Late Feb.

Summerthing. *University Park, Grand Forks (58202). Phone 701/746-0444.* Arts festivals. July.

Limited-Service Hotels

★ ★ **BEST WESTERN TOWN HOUSE.** *710 1st Ave N, Grand Forks (58203). Phone 701/746-5411; toll-free 800/867-9797; fax 701/746-1407. www. bestwestern.com.* Located in the heart of downtown, this family-friendly hotel is across the street from the Civic Auditorium. Some of its many amenities include miniature golf, a casino, a pool area, and some rooms with refrigerators and microwaves. 101 rooms, 2 story. Pets accepted, some restrictions; fee. Check-in 3 pm, check-out noon. High-speed Internet access, wireless Internet access. Restaurant, bar. Indoor pool, whirlpool. Airport transportation available. Casino. **$**
🐾 🏊

★ **C'MON INN.** *3051 32nd Ave, Grand Forks (58201). Phone 701/775-3320; toll-free 800/255-2323; fax 701/780-8141. www.cmoninn.com.* 80 rooms, 2 story. Complimentary continental breakfast. Check-in 3 pm, check-out noon. High-speed Internet access. Fitness room. Indoor pool, whirlpool. **$**
🏃 🏊

★ **COMFORT INN.** *3251 30th Ave S, Grand Forks (58201). Phone 701/775-7503; toll-free 800/424-6423; fax 701/775-7503. www.comfortinn.com.* This affordable, family-friendly hotel is located on the south side of the city and is one block from Columbia Mall. Start the day off right with the complimentary continental breakfast, and then work it off in the indoor pool. 65 rooms, 2 story. Pets accepted, some restrictions; fee. Complimentary continental breakfast. Check-in 2 pm, check-out 11 am. Wireless Internet access. Indoor pool, whirlpool.**$**

★ **FAIRFIELD INN.** *3051 S 34th St, Grand Forks (58201). Phone 701/775-7910; toll-free 800/228-2800; fax 701/775-7910. www.fairfieldinn.com.* Near many businesses and retail shops, this budget-friendly hotel is a good choice for business or leisure travelers. Some rooms have microwaves and refrigerators, and business services are available at the front desk--the pleasant staff will be happy to help with anything you need. 62 rooms, 3 story. Complimentary continental breakfast. Check-in 3 pm, check-out noon. High-speed Internet access. Indoor pool, whirlpool.**$**

★ ★ **HOLIDAY INN.** *1210 N 43rd St, Grand Forks (58203). Phone 701/772-7131; toll-free 800/465-4329; fax 701/780-9112. www.holidayinn.com.* This is the only property in the city with an indoor waterpark. Children will enjoy the pool, children's pool, and game room. And adults will appreciate a relaxing time-out in the whirlpool, or a game of luck in the casino (sans slots). 148 rooms, 2 story. Check-in 4 pm, check-out noon. High-speed Internet access, wireless Internet access. Restaurant, bar. Fitness room. Indoor pool, children's pool, whirlpool. Airport transportation available. Casino.**$**

★ **LAKEVIEW INNS AND SUITES GRAND FORKS.** *3350 S 32nd Ave, Grand Forks (58201). Phone 701/775-5000; toll-free 877/355-3500; fax 701/775-9073. www.lakeviewhotels.com.* This country casual hotel located on the south side of the city is one block from Columbia Mall. The spacious lobby welcomes guests, and the pleasant wood themes and trim work carries a relaxed feel throughout the property. There are VCRs in the guest rooms (major plus for families), and passes for a nearby gym are available. 86 rooms, 3 story. Complimentary continental breakfast. Check-in 3 pm, check-out 11 am. High-speed Internet access, wireless Internet access. Indoor pool, whirlpool.**$**

★ ★ **RAMADA INN.** *1205 N 43rd St, Grand Forks (58203). Phone 701/775-3951; toll-free 888/298-2054; fax 701/775-9774. www.ramada.com.* 100 rooms, 2 story. Pets accepted, some restrictions. Check-in 3 pm, check-out noon. High-speed Internet access, wireless Internet access. Restaurant, bar. Fitness room. Indoor pool, children's pool, whirlpool. Airport transportation available. Business center. Casino.**$**

Restaurant

★ ★ **G F GOODRIBS.** *4223 N 12th Ave, Grand Forks (58203). Phone 701/746-7115; fax 701/775-1051.* This cozy, three dining room steakhouse is popular with both tourists and locals. It's located in a quiet neighborhood near the University of North Dakota campus so it gets busy. The waiting area is large and there is a separate bar area. The extensive menu offers large portions of steaks and seafood--try the prime rib followed by the homemade mud pie. Steak menu. Lunch, dinner, Sun brunch. Closed holidays. Bar. Children's menu. Casual attire. **$$**

Jamestown (C-5)

See also Carrington, Valley City

Settled 1872
Population 15,571
Elevation 1,410 ft
Area Code 701
Zip 58401
Information Jamestown Promotion and Tourism Center, PO Box 388, 212 Third Ave NE; phone 701/252-4835 or toll-free 800/222-4766
Web Site www.jamestownnd.com

Settlers and businessmen in the wake of soldiers and railroad workers established Jamestown as a transportation center guarded by Fort Seward. When farmers discovered they could pay for their rich land with two years' crops, the area developed as a prosperous diversified agricultural sector. The James River, known as the longest unnavigable river in the world, flows through the town. On the northeastern edge of town is Jamestown College (1883).

What to See and Do

Fort Seward Historic Site and Interpretive Center. *Hwy 281 and 8th St NW, Jamestown (58401). Phone 701/251-1875.* Built on the original site of Fort Seward, the center preserves the early military history of the region with a collection of historical documents and artifacts. There is also a picnic area on the grounds. (Apr-Oct, daily) **FREE**

Frontier Village. *Jamestown. On I-94, on the SE edge of town. Phone 701/252-6307.* The big lure here is the "World's Largest Buffalo," a 60-ton concrete sculpture jutting out of the plains, but the adjacent village is a good place to get a glimpse of North Dakota's pioneer past. About a dozen historic structures were relocated here to spare them from the wrecking ball, including a one-room schoolhouse, a barbershop, and a train depot. (May-Sept, daily) Also on-site are the **National Buffalo Museum** (year-round; fee), the home of White Cloud, an albino buffalo. **FREE**

Whitestone Hill Battlefield State Historic Site. *Kulm. 37 miles S on Hwy 281, then 15 miles W on Hwy 13 to Kulm, then 15 miles S on Hwy 56, then E on unimproved road. Phone 701/396-7731.* Most probably triggered by the 1862 Sioux uprising in Minnesota, the September 1863 Battle of Whitestone Hill marked the beginning of a war between the US Cavalry and the Plains Sioux that lasted for more than 20 years. Granite monument of bugler, graves of soldiers; small museum. Picnicking, playgrounds. (Mid-May-mid-Sept, Thurs-Mon) **FREE**

Special Events

Fort Seward Wagon Train. *Jamestown. Phone 701/252-6844.* A weeklong wagon train experience. Wagons are pulled by draft horses or mules; train stops along the way at historical sites. Participants dress and camp in the manner of the pioneers. One week in late June.

Stutsman County Fair. *Jamestown. Phone 701/252-4835.* Late June.

Limited-Service Hotels

★ **COMFORT INN.** *811 SW 20th St, Jamestown (58401). Phone 701/252-7125; fax 701/252-7125. www.comfortinn.com.* 52 rooms, 2 story. Pets accepted. Complimentary continental breakfast. Check-out 11 am. Indoor pool, whirlpool.**$**

★ ★ **DAKOTA INN.** *Hwy 281 S, Jamestown (58402). Phone 701/252-3611; toll-free 800/726-7924; fax 701/252-5711.* 120 rooms, 2 story. Pets accepted; fee. Check-out 11 am. Restaurant, bar. Indoor pool, whirlpool.**$**

★ ★ **GLADSTONE SELECT HOTEL.** *111 2nd St NE, Jamestown (58401). Phone 701/252-0700; toll-free 800/641-1000; fax 701/252-0700. www.gladstone.com.* 111 rooms, 2 story. Pets accepted; fee. Check-in 2 pm, check-out 11 am. Restaurant, bar. Fitness room. Indoor pool, whirlpool.**$**

Kenmare (A-2)

See also Minot

Settled 1897
Population 1,214
Elevation 1,850 ft
Area Code 701
Zip 58746
Information Chamber of Commerce, 320 Central Ave, PO Box 517; phone 701/385-4275
Web Site www.kenmarend.com

In the center of a rich farming area that produces durum wheat and sunflowers, Kenmare also enjoys the beauties of nature from its hillside location overlooking Middle Des Lacs Lake. At one time, grain was shipped down the lake by steamboat from the Canadian border area for shipment by rail to US markets.

What to See and Do

Des Lacs National Wildlife Refuge. *Kenmare. Refuge headquarters is 1/2 mile W of town. Phone 701/385-4046.* Rings Upper, Middle, and Lower Des Lacs Lakes, a 30-mile finger of water pointing down from Canadian border. A 6-mile stretch of the Upper Lake has a picnic site (Memorial Day-Labor Day, daily). The Taskers Coulee Recreational Area (3 miles SW of town) offers picnicking, bird-watching (Memorial Day-Labor Day, daily). (Mon-Fri; closed holidays). **FREE**

Lake Darling. *Kenmare. 6 miles N on Hwy 52, then 18 miles E on Hwy 5, then S.* (See Upper Souris National Wildlife Refuge in MINOT.)

Mandan (C-3)

See also Bismarck

Settled 1881
Population 15,177
Elevation 1,651 ft
Area Code 701
Zip 58554
Information Bismarck-Mandan Convention & Visitors Bureau, 1600 Burnt Boat Dr, Bismarck 58503; phone 701/222-4308 or toll-free 800/767-3555
Web Site www.bismarckmandancvb.com

The Mandan originally farmed this area, and today the agricultural tradition persists in the dairy and dry farms that surround the city. Lignite, a soft coal, is mined in this region. Mandan has been an important railroad city since the tracks crossed the Missouri River the year the city was founded.

What to See and Do

Cross Ranch Nature Preserve. *The Nature Conservancy, 1401 River Rd, Center (58530). 30 miles N via Hwy 1806 (gravel). Phone 701/794-8741.* This 6,000-acre nature preserve has mixed grass prairies, Missouri River floodplain forest, upland woody draws. Bison herd. Hiking and self-guided nature trails. (Daily) **FREE**

Five Nations Art Depot. *401 W Main St, Mandan (58554).* Home to Native American arts and crafts; works available to purchase. (Daily) **FREE**

★**Fort Abraham Lincoln State Park.** *4480 Fort Lincoln Rd, Mandan (58554). 7 miles S on Hwy 1806. Phone 701/667-6340.* Historic site marks fort which Custer commanded prior to his "last stand." Reconstructed fort buildings; tours (Memorial Day-Labor Day) and Mandan earthlodge village. Fishing, hiking, cross-country skiing, snowmobiling, picnicking, playground, concession, camping. Visitor center, amphitheater, museum, summer interpretive program. **$$**

Huff Hills Ski Area. *Hwy 1806, Mandan (58554). 15 miles S on Hwy 1806. Phone 701/663-6421. www.huffhills.com.* Two double chairlifts. Rentals (snowboard and ski). Chalet. Longest run 3,600 feet; vertical drop 425 feet. (Mid-Nov-Mar, Thurs-Sun) **$$$$**

Railroad Museum. *Mandan. N of Mandan on Old Red Trail.* Houses exhibits from early 1900s. Handmade models, photographs, and uniforms; miniature train carries passengers on Sunday. (Memorial Day-Labor Day, afternoons) **FREE**

Special Events

Buggies 'n Blues. *205 2nd Ave NW, Mandan (58554). Phone 701/224-1378.* Live entertainment, more than 300 classic roadsters on display. Early June.

Jaycees Rodeo Days. *Mandan. Phone 701/220-2959.* Rodeo, parade, midway, and arts and crafts. Early July.

Stock Car Racing. *Dacotah Speedway, 2500 Longspur Trail, Mandan (58554). Phone 701/663-9821.* Cars race on a 3/8-mile dirt, high-banked, oval track. Fri. Mid-May-early Sept.

Limited-Service Hotel

★ ★ **BEST WESTERN SEVEN SEAS INN & CONFERENCE CENTER.** *2611 Old Red Trail, Mandan (58554). Phone 701/663-7401; toll-free 800/597-7327; fax 701/663-0025. www.bestwestern.com.* 103 rooms, 3 story. Pets accepted. Check-in 3 pm, checkout noon. High-speed Internet access. Restaurant, bar. Indoor pool, whirlpool. Business center. **$**

Medora (C-1)

See also Dickinson

Founded 1883
Population 101
Elevation 2,271 ft
Area Code 701
Zip 58645
Information Chamber of Commerce, PO Box 186; phone 701/623-4910
Web Site www.medorand.com

This village is a living museum of two of the most colorful characters found on the raw badlands frontier: young, bespectacled Theodore Roosevelt, and the hot-blooded, visionary Marquis de Mores. The Marquis, a wealthy Frenchman, established the town and named it for his wife, daughter of a New York banker. He built a packing plant and icehouses, then planned to slaughter cattle on the range and ship them to metropolitan markets in refrigerated railroad cars. The plan fizzled, but not before the mustachioed Frenchman left his stamp on the community. Roosevelt came here in 1883 and won respect as part owner of the Maltese Cross and Elkhorn ranches and as organizer and first president of the Little Missouri Stockmen's Association.

What to See and Do

★ **Chateau de Mores State Historic Site.** *3448 Chateau Rd, Medora (58645). 1 mile W, off Hwy 10, I-94. Phone 701/623-4355.* The site commemorates the life of Antoine de Vallombrosa, the Marquis de Mores. The Marquis busied himself with many undertakings such as a stagecoach line, an experiment with refrigerated railroad cars, and a beef packing plant. Remaining are the ruins of a packing plant; a 26-room, two-story frame mansion filled with French furnishings; also library, servants' quarters, relic room displaying the Marquis's saddles, guns, boots, coats, and other possessions. An interpretive center is on the grounds. The site is not heated. Picnicking available. Station-guided tours (mid-May-mid-Sept, daily; rest of year, by appointment; closed Jan 1, Thanksgiving, Dec 25). **$$**

Historic buildings. *Medora. On or near Hwy 10, I-94.* **Rough Riders Hotel** (1884) provided the name of T. R.'s regiment in the Spanish-American War; remodeled. **St. Mary's Catholic Church** (1884), built by the Marquis. **Joe Ferris Store** (1885), owned by Roosevelt partner; remodeled (1965).

Theodore Roosevelt National Park-South Unit. *Medora. Phone 701/623-4466.* (see)

Special Event

Medora Musical. *1 Main St, Medora (58645). Phone 701/623-4444; toll-free 800/633-6721.* Outdoor musical extravaganza; western songs, dance. Early June-early Sept.

Limited-Service Hotel

★ **AMERICINN MEDORA.** *75 E River Rd S, Medora (58645). Phone 701/623-4800; fax 701/623-4890. www.americinn.com.* 56 rooms, 2 story. Pets accepted, some restrictions; fee. Complimentary continental breakfast. Check-in 4 pm, check-out 11 am. Indoor pool, whirlpool. **$**

Minot (B-3)

See also Kenmare, Rugby

Settled 1886
Population 34,544
Elevation 1,580 ft
Area Code 701
Zip 58701
Information Convention & Visitors Bureau, 1020 S Broadway, PO Box 2066, 58702; phone 701/857-8206 or toll-free 800/264-2626
Web Site www.visitminot.org

Minot's advance from tepee and tarpaper to a supersonic-age city has been so vigorous that it lays claim to being the "Magic City." Where buffalo bones were once stacked by "plainscombers" stands a city rich from agriculture,

The Little Missouri Badlands

Medora sits at the base of the dramatic Little Missouri Badlands, a deeply eroded gorge that exposes hundreds of millions of years of sedimentary deposits in colorful horizontal striations. Medora itself is a fascinating historical town: Teddy Roosevelt lived near here in the 1880s, as did the flamboyant Marquis de Mores, a French nobleman who journeyed to Dakota Territory to live out his cowboy fantasies. Before setting out to explore bluffs that rise behind the town, be sure to visit the Chateau de More, the luxurious frontier home built by the Marquis. When it was built in 1883, this 26-room mansion was the finest and most modern private home for hundreds of miles.

The Maah Daah Hey Trail is 100 miles long and connects the northern and southern sections of the Theodore Roosevelt National Park, passing through the Little Missouri National Grassland. The following hike covers 4.5 miles at the trail's southern extreme and explores the scenic badlands above Medora, passing through the fascinating and ruggedly beautiful badlands ecosystem, home to prairie wildlife including pronghorn antelope, coyotes, white-tail deer, prairie dogs, and

rattlesnakes. This section of the Maah Daah Hey Trail makes a wonderful -day hike for fit hikers.

Begin the hike at Sully Creek State Park, 2 miles south of Medora (the Maah Daah Hey Trail is also popular with mountain bikers, so be aware that you'll share the trail). The trail crosses the Little Missouri River, which is ankle-deep and easily waded in summer, and follows the river valley through stands of cottonwood, willow, and silver sage. The trail then begins to climb up the face of a badland mesa, eventually reaching a plateau. From a rocky escarpment, enjoy a magnificent overlook onto Medora nestled in the Little Missouri River breaks. Continue north on the trail through prairie grassland to a side path, the Canyon Trail, which drops steeply down a rugged canyon wall to a prairie dog town. Follow the trail north, through a self-closing gate, to where the Canyon Trail rejoins the Maah Daah Hey. From here, hikers have a choice of returning to Medora along a gravel road or continuing north through more badlands landscape to the South Unit of the Theodore Roosevelt National Park headquarters.

lignite coal reserves, oil pools, industries, and railroad yards on both sides of the Mouse River. Minot is the commercial center of a radius that sweeps into Canada. Minot State University is located here.

What to See and Do

Minot AFB. *201 Summit Dr, Minot (58705). 13 miles N on Hwy 83. Phone 701/723-6212.* Air Combat Command base for B-52 bombers, UH-1 helicopters, and Minuteman III missiles under 91st Space Wing. **FREE**

Oak Park. *4th Ave NW between 10th and 16th sts NW, Minot.* Heated swimming pool, wading pool, bathhouse, lifeguards (fee; schedule same as Roosevelt Park); exercise trail; picnicking, playground, fireplaces. Park (daily). **FREE**

Roosevelt Park and Zoo. *1219 Burdick Expy E, Minot (58701). Phone 701/857-4166.* Includes 90 acres of formal lawns and sunken gardens. On the grounds are a swimming pool, water slide, and bathhouse, lifeguards on duty (late May-early Sept, daily; fee). Also in the park are picnic facilities, playgrounds, tennis courts, mini train (fee), carousel (fee), a bandshell, and a 28-acre zoo (May-Sept, daily; fee). Park (daily).

Scandinavian Heritage Center. *Broadway and 11th Ave, Minot (58701). Phone 701/852-9161.* A 220-year-old house from Sigdal, Norway; Danish windmill; flag display; statues of famous people. (Daily; Memorial Day-Labor Day, weekends)

Upper Souris National Wildlife Refuge. *17705 212th Ave NW, Berthold (58718). Refuge headquarters are 7 miles N of Foxholm. 18 miles NW on Hwy 52 to Foxholm, then continue 7 miles N, or travel 15 miles N on Hwy 83, then 12 miles W on County 6. Phone 701/468-5467.* Lake Darling, a 20-mile lake within the refuge, is home to more than 290 species of birds. Ice fishing and open-water fishing for walleye, northern pike, smallmouth bass, and perch in designated areas, boat and bank fishing in summer, canoe areas; picnic facilities, 3-mile auto tour route, hiking trails. **FREE**

Ward County Historical Society Museum and Pioneer Village. *State Fairgrounds, 2505 Burdick Expy E, Minot (58701). Phone 701/839-0785.* First county courthouse, early schoolhouse, depot, blacksmith shop, pioneer cabin, church, and ten-room house, barbershop, dental parlor; museum with antiques. (May-Sept, limited hours; also by appointment) **$**

Special Events

Norsk Hostfest. *All Seasons Arena, 1020 S Broadway, Minot (58702). Phone 701/852-2368* Norwegian folk festival. Mid-Oct.

North Dakota State Fair. *State Fairgrounds, 2005 Burdick Expy E, Minot (58702). Phone 701/857-7620. www.ndstatefair.com.* State Fairgrounds. 4-H, livestock, commercial exhibits; horse and tractor pulls, carnival, machinery show, concerts, auto races, demolition derby. Early July.

Limited-Service Hotels

★ **BEST WESTERN KELLY INN.** *1510 26th Ave SW, Minot (58701). Phone 701/852-4300; toll-free 800/735-5868; fax 701/838-1234. www.bestwesternminot .com.* 100 rooms, 2 story. Pets accepted, some restrictions. Complimentary continental breakfast. Check-in 3 pm, check-out 11 am. High-speed Internet access. Indoor pool, whirlpool.**$**

★ **COMFORT INN.** *1515 22nd Ave SW, Minot (58701). Phone 701/852-2201; toll-free 800/228-5150; fax 701/852-2201. www.comfortinn.com.* 140 rooms, 3 story. Pets accepted, some restrictions. Complimentary continental breakfast. Check-out 11 am. Indoor pool, whirlpool.**$**

Full-Service Hotel

★★ **HOLIDAY INN.** *2200 Burdick Expy E, Minot (58701). Phone 800/468-9968; toll-free 800/468-9968; fax 701/852-2630. www.holiday-inn.com.* 172 rooms, 7 story. Pets accepted, some restrictions. Check-in 3 pm, check-out noon. High-speed Internet access. Two restaurants, two bars. Fitness room. Indoor pool, whirlpool.**$**

Rugby (B-4)

See also Minot

Founded 1886
Population 2,909
Elevation 1,545 ft
Area Code 701
Zip 58368
Information Chamber of Commerce & Convention Visitor Bureau, 224 Hwy 2 SW; phone 701/776-5846

Web Site www.rugbynorthkdakota.com

The geographical center of North America has been located by the US Geological Survey as 1/2 mile south of Rugby. The location is marked by a monument.

What to See and Do

Geographical Museum and Pioneer Village. *102 Hwy 2 SE, Rugby (58368). Phone 701/776-6414.* A rather unusual museum featuring 27 buildings from Pierce County and the surrounding area. Each building is furnished with materials from the period when it was in use. Gun collections, displays of farm implements, dolls, and glass items. (May-Sept, daily) **$$**

Theodore Roosevelt National Park (B-1)

The 70,447 scenic acres of spectacular badlands that compose this park are the state's foremost tourist attraction. This national park is a monument to Theodore Roosevelt, who, in addition to all of his other vigorous pursuits, was the nation's champion of conservation of natural resources. Roosevelt, who came to the badlands in September 1883 to hunt buffalo and other big game, became interested in the open-range cattle industry and purchased interest in the Maltese Cross Ranch near Medora (see). He returned the next year and established another ranch, the Elkhorn, about 35 miles north of Medora. The demands of his political career and losses in cattle production eventually forced him to abandon his ranching ventures.

The park preserves the landscape as Roosevelt knew it. General Sully, during his campaign against the Sioux in 1864, described it as "hell with the fires out... grand, dismal, and majestic." Wind and water have carved from a thick series of flat-lying sedimentary rocks, curiously sculptured formations, tablelands, buttes, canyons, and rugged hills. Exposed in eroded hillsides are thick, dark layers of lignite coal that sometimes are fired by lightning and burn slowly for many years, often baking adjacent clay layers into a red, brick-like substance called scoria, or clinker.

Many forms of wildlife inhabit the area. Elk and bison have been reintroduced here and may be seen by visitors. There are several large prairie dog towns; mule and whitetail deer are abundant; wild horses can be seen in the South Unit; and the area is rich in bird life including hawks, falcons, eagles, and other more common species.

The park is divided into three units: the South Unit is accessible from I-94 at Medora, where there is a visitor center (daily) and Roosevelt's Maltese Cross cabin; the Elkhorn Ranch Site on the Little Missouri River can be reached only by rough dirt roads, and visitors should first obtain current information from rangers at the Medora Visitor Center, phone 701/623-4466, before attempting the trip; the North Unit is accessible from US 85, near Watford City, and this unit also has a visitor center. An additional visitor center is located at Painted Canyon Scenic Overlook on I-94 (April-October, daily). There are self-guided trails, picnic areas, camping (standard fees, daily), and evening campfire programs in both the North and South Units (June-mid-September). The park is open all year (fee). Visitor centers are closed January 1, Thanksgiving, December 25. Golden Eagle and Golden Age passports are accepted (see MAKING THE MOST OF YOUR TRIP).

Valley City (C-5)

See also Jamestown

Settled 1872
Population 7,163
Elevation 1,222 ft
Area Code 701
Zip 58072
Information Valley City Area Chamber of Commerce, 205 NE 2nd St, PO Box 724; phone 701/845-1891
Web Site www.hellovalley.com

The railroad and the first settlers arrived here simultaneously to establish a community then known as Worthington. Later, as the seat of Barnes County, the town in the deeply forested Sheyenne River Valley changed to its present name. The grain fields and dairy farms of the surrounding area provide the basis of its economy.

What to See and Do

Baldhill Dam and Lake Ashtabula. *11 miles NW on county rd. Phone 701/845-2970.* Impounds Sheyenne River and Baldhill Creek in water supply project, creating 27-mile-long Lake Ashtabula; eight recreational areas. Swimming, water-skiing, fishing, boating (ramps); picnicking (shelters), concessions, camping (hookups; fee). Fish hatchery. (May-Oct)

Clausen Springs Park. *4 miles W on I-94, then 16 miles S on Hwy 1, then 1 mile E, 1/2 mile S following signs.* A 400-

acre park with a 50-acre lake. Fishing, canoes, boating (electric motors only); nature trails, bicycling, picnicking, playground, camping, tent and trailer sites (electric hookups, fee). (May-Oct, daily)

Fort Ransom State Park. *5981 Walt Hjelle Pkwy, Fort Ransom (58033). Phone 701/973-4331; toll-free 800/807-4723. www.ndparks.com/Parks/frsp.htm.* Former frontier Army post. The park also preserves a historic farm that re-creates the life of early Minnesota homesteaders. Sodbuster Days festival is held the second weekends in July and Sept. Arts and crafts festival is the last weekend in Sept. Downhill ski resort. Camping, picnic areas, Hiking, cross-country skiing, and snowmobiling.

Little Yellowstone Park. *4 miles W on I-94, then 19 miles S on Hwy 1, then 6 miles E off Hwy 46.* Picnicking, camping (electric hookups, fee) in sheltered portion of rugged Sheyenne River Valley; fireplaces, shelters, rustic bridges. (May-Oct, daily)

Valley City State University. *101 College St SW, Valley City (58072). S side of town. Phone 701/845-7101. www.vcsu. edu.* (1890) (1,100 students) Teacher education, business, computer information systems, liberal arts. Planetarium, Medicine Wheel Park on campus. Campus tours.

Special Event

Dakota Soap Box Derby. *Phone 701/845-1891.* Two-day downhill gravity race. First weekend in June.

Limited-Service Hotel

★ **WAGON WHEELS INN.** *455 Winter Show Rd, Valley City (58072). Phone 701/845-5333.* 88 rooms, 1 story. Indoor pool, whirlpool. **$**
☒

Restaurant

★ **DUTTON'S PARLOUR.** *256 Central Ave N, Valley City (58072). Phone 701/845-3390.* Located in downtown Valley City, this turn-of-the-century ice-cream parlor offers homemade lunch and sandwich items. American menu. Breakfast, lunch. **$**

Wahpeton (D-6)

See also Fargo

Settled 1871

Population 8,751
Elevation 963 ft
Area Code 701
Zip 58075
Information Visitors Center, 118 N 6th St; phone 701/642-8559 or toll-free 800/892-6673
Web Site www.wahpchamber.com

Where the waters of the Bois de Sioux and Otter Tail rivers integrate to become the Red River of the North, Wahpeton, derived from an Indian word meaning "dwellers among the leaves," is situated at the start of the Red River. Wahpeton is the marketplace for a large segment of the southeast corner of the state.

What to See and Do

Chahinkapa Park. *1900 N 4th St, Wahpeton (58074). 1st St and 7th Ave N, on banks of Red River of the North. Phone 701/642-2811.* Chahinkapa Zoo includes petting zoo; many North American animals, several exotic displays, nature center. Restored 1926 **Prairie Rose Carousel** (Memorial Day-Labor Day; fee). Swimming, water slide (fee), trails, basketball, tennis, 18-hole golf, softball; picnicking; camping (fee). **$$**

☒ **Fort Abercrombie State Historic Site.** *20 miles N, 1/2 mile E off Hwy 81. Phone 701/553-8513.* The first federal military post in the state, rebuilt on authentic lines; blockhouses, guardhouse, stockade. Built on the west bank of the Red River, the fort regulated fur trade, kept peace between the Chippewa and the Sioux, and served as a gateway through which wagon trains, stagecoaches, and Army units moved west. Established in 1858, abandoned in 1859, reoccupied in 1860 and moved to present site, repelled a six-week siege in 1862, and abandoned in 1877. A museum interprets the history of the fort; displays of relics and early settlers' possessions (mid-May-mid-Sept, daily; fee). Picnicking. **FREE**

Kidder Recreation Area. *4th Stand 18 1/2 Ave N, Wahpeton (58075). Phone 701/642-2811.* Fishing, boating (docks, ramp); picnicking. **FREE**

Richland County Historical Museum. *11 7th Ave N, Wahpeton (58075). 2nd St and 7th Ave N. Phone 701/642-3075.* Pioneer artifacts trace county's history; display of Rosemeade pottery. (Apr-Nov, limited hours) **FREE**

Special Event

Carousel Day. *Phone 701/642-8709.* Second weekend in June.

Williston (D-6)

See also Fargo

Settled 1870
Population 13,131
Elevation 1,880 ft
Area Code 701
Zip 58801
Information Convention & Visitors Bureau, 10 Main St; phone 701/774-9041 or toll-free 800/615-9041
Web Site www.willistonndtourism.com

The city, which was first called "Little Muddy, has grown from its origin as a small supply center for ranchers. As the area populated, the production of grains became an important business. The refining of high-grade petroleum has also had a major effect on the local economy since it was discovered in the early 1950s. Today, Williston is a trading center for some 90,000 people.

What to See and Do

Buffalo Trails Museum. *Main St, Epping (58843). 6 miles N on Hwy 2, 85, then 13 miles E on County Rd 6. Phone 701/859-4361.* Seven-building complex with dioramas of Native American and pioneer life; fossils; interior of homesteader's shack; regional historical exhibits. (June-Aug, daily; Sept-Oct, Sun only; other days and May by appointment) **$**

Fort Buford State Historic Site. *15349 39th Ln NW, Williston (58801). 7 miles W on Hwy 2, then 17 miles SW on Hwy 1804. Phone 701/572-9034.* Established near the confluence of the Missouri and Yellowstone rivers in 1866, Fort Buford served primarily as the distribution point for government annuities to peaceful natives in the vicinity. During the war with the Sioux in the 1870s and 1880s, the post became a major supply depot for military field operations. The fort is perhaps best remembered as the site of the surrender of Sitting Bull in 1881. Original features still existing on the site include a stone powder magazine, the post cemetery, and a museum. Picnicking. Interpretive center. (Mid-May-mid-Sept, daily; rest of year, by appointment) **$$**

Fort Union Trading Post National Historic Site. *15550 Hwy 1804, Williston (58801). 7 miles W on Hwy 2, then SW on Hwy 1804 W. Phone 701/572-9083. www.nps.gov/fous.* The American Fur Company built this fort in 1829 at the confluence of the Yellowstone and Missouri rivers. During the next three decades, it was one of the most important trading depots on the western frontier. In 1867, the government bought the fort, dismantled it, and used the materials to build Fort Buford 2 miles away. Much of the fort has been reconstructed. A National Park Service visitor center is located in the Bourgeois House. Guided tours and interpretive programs are available in summer. Site (daily). **FREE**

Lewis and Clark State Park. *4904 119th Rd NW, Williston (58843). 19 miles SE off Hwy 1804. Phone 701/859-3071. www.ndparks.com/parks/lcsp.htm.* Situated on a northern bay in Lake Sakakaweaa man-made body of water created by damming the Missouri River--this state park is so named because the Lewis and Clark expedition camped nearby twice, on their 1805 westward journey in search of the fabled Northwest Passage and on the return trip east the next year. Today, the park is popular primarily because of its good marina, a jumping-off point for boaters and anglers. (The latter even flock here in winter when the surface is frozen.) Of the fish lurking below, the most remarkable are immense paddlefish, prehistoric-looking beasts once thought to be extinct, and endangered pallid sturgeon, which grow up to 6 feet in length. The wildlife on land, including deer, badgers, porcupines, and a diverse bird population, is also notable. A good trail system allows for hiking and cross-country skiing; rental cabins and a large campground round out the facilities. **$**

Lewis and Clark Trail Museum. *Hwy 85, Alexander (58831). 19 miles S on Hwy 85. Phone 701/828-3595.* Located on the first leg of the Corps of Discovery's westward route (south of Williston and the Missouri River in Alexander), this museum covers not only Lewis and Clark but also early homesteaders in North Dakota. The most notable exhibit is a scale model of Fort Mandan, where the party stayed during the winter of 1804-1805. (Memorial Day-Labor Day, daily) **$**

Spring Lake Park. *3 miles N on Hwy 2, 85.* Landscaped park area, lagoons. Picnicking. (Daily) **FREE**

Special Events

Fort Buford 6th Infantry State Historical Encampment. *Phone 701/572-9034.* Reenactment of Indian Wars frontier army exercises. July.

Fort Union Trading Post Rendezvous. *15550 Hwy 1804, Williston (58801). Phone 701/572-9083.* Mid-June.

South Dakota

This land was once dominated by the proud and mighty Sioux. They, along with mountain men who trapped for the American Fur Company, the Missouri Fur Company, and the Hudson's Bay Company, slowly gave way to settlers. Today, most Sioux descendants live on nine reservations in South Dakota. Many South Dakota museums and shops display and sell Native American art and artifacts.

Many settlers who came for the free land offered under the Homestead Act of 1862 built sod houses on the prairies; others, who came for gold discovered in 1874, set up gold rush camps in the Black Hills. Three groups of immigrants: Germans, Scandinavians, and Czechs, retain their traditional customs and cookery in their home life. Several colonies of Hutterites prosper in the eastern part of the state.

In South Dakota, human achievements are strikingly contrasted with nature's design. Near the town of Wall are the Badlands, a colorful and spectacular result of eons of erosion. In the Black Hills, the largest sculpture in the world, the Crazy Horse Memorial, is being created. The combination of natural wonders with Native American and frontier legend is a made-to-order attraction for tourists.

The wide-open spaces of eastern and central South Dakota are famous for pheasant and offer some of the finest hunting in the nation. The Missouri River, with its four great lakes, is a paradise for those who love water recreation. Walleye fishing in the area is superlative. Fishing for northern pike is also superb, especially in Lake Oahe, where they often reach trophy size.

Population: 696,004
Area: 75,953 square miles
Elevation: 962-7,242 feet
Peak: Harney Peak (Pennington County, in Black Hills)
Entered Union: November 2, 1889 (40th state, same day as North Dakota)
Capital: Pierre
Motto: Under God, the people rule
Nickname: Mount Rushmore State; Coyote State
Flower: Pasque
Bird: Chinese Ring-Necked Pheasant
Tree: Black Hills Spruce
Fair: August in Huron
Time Zone: Central and Mountain
Web Site: www.travelsd.com
Fun Facts:
- Sculptor Gutzon Borglum began drilling into the 6,200-foot Mount Rushmore in 1927. The creation of the Shrine to Democracy took 14 years and cost a mere $1 million, though it's now deemed priceless.
- With more than 82 miles of mapped passages, Wind Cave contains the world's largest display of a rare formation called boxwork.

Throughout the state, hundreds of markers inform visitors of history or natural phenomena. Many sites of natural, historical, and cultural significance are also preserved in a number of the state parks and recreation areas.

When to Go/Climate

Unpredictable, sometimes erratic weather conditions are common in South Dakota. Summers are hot and humid, although less so than in other Midwestern states. September brings cool temperatures, while winter can get downright frigid, and it has been known to snow as late as May.

Calendar Highlights

June

L. Frank Baum Oz Festival *(Aberdeen).* *At Wylie Park; Phone 605/645-3310 or toll-free 800/645-3851.* Oz characters, storytelling, book memorabilia, educational lectures. Art and food vendors, band concerts.

10K Volksmarch *(Crazy Horse Memorial). Phone 605/673-4681.* Only time mountaintop is open to the public.

July

Corvette Classic *(Spearfish). Main St. Phone 605/336-7140 or 605/642-2626.* Sports car enthusiasts gather each summer for their convention. Highlight is Main Street Show and Shine, when hundreds of Corvettes line Main Street.

Summer Festival *(Brookings). Pioneer Park. Phone 605/692-6125.* Largest arts and crafts festival in the state. Entertainment, food.

August

Central States Fair *(Rapid City). Central States Fairground. Phone 605/355-3861.* Rodeo, carnival, horse and tractor pulls, auto races, demo derby.

South Dakota State Fair *(Huron). Phone 605/353-7340.* Largest farm machinery exhibit in the Midwest. Carnival, entertainment, horse shows, car races, rodeos, livestock.

September

Corn Palace Festival *(Mitchell). Phone Chamber of Commerce, 605/996-5667, 605/996-6223, or toll-free 800/257-2676.* Music and entertainment.

AVERAGE HIGH/LOW TEMPERATURES (F)

Rapid City

Jan 34/11	May 68/42	Sep 74/46
Feb 38/15	Jun 78/52	Oct 63/35
Mar 46/22	Jul 86/58	Nov 47/23
Apr 58/32	Aug 85/56	Dec 36/13

Sioux Falls

Jan 24/3	May 71/46	Sep 73/49
Feb 30/10	Jun 81/56	Oct 61/36
Mar 42/23	Jul 86/62	Nov 43/23
Apr 59/35	Aug 83/59	Dec 28/9

Parks and Recreation

Water-related activities, hiking, riding, various other sports, picnicking and visitor centers, as well as camping, are available in many of South Dakota's parks. Entrance fee (daily). Annual $20/carload permit is good at all state parks and recreation areas or $2/person daily (Custer, $3 May-Oct); under age 12 free. There is a camping fee at most areas ($10-$13/site per night; electricity $3). Cabins (where available) $32/night. All areas open daily. Pets on leash only. For further information, write to the Division of Parks and Recreation, Department of Game, Fish, and Parks, 523 E Capitol Ave, Pierre 57501-3182; phone 605/773-3391. Phone toll-free 800/710-2267 for reservations at parks.

FISHING AND HUNTING

Nonresident: annual fishing license $59; family $59 (allows one limit); visitor's three-day $30; one-day $12; no license required for nonresidents under 16, but fish taken will be counted as part of the string limit of a licensed accompanying adult. Nonresident: big game $155-$205; small game $100 (good for two five-day periods). Nonresident waterfowl license $105 (good for ten consecutive days except in southeast counties); nonresident turkey license $75-$85; nonresident predator license $35.

All nonresident big game firearm licenses are issued through a computer lottery.

Regulations, seasons, and limits for both fish and game vary in different waters and areas of South Dakota. For detailed information, write to the Department of Game, Fish, and Parks, 523 E Capitol Ave, Pierre 57501 or phone 605/773-3485.

Driving Information

Children under 5 years must be in approved child

passenger restraint systems anywhere in a vehicle: ages 2-5 may use regulation safety belts; age 1 and under must use approved safety seats. Phone 605/773-4493.

INTERSTATE HIGHWAY SYSTEM

The following alphabetical listing of South Dakota towns in this book shows that these cities are within 10 miles of the indicated interstate highways. Check highway map for the nearest exit.

Highway Number	Cities/Towns within 10 miles
Interstate 29	Beresford, Brookings, Sioux Falls Sisseton, Vermillion, Watertown.
Interstate 90	Badlands National Park, Belle Fourche, Chamberlain, Deadwood, Mitchell, Murdo, Rapid City, Sioux Falls, Spearfish, Sturgis, Wall.
Interstate 229	Sioux Falls.

BLACK HILLS AND BUFFALO: THE PETER NORBECK SCENIC BYWAY

This route passes through the rugged high country of the Black Hills, an isolated, pine-covered mountain range that rises from the northern prairies. Although the Black Hills look gently domed from a distance, in fact they are highly eroded, with many steep canyons, rocky peaks, and precipitous winding roads.

From Keystone, follow Highway 16A south into the Black Hills, ascending one of the most scenicand challengingroads in the Black Hills. Called the Iron Mountain Road, this road passes over three Pigtail Bridges, trestles that spiral up a mountain slope too steep for traditional switchbacks. The road was also designed so that drivers emerge from the tunnels with Mount Rushmore perfectly framed in the distance. The Norbeck Memorial Overlook, at 6,445 feet, is named for Black Hills conservationist Peter Norbeck and is the highest point reached by paved road in the Black Hills. From here you can take in views that include Mount Rushmore, the granite cliffs and forests of the Black Elk Wilderness, and hundreds of miles of distant prairie.

Continuing south, the route passes into Custer State Park, the star of the South Dakota state park system. Custer State Park is home to the world's largest free-roaming buffalo herd, and hikers are apt to glimpse deer, elk, beaver, coyote, and raptors, as well as hear the trill of songbirds.

At Hermosa junction, continue on Highway 16A west into the park. Stop by the Peter Norbeck Visitors Center for information on hiking and other recreation, and visit the State Game Lodge and Resort, a venerable hotel built in 1920 that served as the Summer White House for President Calvin Coolidge.

Continue west on Highway 16A. Legion Lake, near the junction with Highway 87, has a campground,

swimming beach, picnic area, and rustic lodge. Turn north on Highway 87 to join the Needles Highway, which passes through a maze of spired granite formations that rise above the Black Hill's heavy forest mantle. To carve a road through this precipitous landscape, engineers had to blast tunnels and corkscrew roadbeds down sheer cliffs. Rock climbing is a popular sport along the spires of the Needles formations; watch for brightly clad climbers clambering up the sheer rock faces. Less ambitious visitors can hike one of the many trails in this part of the Black Hills.

Continue north on Highway 87, passing Sylvan Lake, a cliff-lined lake popular for canoeing and swimming. Boat rentals and lodgings are available from the Sylvan Lake Lodge, whose buildings were inspired by Frank Lloyd Wright. From Sylvan Lake, continue north, climbing steeply through more tunnels and up more pigtail switchbacks to the junction with Highway 244 and roll east across the forested uplands. To the south is Mount Harney, which boasts an elevation of 7,242 feet, making it the continent's highest point east of the Rocky Mountains. Whether you first see the crowds and tour buses or the carved busts of past presidents, you'll soon know you're near Mount Rushmore National Monument. Designed by Gutzon Borglum in the 1930s, the 60-feet-high carvings on Mount Rushmore are both more and less than you imagine them to be. Stop at the new visitor center and museum and explore the Presidential Trail, a walking trail and boardwalk that provide spectacular close-up views of the mountain sculpture. From Mount Rushmore, continue east, dropping down the steep switchbacks to Keystone. **(Approximately 70 miles)**

Additional Visitor Information

A state highway map and the annual *South Dakota Vacation Guide* are free from the South Dakota Department of Tourism, 711 E Wells Ave, Pierre 57501-3369; phone toll-free 800/732-5682. A periodical also worth looking at is *South Dakota Conservation Digest,* bimonthly, from South Dakota Department of Game, Fish, and Parks, 445 E Capitol Ave, Pierre 57501.

There are 13 information centers (mid-May-Sept, daily) at rest areas along I-90 near Chamberlain, Tilford, Salem, Spearfish, Valley Springs, Vivian, and Wasta; and along I-29 near New Effington, Vermillion, and Wilmot.

Aberdeen (A-5)

See also Redfield, Webster

Settled 1880
Population 24,927
Elevation 1,304 ft
Area Code 605
Zip 57401
Web Site www.aberdeencvb.com
Information Convention & Visitors Bureau, 514-1/2 S Main St, PO Box 1179, 57402-1179; phone 605/225-2414 or toll-free 800/645-3851

The roots of Aberdeen's commerce are the three railroads that converge here and make it a wholesale and distribution center, giving it the fitting nickname "Hub City." Alexander Mitchell, a railroader of the 19th century, named the town for his Scottish birthplace. German-Russian immigrants arrived in 1884. Hamlin Garland, author of *Son of the Middle Border,* and L. Frank Baum, author of *The Wizard of Oz,* lived here.

What to See and Do

Dacotah Prairie Museum. *21 S Main St*, Aberdeen (57401). *Phone 605/626-7117*. Pioneer and Native American artifacts; area history and art. **Hatterscheidt Wildlife Gallery** features specimens from around the world. (Tues-Sun; closed holidays)**FREE**

Mina State Recreation Area. *37908 Youth Camp Rd, Aberdeen (57401). 11 miles W off Hwy 12. Phone 605/225-5325; toll-free 800/710-2267.* On 300 acres.

Swimming, bathhouses; fishing; boating (ramps, dock). Hiking. Picnicking (shelters), playground. Camping (electrical hookups). Interpretive programs. Standard fees.

Richmond Lake State Recreation Area. *37908 Youth Camp Rd, Aberdeen (57401). 10 miles NW via Hwy 12, County 6, and County 13. Phone 605/225-5325; toll-free 800/710-2267.* On 346 acres. Swimming, bathhouses; fishing; boating (ramps, dock). Hiking. Picnicking (shelters), playground. Camping (electrical hookups). Interpretive program. Standard fees.

Wylie Park. *2202 24th Avenue NW, Aberdeen (57401). 1 mile N on Hwy 281. Phone 605/626-3512.www.aberdeen. sd.us/parks/wylie.html.* A whimsical, kid-focused source of community pride, Wylie Park is best known for its colorful theme parks, Storybook Land and the Land of Oz. Since the early 1970s, thousands of volunteers have collaborated on sculptures, structures, and playthings that sport a fairy-tale theme. (The plan was spurred in part by a famous former resident: L. Frank Baum lived in Aberdeen before he penned *The Wizard of Oz.* Today, the parks feature a train, a carousel, a castle (with a stage that hosts free performances), two mazes, and fanciful creations ranging from Jack and Jill's Hill and Captain Hook's Ship to the Cowardly Lion's Den and Munchkinland. Beyond the theme parks, there is a campground, a man-made lake (with boat rentals), 2 miles of paved trails, a zoo, a mini-golf course, and a water slide. (Late Apr-mid-Oct, daily) **FREE**

Special Events

L. Frank Baum Oz Festival. *Wylie Park, Aberdeen (57401). Phone 605/626-3310; toll-free 800/645-3851.* June.

Pari-mutuel horse racing. *Brown County Fairgrounds, 4450 Brown County 10, Aberdeen (57401). Phone 605/225-2414.* Quarterhorse and Thoroughbred racing. Three weekends in May.

Snow Queen Festival. *Phone 605/225-2414.* Two weekends in Jan.

Limited-Service Hotels

★ ★ **BEST WESTERN RAMKOTA HOTEL.** *1400 NW 8th Ave, Aberdeen (57401). Phone 605/229-4040; toll-free 800/780-7234; fax 605/229-0480.www. ramkota.com.*154 rooms, 2 story. Pets accepted.

Check-in 2 pm, check-out 11 am. Restaurant, bar. Fitness room. Indoor pool, whirlpool. Business center. **$**

★ ★ RAMADA INN & CONVENTION CENTER.

2727 SE 6th Ave, Aberdeen (57401). Phone 605/225-3600; toll-free 800/272-6232; fax 605/225-6704. www. ramada.com. 152 rooms, 2 story. Pets accepted. Complimentary continental breakfast. Check-in 2 pm, check-out noon. High-speed Internet access. Restaurant, bar. Indoor pool, whirlpool. **$**

Restaurant

★ ★ **THE FLAME.** *2 S Main St, Aberdeen (57401). Phone 605/225-2082; fax 605/225-5001.* American menu. Lunch, dinner. Closed Sun; Thanksgiving, Dec 25, Easter. Bar. Children's menu. Casual attire. **$$**

Badlands National Park (C-2)

Web Site www.nps.gov/badl

75 miles E of Rapid City via I-90, Hwy 240.

This fantastic, painted landscape of steep canyons, spires, and razor-edged ridges was made a national monument by President Franklin D. Roosevelt in 1939 and became a national park in 1978. Its stark and simple demonstration of geologic processes has an unusual beauty. Soft clays and sandstones deposited as sediments 26 to 37 million years ago by streams from the Black Hills created vast plains, which were inhabited by the saber-toothed cat, the rhinoceros--like bronto--there, and ancestors of the present-day camel and horse. Their fossilized bones make the area an enormous prehistoric graveyard. Herds of bison, gone for many years, roam the area again. Pronghorn antelope, mule deer, prairie dogs, and Rocky Mountain bighorn sheep can also be seen.

More than 600 feet of volcanic ash and other sediments were laid down. About 500,000 years ago, streams began carving the present structures, leaving gullies and multicolored canyons.

The Ben Reifel Visitor Center, with exhibits and an audiovisual program, is open all year at Cedar Pass (daily; closed Jan 1, Thanksgiving, Dec 25). The Touch Room is open to children of all ages. Evening programs and activities conducted by ranger-naturalists are offered during the summer. Camping is available at Cedar Pass (fee) and Sage Creek (free). The White River Visitor Center, 60 miles southwest of the Ben Reifel Visitor Center, features colorful displays on the history and culture of the Oglala Sioux. Per-vehicle fee; Golden Eagle, Golden Age, and Golden Access Passports are accepted (see MAKING THE MOST OF YOUR TRIP). For further information, contact PO Box 6, Interior 57750; phone 605/433-5361.

Belle Fourche (B-1)

See also Deadwood, Lead, Spearfish, Sturgis

Founded 1890
Population 4,335
Elevation 3,023 ft
Area Code 605
Zip 57717
Information Chamber of Commerce, 415 5th Ave; phone 605/892-2676 or toll-free 888/345-5859
Web Site www.bellefourche.org

Belle Fourche, rich in Western heritage, is a destination for those in search of the West. Cowboys and sheepherders once fought a range war here. Belle Fourche, seat of Butte County, still ships the largest volume of livestock of any town in western South Dakota, Wyoming, or Montana and is the wool-shipping capital of the nation. Industry includes bentonite (industrial clay) mills and mines. However, around July 4 there is little work done, for the Black Hills Roundup, one of the West's outstanding rodeos, keeps the town at fever pitch. The geographical center of the United States, with Alaska included, is marked at a point 20 miles north of Belle Fourche on Highway 85.

What to See and Do

Belle Fourche Reservoir and Orman Dam. *NE of town off Hwy 212.* Recreation on 52-mile shoreline. Swimming, water-skiing, windsurfing. Walleye and northern pike fishing.

Johnny Spaulding Cabin. *4065 Bitter Lakes Rd, Belle Fourche (57717). 801 State St opposite Post Office.* Two-story cabin, built in 1876 and restored. (June-Aug, Mon-Sat) **FREE**

Tri-State Museum. *831 State St, Belle Fourche (57717). Phone 605/892-3705.* Regional and historical exhibits; fossils; dolls. (Mid-May–mid-Sept, daily; closed Labor Day) **FREE**

Special Events

All Car Rally. *7116 Hatchway Rd, off Hwy 190, Belle Fourche (57717). Phone 605/892-2676.* Early June.

Black Hills Roundup. *415 5th Ave, Belle Fourche (57717). Phone 605/892-2676.* Rodeo. For ticket prices and reservations please call. Early July.

Butte County Fair. *17 miles E on Hwy 212. Phone 605/892-2676.* Mid-Aug.

Beresford (D-6)

See also Sioux Falls, Vermillion, Yankton

Population 1,849
Elevation 1,498 ft
Area Code 605
Zip 57004
Information Chamber of Commerce, PO Box 167;
phone 605/763-2021
Web Site www.bmtc.net/~chamber

What to See and Do

Union Grove State Park. *11 miles S off I-29. Phone 605/987-2263.* Approximately 500 acres. Hiking, bridle trails. Picnicking. Camping. Standard fees. **$$**

Black Hills (C-1)

See also Crazy Horse Memorial, Custer, Custer State Park, Deadwood, Hill City, Hot Springs, Jewel Cave National Monument, Keystone, Lead, Mount Rushmore National Memorial, Rapid City, Spearfish, Sturgis, Wind Cave National Park,

Web Site *www.blackhills.com*

Magnificent forests, mountain scenery, ghost towns, Mount Rushmore National Memorial, Harney Peak (highest mountain east of the Rockies), Crazy Horse Memorial, swimming, horseback riding, rodeos, hiking, skiing, and the Black Hills Passion Play make up only a partial list of attractions. Memories of Calamity Jane, Wild Bill Hickock, and Preacher Smith haunt the old Western towns. Bison, deer, elk, coyotes, mountain goats, bighorn sheep, and smaller animals make this area home.

Black Hills National Forest includes 1,247,000 acres--nearly half of the Black Hills. The forest offers 28 campgrounds, 20 picnic grounds, and one winter sports area. Daily fees are charged at most campgrounds. Headquarters are in Custer. For information and a map ($4) of the National Forest write Forest Supervisor, train 2, Box 200, Custer 57730. Two snowmobile trail systems, one in the Bearlodge Mountains and the other in the northern Black Hills, offer 330 miles of some of the best snowmobiling in the nation. There are also 250 miles of hiking, bridle, and mountain biking trails.

There is a whimsical story that explains the formation of the Black Hills. Paul Bunyan had a stove so large that boys with hams strapped to their feet skated on the top to grease it for the famous camp flapjacks. One day when the stove was red hot, "Babe," Paul's favorite blue ox, swallowed it whole and took off. He died of a combination of indigestion and exhaustion. Paul, weeping so copiously his tears eroded out the Badlands, built the Black Hills as a cairn over his old friend.

Geologists, however, state that the Black Hills were formed by a great geologic uplift that pushed a mighty dome of ancient granite up under the sandstone and limestone layers. Water washed away these softer rocks, exposing the granite. This uplift was slow. It may still be going on. The Black Hills offers rich rewards in gold and silver from the famous Homestake and other mines. Pactola Visitor Center, on Highway 385 at Pactola Reservoir, west of Rapid City, has information and interpretive exhibits on Black Hills history, geology, and ecology (Memorial Day–Labor Day).

Brookings (C-6)

See also Huron, Madison, Watertown

Founded 1879
Population 16,270
Elevation 1,623 ft
Area Code 605
Zip 57006
Information Chamber of Commerce/Convention & Visitor Bureau, 2308 E 6th St, PO Box 431; phone 605/692-6125 or toll-free 800/699-6125
Web Site www.brookingssd.com

Research done at South Dakota State University has helped make Brookings the agricultural capital of the state; it has developed diversified farming and the manufacturing of devices for seed cleaning, counting, and planting.

What to See and Do

McCrory Gardens. *2308 6th St E, Brookings (57007).* Twenty acres of formal gardens and 45 acres of arboretum. (Daily) **FREE**

Oakwood Lakes State Park. *46109 202nd St, Bruce(57220). 8 miles N of Brookings on I-29, then 13 miles W on County Rd 6.Phone 605/627-5441.* On 255 acres. Swimming; fishing; boating, canoeing. Hiking. Picnicking, playground. Camping (electrical hookups, dump station). Visitor center (daily). Interpretive program. Standard fees.

South Dakota Art Museum. *1000 Medary Ave, Brookings (57007). Phone 605/688-5423.*Features Harvey Dunn paintings of pioneers, Oscar Howe paintings; Native American arts; South Dakota collection; changing exhibits. (Daily; closed holidays) **DONATION**

South Dakota State University. *NE part of town. Phone 605/688-4541.* (1881) (8,090 students.) McCrory Gardens and South Dakota Arboretum, 65 acres of horticultural gardens includes 15 acres of theme gardens. Guided tours on request. Also on campus is

> **Agricultural Heritage Museum**. *11th St and Medary Ave, Brookings (57006). Phone 605/688-6226.* Displays on the development of South Dakota agriculture. (Daily; closed holidays) **FREE**

Special Event

Summer Art Festival. *Pioneer Park, Brookings (57008). Phone 605/692-6125.* Largest arts and crafts festival in the state. Entertainment, food. Second weekend in July.

Limited-Service Hotel

★ ★ **BROOKINGS INN.***2500 E 6th St, Brookings (57006). Phone 605/692-9471; toll-free 877/831-1562; fax 605/692-5807. www.brookingsinn.net.* 125 rooms, 2 story. Pets accepted, some restrictions. Complimentary continental breakfast. Check-out noon. Restaurant, bar. Fitness room. Indoor pool, whirlpool. Business center.**$**

Restaurant

★ ★ **THE RAM & O'HARE'S.** *327 Main Ave, Brookings (57006). Phone 605/692-2485.* Located in a restored 1920 bank, this downtown local favorite offers three levels of dining. Old area photographs and artifacts fill the walls. American menu. Lunch, dinner. Closed Sun; Thanksgiving, Dec 25, Easter. Bar. Children's menu. Casual attire. **$$**

Chamberlain (C-4)

See also Pine Ridge, Platte, Winner

Population 2,347
Elevation 1,465 ft
Area Code 605
Zip 57325
Information Chamberlain-Oacoma Area Chamber of Commerce, 115 W Lawler; phone 605/734-4416
Web Site www.chamberlainsd.org

This town on the Missouri River is situated in the middle of the state, between corn farms and western cattle ranches.

What to See and Do

Akta Lakota Museum. *N Main St, Chamberlain (57326). On campus of St. Joseph's Indian School (I-90, exit 263). Phone 605/734-3452; toll-free 800/798-3452.* Features large collection of Sioux artifacts and handcrafts, as well as several dioramas that depict daily life on the prairie. Also features large collection of Native American paintings and sculpture. Gift shop carries an extensive selection of books of Native American history and culture, as well as locally made jewelry and art. (Mon-Fri; Memorial Day-Labor Day, daily) **FREE**

American Creek Recreational Area. *Main St, Chamberlain (57325). N end of Main St, Hwy 50. Phone 605/734-5151.* On Lake Francis Case; swimming (May-Oct, fee), sand beaches, water-skiing; fishing; boat docks. Picnicking; camping (Apr-Oct; fee). Park (daily; ranger, Apr-Oct).

Big Bend Dam-Lake Sharpe. *21 miles NW via Hwy 50. Phone 605/245-2255.* One of a series of six dams on the Missouri River built by the US Army Corps of Engineers as units in the "Pick-Sloan Plan" for power production, flood control, and recreation. Guided tours of powerhouse (June-Aug, daily; rest of year, by appointment). Visitor center at dam site (mid-May-mid-Sept, daily). Many recreation areas along reservoir have swimming, fishing; boating (docks, ramps, fee); winter sports; picnicking; camping (May-mid-Sept, fee). **FREE**

Limited-Service Hotels

★ **BEST WESTERN LEE'S MOTOR INN.** *220 W King Ave, Chamberlain (57325). Phone 605/734-5575; toll-free 800/780-7234; fax 605/234-6555. www. bestwestern.com.* 60 rooms, 2 story. Complimentary continental breakfast. Check-out 11 am. Fitness room. Indoor pool, whirlpool. **$**

★ **OASIS KELLY INN.** *1100 E Hwy 16, Oacoma (57365). Phone 605/734-6061; toll-free 800/635-3559; fax 605/734-4161.* 69 rooms, 2 story. Pets accepted, some restrictions. Complimentary continental breakfast. Check-out 11 am. Bar. Indoor pool, whirlpool. Airport transportation available. **$**

Restaurant

★ **AL'S OASIS.** *1-90, exit 260, Oacoma (57365). Phone 605/734-6051; fax 605/734-6927. www.alsoasis. com.* American menu. Breakfast, Lunch, dinner. Closed Jan 1, Thanksgiving, Dec 25, Bar. Children's menu. **$$**

Crazy Horse Memorial (C-1)

See also Custer, Black Hills

Web Site www.crazyhorse.org

Avenue of the Chiefs, Crazy Horse (57730). 5 miles N of Custer off Hwy 16, 385. Phone 605/673-4681.

This large sculpture, still being carved from the granite of Thunderhead Mountain, was the life work of Korczak Ziolkowski (1908-1982), who briefly assisted Gutzon Borglum on Mount Rushmore. With funds gained solely from admission fees and contributions, Ziolkowski worked alone on the memorial, refusing federal and state funding. The work is being continued by the sculptor's wife, Ruth, and several of their children.

The sculpture will depict Crazy Horse—the stalwart Sioux chief who helped defeat Custer and the United States Seventh Cavalry--astride a magnificent horse. It is meant to honor not only Crazy Horse and the unconquerable human spirit, but also all Native American tribes. It is merely a part of what is planned by Ziolkowski's family and the Crazy Horse Memorial Foundation. Near the mountain, Ziolkowski visualized a great Native American center with a museum, medical training center, and university.

Crazy Horse's emerging head and face are nearly nine stories tall. When completed in the round, the mountain carving will be 563 feet high and 641 feet long--the largest sculpture in the world. To date, 8.4 million tons of granite has been blasted off the mountain. Audiovisual programs and displays show how the mountain is being carved.

The Indian Museum of North America is on the grounds and houses some 20,000 artifacts in three wings. A Native American educational and cultural center opened in 1997. The visitor complex also includes the sculptor's log studio/home and workshop filled with sculpture, fine arts, and antiques. A restaurant is open daily (in season). Memorial (dawn-dusk; closed Dec 25).

Special Events

10K Volksmarch. *Crazy Horse Memorial. Phone 605/673-4681.* The only time the mountaintop is open to the public. First full weekend June.

Night blasting. *Crazy Horse Memorial.* Late June and early Sept.

Custer (C-1)

See also Black Hills, Crazy Horse Memorial, Custer State Park, Hill City, Hot Springs, Jewel Cave National Monument, Keystone, Mount Rushmore National Memorial, Rapid City, Wind Cave National Park

Settled 1876
Population 1,741
Elevation 5,318 ft
Area Code 605
Zip 57730
Information Custer County Chamber of Commerce, 615 Washington St; 605/phone 673-2244 or toll-free 800/992-9818
Web Site www.custersd.com

This is where a prospector with Lieutenant Colonel Custer's expedition of 1874 discovered gold, prompting the gold rush of 1875-1876. Main Street was laid out in the 1880s, wide enough for wagons pulled by teams of oxen to make U-turns. Custer is the seat of Custer County, headquarters of the Black Hills National Forest (see BLACK HILLS) and center of an area of great mineral wealth. Gold, quartz, beryl, mica, and gypsum are some of the minerals that are mined in commercial quantities. Lumbering, tourism, and ranching are also important to the economy. Custer is a popular area for winter sports activities.

What to See and Do

Custer County Courthouse Museum. *411 Mount Rushmore Rd, Custer (57730). Phone 605/673-2443.* (1881) Features historical and cultural memorabilia of Custer County. (May-Oct, daily) Also here is

> **1875 Log Cabin.** *Way Park, Custer (57730).* Oldest cabin in the Black Hills. Preserved as a pioneer museum. (Days same as Courthouse Museum)**$**

Flintstones Bedrock City. *Hwys 16 and 385, Custer (57730). Phone 605/673-4079.* Adventures with the modern stone-age family: Fred, Wilma, Barney, Betty, Pebbles, Bamm Bamm and Dino. Village tour; train ride; concessions. Campground. (Mid-May-mid-Sept, daily) **$$$**

Golden Circle Tours. *1 mile E on Hwy 16A, Custer (57730). Phone 605/673-4349.* Mini-bus tours of the area. (May-Sept, daily) **$$$$**

Mountain Music Show. *Flintstone Theater, 1160 Camino Cruz Blanca, Custer (57730). 3 miles N on Hwy 16, 385. Phone 605/673-2405.* Country music show with comedy; family entertainment. (Late May-Labor Day, daily) **$$$**

National Museum of Woodcarving. *Hwy 16 W, Custer (57730) 2 miles W on Hwy 16. Phone 605/673-4404.* Features woodcarvings by an original Disney animator and other professional woodcarvers; Wooden Nickel Theater, museum gallery, carving area, and snack bar. (May-Oct, daily)

Special Event

Gold Discovery Days. *Phone 605/673-2244.* Pageant of Paha Sapa, festival, carnival, parade, balloon rally. Late July.

Limited-Service Hotels

★**BAVARIAN INN.** *Hwy 16 and 385 N, Custer (57730). Phone 605/673-2802; toll-free 800/657-4312; fax 605/673-4777. www.bavarianinnsd.com.* 65 rooms, 2 story. Closed Dec-Feb. Pets accepted; fee. Complimentary continental breakfast. Check-in 2 pm, check-out noon. Indoor pool, outdoor pool, whirlpool.**$**

★★**STATE GAME LODGE.** *Hwy 16A, Custer (57730). Phone 605/255-4541; toll-free 800/658-3530; fax 605/255-4706. www.custerresorts.com.* 68 rooms, 3 story. Closed Oct-Apr. Pets accepted, some restrictions; fee. Check-in 2 pm, check-out 10 am. Restaurant, bar.**$**

★★**SYLVAN LAKE RESORT.** *Needles Hwy and Harney Peak, Custer (57730). Phone 605/574-2561; toll-free 800/658-3530; fax 605/574-4943. www.custerresorts.com.* 33 rooms, 3 story. Closed Nov-Apr, Pets accepted, some restrictions; fee. Check-in 2 pm, check-out 10 am. Restaurant.**$**

Specialty Lodging

CUSTER MANSION BED & BREAKFAST. *35 Centennial Dr, Custer (57730). Phone 605/673-3333; toll-free 877/519-4948; fax 605/673-6696. www.custermansionbb.com.* 6 rooms, 2 story. Complimentary full breakfast. Check-in 3-7 pm. Check-out 11 am.**$**

Restaurant

★ **ELK CANYON STEAKHOUSE.** *511 Mount Rushmore Rd, Custer (57730). Phone 605/673-4477; fax 605/673-2997.* Steak menu. Breakfast, lunch, dinner, brunch. Bar. Children's menu. Casual attire. **$$**

Custer State Park (C-1)

See also Black Hills, Custer, Hot Springs, Keystone

Web Site www.custerstatepark.info

5 miles E on Hwy 16A. Phone 605/255-4141.

This is one of the largest state parks in the United States—73,000 acres. A mountain recreation area and game refuge, the park has one of the largest publically owned herds of bison in the country (more than 1,400), as well as Rocky Mountain bighorn sheep, mountain goats, burros, deer, elk, and other wildlife. Four man-made lakes and three streams provide excellent fishing and swimming. Near the park is the site of the original gold strike of 1874 and replica of the Gordon stockade, built by the first gold rush party in 1874.

Peter Norbeck Visitor Center (May-Oct, daily) has information about the park and naturalist programs, which are offered daily (May-Sept). Paddleboats; horseback riding, hiking, bicycle rentals, Jeep rides, camping, hayrides, chuchkwagon cookouts. A park entrance license is required. Per vehicle $10 or per person $5.

The Black Hills Playhouse, in the heart of the park, is the scene of productions for 11 weeks (mid-June-late Aug, schedule varies)

Deadwood (B-1)

See also Belle Fourche, Black Hills, Hill City, Lead, Rapid City, Spearfish, Sturgis,

Population 1,830
Elevation 4,537 ft
Area Code 605
Zip 57732
Information Deadwood Area Chamber of Commerce & Visitors Bureau, 735 Main St; phone 605/578-1876 or toll-free 800/999-1876
Web Site www.deadwood.org

This town is best known for gold and such Wild West characters as Calamity Jane, Preacher Smith, and Wild Bill Hickock. The main street runs through Deadwood Gulch; the rest of the town crawls up the steep canyon sides. A bust of Hickock by Korczak Ziolkowski--creator of the Crazy Horse Memorial--stands on Sherman Street. At the height of the 1876 gold rush, 25,000 people swarmed over the hillsides to dig gold. When gold was first struck at Deadwood, nearly the entire population of Custer rushed to Deadwood; predictably, at the height of a newer strike, nearly the entire population of Deadwood rushed to the town of Lead. Recently legalized gambling has given Deadwood another boom.

The Nemo Ranger District office of the Black Hills National Forest (see BLACK HILLS) is located in Deadwood.

What to See and Do

Adams Museum. *Sherman and Deadwood sts, Deadwood (57732). Phone 605/578-1714.* Exhibits of local interest. (May-Sept, daily; rest of year, Mon-Sat) **FREE**

Boot Hill Tours. *Departs from cafe at center of Main St. Deadwood (57732). Phone 605/578-3758.* One-hour narrated open-air bus tours through historic Deadwood and Mount Moriah Cemetery ("Boot Hill"). Visit graves of Wild Bill Hickock and Calamity Jane. Reservations required for groups. (June-early Oct, daily)**$$$**

Broken Boot Gold Mine. *1200 Main St, Deadwood (57732). S edge of town on Hwy 14A. Phone 605/578-9997.* See how gold was mined in the historic gold camp days; underground guided tour. (Mid-May-mid-Sept, daily) **$$**

Casino gambling. *On historic Main St, Deadwood (57732).* Most facilities have dining and lodging available. **First Gold Hotel,** 270 Main St, phone 605/578-9777 or toll-free 800/274-1876; **Four Aces,** 531 Main St, phone toll-free 800/834-4384; **Gold Dust,** 688 Main St, phone 605/578-2100 or toll-free 800/456-0533; **Historic Franklin Hotel,** 700 Main St, phone 605/578-2241 or toll-free 800/688-1876; **Midnight Star,** 677 Main St, phone toll-free 800/999-6482; **Miss Kitty's,** 649 Main St, phone 605/578-1811; **Silverado,** 709 Main St, phone 800/584-7005; **Wild West Winners Club,** 622 Main St, phone 605/578-1100 or toll-free 800/500-7711.

Mount Moriah Cemetery. "Boot Hill" of Deadwood. Graves of Wild Bill Hickock, Calamity Jane, Preacher Smith, Seth Bullock, and others.

Old Style Saloon #10. *57 Main St, Deadwood (57732). Phone 605/578-3346.* Collection of Western artifacts, pictures, guns; this is the saloon in which Wild Bill Hickock was shot. Entertainment (four shows per day, Memorial Day-Labor Day), gambling, refreshments, restaurant. (Daily; closed Dec 25) **FREE**

Original Deadwood Tour. *677 Main St, Deadwood (57732). Departs from Midnight Star. Phone 605/578-2091.* One-hour narrated open-air bus tours through historic Deadwood and "Boot Hill." Reservations recommended. (May-late Sept, daily) **$$$**

Special Events

Days of '76. *Rodeo at Amusement Park, Deadwood (57732). Phone toll-free 800/999-1876.* 1 mile N. Historic parade down Main Street; reenactment of early days. Last weekend in July.

Deadwood Jam. *Deadwood (57732). Phone toll-free 800/999-1876.* Free concert and entertainment. Second week in Sept.

Ghosts of Deadwood Gulch Wax Museum. *Old Town Hall, Lee and Sherman sts, Deadwood (57732). Phone 605/578-1714.* Old Town Hall. Audiovisual tour of more than 70 life-size wax figures depicting 19 historic episodes in the settling of the Dakota Territory. Daily. Mid-May-Sept.

Kool Deadwood Nites. *Deadwood (57732). Phone toll-free 800/999-1876.* Free concert, show, adult prom. Third week in Aug.

Trial of Jack McCall. *Old Town Hall, Lee and Sherman sts, Deadwood (57732).* Reenactment of McCall's capture and trial for killing Wild Bill Hickock. June-Aug.

Limited-Service Hotel

★ ★ **BULLOCK HOTEL & CASINO.** *633 Main St, Deadwood (57732). Phone 605/578-1745; toll-free 800/336-1876; fax 605/578-1382. www.bullockhotel. com.* 28 rooms, 3 story. Check-in 3 pm, check-out 11 am. High-speed Internet access. Restaurant, bar. Fitness room. Casino. **$**

🕴

Restaurant

★ ★ ★ **JAKE'S ATOP THE MIDNIGHT STAR.** *677 Main St, Deadwood (57732). Phone 605/578-1555; toll-free 800/999-6482; fax 605/578-2739. www. themidnightstar.com.* Located on the top floor of the

Midnight Star Casino, this elegant dining room serves American favorites. Piano entertainment is provided five nights a week. American menu. Dinner. Closed Dec 24. Bar. Children's menu. Casual attire. Reservations recommended. **$$**

Hill City

See also Black Hills, Custer, Custer State Park, Deadwood, Jewel Cave National Monument, Keystone, Mount Rushmore National Memorial, Rapid City, Wind Cave National Park,

Settled 1876
Population 650
Elevation 4,979 ft
Area Code 605
Zip 57745
Information Chamber of Commerce, 324 Main St; **phone** 605/574-2368 or toll-free 800/888-1798
Web Site www.hillcitysd.com

Hill City is a beautiful mountain town in the heart of the Black Hills. The Black Hills Institute of Geological Research and a Ranger District office of the Black Hills National Forest (see BLACK HILLS) are located here.

What to See and Do

1880 Train. *Hill City Depot, 222 Railroad Ave, Hill City (57745). Phone 605/574-2222.* Steam train runs on gold rush era track; vintage railroad equipment. Two-hour round trip between Hill City and Keystone through national forest, mountain meadowlands. Vintage car restaurant, gift shop. (Mid-May-mid-Oct, daily) **$$$$**

Recreation areas. *In Black Hills National Forest.* **Sheridan Lake.** 4 miles NE on Hwy 16, then 2 miles NE on Hwy 385. Swimming beaches. **Pactola Lake.** 4 miles NE on Hwy 16, then 12 1/2 miles NE off Hwy 385. Both areas offer fishing; boating (ramps, rental). Picnicking; camping supplies, grocery. Tent and trailer sites (fee). Visitor center (Memorial Day-Sept, daily). **Deerfield Lake.** 16 miles NW on Forest Highway. Fishing; waveless boating only (ramps). Picnicking. Camping (fee). Contact Forest Supervisor, train 2, Box 200, Custer 57730.

Wade's Gold Mill. *12401 Deerfield Rd, Hill City (57745). 3/4 miles NW. Phone 605/574-2680.* Authentic mill showing four methods of recovering gold. Panning for gold (fee). (Memorial Day-Labor Day, daily)

Special Event

Heart of the Hills Celebration. *Phone 605/574-2368.* Parade, barbecue, timber and logging show. Third weekend in June.

Limited-Service Hotel

★ ★ **BEST WESTERN GOLDEN SPIKE INN & SUITES.** *106 Main St (Hwy 16, 385), Hill City (57745). Phone 605/574-2577; toll-free 800/780-7234; fax 605/574-4719. www.bestwesterngoldenspike.com.* 87 rooms, 2 story. Closed mid-Nov-mid-Mar. Pets accepted; fee. Check-in 4 pm, check-out 11 am. Restaurant. Fitness room. Indoor pool, outdoor pool, whirlpool. **$**

Restaurant

★ ★ **ALPINE INN.** *225 Main St, Hill City (57745). Phone 605/574-2749.* American, German menu. Lunch, dinner. Closed Sun; Jan 1, Thanksgiving, Dec 25. Casual attire. **$**

Hot Springs (D-1)

See also Black Hills, Custer, Custer State Park, Keystone, Pine Ridge, Wind Cave National Park

Settled 1879
Population 4,325
Elevation 3,464 ft
Area Code 605
Zip 57747
Information Chamber of Commerce, 801 S 6th St;
phone 605/745-4140 or toll-free 800/325-6991
Web Site www.hotsprings-sd.com

Hot Springs, seat of Fall River County, is on the southeast edge of Black Hills National Forest. Many local buildings are of pink, red, and buff sandstone. A Ranger District office of the Nebraska National Forest is located here.

What to See and Do

Angostura Reservoir State Recreation Area. *10 miles SE off Hwy 18., Hot Springs (57747). Phone 605/745-*
6996. On 1,480 acres. Swimming; fishing; boating, canoeing. Hiking. Picnicking, concession, lodging. Camping nearby. Interpretive program.

Black Hills Wild Horse Sanctuary. *Rocky Ford Rd, Hot Springs (57747). 13 miles S. Phone 605/745-5955; toll-free 800/252-6652. www.gwtc.net/~iram.* Nestled between the Black Hills and Hell Canyon, the Wild Horse Sanctuary provides a home for wild horses, which were threatened with annihilation before 1970s protection led to a population boom that pressured the horses' habitat to its limits. Established in 1988 and managed by IRAM (Institute of the Range and the American Mustang), the unspoiled 11,000-acre sanctuary now supports a population of about 400 free-roaming mustangs. Guided tours are available; a picnic area and gift shop are on-site. (Apr-Oct, daily; rest of year by reservation only) **$$$$**

Evans Plunge. *1145 N River St, Hot Springs (57747). N edge of town on Hwy 385. Phone 605/745-5165.* Large indoor, natural warm water pool. Also health club with sauna, steam bath, spas and exercise equipment; indoor water slides. Outdoor pool with water slide open during summer months. (Daily; closed Dec 25) **$$$**

Fall River County Museum. *300 N Chicago St, Hot Springs (57747). Phone 605/745-5147.* Artifacts and memorabilia documenting history of Black Hills. In former school (1893). (Memorial Day-Labor Day, Mon-Sat) **FREE**

⭐ **Historic District.** *Near town center.* Thirty-nine Richardsonian-Romanesque buildings, constructed of locally quarried sandstone. Architectural guide, narrated tours available at the Chamber of Commerce. **FREE**

Hot Springs Historic District. *River St, Hot Springs (57747).* The presence of underground springs catalyzed the development of Hot Springs in the 1880s, with River Street being the initial epicenter of the boom. In all, the district includes 130 buildings on more than 3,000 acres, including 39 impressive Richardsonian-Romanesque specimens made of locally quarried sandstone. Several are occupied by spas fed by the springs; others house eateries and art galleries.

⭐ **Mammoth Site of Hot Springs.** *Southern city limits on Hwy 18 truck bypass. Hot Springs (57747). Phone 605/745-6017.* Excavation of a remarkable concentration of mammoth skeletons; to date the remains of 51 mammoths, a camel, and a giant short-faced bear have been unearthed. (Daily)**$$$**

Huron (C-5)

See also Brookings, Mitchell

Founded 1879
Population 12,448
Elevation 1,275 ft
Area Code 605
Zip 57350
Information Huron Convention & Visitors Bureau, 15 4th St SW; phone 605/352-0000 or toll-free 800/487-6673
Web Site www.huronsd.com

Huron, seat of Beadle County, is also the administrative center for a number of federal and state agencies. It is a trade and farm products processing center for a 10,500-square-mile area. Twelve city parks feature swimming, picnicking, golf, tennis, and ballfields. The area offers excellent northern and walleye fishing, and good pheasant hunting brings enthusiasts here when the season opens in mid-October.

What to See and Do

Centennial Center. *48 4th St SE, Huron (57350). Phone 605/352-1442.*Gothic stone structure (1887) houses state centennial memorabilia, Native American artifacts, railroad items, and memoirs of Hubert and Muriel Humphrey. (Mon-Fri, afternoons; also by appointment)

Dakotaland Museum. *8 blocks W on Hwy 14 at State Fairgrounds. Phone 605/352-4626.*Pioneer exhibits, log cabin. (Memorial Day-Labor Day, Mon-Fri) **$**

Gladys Pyle Historic Home. *376 Idaho Ave SE, Huron (57350). Phone 605/352-2528.* (1894) This Queen Anne-style house was the residence of the first elected female US senator. Stained glass, carved woodwork, original furnishings. (Daily, afternoons only) **$**

Hubert H. Humphrey Drugstore. *233 Dakota S, Huron (57350). Phone 605/352-4064.* Mid-1930s atmosphere; owned by the former senator and vice-president until his death; still owned by Humphrey family. (Mon-Sat) **FREE**

Laura Ingalls Wilder Home. *105 Olivet Ave, De Smet (57231). Phone 605/854-3383. www.lauraingallswilder. com.* Laura Ingalls Wilder and her family lived in these houses 1887-1928, and they figure into her book *Little Town on the Prairie.* Tours are offered of the two houses, and interested visitors can follow a self-guided tour of 16 other De Smet sites mentioned by Ingalls in her books. (Daily)**$$**

Laura Ingalls Wilder Memorial. *105 Olivet Ave, De Smet (57231). Phone 605/854-3383. www.laura ingallswilder.com.* Laura Ingalls Wilder wrote a series of children's books based on her childhood experiences in De Smet. Here are restored surveyors' house, the family home from 1879-1880; original family home (1887); replica of period schoolhouse; memorabilia; many other sites and buildings mentioned in her books. Guided tours (daily).**$$$**

Special Events

Laura Ingalls Wilder Pageant. *De Smet (57231). Phone toll-free 800/776-3594.* Last weekend in June and first two weekends in July. **$$**

Parade of Lights. *Huron (57350). Phone 605/352-0000.* Day after Thanksgiving.

South Dakota State Fair. *State Fairgrounds, 890 3rd St SW, Huron (57350). W on Hwy 14, at 3rd St SW and Nevada Ave SW. Phone 605/353-7340.* Early Aug.

State Fair Speedway. *Hwy 14 W, Huron (57350). Phone 605/352-4848.* South Dakota's largest racing program. Late Apr-early Sept.

Limited-Service Hotel

★ ★ **CROSSROADS HOTEL & CONVENTION CENTER.** *100 4th St SW, Huron (57350). Phone 605/352-3204; toll-free 800/876-5858. www.crossroas hotel.com.*This hotel is located near downtown in an area that gives a small-town feeling with many shops and restaurants.100 rooms, 3 story. Pets accepted, some restrictions; fee. Check-out 11 am. Restaurant, bar. Indoor pool, whirlpool. Airport transportation available.**$**

Jewel Cave National Monument (C-1)

See also Custer, Hill City

Web Site www.nps.gov/jeca

14 miles W on Hwy 16

On a high rolling plateau in the Black Hills is Jewel Cave, with an entrance on the east side of Hell Canyon. More than 100 miles of passageways make this cave system the second-longest in the United States. Formations of Jewel-like calcite crystals produce unusual effects. The surrounding terrain is covered by ponderosa pine. Many varieties of wildflowers bloom from early spring through summer on the 1,274-acre monument.

There is a guided 1 1/4-hour scenic tour of the monument (May-Sept) and a 1 1/2-hour historic tour (Memorial Day-Labor Day; age 6 years or older only). There is also a four-to-five-hour spelunking tour (June-Aug); advance reservations required; minimum age 16. *Note:* all tours recommended only for those in good physical condition. For spelunking, wear hiking clothes and sturdy, lace-up boots. Visitor center. (Daily) Tours: scenic, historic, or spelunking.

Keystone (C-1)

See also Black Hills, Custer, Custer State Park, Hill City, Hot Springs, Mount Rushmore National Memorial Rapid City, Wind Cave National Park,

Population 232
Elevation 4,323 ft
Area Code 605
Zip 57751
Information Chamber of Commerce, PO Box 653; phone 605/666-4896 or toll-free 800/456-3345
Web Site www.keystonechamber.com

Sculptor Gutzon Borglum began drilling into the 6,200-foot Mount Rushmore in 1927. The creation of the Shrine to Democracy took 14 years and a cost a mere $1 million, though it's now deemed priceless.

Keystone is the entrance to Mount Rushmore and Custer State Park. A former mining town supplying miners for the Peerless, Hugo, and the Holy Terror

Gold Mine, it was also home to Carrie Ingalls and the men who carved Mount Rushmore.

What to See and Do

Big Thunder Gold Mine. *604 Blair St, Keystone (57751). 5 blocks E of stop light. Phone 605/666-4847.* Authentic 1880s gold mine. Visitors may dig gold ore or pan it by the stream. Guided tours; historic film. (May-Oct, daily) **$$$**

Borglum Historical Center. *342 Winter St, Keystone (57751). Hwy 16A, in town. Phone 605/666-4449; toll-free 800/888-4369.* Born in Idaho, Gutzon Borglum (1867-1941) won acclaim for his early paintings and was sent by patrons to study in Paris. After he returned to the United States, his lifelike sculptures started generating a buzz in the national arts community. Sculpting success led Borglum in 1916 to propose carving the likeness of Robert E. Lee into Stone Mountain in Georgia, a project that he left in 1925 after clashing with financiers. At the age of 60, he embarked on the work that immortalized his famecarving the presidents' faces on Mount Rushmore. (Borglum died just before its completion; his son Lincoln finished the sculpture.) The Borglum Historical Center tells the story of Gutzon's remarkable life, focusing on his Mount Rushmore days. The center's exhibits include a full-size replica of Lincoln's eye from the monument, assorted artworks by Borglum, and a documentary about the Mount Rushmore project, narrated by US Senator (and South Dakotan) Tom Daschle. (May, Sept: daily 9 am-5 pm; June-Aug: daily 8 am-6 pm)**$$$**

Cosmos of the Black Hills. *Hwy 16 W, Rapid City (57701). 4 miles NE, 1/2 mile off Hwy 16. Phone 605/343-9802.* Curious gravitational and optical effects. Guided tours every 12 minutes. (Apr-Oct, daily) **$$$**

Parade of Presidents Wax Museum. *609 Hwy 16A, Keystone (57751). S on Hwy 16A, at E entrance to Mount Rushmore. Phone 605/666-4455.* Nearly 100 life-size wax figures depict historic scenes from nation's past. (May-Sept, daily)**$$$**

Rushmore Aerial Tramway. *203 Cemtery Rd, Keystone (57751). S on Hwy 16A. Phone 605/666-4478.* This 15-minute ride allows a view of the Black Hills and Mount Rushmore across the valley. (May-mid-Sept, daily)**$$$**

Rushmore Cave. *13622 Hwy 40, Keystone (57751). 5 miles E via Hwy 40, turn at Keystone traffic light. Phone 605/255-4467.* Guided tours (May-Oct, daily).**$$$**

Limited-Service Hotel

**★BEST WESTERN FOUR PRESIDENTS
LODGE.** *24075 Hwy 16A, Keystone (57751). Phone
605/666-4472; toll-free 800/780-7234; fax 605/666-4574.
www.fourpresidents.com.* 49 rooms, 3 story. Closed
Nov-Mar. Complimentary continental breakfast.
Check-in 2:30 pm, check-out 11 am. High-speed Internet access. Fitness room. Indoor pool, whirlpool.**$**
🏃 🏊

Lead(C-1)

*See also Belle Fourche, Black Hills, Deadwood, Rapid
City, Spearfish, Sturgis,*

Founded 1876
Population 3,632
Elevation 5,400 ft
Area Code 605
Zip 57754
Information Deadwood Area Chamber of Commerce
& Visitors Bureau, 735 Historic Main St, Deadwood
57732; phone 605/578-1876 or toll-free 800/999-1876
Web Site www.lead.sd.us

The chain of gold mines that began in Custer and
spread through the Black Hills to Deadwood ended
in Lead. The discovery of gold here in 1876 eventually
led to the development of the Homestake Mine, one
of the largest gold producers in this hemisphere. Lead
is located on mountaintops with the Homestake Mine
burrowing under the town.

What to See and Do

⭐ **Black Hills Mining Museum.** *323 W Main St, Lead
(57754). Phone 605/584-1605.*Exhibits trace development of mining in the Black Hills since 1876; includes
guided tour of underground mine; gold panning;
historic displays. (Daily)**$$**

Deer Mountain. *3 miles S on Hwy 85. Lead (57754).
Phone 605/584-3230; toll-free 888/410-3337. www.
skideermountain.com.* Triple chairlift, two Pomalifts;
patrol, school, rentals; cafeteria, bar. Cross-country
trails. Night skiing. Halfpipe for snowboards. Vertical
drop 850 feet. (Mid-Dec -early Jan: Wed-Thurs, Sun;
closed Dec 25)**$$$$**

Homestake Gold Mine Surface Tours. *160 W Main St,
Lead (57754). Phone 605/584-3110.* (Since 1876) A
one-hour tour of surface workings in an 8,000-foot
mine; explanation of gold production. (May-Sept,
daily; closed holidays)**$$**

Terry Peak. *3 miles SW on Hwy 85, then N, in Black Hills
National Forest. Phone 605/584-2165. www.terrypeak.com.*
Two quads, two triple, one double chairlifts, Mitey-Mite;
patrol, school, rentals; snowmaking; two chalets; snack
bar, cafeteria, bar. Longest run 1 1/4 miles; vertical drop
1,052 feet. (Thanksgiving-Easter, daily)**$$$$**

Limited-Service Hotel

★ ★ GOLDEN HILLS INN. *900 Miners Ave, Lead
(57754). Phone 605/584-1800; toll-free 888/465-3080;
fax 605/584-3933. www.goldenhills.com.* 100 rooms, 5
story. Pets accepted, some restrictions; fee. Complimentary continental breakfast. Check-in 3 pm, check-
out 11 am. Restaurant, bar.**$**

Madison (C-6)

See also Brookings, Sioux Falls

Founded 1875
Population 6,257
Elevation 1,670 ft
Area Code 605
Zip 57042
Information Greater Madison Chamber of Commerce,
315 S Egan Ave, PO Box 467; phone 605/256-2454
Web Site www.madison.sd.us/chamber

Madison, seat of Lake County, is the marketing,
processing, and trade center for meat, grain, and dairy
products and has some diversified industry. Madison
is well-known for its pheasant hunting as well as walleye fishing at many area lakes.

What to See and Do

Dakota State University. *Egan Ave and NE 8th St,
Madison (57042). Phone 605/256-5111. (1881)* (1,400
students.) Karl E. Mundt Library contains archives of
the South Dakota senator. The Dakota Prairie Playhouse offers varied entertainment; located off campus
at 1205 North Washington Avenue. On campus is

Smith-Zimmermann State Museum. *221 NE 8th St,
Madison (57042). Phone 605/256-5308.* History of
eastern South Dakota from 1860 to 1940. (Tues-
Fri, daily) **FREE**

Lake Herman State Park. *2 miles W off Hwy 34. Phone 605/256-5003.* On 226 acres. Swimming; fishing; boating, canoeing. Hiking. Picnicking, playground. Interpretive program, children's activities. Camping (electrical hookups, dump station).

Prairie Village. *45205 Hwy 34, Madison (57042). 2 miles W on SD 34. Phone 605/256-3644; toll-free 800/693-3644. www.prairievillage.org.* Replica of pioneer town; 40 restored buildings, antique tractors, autos; steam merry-go-round (1893) and three steam trains. (May-Sept, daily) Limited camping.**$$**

Special Event

Steam Threshing Jamboree. *Prairie Village, 45205 Hwy 34, Madison (57042). Phone 605/256-3644; toll-free 800/693-3644. www.prairievillage.org.* Prairie Village. Antique farm machinery; plowing; parades, arts and crafts display; steam merry-go-round, train rides. Last weekend in Aug.

Milbank(B-6)

See also Watertown

Population 3,879
Elevation 1,150 ft
Area Code 605
Zip 57252
Information Milbank Area Chamber of Commerce, 401 S Main St; phone 605/432-6656 or toll-free 800/675-6656
Web Site www.milbanksd.com

Milbank, the county seat of Grant County, is set in the Whetstone Valley, where granite production and the dairy industry figure prominently. Milbank is the birthplace of American Legion baseball, proposed here on July 17, 1925.

What to See and Do

Hartford Beach State Park. *15 miles N on Hwy 15. Phone 605/432-6374.* On 331 acres. Swimming, bathhouse; fishing; boating, canoeing. Hiking. Picnicking, playground. Camping (fee; hookups, dump station).

Historic Gristmill. *E on Hwy 12.* (1886) Picturesque English-style gristmill (not operating), open to public. Operates as tourist information center May-August.

Special Event

Train Festival. *Phone toll-free 800/675-6656.* Ride the rails on the Whetstone Valley Express. Second weekend in Aug.

Mission(D-3)

See also Murdo, Winner

Population 730
Elevation 2,581 ft
Area Code 605
Zip 57555
Information Rosebud Sioux Tribal Office, PO Box 430, Rosebud 57570; phone 605/747-2381

This is a trading center for the Rosebud Sioux Reservation.

What to See and Do

Buechel Memorial Lakota Museum. *350 S Oak St, St. Francis (57572). 5 miles W on Hwy 18, then 16 miles SW on Bureau of Indian Affairs Rd. Phone 605/747-2745.* Lakota Sioux artifacts. (Late May-Sept, daily) **FREE**

Ghost Hawk Park. *3 miles NW of Rosebud on Bureau of Indian Affairs Rd; on Little White River.* Swimming; fishing. Picnicking, playground. Camping (fee). (Mid-May-Sept, daily)

Rosebud. *Headquarters for Rosebud Reservation, 11 Legion Ave, Rosebud (57570). 5 miles W on Hwy 18, then 8 miles SW on Bureau of Indian Affairs Rd. Phone 605/747-2381.* Powwows can be seen Saturday-Sunday nights during summer. Inquire for swimming, fishing, golf in area.

Special Event

Rosebud Sioux Tribal Fair and Powwow. *11 Legion Ave, Rosebud, Mission (57570). Phone 605/747-2381.* Dances, traditional buffalo dinner; arts and crafts exhibits. Late Aug.

Mitchell (C-5)

See also Huron

Founded 1879
Population 13,798

Elevation 1,293 ft
Area Code 605
Zip 57301
Information Chamber of Commerce, 601 N Main St, PO Box 1026; phone 605/996-6223 or toll-free 866/273-2676
Web Site www.cornpalace.org

This is a tree-shaded town in the James River Valley, where agriculture is celebrated with a colorful nine-day festival each September. The economy is based on agriculture, light industry, and tourism. Pheasant shooting attracts hunters from around the country.

What to See and Do

 The Corn Palace. *601 N Main St, Mitchell (57301) Phone 605/996-5031; toll-free 866/273-2676. www. cornpalace.org.* Mitchell dubs itself as "the Corn capital of the world," a designation backed up by this one-of-a-kind community center. Since 1921, locals have decorated the exterior of the turreted, czarist Russia-style palace with different murals each year, but with a twist: The medium is not paint, but thousands of bushels of corn and other South Dakota grains. The initial intent of the place was to prove the fertility of South Dakota soil, but it has since evolved into a roadside tourist attraction. The Corn Palace festival, held annually in September, celebrates the annual fall harvest with concerts, a carnival midway, and other festivities. After the harvest, pigeons devour the palace's second skin, leaving the grand facade blank and longing for redecoration the following spring. (Daily 8am-5pm, until 9pm in summer)**FREE**

Dakota Discovery Museum. *1300 E University Ave, Mitchell (57301). Phone 605/996-2122.*Seven-building complex features Case Art Gallery; 1886 restored house, 1885 territorial school, 1900 railroad depot; pioneer life exhibits, horse-drawn vehicles; American Indian Gallery; 1909 country church; changing exhibits. (May-Sept, daily; rest of year, by appointment) **$$**

Enchanted World Doll Museum. *615 N Main, Mitchell (57301). Phone 605/996-9896.*More than 4,800 antique and modern dolls displayed in scenes from fairy tales and story books; dollhouses; accessories. (June-Sept, daily; Mar-May and Oct-Nov, Mon-Fri) **$$**

Lake Mitchell. *Main St and Lakeshore Dr, Mitchell (57301). 1 1/2 miles N on Hwy 37.* Swimming, fishing, boating (rentals). Playground, grocery. Camping (elec-

trical and sewer hookups, fee). (Mid-Apr-late Oct)

Prehistoric Indian Village National Historic Landmark Archaeological Site. *3200 Indian Village Rd, Mitchell (57301). 2 miles N via Hwy 37, exit 23rd Ave to Indian Village Rd, then N. Phone 605/996-5473.* Ongoing study of 1,000-year-old Native American village. Boehnen Memorial Museum; excavation and exhibits; guided tours; visitor center. (May-Oct, daily; rest of year, by appointment) **$$**

Soukup and Thomas International Balloon and Airship Museum. *700 N Main St, Mitchell (57301). Phone 605/996-2311.*Exhibits detailing history of ballooning from 1700s to present; *Hindenburg* china, antiques. Video presentations. (Memorial Day-mid-Sept, daily; rest of year, Mon-Tues, and Thurs-Sun, afternoons)

Special Events

Corn Palace Festival. *Phone 605/996-5567.* Late Aug-early Sept.

Corn Palace Stampede. *Phone 605/996-3662.* Rodeo. Third weekend in July.

Dakotafest. *Phone 605/996-5567.* Third Tues-Thurs in Aug.

Limited-Service Hotels

★ **COMFORT INN.** *117 S Burr St, Mitchell (57301). Phone 605/996-1333; toll-free 866/996-1333; fax 605/996-6022. www.comfortinn.com.* 60 rooms, 2 story. Complimentary continental breakfast. Check-in 2 pm, check-out 11 am. High-speed Internet access. Indoor pool, whirlpool. Business center.**$**

★ **DAYS INN.** *1506 S Burr St, Mitchell (57301). Phone 605/996-6208; fax 605/996-5220. www.daysinn. com.* 68 rooms, 2 story. Complimentary continental breakfast. Check-in 3 pm, check-out 11 am. High-speed Internet access, wireless Internet access. Indoor pool, children's pool, whirlpool. Business center.**$**

Full-Service Hotel

★ ★ **HOLIDAY INN.** *1525 W Havens St, Mitchell (57301). Phone 605/996-6501; toll-free 800/888-4702; fax 605/996-3228. www.holiday-inn.com/mitchellsd.* 153 rooms, 2 story. Pets accepted, some restrictions;

fee. Check-in 3 pm, check-out noon. Restaurant, bar. Fitness room. Indoor pool, children's pool, whirlpool. Airport transportation available.**$**

Restaurant

★ ★ **CHEF LOUIE'S.** *601 E Havens, Mitchell (57301). Phone 605/996-7565.* Steak menu. Dinner. Closed Sun; holidays. Bar. Children's menu. Casual attire. **$$**

Mobridge (A-3)

Founded 1906
Population 3,768
Elevation 1,676 ft
Area Code 605
Zip 57601
Information Chamber of Commerce, 212 Main St; **phone** 605/845-2387 or toll-free 888/614-3474
Web Site www.mobridge.org

The Milwaukee Railroad built a bridge across the Missouri River in 1906 at what was once the site of an Arikara and Sioux village. A telegraph operator used the contraction "Mobridge" to indicate his location. The name has remained the same. Today, Mobridge is centered in farm and ranch country and is still home for a large Native American population. Located on the Oahe Reservoir, Mobridge is noted for its ample fishing and recreational activities.

What to See and Do

Klein Museum. *1820 W Grand Crossing, Mobridge (57601). 2 miles W on Hwy 12. Phone 605/845-7243.* Changing art exhibits; local pioneer artifacts and antiques; Sioux and Arikara artifacts; farm machinery collection; restored schoolhouse. (June-Aug: daily; Apr- May-Sept-Oct: Mon, Wed-Sun; closed Easter, Labor Day)**$**

Recreation Areas. Indian Creek. *2 miles E on Hwy 12, then 1 mile S. Phone 605/845-2252.* **Indian Memorial.** 2 miles W off Hwy 12. Both on Oahe Reservoir (see PIERRE). Swimming, bathhouse; boating (ramps, marinas); fishing. Picnicking, playgrounds. Tent and trailer sites (Memorial Day-Labor Day; hookups, dump station; fee).

Scherr Howe Arena. *212 N Main St, Mobridge (57601). Phone 605/845-3700.* Colorful murals by Oscar Howe, a Dakota Sioux and art professor at the University of South Dakota, depict history and ceremonies of Native Americans. (Mon-Sat; closed holidays)**FREE**

Sitting Bull Monument. *3 miles W on Hwy 12, then 4 miles S on County 1806.* Korczak Ziolkowski sculpted the bust for this monument. The burial ground on the hill affords a beautiful view of the Missouri River and surrounding country.

Limited-Service Hotel

★ ★ **BEST VALUE WRANGLER INN.** *820 W Grand Crossing, Mobridge (57601). Phone 605/845-3641; toll-free 888/884-3641; fax 605/845-3641.www.wranglerinn.com.* 60 rooms, 2 story. Check-in 3 pm, check-out 11 am. High-speed Internet access. Restaurant, bar. Indoor pool, whirlpool. Business center.**$**

Mount Rushmore National Memorial
(C-1)

See also Black Hills, Custer, Hill City, Keystone, Rapid City

Web Site www.nps.gov/moru

25 miles SW of Rapid City off Hwy 16A and Hwy 244

The faces of four great American presidents—Washington, Jefferson, Lincoln and Theodore Roosevelt—stand out on a 5,675 foot mountain in the Black Hills of South Dakota, as grand and enduring as the contributions of the men they represent. Senator Peter Norbeck was instrumental in the realization of the monument. The original plan called for the presidents to be sculpted to the waist. It was a controversial project when sculptor Gutzon Borglum began his work on carving in 1927. With crews often numbering 30 workers, he continued through 14 years of crisis and heartbreak and had almost finished by March, 1941, when he died. Lincoln Borglum, his son,brought the project to a close in October of that year. Today, the memorial is host to almost 3 million visitors a year. To reach it, follow the signs south from Interstate 90 on Highway 16. Then take Highway 16A through Keystone to Highway 244 and the Memorial entrance. The orientation center, administrative and information headquarters, gift shop, and a snack bar (daily) are on the grounds; Buffalo Room Cafeteria. Evening program followed by sculpture lighting and other interpretive programs (mid-May-mid-Sept, daily). Sculptor's studio. museum (summer). Phone 605/574-2523. Per vehicle $5-$10.

Murdo (C-4)

See also Mission

Founded 1906
Population 679
Elevation 2,326 ft
Area Code 605
Zip 57559
Information Chamber of Commerce, PO Box 242; phone 605/669-3333
Web Site www.murdosd.com

The old fort Pierre-Custer stage route and one of the main routes of the old Texas Cattle Trail passed through the site where Murdo is now located. The town is named for pioneer cattleman Murdo McKenzie. Seat of Jones County, Murdo is still dominated by the cattle business. It is on the dividing line between Mountain and Central time.

Limited-Service Hotel

★ **BEST WESTERN GRAHAM'S.** *301 W 5th St, Murdo (57559). Phone 605/669-2441; toll-free 800/780-7234; fax 605/669-3139. www.bestwestern.com.* 45 rooms. Pets accepted, some restrictions. Complimentary continental breakfast. Check-in 1pm, check-out 11am. Outdoor pool.**$**

Pierre (C-3)

Settled 1880
Population 12,906
Elevation 1,484 ft
Area Code 605
Zip 57501
Information Chamber of Commerce, 800 W Dakota, PO Box 548; phone 605/224-7361 or toll-free 800/962-2034
Web Site www.pierre.org

Pierre (PEER) is the capital of South Dakota, an honor for which it campaigned hard and won, in part, because of its central location--the geographic center of the state. The town's prosperity was built by cattle ranchers from the west, farmers from the east, local businesspeople, and government officials.

What to See and Do

Cultural Heritage Center. *900 Governors Dr, Pierre (57501). Phone 605/773-3458.* This fine historical museum north of the South Dakota State Capitol is home to collections of artifacts used by ranchers, miners, and Native Americans of the state's past. On display is the Verendrye Plate, buried by French brothers who explored this area in 1743 (making them the first Europeans to visit to the state), and more than 1,300 artifacts depicting the history of the Sioux tribes who inhabited the state long before the Verendryes's expedition. (Mon-Fri 9 am-4:30 pm, Sat-Sun 1-4:30 pm; closed Jan 1, Thanksgiving, Dec 25)**$**

Farm Island State Recreation Area. *1301 Farm Island Rd, Pierre (57501). 4 miles E off Hwy 34.* On 1,184 acres. Swimming, bathhouse; fishing; boating, canoeing. Hiking. Picnicking, playground. Interpretive program. Camping (electrical hookups, dump station). Visitor center (May-Sept, daily). Standard fees.

Fighting Stallions Memorial. Replica of a carving by Korczak Ziolkowski honors Governor George S. Mickelson and seven others who died in an airplane crash in 1993.

Oahe Dam and Reservoir. *28563 Power House, Pierre (57501). 6 miles N on Hwy 1804, 1806.Phone 605/224-5862.*This large earthfill dam (9,300 feet long, 245 feet high) is part of the Missouri River Basin project. Lobby with exhibits (late May-early Sept, daily; rest of year Mon-Fri; free). Recreation areas along reservoir offer water skiing; fishing, boating. Nature trails. Picnicking. Primitive and improved camping (mid-May-mid-Sept; fee).

South Dakota Discovery Center and Aquarium. *805 W Sioux Ave, Pierre (57501). Phone 605/224-8295. www.sd-discovery.com.* The focus of this kids' museum is interactivity. Visitors of all ages can encase themselves in a Body Bubble, explore a maze laden with displays about the lifestyles of wild animals, or dismantle retired appliances at the Take Apart Table. The modest aquarium houses fish native to South Dakota. Summer workshops allow kids to dig deeper into a science of their choosing. (Daily until 5 pm; opening time varies by season)**$**

State Capitol. *500 E Capitol Ave, Pierre (57501). Phone 605/773-3765.*Built of Bedford limestone, local boulder granite and marble. Guided tours (Daily). **FREE** Adjacent is

> **Flaming Fountain.** *On the NW shore of Capitol Lake.* The artesian well that feeds this fountain has a natural sulphur content so high that the waters can be lit. The fountain serves as a memorial to war veterans.

State National Guard Museum. *301 E Dakota, Pierre (57501). Phone 605/224-9991.*Historical guard memorabilia. (Mon, Wed, Fri afternoons)

Limited-Service Hotels

★ ★ **BEST WESTERN RAMKOTA HOTEL.** *920 W Sioux Ave, Pierre (57501). Phone 605/224-6877; toll-free 800/780-7234; fax 605/224-1042. www.ramkota hotels.com.* 151 rooms, 2 story. Pets accepted. Check-in 2 pm, check-out noon. High-speed Internet access. Restaurant, bar. Fitness room. Indoor pool, outdoor pool, whirlpool. Airport transportation available. Business center. **$**

★ **DAYS INN.***520 W Sioux Blvd, Pierre (57501). Phone 605/224-0411; toll-free 800/329-7466; fax 605/224-2219. www.daysinn.com.* 79 rooms, 2 story. Check-in 4 pm, check-out 11 am. Fitness room.**$**

Restaurant

★★★**LA MINESTRA.** *106 E Dakota Ave, Pierre (57501). Phone 605/224-8090. www.laminestra.com.* Set in the historic downtown district in an 1896 building, La Minestra features original wainscoting and tin walls and ceilings. The restaurant serves upscale Italian cuisine in a wonderful ambience. Lunch Mon-Fri, dinner. Closed Sun. Bar. Reservations not accepted. **$$$**

Pine Ridge (D-2)

See also Badlands National Park, Hot Springs

Population 2,596
Elevation 3,232 feet
Area Code 605
Zip 57770
Web Site www.pineridgechamber.com

This is the administrative center for the Oglala Sioux nation at the Pine Ridge Indian Reservation.

What to See and Do

Red Cloud Indian School Heritage Art Museum. *Holy Rosary Mission, 100 mission Dr, Pine Ridge (57770). 4 miles W on Hwy 18. Phone 605/867-5491.* Features works by various Native American tribes. (June-Aug, daily; rest of year, Mon-Fri) **FREE**

★ **Wounded Knee Historical Site.** *8 miles E on Hwy 18, then 7 miles N on an unnumbered paved road.* On December 29, 1890, almost 150 Minniconjou Sioux, including women and children, were shot by the US Army on these grounds. A monument marks their mass grave. (Daily dawn-dusk)**FREE**

Special Event

Oglala Nation Fair and Rodeo. *Phone 605/867-5821.* Powwow and dance contest with participants from 30 tribes; displays; activities. Early Aug.

Platte (D-5)

See also Chamberlain

Settled 1882
Population 1,311
Elevation 1,612 feet
Area Code 605
Zip 57369
Information Chamber of Commerce, PO Box 393;
phone 605/337-2275 or toll-free 800/510-3272
Web Site www.plattesd.org

Settled by immigrants from the Netherlands, Platte has a strategic location at the end of a railroad line.

What to See and Do

Fort Randall Dam-Lake Francis Case. *Hwy 18, Pickstown (57367). 7 miles E on Hwy 44, then 24 miles S on Hwy 50, then 6 miles S on Hwy 18, 281.Phone 605/487-7847.*Part of the Missouri River Basin project, Fort Randall Dam is 10,700 feet long and 165 feet high. Powerhouse guided tours (Memorial Day-Labor Day, daily). Many recreation areas along reservoir have swimming, fishing, boating, picnicking; camping (May-Oct; fee, electricity additional). The project also includes the former site of Fort Randall just below the dam. Contact Lake Manager, PO Box 199, Pickstown 57367.

Platte Creek State Recreation Area. *8 miles W on Hwy 44, then 6 miles S on Hwy 1804. Phone 605/337-2587.* On 190 acres. Fishing; boating (ramp), canoeing. Picnicking. Camping (electrical hookups, dump station).

Snake Creek State Recreation Area. *35316 Hwy 44, Platte (57369). 14 miles W off Hwy 44. Phone 605/337-2587.* On 735 acres. Swimming, bathhouse; fishing; boating (ramp), canoeing. Picnicking, concession. Camping (electrical hookups, dump station). Standard fees.

Rapid City (C-1)

See also Black Hills, Custer, Deadwood, Hill City, Keystone, Lead, Mount Rushmore National Memorial, Spearfish, Sturgis, Wall

Founded 1876
Population 54,523
Elevation 3,247 ft
Area Code 605
Information Convention & Visitors Bureau, 444 Mount Rushmore Rd N, PO Box 747, 57709; phone 605/343-1744 or toll-free 800/487-3223
Web Site www.rapidcitycvb.com

In the last few decades' tourism has replaced gold mining as one of the chief industries of Rapid City. Founded only two years after gold was discovered in the Black Hills, Rapid City is a boom town that came to stay. It is the seat of Pennington County, second-largest city in South Dakota and home of Ellsworth Air Force Base. There is a substantial industrial life based on mining, lumbering, and agriculture. The Pactola Ranger District office of the Black Hills National Forest (see BLACK HILLS) is located in Rapid City.

What to See and Do

Bear Country USA. *13820 S Hwy 16, Rapid City (57702). 8 miles S via Hwy 16. Phone 605/343-2290. www.bearcountryusa.com.* Drive-through wildlife park with bears, mountain lions, wolves, elk, deer, buffalo, antelope, bighorn sheep, and Rocky Mountain goats. (Late May-mid-Oct, daily)**$$$$**

Black Hills Caverns. *2600 Cavern Rd, Rapid City (57702). 4 miles W on Hwy 44.Phone 605/343-0542.* Series of chambers connected by a fissure 160 feet high at some points; many types of formations, including amethyst and boxwork. Three different tours. (May- mid-Oct, daily)**$$$**

Black Hills Petrified Forest. *8228 Elk Creek Rd, Rapid City (57769). 11 miles NW on I-90, exit 46, then 1 mile E on Elk Creek Rd. Phone 605/787-4560.* Includes interpretive film on the Black Hills geology and petrifaction process; five-block walk-through area of logs ranging from 5-100 feet in length and up to 3-5 feet in diameter and stumps 3-5 feet in height. Self-guided tours. Rock, fossil, and mineral museum; gift and rock/lapidary shops. (Memorial Day-Labor Day, daily; weather permitting) Campground nearby. **$$$**

Black Hills Reptile Gardens. *8955 S Hwy 16, Rapid City (57702). 6 miles S on Hwy 16. Phone 605/342-5873.* Includes reptile exhibit, alligator show, birds-of-prey show, snake lecture, jungle orchid trail, giant tortoises. (Apr-Oct, daily)**$$$**

Chapel in the Hills. *3788 Chapel Ln, Rapid City (57702). SW off Jackson Blvd. Phone 605/342-8281.* Replica of 12th-century Borgund Stavkirke. Vespers during summer months.

Circle B. *22735 Hwy 385, Rapid City (57702). 15 miles W via Hwy 44, then 1 mile N on State Rd 385. Phone 605/348-7358.* Also covered wagon ride, shoot-outs. Supper (early June-Sept, daily; reservations required). **$$$$**

Crystal Cave Park. *7770 Nameless Cave Rd, Rapid City (57703). 3 miles W via Hwy 44. Phone 605/342-8008.* Park with nature trail leading to replica of Native American village, petrified garden, rock and mineral display and cave; picnic grounds. (Mid-May-Sept, daily)**$$$**

Dahl Arts Center. *713 7th St, Rapid City (57701). Phone 605/394-4101.* Visual arts center with three galleries. Mural Gallery with 200-foot cyclorama depicting 200 years of US history; narration. Two regional artists' galleries. (Daily; closed holidays)**FREE**

Dinosaur Park. *940 Skyline Dr, Rapid City (57701). W on Quincy St to Skyline Dr. Phone 605/343-8687.* Life-size steel and cement models of dinosaurs once numerous in the area. (Daily)**FREE**

Flying T Chuckwagon. *8971 S Hwy 16, Rapid City (57702). 6 miles S via Hwy 16; adjacent to Reptile Gardens. Phone 605/342-1905.* Supper and show (late May-mid-Sept, daily). Reservations accepted. **$$$$**

Gray Line Sightseeing Tours. *1600 E St. Patrick St, Rapid City (57703). Phone 605/342-4461.* Trips to Black Hills and Badlands.

The Journey. *222 New York St, Rapid City (57701). Phone 605/394-6923. www.journeymuseum.org.* This important historical center utilizes state-of-the-art technology to reveal the geography, people, and historical events that shaped the history of the Black Hills. Fully interactive exhibits take visitors back in time to discover the land as it was 2 1/2 billion years ago and trace its development to today. Home to five substantial collections of artifacts, memorabilia, and specimens from the area. The gallery features traveling exhibits and is a workplace for artists and craftspeople. Museum store. (Daily) **$$**

Sitting Bull Crystal Cave. *255 Texas St, Rapid City (57701). 9 miles S on Hwy 16. Phone 605/342-2777.* Believed to be only dogtooth spar cave in North America. (Mid-May-mid-Oct, daily)**$$$**

South Dakota School of Mines and Technology. *501 St. Joseph St, Rapid City (57701). Phone 605/394-2400; toll-free 800/544-8162. www.sdsmt.edu.* (1885) (2,358 students) Computer and scanning electron microscope laboratories. On campus is

> **Museum of Geology.** *O'Harra Memorial Building, 501 E St. Joseph, Rapid City (57701). Phone 605/394-2467.* Exceptional display of minerals, fossils, gold samples and other geological material; first Tyrannosaurus rex skull found in South Dakota. (Mon-Sat, Sun afternoons; closed holidays) **FREE**

Stagecoach West. *2255 Moon Meadows Dr, Rapid City (57702). Phone 605/343-3113.* Lecture tours to Mount Rushmore, Custer State Park, Crazy Horse Memorial, Black Hills. (May-Sept, daily) Contact PO Box 264, 57709. **$$$$**

Storybook Island. *1301 Sheridan Lake Rd, Rapid City (57702). 2 miles SW. Phone 605/342-6357. www.storybookisland.org.* Fairyland park illustrating children's stories and rhymes; outdoor settings with music and animation. (Late May-early Sept: daily 9 am-7 pm, weather permitting) **FREE**

Thunderhead Underground Falls. *10940 W Hwy 44, Rapid City (57702). 10 miles W via Hwy 44. Phone 605/343-0081.* One of the oldest (1878) gold mining tunnels in Black Hills area; stalactites and gold-bearing granite formations. Falls are 600 feet inside the mine. (May-Oct, daily)**$$**

Special Events

Black Hills Autumn Exposition - Black Hills Powwow. *Phone 605/341-0925.* Mid-Oct.

Central States Fair. *Central States Fairground, 800 San Francisco St, Rapid City (57701). Phone 605/355-3861.* Rodeo, carnival, horse and tractor pulls, auto races, demo derby. Mid-Aug.

Limited-Service Hotels

★ ★ **ALEX JOHNSON.** *523 Sixth St, Rapid City (57701). Phone 605/342-1210; toll-free 800/888-2539; fax 605/342-1210. www.alexjohnson.com.*143 rooms, 10 story. Pets accepted; fee. Check-in 3 pm, check-out 11 am. Restaurant, bar. Airport transportation available. Business center.**$**
🖪 🔦 🕴

★ **AMERICINN RAPID CITY.** *1632 Rapp St, Rapid City (57701). Phone 605/343-8424; toll-free 800/634-3444; fax 605/343-2220. www.americinn.com.* 64 rooms, 3 story. Check-in 3 pm, check-out 11 am. High-speed Internet access. Fitness room. Indoor pool, whirlpool.**$**
🕴 ⛱

★ ★ **BEST WESTERN RAMKOTA HOTEL.** *2111 N Lacrosse St, Rapid City (57701). Phone 605/343-8550; toll-free 800/780-7234; fax 605/343-9107. www.ramkota.com.* 267 rooms, 2 story. Pets accepted, some restrictions. Check-in 3 pm, check-out noon. High-speed Internet access, wireless Internet access. Restaurant, bar. Fitness room. Indoor pool, whirlpool. **$**
🔦 🕴 ⛱

★ **BEST WESTERN TOWN 'N COUNTRY.** *2505 Mount Rushmore Rd, Rapid City (57701). Phone 605/343-5383; toll-free 877/666-5383; fax 605/343-9670. www.bestwestern.com.* 99 rooms, 2 story. Complimentary continental breakfast. Check-in 3 pm, check-out 11 am. High-speed Internet access. Outdoor pool, whirlpool. Airport transportation available.**$**
⛱

★ **DAYS INN.** *1570 Rapp St, Rapid City (57701). Phone 605/348-8410; toll-free 800/329-7466; fax 605/348-3392. www.daysinnrapidcity.com.* 77 rooms, 2 story. Complimentary continental breakfast. Check-in 3 pm, check-out 11 am. Fitness room. Indoor pool, whirlpool. Airport transportation available. **$**
🏃 ⌧

★ ★ **HOLIDAY INN.** *505 N 5th St, Rapid City (57701). Phone 605/348-4000; toll-free 800/465-4329; fax 605/348-9777.www.holidayinnrapidcity.com.* 205 rooms, 8 story. Pets accepted; fee. Check-in 4 pm, check-out noon. High-speed Internet access. Restaurant, bar. Fitness room. Indoor pool, whirlpool. Airport transportation available. Business center. **$**
🐾 🏃 ⌧ 🎿

Full-Service Hotel

★ ★ **RAMADA INN.** *1721 N Lacrosse St, Rapid City (57701). Phone 605/342-1300; fax 605/342-0663. www.ramadamtrushmore.com.* 139 rooms, 4 story. Pets accepted; fee. Check-in 2 pm, check-out noon. Restaurant, bar. Fitness room. Indoor pool, whirlpool. Airport transportation available. Business center. **$**
🐾 🏃 ⌧ 🎿

Specialty Lodging

ABEND HAUS COTTAGES & AUDRIE'S BED & BREAKFAST. *23029 Thunderhead Falls Rd, Rapid City (57702). Phone 605/342-7788. www.audriesbb.com.* 10 rooms, 2 story. No children allowed. Complimentary full breakfast. Check-in 4-9 pm, check-out 11 am. **$**

Restaurants

★ **FIREHOUSE BREWING CO.** *610 Main St, Rapid City (57701). Phone 605/348-1915; fax 605/348-9972. www.firehousebrewing.com.* American menu. Lunch, dinner. Closed Jan 1, Thanksgiving, Dec 25. Bar. Children's menu. Casual attire. Outdoor seating. **$$**

★ **FLYING T. CHUCKWAGON SUPPER & SHOW.** *8971 S Hwy 16, Rapid City (57702). Phone 605/342-1905. www.flyingt.com.* American menu. Dinner. Closed mid-Sept-late May. **$**

★ ★ **GREAT WALL.** *315 E North St, Rapid City (57701). Phone 605/348-1060; fax 605/348-1183. www.greatwalltogo.com.* Chinese menu. Lunch, dinner. Children's menu. Casual attire. **$$**

★ ★ **IMPERIAL.** *702 E North St, Rapid City (57701). Phone 605/394-8888; fax 605/394-9532.*Chinese menu. Lunch, dinner. Closed Thanksgiving, Dec 24-25. Children's menu. Casual attire. **$$**

Redfield (B-5)

See also Aberdeen

Population 2,770
Elevation 1,303 ft
Information Chamber of Commerce, 626 N Main St;
phone 605/472-0965
Web Site www.redfield-sd.com

What to See and Do

Fisher Grove State Park. *17290 Fishers Ln, Frankfort (57440). 7 miles E on US 212. Phone 605/472-1212.* On 277 acres. Fishing; boating, canoeing. Hiking, golf. Picnicking, playground. Camping (electrical hookups, dump station). Standard fees.

Spink County Historical Memorial Museum. *210 E 7th Ave, Redfield (57469). SE corner Courthouse Sq. Phone 605/472-0758.* Early-day furniture, household items, tools, machinery; collections of mounted birds, butterflies, other insects. (June-Aug, daily) **$**

Sioux Falls

See also Beresford, Luverne, Madison

Founded 1856
Population 100,814
Elevation 1,442 ft
Area Code 605
Information Chamber of Commerce & Convention and Visitors Bureau, 200 N Phillips Ave, Suite 102; 57104; phone 605/336-1620 or toll-free 800/333-2072
Web Site www.siouxfallscvb.com

At the falls of the Sioux River, this city has been developing at a constant pace since it was reestablished in 1865, having been abandoned in 1862 after threats of a Lakota attack. Its prosperity is based on diversified industry and farming. Cattle are shipped from a three-state area, slaughtered, and packed here, then shipped east. Manufactured goods from the East are distributed throughout much of South Dakota from Sioux Falls.

A City of Parks

Sioux Falls has a handsome Victorian town center accented with progressive cultural institutions; with over 60 parks, it's a walker's dream. No wonder the community repeatedly leads many surveys of most livable small cities in the nation. Begin a walking tour at the Falls Park Visitor Information Center, near the corner of Phillips and 6th Avenue. From the center's observation tower, take in views of her town and its namesake waterfalls

.Falls Park contains a number of attractions, including terraced rock formations over which the Big Sioux River tumbles in a series of waterfalls. Trails lead to the falls and to picnic areas scattered around the park; at night, light programs play across the falls. At the north end of the park is the Horse Barn Arts Center, an artists cooperative housed in an old stone barn. The second-floor gallery features exhibits of local artists and crafters.

Continue south on Philips Avenue, past the Sioux Falls Brewing Company (431 N Phillips Ave), which is housed in a classic stone-and-brick storefront, to 6th Street. West on 6th lies the modern downtown core of Sioux Falls, plus the city's Historic District. The Old Courthouse Museum, at 6th Street and Main Avenue, is a grand structure built of local quartzite that now serves as a historical museum, activity center for kids, and gift shop featuring local crafts. In summer, live music plays in the neighboring plaza.

Continue south on Main to 8th Street, and turn west to Duluth Avenue. The Pettigrew Home and Museum, 8th Street and Duluth Avenue, is the Queen Anne Victorian home of South Dakota's first US Senator. This beautifully restored home contains period furniture and artifacts from the frontier era

of Sioux Falls. Follow 8th Street, past more Victorian homes, to Grange Avenue. Turn north and continue to 6th Street and Terrace Park. The Shoto-Teien Japanese Gardens, with formal gardens, pagodas, and exotic Asian plants, flank Covell Lake in the park. If it's a warm day and you've got kids in tow, the swimming pools and water slides of Terrace Park Aquatic Center are a perfect spot to cool down.

From Terrace Park, walk south on Grange Avenue to 12th Street, and turn west. The 205-acre Sherman Park, at 12th and Kiwanis Avenue, contains the Great Plains Zoo and Delbridge Museum of Natural History, plus a memorial for the USS *South Dakota*, the most decorated battleship in World War II. The park also features a number of unexcavated Native American burial mounds.

From Sherman Park, head back east toward downtown along 12th Avenue. At Main Avenue is Sioux Falls's largest entertainment, cultural, and educational facility, the Washington Pavilion of Arts and Science. Formerly the city's original high school, the complex is a model of architectural repurposing. The pavilion contains the Visual Arts Center, with a permanent collection of regional artists, plus changing exhibitions and art shows. Also in the pavilion are the Wells Fargo Cinedome Theater, Kirby Science Discovery Center, Husby Performing Arts Center, restaurants, and gift shops.

Continue east along 11th Street, passing a full-size casting of Michelangelo's *David* just before crossing the Big Sioux River. From here, drop down onto the Sioux River Greenway, and follow the hiking and biking trail north to Falls Park

Jean Nicolet saw the falls here in 1839 and described them impressively. The Dakota Land Company of Minnesota (1856) and the Western Town Company (1857) of Dubuque set out to develop the area and apparently worked together successfully. In September, 1858, the thirty-odd residents elected members to a Territorial Legislature, casting (it is said) votes for all their relatives as well as for themselves. On July 2, 1859, the first Sioux Falls newspaper, the *Democrat,* appeared.

Sioux Falls is the center for EROS (Earth Resources Observation Systems), an international center for space and aircraft photography of the Earth.

What to See and Do

Augustana College. *29th St and Summit Ave, Sioux Falls (57197). Phone 605/274-0770; toll-free 800/727-2844. www.augie.edu.* (1860) (2,100 students) Gilbert

Science Center with Foucault pendulum, miniature dioramas of state wildlife. Center for Western Studies has museum and archival center on Western heritage. Art exhibits. Replica of Michelangelo's statue of Moses is on campus. Tours.

Sherman Park. Formal flower garden, ballfields, picnicking. Kiwanis Avenue from 12th to 22nd streets. Also here are

Delbridge Museum of Natural History. *805 S Kiwanis Ave, Sioux Falls (57104). Phone 605/367-7003.* Included in the zoo admission. Displays cover five different climactic eco-zones and feature 150 mounted animal specimens, including a giant pandaa rarity in the United States. (Daily)

Great Plains Zoo. *805 S Kiwanis Ave, Sioux Falls (57104). Phone 605/367-7003.* The centerpiece of Sherman Park, the Great Plains Zoo focuses on animals native to places outside of South Dakota: black rhinos, red pandas, and Galapagos tortoises are among the 400 residents (representing 100 species in all). The zoo replicates a variety of ecosystems, including the Australian Outback and the banks of the Nile River, to give visitors a better understanding of how the animals live in the wild. A seasonal train takes riders on a behind-the-scenes look at the African Savannah exhibit, and summertime shows give kids a closer look at some of the animals. (Daily; hours vary by season) **$$**

⭐ **Siouxland Heritage Museums.** Unified museum system composed of two sites:

Old Courthouse Museum. *200 W 6th St, Sioux Falls (57104). Phone 605/367-4210.* Restored Richardsonian-Romanesque quartzite stone courthouse (1890) contains exhibits of Siouxland history, special exhibits on local culture. (Daily; closed holidays) **FREE**

Pettigrew Home and Museum. *131 N Duluth Ave, Sioux Falls (57104). Phone 605/367-7097.* Restored Queen Anne historic house (1889) furnished to show life of state's first senator; galleries of Native American items and cultural history of the Siouxland. (Daily; closed holidays) **FREE**

University of Sioux Falls. *22nd St and Prairie Ave, Sioux Falls (57105). Phone 605/331-5000; toll-free 800/888-1047. www.thecoo.edu.* (1883) (1,325 students) Has Lorene B. Burns Indian Collection and Lucy Borneman Chinese Collection (Academic year, daily; summer,

Mon-Fri; closed school vacations). The historic Yankton Trail crossed this area; marker indicates the site.

USS *South Dakota* Battleship Memorial. *W 12th St and Kiwanis Ave, Sioux Falls (57101). Phone 605/367-7060.* The USS *South Dakota* was the first ship to fire on Japanese enemies in World War II and played a role in every major Pacific battle between 1942 and 1945. Located in Sherman Park, the memorial pays honor to the crew that served on the *South Dakota* and has the same dimensions as the ship, sold off by the Navy in 1962, and features many items that were once onboard. A small museum is also on-site. (Memorial Day-Labor Day, daily)

Limited-Service Hotels

★ **AMERICINN.** *3508 S Gateway Blvd, Sioux Falls (57106). Phone 605/361-3538; toll-free 800/634-3444; fax 605/361-5204. www.americinn.com.* 65 rooms, 2 story. Complimentary continental breakfast. Check-in 3 pm, check-out 11 am. High-speed Internet access. Indoor pool, whirlpool. **$**
🏊

★ **BAYMONT INN.** *3200 S Meadow Ave, Sioux Falls (57106). Phone 605/362-0835; toll-free 877/229-6668; fax 605/362-0836. www.baymontinns.com.* 78 rooms, 3 story. Pets accepted; fee. Complimentary continental breakfast. Check-in 1 pm, check-out noon. High-speed Internet access, wireless Internet access. Indoor pool, whirlpool. **$**
🐾 🏊

★ ★ **BEST WESTERN RAMKOTA HOTEL.** *2400 N Louise Ave, Sioux Falls (57107). Phone 605/336-0650; toll-free 800/780-7234; fax 605/336-1687. www.ramkota.com.* 226 rooms, 2 story. Pets accepted, some restrictions. Check-out 11 am. Restaurant, bar. Indoor waterpark, outdoor pool, whirlpool. Airport transportation available. **$**
🐾 🏊

★ **COMFORT INN.** *3216 S Carolyn Ave, Sioux Falls (57106). Phone 605/361-2822; toll-free 800/252-7466; fax 605/361-2822. www.comfortinn.com.* 65 rooms, 2 story. Pets accepted; fee. Complimentary continental breakfast. Check-in 2 pm, check-out 11 am. Indoor pool, whirlpool. **$**
🐾 🏊

★ **COMFORT SUITES.** *3208 Carolyn Ave, Sioux Falls (57106). Phone 605/362-9711; toll-free 800/424-6423; fax 605/362-9711. www.comfortsuites.com.* 61 rooms, 3 story. Pets accepted; fee. Complimentary continental breakfast. Check-in 3 pm, check-out 11 am. High-speed Internet access, wireless Internet access. Indoor pool, whirlpool. **$**
🐾 🏊

★ **DAYS INN.** *3401 Gateway Blvd, Sioux Falls (57106). Phone 605/361-9240; fax 605/361-5419. www.siouxfallsdaysinnempire.com.* 80 rooms, 2 story. Complimentary continental breakfast. Check-in 3 pm, check-out noon. Airport transportation available. **$**

★ ★ **HOLIDAY INN.** *100 W 8th St, Sioux Falls (57104). Phone 605/339-2000; toll-free 800/465-4329; fax 605/339-3724. www.holiday-inn.com/fsd-cityctr.* 299 rooms, 10 story. Check-in 3 pm, check-out noon. High-speed Internet access. Restaurant, bar. Fitness room. Indoor pool, whirlpool. Airport transportation available. Business center. **$**
🧍 🏊 🏃

★ **KELLY INN - SIOUX FALLS.** *3101 W Russell, Sioux Falls (57107). Phone 605/338-6242; toll-free 800/635-3559; fax 605/338-5453. www.kellyinnsiouxfalls.com.* 43 rooms, 2 story. Pets accepted. Complimentary continental breakfast. Check-in 2 pm, check-out 11 am. High-speed Internet access, wireless Internet access. Whirlpool. Airport transportation available. **$**
🐾

★ ★ **RAMADA INN &SUITES AIRPORT.** *1301 W Russell St, Sioux Falls (57104). Phone 605/336-1020; toll-free 866/336-1020; fax 605/336-3030. www.ramada.com.* 153 rooms, 2 story. Pets accepted, some restrictions; fee. Check-in 4 pm, check-out noon. Restaurant, bar. Fitness room. Indoor pool, whirlpool. Airport transportation available. **$**
🐾 🧍 🏊

Full-Service Hotels

★ ★ **RADISSON ENCORE HOTEL-SIOUX FALLS.** *4300 W Empire Pl, Sioux Falls (57106). Phone 605/361-6684; toll-free 800/333-3333; fax 605/362-0916. www.radisson.com.* This property is conveniently located near the Sioux Falls International Airport. 105 rooms, 3 story. Complimentary continental breakfast. Check-in 4 pm, check-out noon. High-speed Internet access, wireless Internet access. Restaurant, bar. Fitness room. Indoor pool, whirlpool. Airport transportation available. Business center. **$**
🧍 🏊

★ ★ ★ **SHERATON SIOUX FALLS & CONVENTION CENTER.** *1211 N West Ave, Sioux Falls (57104). Phone 605/331-0100; toll-free 800/325-3535; fax 605/373-1033. www.jqhhotels.com.* 184 rooms, 6 story. Pets accepted, some restrictions. Check-in 3 pm, check-out noon. High-speed Internet access, wireless Internet access. Restaurant, bar. Fitness room. Indoor pool, whirlpool. Airport transportation available. Business center. **$**
🐾 🧍 🏊 🏃

Restaurant

★ ★ ★ **C. J. CALLAWAY'S.** *500 E 69th St, Sioux Falls (57109). Phone 605/334-8888; fax 605/334-1998. www.cjcallaways.com.* Overlooking Prairie Green Golf Course, this handsome, country-club-style restaurant offers creatively prepared regional fare. American menu. Dinner. Closed Sun; holidays. Bar. Children's menu. Casual attire. Reservations recommended. Outdoor seating. **$$**

Sisseton (A-6)

See also Webster

Population 2,181
Elevation 1,204 ft
Area Code 605
Zip 57262
Web Site www.sisseton.com

What to See and Do

Fort Sisseton State Park. *20 miles W on Hwy 10, then S on Hwy 25. Phone 605/448-5701.* Established in 1864 to protect settlers, the fort housed 400 soldiers and contained more than 45 wooden, stone-and-brick buildings. The post was abandoned in 1889; during the 1930s it was used as a federal transient camp by the Works Progress Administration, which restored 14 of the fort's brick and stone buildings. Hiking trail, picnicking. Camping. Visitor center with historical exhibits (Memorial Day-Labor Day, daily).

Roy Lake State Park. *Roy Lake Rd, Sisseton (57247). 18 miles W on Hwy 10, then 3 miles SW near Lake City.*

Phone 605/448-5701. On 509 acres. Swimming beach, bathhouse; fishing; boating, canoeing. Hiking. Picnicking, playground, concession. Camping (electrical hookups, dump station), cabins. Reservations accepted after January 1 annually. Standard fees. **$$**

Special Event

Fort Sisseton Historical Festival. *Fort Sisseton State Park, 11545 Northside Dr, Lake City (57247). Phone 605/448-5701.* Includes muzzleloading rendezvous, cavalry and infantry drills, square dancing, melodrama, frontier crafts and dutch oven cook-off. Late May.

Restaurant

★ **AMERICAN HEARTH.** *10 Hickory St E, Sisseton (57262). Phone 605/698-3077.* American menu. Breakfast, lunch, dinner. Children's menu. Casual attire. **$**

Spearfish (B-1)

See also Belle Fourche, Black Hills, Deadwood, Lead, Rapid City, Sturgis

Population 6,966
Elevation 3,643 ft
Area Code 605
Zip 57783
Information Chamber of Commerce, 106 W Kansas, PO Box 550; phone 605/642-2626 or toll-free 800/626-8013
Web Site www.spearfish.sd.us

The fertile valley in which Spearfish lies is at the mouth of Spearfish Canyon, famous for its scenery and fishing. A Ranger District office of the Black Hills National Forest (see BLACK HILLS) is located in Spearfish.

What to See and Do

Black Hills State University. *1200 University St, Spearfish (57783). Phone 605/642-6343; toll-free 800/255-2478. www.bhsu.edu.(1883)* (3,836 students) Located in the northern Black Hills overlooking the community. Library has Lyndle Dunn wildlife art, Babylonian tablets and Rachetts porcelain miniature dolls of First Ladies. Donald E. Young Sports and Fitness Center open to public (fees). Walking tours.

City Campgrounds. *404 S Canyon St, Spearfish (57783). I-90, exit 12, left at second light. Phone 605/642-1340.* Includes 150 campsites, 57 with hookups (additional fee). Fishing. (Mid-May-Oct, daily) **$$$**

D. C. Booth Historic National Fish Hatchery. *423 Hatchery Cir, Spearfish (57783). Phone 605/642-7730. dcbooth.fws.gov.* Operated by the Fish and Wildlife Service from 1899 to the mid-1980s, the D. C. Booth Historic Fish Hatchery is now a museum covering the history of aquaculture in the western United States. While in operation, the hatchery propagated trout to stock the waters of the Black Hills region and managed the fisheries of Yellowstone National Park. Fish are still viewable through an underwater viewing area, and visitors can also explore displays covering everything from fish cars (railroad cars once used to transport fish stock) to the Fish Culture Hall of Fame. (Grounds daily dawn-dusk; tours mid-May-mid-Sept) **FREE**

Eagle Aviation Air Tours. *310 Aviaion Pl, Spearfish (57783). Phone 605/642-4112; toll-free 800/843-8010.* Airplane tours of the Gold Country, Devils Tower, Mount Rushmore, and the Badlands. Minimum two persons per ride. **$$$$**

High Plains Western Heritage Center. *825 Heritage Dr, Spearfish (57783). Phone 605/642-9378. www.western-heritagecenter.com.* Covering pioneer life in the Dakotas, Montana, Wyoming, and Nebraska, this history museum includes artwork, artifacts, and snazzy custom saddles and Western furnishings. Among the exhibits is the original stagecoach that ran the Deadwood-to-Spearfish route and displays covering mining, forestry, and rodeo. Outside, there is a furnished log cabin, a one-room schoolhouse, a seasonal farm with small animals, and pastures populated by bison and longhorn cattle year-round. (Daily 9 am-5 pm; closed holidays) **$$**

Spearfish Canyon. *Phone 605/642-8166. www.spearfish.com/canyon.* Carved over the last 60 million years by Spearfish Creek slicing through layers of limestone and sandstone, this scenic, pine-laden canyon is a popular recreation destination in the summer months. Rife with plant and animal life (not to mention cabins and resorts), the winding gorge is 1,000 feet deep at its deepest, punctuated by waterfalls and dubbed the most magnificent canyon in the West by renowned architect Frank Lloyd Wright. Highway 14A, running from Spearfish up 20 miles to Cheyenne Crossing, on its floor has a popular motorcycling and biking route. There is no motorized-vehicle access to the canyon's rims, but there are a few hiking trails that climb its steep walls. Fly-fishing in Spearfish Creek, with trout being the prime catch, is also popular, as are snowmobiling and cross-country skiing in the winter. There are a few campgrounds in the canyon.

Special Events

Black Hills Passion Play. *Amphitheater, 400 St. Joe St, Spearfish (57783). Phone 605/642-2646.* Dramatization of last days of Jesus Christ, presented on 350-foot outdoor stage. Tues, Thurs and Sun. June-Aug.

Corvette Classic. *Main St, Spearfish (57783). Phone 605/642-2626.* Sports car enthusiasts gather each summer for their convention. Highlight is Main Sreeet Show and Shine, when hundreds of corvettes line Main Street. Mid-July.

Matthews Opera House. *614 Main, Spearfish (57783). Phone 605/642-7973.* June-Aug.

Limited-Service Hotels

★ **BEST WESTERN BLACK HILLS LODGE.** *540 E Jackson, Spearfish (57783). Phone 605/642-7795; toll-free 800/780-7234; fax 605/642-7751. www.bestwestern.com.* 49 rooms, 2 story. Pets accepted; fee. Complimentary continental breakfast. Check-in 3 pm, check-out 11 am. High-speed Internet access. Outdoor pool, two whirlpools. **$**
🐾 🏊

★ **FAIRFIELD INN.** *2720 E 1st Ave, Spearfish (57783). Phone 605/642-3500; toll-free 800/450-4442; fax 605/642-3500. www.fairfieldinn.com.* 57 rooms, 3 story. Complimentary continental breakfast. Check-in 3 pm, check-out 11 am. Indoor pool, whirlpool.**$**
🏊

★ ★ **HOLIDAY INN.** *305 N 27th St, Spearfish (57783). Phone 605/642-4683; toll-free 800/999-3541; fax 605/642-0203. www.holidayinn-spearfish.com.* 145 rooms, 2 story. Pets accepted; fee. Check-in 3 pm, check-out noon. High-speed Internet access. Restaurant, bar. Fitness room. Indoor pool, whirlpool. Airport transportation available. **$**
🐾 🏃 🏊

★ ★ **SPEARFISH CANYON RESORT.** *10619 Roughlock Falls Rd, Spearfish (57754). Phone 605/584-3435; toll-free 877/975-6343; fax 605/584-3990. www.spfcanyon.com.* 54 rooms, 2 story. Pets accepted; fee.

Check-in 3 pm, check-out 11 am. Bar. Whirlpool. **$**

Sturgis (B-1)

See also Belle Fourche, Black Hills, Deadwood, Lead, Rapid City, Spearfish,

Founded 1878
Population 5,330
Elevation 3,440 ft
Area Code 605
Zip 57785
Information Chamber of Commerce, 2040 Junction Ave, PO Box 504; phone 605/347-2556
Web Site www.sturgis-sd.org

Originally a "bullwhackers" (wagon drivers) stop on the way to Fort Meade, this was once known as "Scooptown" because soldiers who came in were "scooped" (cleaned out) by such characters as Poker Alice, a famed cigar-smoking scoop-expert. Now Sturgis is a bustling Black Hills trade center.

What to See and Do

Bear Butte State Park. *N Hwy 79, Sturgis (57785). 6 miles NE off Hwy 79. Phone 605/347-5240. www.state.sd.us/gfp/sdparks/bearbutt/bearbutt.htm.* Called Mato Paha (or Bear Mountain) by the Lakota people, the defining feature here is not actually a flat-topped butte, but a singular mountain (4,422 feet above sea level) rising from the plains. For generations, the mountain has been a spiritually significant site for the Lakota and Cheyenne people, and thousands of worshippers continue to visit the ceremonial area at its base every year. The 1.7-mile Summit Trail takes hikers on a steep path (gaining 1,253 feet) to the peak, where four states are visible, and the park also serves as the northern trailhead for the 111-mile Centennial Trail into the Black Hills. A bison herd also roams free within the park's boundaries. The visitor center features displays on the area's ecology and history, and there is a small campground and a lake with a boat ramp in the park. Visitor center (May-early Sept, daily 8 am-6 pm). Park (daily 8 am-7 pm).

Fort Meade Museum. *1 mile E on Hwy 34, 79. Fort Meade (57741) Phone 605/347-9822.*On site of original Fort Meade (1878-1944), to which surviving members of the Seventh Cavalry came after the Custer Massacre. Old cavalry quarters, post cemetery; museum has displays of artifacts, documents. Video presentation. (May-Sept, daily)

Wonderland Cave. *Alpine and Vanocker rds, Nemo (57759). S via I-90, exit 32, then 15 miles S on Vanocker Canyon Rd or S of Deadwood on Hwy 385. Phone 605/578-1728.* Scenic tours of underground caverns 60 million years old; two-level living cave with largest variety of crystal formations in the Northwest. Picnicking, snack bar; gift shop; hiking trails. (May-Oct, daily) **$$$**

Special Event

Sturgis Rally. *www.sturgis-rally.com.* The biggest motorcycle rally in the country isn't just for wild bikers anymore--it attracts lawyers, doctors, and virtually everybody else who's ever revved a Harley-Davidson. The inaugural rally was held by the local motorcycle club, the Jackpine Gypsies, in 1938, and was quite modest: nine racers riding in front of a small audience. The annual August event has since snowballed into an extravaganza that draws in a crowd in excess of 450,000, and over 100 marriage licenses have been issued to attending couples in recent years. During the rally, five blocks of Sturgis's historic Main Street are open to motorcycle traffic only, creating a wild picture of wall-to-wall bikes and people. The schedule includes motorcycle races and tours, and there are hundreds of vendors selling everything from leather of all descriptions to exotic foods. But beware--the hotels, campgrounds, and restaurants in Sturgis book up months before the bikes roar into town. Mid-Aug.

Limited-Service Hotel

★ **DAYS INN.** *2630 Lazelle St, Sturgis (57785). Phone 605/347-3027; toll-free 800/329-7466; fax 605/347-0291. www.daysinn.com.* 53 rooms, 2 story. Pets accepted, some restrictions; fee. Complimentary continental breakfast. Check-in noon, check-out 11 am. Whirlpool. **$**

Vermillion (D-6)

See also Beresford, Crofton, Sioux City, Yankton

Settled 1859
Population 10,034
Area Code 605
Zip 57069
Information Chamber of Commerce, 906 E Cherry St;
phone 605/624-5571 or toll-free 800/809-2071
Web Site www.vermillionchamber.com

Vermillion, the seat of Clay County, was settled originally below the bluffs of the Missouri River until the flood of 1881 changed the river's course, forcing residents to higher ground. Located in a portion of the state that was claimed twice by France and once by Spain before being sold to the United States, Vermillion has prospered and now prides itself as being a combination of rich farmland, good industrial climate, and home to the University of South Dakota.

What to See and Do

Clay County Recreation Area. *4 miles W, 1 1/2 miles S off Hwy 50, on banks of Missouri River. Phone 605/987-2263.* On 121 acres. Fishing; boating, canoeing (landing). Picnicking.

University of South Dakota. *Dakota St, Vermillion (57069). On Hwy 50 Bypass. Phone 605/677-5326; toll-free 877/269-6837. www.usd.com.* (1862) (7,300 students) On campus is the DakotaDome, a physical education, recreation and athletic facility with an air-supported roof. Art galleries and theaters are located in the Warren M. Lee Center for the Fine Arts and Coyote Student Center. Tours. Also on campus is

Shrine to Music Museum. *414 E Clark St, Vermillion (57069). Clark and Yale sts. Phone 605/677-5306.* More than 6,000 antique musical instruments from all over the world and from all periods. (Daily; closed Jan 1, Thanksgiving, Dec 25) **FREE**

W. H. Over State Museum. *1110 Ratingen St, Vermillion (57069). Phone 605/677-5228.* State museum of natural and state history. Exhibits include life-size diorama of a Teton Dakota village; the Stanley J. Morrow collection of historical photographs; and pioneer artifacts. Changing gallery. Gift shop. (Daily; closed holidays) **FREE**

Limited-Service Hotel

★ **COMFORT INN.** *701 W Cherry St, Vermillion (57069). Phone 605/624-8333; toll-free 800/228-5150; fax 605/624-8333. www.choicehotels.com.* 46 rooms, 2 story. Pets accepted; fee. Complimentary continental breakfast. Check-in 3 pm, check-out 10 am. High-speed Internet access. Fitness room. Indoor pool, whirlpool. **$**

Restaurant

★ **SILVER DOLLAR.** *1216 E Cherry (Hwy 50), Vermillion (57069). Phone 605/624-4830.* American menu. Lunch, dinner, brunch. Bar. Children's menu. Casual attire. **$$**

Wall (C-2)

See also Rapid City

Founded 1907
Population 834
Elevation 2,818 ft
Area Code 605
Zip 57790
Web Site www.wall-badlands.com

Established as a station on the Chicago & North Western Railroad in 1907, Wall is a gateway to Badlands National Park (see). The town is a trading center for a large area of farmers and ranchers, and it is noted for its pure water, which is brought up from wells 3,200 feet deep. A Ranger District office of the Nebraska National Forest is located here.

What to See and Do

Wall Drug Store. *510 Main St*, Wall (57790). *On Hwy 14, I-90, Hwy 240. Phone 605/279-2175. www.walldrug. com.* Ted and Dorothy Hustead bought the Wall Drug pharmacy in 1931, in the midst of the Great Depression. Business was lukewarm for five years until Ted started putting up signs advertising free ice water. It worked. Now in the hands of a third Hustead generation, Wall Drug is a sprawling tourist outpost that attracts upwards of 20,000 visitors on hot summer days, pouring some 5,000 glasses of ice cold water in the process. The signs remain integral, and thousands are in existence along I-90, in European cities like Amsterdam and London, and even in people's homes. All this advertising has helped the Husteads build an empire that includes not just a drugstore, but also a shopping mall, a 500-seat restaurant, a jackalope to climb on for a photo op, and numerous robots that will gladly perform for a quarter. Studies have shown that about three-quarters of I-90's traffic exits at Wall, South Dakota. (Daily 6:30 am-6 pm; closed holidays) **FREE**

Limited-Service Hotel

★ **DAYS INN.** *210 10th Ave and Norris, Wall (57790). Phone 605/279-2000; toll-free 800/329-7466; fax 605/279-2004. www.daysinn.com.* 32 rooms, 2 story. Pets accepted, some restrictions; fee. Complimentary continental breakfast. Check-in 2 pm, check-out 11 am. Whirlpool. **$**

Restaurant

★ **WALL DRUG.** *510 Main St, Wall (57790). Phone 605/279-2175; fax 605/279-2699. www.walldrug.com.* American menu. Breakfast, lunch, dinner. Closed holidays. Children's menu. Casual attire. **$**

Watertown (B-6)

See also Brookings, Milbank

Founded 1879
Population 17,592
Elevation 1,739 ft
Area Code 605
Zip 57201
Information Convention & Visitors Bureau, 1200 33 St SE, Ste 209, PO Box 1113; phone 605/886-5814 or toll-free 800/658-4505
Web Site www.watertownsd.com

Originally called Waterville, the settlement owed its boom to the railroads. Two large lakes, Kampeska and Pelican, are on the edges of town.

What to See and Do

Bramble Park Zoo. *901 6th Ave NW (Hwy 20), Watertown (57201). Phone 605/882-6269.* Municipal zoo (21 acres) features more than 500 birds and mammals of 130 different species. Live animal encounters; picnic area, playground; discovery center features displays and hands-on programs. (Daily, weather permitting) **$$**

Codington County Heritage Museum. *27 1st Ave SE, Watertown (57201). Phone 605/886-7335.* Exhibits depict pioneer history, local history through World War II, and Native American artifacts. (Tues-Sat, afternoons) **FREE**

Mellette House. *421 5th Ave NW, Watertown (57201). Phone 605/886-4730.* (1883) Built by Arthur C. Mellette, last territorial and first state governor of South Dakota. Original Victorian furnishings, heirlooms, family portraits. (May-Sept, Tues-Sun, afternoons) **FREE**

Redlin Art Center. *1200 33rd St SE, Watertown (57201). Jct Hwy 212 and I-29. Phone 605/882-3877.* Houses over 100 of Terry Redlin's original oil paintings. Center also includes the only planetarium in the state, an amphitheater, gift shop and Glacial Lakes and Prairie Tourism Association. (Daily; seasonal schedule) **FREE**

Stokes-Thomas City Park on Lake Kampeska. *NW on Hwy 20. Watertown (57201). Phone 605/882-6260.* Parks along shore offer swimming, bathhouses, water-skiing; fishing; boating (launch). Picnicking. Camping, trailer sites. Standard fees. There is also a 25-mile scenic drive around the lake.

Limited-Service Hotel

★ ★ **BEST WESTERN RAMKOTA HOTEL.** *1901 SW 9th Ave, Watertown (57201). Phone 605/886-8011; toll-free 800/780-7234; fax 605/886-3667. www. ramkota.com.* 101 rooms, 2 story. Pets accepted, some restrictions. Check-in 3 pm, check-out noon. High-speed Internet access. Restaurant, bar. Indoor pool, whirlpool. Airport transportation available. **$**

Webster (A-5)

See also Aberdeen, Sisseton

Founded 1881
Population 2,017
Elevation 1,847 ft
Area Code 605
Zip 57274
Information Chamber of Commerce, 513 Main, PO Box 123; phone 605/345-4668
Web Site www.webstersd.com

What to See and Do

Museum of Wildlife, Science and Industry. *W Hwy 12, Webster (57274). Exit 207 off I-29. Phone 605/345-4751.* Antique automobiles, tractors; international animal display. (Daily) **Donation**

Waubay National Wildlife Refuge. *19 miles NE via Hwy 12, then 7 miles N on County Rd 1. Phone 605/947-4521.* This 4,694-acre wildlife refuge has nature and bird-watching trails; 100-foot tall observation tower; outdoor classroom activities and wildlife exhibits. (Mon-Fri)

Special Event

Day County Fair. *Phone 605/345-4668.* Grandstand shows, animals on display, special programs. Fair is over 110 years old. Aug.

Wind Cave National Park (C-1)

See also Black Hills, Custer, Hill City, Hot Springs, Keystone

Web Site www.nps.gov/wica/

11 miles N of Hot Springs on Hwy 385.

Wind Cave, one of many caves in the ring of limestone surrounding the Black Hills, is a maze of subterranean passages known to extend more than 79 miles. It is named for the strong currents of wind that blow in or out of its entrance according to atmospheric pressure. When the pressure decreases, the wind blows outward; when it increases, the wind blows in. It was the rushing sound of air coming out of the entrance that led to its discovery in 1881. The cave and surrounding area became a national park in 1903; today, it comprises 44 square miles.

Wind Cave is a constant 53 F. Various one- to two-hour guided tours (daily; no tours Thanksgiving, Dec 25) and four-hour tours (June-mid-Aug, daily). Tours are moderately strenuous. A sweater or jacket is advised; shoes must have low heels and nonslip soles.

On the surface are prairie grasslands, forests, and a wildlife preserve the home of bison, pronghorn elk, deer, prairie dogs, and other animals. The Centennial Trail, a 111-mile, multi-use trail, takes visitors from one end of the Black Hills to the other. The trail begins here and ends at Bear Butte State Park (see STURGIS). In addition, there is hiking, bicycling, picnicking, and camping at Elk Mountain near headquarters. Visitor center (daily; closed Thanksgiving, Dec 25). Hours may vary throughout the year. Park (daily). Phone 605/745-4600.

Winner (D-4)

See also Chamberlain, Mission

Founded 1909
Population 3,354
Area Code 605
Zip 57580
Information Chamber of Commerce, Tripp County Courthouse, PO Box 268; phone 605/842-1533 or toll free 800/658-3079

Web Site www.winnersd.org

Winner is a sports-oriented town; a pheasant hunting autumn follows a baseball summer. It is the seat of Tripp County and one of the largest producers of cattle and wheat in the state.

Special Events

Regional High School Rodeo. *Phone 605/842-2919.* Early June.

Shrine Circus. *Phone 605/842-1533.* July

Yankton (D-6)

See also Beresford, Vermillion

Settled 1859
Population 12,703
Elevation 1,205 feet
Area Code 605
Zip 57078
Information Chamber of Commerce, 218 W 4th St, PO Box 588; phone605/665-3636 or toll-free 800/888-1460
Web Site www.yanktonsd.com

The first capital of Dakota Territory (1861-1883), Yankton has restored homes and mansions dating to territorial days.

What to See and Do

Dakota Territorial Capitol. *Riverside Park, Yankton (57078).* Replica of the first capitol of Dakota Territory. Original building (1862) was auctioned for scrap after the territorial capital was moved to Bismarck in 1883. **FREE**

Dakota Territorial Museum. *Westside Park, 610 Summit Ave, Yankton (57078). Phone 605/665-3898.* Museum in complex includes restored Dakota Territorial Legislative Council Building; railroad depot, caboose; rural schoolhouse; blacksmith shop; 1870 parlor, 1900 bedroom, grandma's kitchen; military display. (Memorial Day-Labor Day: daily Tues-Sun; rest of year: Mon-Fri) **$**

Lewis and Clark Lake/Gavins Point Dam. *5 miles W on Hwy 52. Phone 402/667-7873.*This reservoir of Missouri River has 15 developed recreation areas for camping (fee), swimming beaches, boat and fish-

ing access. Primitive areas for hunting, scenic drives, hiking. Other attractions include tour of powerhouse, visitor center, fish hatchery and aquarium, and campground programs. **FREE**

Special Events

Great Plains Oldtime Fiddlers Contest. *Phone 605/665-3636.* Mid-Sept.

Riverboat Days. *Phone 605/665-1657.* Entertainment, crafts, food, rodeo. Third weekend in Aug.

Limited-Service Hotel

★ **DAYS INN.** *2410 Broadway, Yankton (57078). Phone 605/665-8717; toll-free 800/329-7466; fax 605/665-8841. www.daysinn.com.* 46 rooms, 2 story. Pets accepted; fee. Complimentary continental breakfast. Check-in 2 pm, check-out 11 am. Whirlpool. **$**

Sportech

**Ticket must be cashed by
March 31st of the year
following the year of purchase.**

Sportech

D-0770-E682-8569

Race 9

11-MAY-19 8:01M

BELMONT

$2 WIN		$
2		
$3 SHOW		$3
2		
BETS	TOTAL	$5

11 WE 22502   11-MAY-19   12:57

D-0770-E682-8569

Wyoming

From the high western plateaus of the Great Plains, the state of Wyoming stretches across the Continental Divide and into the Rocky Mountains. This is a land of scenic beauty and geographic diversity; mountain ranges, grasslands, and desert can all be found within Wyoming's borders.

The first Europeans to explore this region were French; brothers Louis and Francés François Verendrye trapped here in 1743. The first American to enter what is now Yellowstone National Park was John Colter, a member of the Lewis and Clark expedition, who was here during the winter of 1807-1808. The 1820s saw a number of trappers and fur traders become established in the area. The territory became the site of important stops along the pioneer trails to the West Coast in the 1840s-1860s.

The pioneer trails across Wyoming allowed pioneers to cross the rugged spine of the Rocky Mountains on an easy grade, following grass and water over the Continental Divide. Of the approximately 350,000 individuals who made their way along the various westward trails, some 21,000 died en route, claimed by disease, accidents, and mountain snow. After 1847, thousands of Mormons came along the Mormon Trail to join Brigham Young's settlement at Salt Lake. The situation improved dramatically for those bound for the West when the Union Pacific Railroad pushed across Wyoming during 1867-1869. The "iron horse" made the journey considerably safer and easier, not to mention faster. Permanent settlement of the West then began in earnest.

The hard existence wrought from a sometimes inhospitable land bred a tough, practical people who

Population: 493,782

Area: 96,988 square miles

Elevation: 3,100-13,804 feet

Peak: Gannett Peak (between Fremont and Sublette counties)

Entered Union: July 10, 1890 (44th state)

Capital: Cheyenne

Motto: Equal Rights

Nickname: Equality State, Cowboy State

Flower: Indian Paintbrush

Bird: Meadowlark

Fair: August in Douglas

Tree: Cottonwood

Time Zone: Mountain

Web Site: www.state.wy.us

Fun Fact:
- Wyoming was the first state to give women the right to vote.

recognized merit when they saw it. While still a territory, Wyoming in 1869 became the first area in the United States to grant women the right to vote. Subsequently, Wyomingites were the first in the nation to appoint a woman justice of the peace, the first to select women jurors, and the first to elect a woman, Nellie Tayloe Ross, governor in 1924. This reputation has earned Wyoming the nickname "the Equality State."

The civic-mindedness of its citizens spread beyond the political arena with equal vigor. Wyoming introduced the nation's first county library system and instituted a public education system that today ranks among the finest in the United States.

Cattle and sheep outnumber people by more than five to one in Wyoming, which is the least populated state in the country. It is, therefore, easy to see how the cowboy has become such a promi-

Calendar Highlights

June

Plains Indian Powwow *(Cody). Phone 307/587-4034.* People from tribes throughout the western plains states and Canada gather to compete. Dancing and singing; ceremonial and traditional tribal dress.

July

1838 Mountain Man Rendezvous *(Riverton). Phone 307/856-7306.* Council fire, primitive shoots, hawk and knife throw, games, food. Camping available.

Central Wyoming Fair and Rodeo *(Casper). Fairgrounds. Phone 307/235-5775.*

Cheyenne Frontier Days *(Cheyenne). Phone toll-free 800/227-6336.* Frontier Park Arena. One of the country's most famous rodeos; originated in 1897. Parades, carnivals; USAF Thunderbirds flying team; pancake breakfast; entertainment, square dancing nightly.

Legend of Rawhide *(Lusk). Phone 307/334-2950.* Live show performed since 1946. Concert, dances, trade show, golf tournament, gun show, parade, pancake breakfast.

Red Desert Round-Up *(Rock Springs). Phone 307/352-6789.* One of the largest rodeos in the Rocky Mountains region.

August

Gift of the Waters Pageant *(Thermopolis). Phone toll-free 800/786-6772.* Hot Springs State Park. Commemorates the deeding of the world's largest mineral hot springs from the Shoshone and Arapahoe to the people of Wyoming in 1896. Pageant features Native American dances, parade, buffalo barbecue.

September

Jackson Hole Fall Arts Festival *(Jackson). Phone 307/733-3316.* A three-week celebration of the arts featuring special exhibits in more than 30 galleries, demonstrations, special activities. Also dance, theater, mountain film festival, Native American arts, and culinary arts.

---

nent symbol here. The bucking horse insignia has appeared on Wyoming license plates since 1936. It also appears in various versions on road signs, storefronts, and newspapers.

Mineral extraction is the principal industry in Wyoming, which has the largest coal resources in the country. Tourism and recreation ranks second, with approximately 4 million visitors per year entering the state. Generally, they come to visit the numerous national parks, forests, and monuments. But Wyoming offers a wide range of attractions, from abundant camping to rustic guest ranching, all set among some of the finest natural beauty to be found in the nation.

The country's first national park (Yellowstone), first national monument (Devils Tower), and first national forest (Shoshone) are all located in Wyoming.

When to Go/Climate

Wyoming's climate is relatively cool and dry, although spring can be wet in the lower elevations and winter can be dangerous. Blizzards are frequent and have been known to arise from November through June. Temperatures can vary greatly on any given day in both spring and fall.

AVERAGE HIGH/LOW TEMPERATURES (°F)

Cheyenne

Jan 38/15	**May** 65/39	**Sep** 71/44
Feb 41/18	**Jun** 74/48	**Oct** 60/34
Mar 45/22	**Jul** 82/55	**Nov** 47/24
Apr 55/30	**Aug** 80/53	**Dec** 39/17

Lander

Jan 31/8	**May** 66/40	**Sep** 72/44
Feb 37/14	**Jun** 77/49	**Oct** 60/34
Mar 46/22	**Jul** 86/56	**Nov** 43/20
Apr 56/31	**Aug** 84/54	**Dec** 32/9

Parks and Recreation

Water-related activities, hiking, various other sports, picnicking, and visitor centers, as well as camping, are available in many of Wyoming's parks. State parks are open all year, but some facilities may be closed from November to March. The entrance fee per vehicle is $4 for nonresidents, $2 for residents; an annual use permit is $40 for nonresidents, $25 for residents. Overnight camping is $12 for nonresidents, $6 for residents. The entrance fee for state historical sites is $2 for nonresidents, $1 for residents. Camping is limited to 14 days per site unless otherwise posted. Pets are allowed under control. For further information, contact the Wyoming State Parks & Historic Sites, 122 W 25th, Herschler Building 1-E, Cheyenne 82002; phone 307/777-6323; www.wyo-park.com.

FISHING AND HUNTING

For anglers, there are 16,000 miles of fishing streams, 270,000 acres of fishing lakes, and 90 fish varieties, among which are 22 game fish. Throughout Wyoming, pronghorn antelope, moose, elk, black bear, white-tailed and mule deer, and bighorn sheep roam the mountain ranges and meadows, which are open to hunters.

Nonresident hunting and fishing license for one elk and one season of fishing: $410. Nonresident deer permit: $220; bighorn sheep permit (one male): $1,510; moose permit (one bull): $1,010; bird or turkey license: $50; small game (cottontail) license: $50 (one-day, $15); nonresident fishing license: annual $65 (one-day, $10). Most hunting licenses must be applied for well in advance of the hunting season and are issued via computer drawing. January 31 is the deadline for elk applications, February 28 for bighorn sheep and moose, and March 15 for deer and antelope. Persons missing the date may apply for any leftover licenses. All license holders except for those purchasing a one-day or five-day fishing license must purchase a conservation stamp for $10 before hunting or fishing; one-time fee per person per year.

Visitors may take a self-guided tour of the visitor center in the headquarters office building, 5400 Bishop Boulevard, Cheyenne.
Further information can be obtained from the State of Wyoming Game and Fish Department, 5400 Bishop Boulevard, Cheyenne 82006, phone 307/777-4600.

Driving Information

Safety belts are mandatory for all persons in the front seat of a vehicle. Children under 3 years or under 40 pounds in weight must be in approved safety seats. For more information, phone 307/772-0824.

INTERSTATE HIGHWAY SYSTEM

The following alphabetical listing of Wyoming towns in this book shows that these cities are within 10 miles of the indicated interstate highways. Check a highway map for the nearest exit.

Highway Number	Cities/Towns within 10 Miles
Interstate 25	Buffalo, Casper, Cheyenne, Douglas, Sheridan, Wheatland.
Interstate 80	Cheyenne, Evanston, Green River, Laramie, Rawlins, Rock Springs.
Interstate 90	Buffalo, Gilette, Sheridan.

Additional Visitor Information

Detailed visitor information is distributed by Wyoming Business Council Tourism Division, I-25 at College Drive, Cheyenne 82002; phone 307/777-7777 or toll-free 800/225-5996. Visitors will find the information provided at Wyoming's several welcome centers helpful in planning their stay in the state. Their locations are as follows: in the northern central part of Wyoming, north on I-90 in Sheridan; at the lower eastern corner, on I-25, south of I-80 in Cheyenne; on the western side, near Grand Teton National Park, on Hwy 89 in Jackson; and in central Wyoming in Casper on Center St, south of I-25 (Mon-Fri); I-80 east at exit 6 in Evanston; I-80, 10 miles east of Laramie (late May-mid-Oct.); and on I-90 in Sundance (late May-mid-Oct.).

DRIVING THE OLD OREGON TRAIL

Between 1843 and 1860, an estimated 53,000 pioneers trekked across the North American continent on the Oregon Trail. This resolute group journeyed up the North Platte River and across Wyoming's Great Divide Basin before crossing the Continental Divide at South Pass, from whence they followed the Snake and Columbia rivers to Oregon. Modern highways parallel the Oregon Trail much of the distance across the state, and many of the same landmarks greet todays travelers.

Begin the tour on Highway 26 near Torrington. Fort Laramie was constructed at the confluence of the North Platte and Laramie rivers, first as a fur trading post and then as a military fort to protect the influx of white settlers from the local Native Americans. Today, the many buildings of the original fort complex have been reconstructed by the National Park Service and serve as a fascinating reminder of frontier life. Thirteen buildings stand around a central parade ground, many filled with period artifacts. The Fort Laramie Museum and Visitor Center houses artifacts, uniforms, and weapons from the fort's heyday.

Just west of Fort Laramie on Highway 26 is Guernsey, where the Register Cliff State Historic Site preserves a sandstone bluff on which migrating pioneers left initials, dates, and other messages carved in stone. The pioneer graveyard near the site is testimony to the hardships of this epic trek. Continue west on I-25 through Douglas, with a town center dominated by a statue of a jackalope, and then on to Glenrock.

Casper, Wyoming's largest city, didnt exist during Oregon Trail days, but the ford on the North Platte River made it a hub for the many trails that brought pioneers to the West. The Oregon, Mormon, Pony Express, California, and Pioneer trails all converged here. Fort Casper was established in 1855 by the army to protect migrating settlers from hostile Indians and over the years served as a military fort, Pony Express station, trading post, and stage stop. The fort was reconstructed during the 1930s by the Civilian Conservation Corps (CCC) according to the original floor plans. Today, the fort buildings serve as museums of the frontier West, complete with living history activities that demonstrate daily life in the 19th century. Also near Casper is the National Historic Trails Interpretive Center, a BLM facility that commemorates the pioneer trails that intersect at Casper.

From Casper, follow Highway 220 west. Independence Rock was named by pioneer William Sublette, who spent July 4, 1830, camped here. Independence Rock became a landmark for Oregon Trail pioneers, who knew that if they reached Independence Rock by July 4, they would get across the mountains to Oregon before snowfall. The pioneers also chiseled names and dates into the rock—among the names carved here are Jesuit missionary Father DeSmet and Mormon leader Brigham Young.

A few miles west of Independence Rock is another landmark of the Oregon Trail. Here the Sweetwater River carves a narrow chasm through a high rock outcrop.

At Muddy Gap, follow Highway 287 west across a desolate desert basin. Roadside markers tell the harrowing story of Oregon Trail pioneers as they passed though this high-elevation wasteland. Follow Highway 28 south as it climbs steadily toward South Pass. Unlike many Rocky Mountain passes, South Pass is not a high mountain divide. Rather, its a high desert plateau covered by sagebrush and short prairie grasses—ideal for Oregon Trail pioneers and their wagon trains.

As the road climbs up to the pass, it passes two historic gold rush towns from the 1870s. Atlantic City, a near-ghost town, still boasts the Mercantile, a steakhouse and saloon thats been serving locals for more than a century. South Pass City preserves 39 acres of abandoned buildings from the days when gold rush fever brought thousands of residents to this lofty corner of Wyoming. **(Approximately 340 miles)**

THE BIG HORN MOUNTAIN SCENIC LOOP

This loop tour departs from Cody, a Wild West town if there ever was one, and travels east across the arid plains to the Big Horn Mountains. This fault-block range rises up precipitously to tower 13,000 feet above the neighboring rangeland. The route passes geological curiosities and sacred Native American sites before dropping back down to traverse the dramatic Big Horn Canyon on its way back to Cody.

Cody is named for Buffalo Bill Cody, the showman famous for his traveling Wild West Show. The town was established in 1895, and though he didn't help found it, Cody was brought in shortly thereafter to promote the town. As befits a showmans adoptive home, the town of Cody overnight became a Wild West tourist destination.

Be sure to visit the complex of downtown museums and galleries that make up the Buffalo Bill Historical Center, particularly the Whitney Gallery of Western Art, which contains one of the worlds foremost collections of 19th-century Western art. As you leave Cody's too-perfect Wild West town center, consider a detour to Old Trail Town, west of town off Highway 20. This open-air museum preserves a collection of 26 historic frontier structures in their authentic state. Included are the actual cabins lived in by the likes of Butch Cassidy, plus the saloons, schoolhouses, and ranch houses that represented everyday life for frontier pioneers.

Travel east of Cody on Highway 14, leaving behind the Yellowstone foothills to cross the increasingly barren ranchland of the Big Horn Basin. The gray, sparsely vegetated buttes and badlands that increasingly dominate the landscape are remnants of volcanic ash deposits from Yellowstones ancient volcanoes. Dunes of ash built up here over millions of years; these are now mined for bentonite, a source material of cement.

Two things characterize this arid prairie: oil, made evident by the rise and fall of rigs scattered to the horizon, and dinosaurs. To get an idea of the plant and reptile Eden that once existed here, stop in Greybull (pronounced "Grable") to visit the Greybull Museum. For a small regional museum, this institution houses an impressive number of significant fossils, including a 5-foot-diameter ammonite and the remnants of a cycad tree forest from 120 million years ago.

Eight miles east of Greybull, on the Red Gulch/Alkali National Back Country Byway is another important paleontological destination. The Red Gulch Dinosaur Tracksite preserves hundreds of dinosaur tracks left

in oozy ocean shoreline mud about 167 million years ago. These tracks were only discovered in 1997 and are, worldwide, some of the only known tracks from the Middle Jurassic Era.

East of the town of Shell, Highway 14 begins to climb up through a wonderland of red hoodoos–the result of iron-rich ash deposits–to the near-vertical face of the Big Horn Mountains. This unusual mountain range was formed by uplifts along vertical fault lines: One side of the fault line has been pushed up over 2 miles into the sky, whereas the other dropped into the Big Horn Basin. The road climbs steeply up the red cliffs, eventually passing through dense forests and–even in midsummersnowfields. Stop at the Shell Falls Viewpoint to gawk at Shell Creek as it tumbles into an extremely narrow canyon cut through limestone and granite.

The top of the Big Horns is a series of rolling mountain peaks flanked by vast alpine meadows, which in summer is spangled with wildflowers and tiny ponds of snowmelt. Watch for beaver dams in the coursing streambeds. Moose and elk are frequently seen in these high-country marshes.

At Burgess Junction, turn west onto Highway 14A. The road begins to drop back down the western face of the Big Horn range. Midway down the mountainside is a side road leading to the Medicine Wheel National Historic Landmark, a fascinating ritual site built by ancient Paleo-Indians. Perhaps dating back 10,000 years, this large ring of rocks with 28 radiating spokes aligned around a central hub is thought to be a Native American Stonehenge. Scientists believe the Medicine Wheel was used to make astronomical calculations and predictions. The Medicine Wheel is a 1-mile hike from the parking area.

Continue the descent of the Big Horns, again reaching arid basin land. The road traverses the now-dammed Big Horn River in its awe-inspiring canyon. Turn north on Highway 37 to catch glimpses of the canyonover 1,000 feet deep in places–threaded by the blue waters of the lake. To the north rise the Pryor Mountains, home to one of the West's last free-ranging herds of wild horses.

From Big Horn Canyon, return east along Highway 14A through Lovell and Powell to Cody. **(Approximately 200 miles)**

Afton (C-1)

See also Alpine

Population 1,394
Elevation 6,239 ft
Area Code 307
Zip 83110
Information Chamber of Commerce, PO Box 1097; phone 307/883-2759 or toll-free 800/426-8833
Web Site www.starvalleychamber.com

An arch across Main Street composed of 3,000 elk horns marks the entrance to the town of Afton. For anglers and big-game hunters there are outfitters and experienced guides here who rarely send their clients home empty-handed. Afton is located in Star Valley, which is noted for its dairy industry. A Ranger District office of the Bridger-Teton National Forest (see JACKSON) is located here.

What to See and Do

Fishing. Excellent brown trout and cutthroat trout fishing year-round on Salt River (within 2 1/2 miles).

Intermittent spring. *7 miles E up Swift Creek Canyon.* Spring flows out of mountain for about 18 minutes, then stops completely for the same period. The theory behind this phenomenon is that a natural siphon exists from an underground lake. Canyon suitable for hiking or horseback riding. Horses, guides available.

Outfitting and Big Game Hunting. Inquire at the Chamber of Commerce.

Alpine (C-1)

See also Afton, Jackson

Population 200
Elevation 5,600 ft
Area Code 307
Zip 83128
Web Site www.alpinewyoming.org

The Palisades Reservoir, just south of town, offers fishing, boating, and tent and trailer camping.

Limited-Service Hotel

★ ★ **Best Western Flying Saddle Lodge.** 118878 Jct Hwys 89 and 26, Alpine (83128). Phone 307/654-7561; toll-free 866/666-2937; fax 307/654-7563. www.flyingsaddle.com. On Snake River. 26 rooms. Pets accepted; fee. Complimentary continental breakfast. Check-in 2 pm, check-out 11 am. Restaurant, bar. Fitness room. Outdoor pool, whirlpools. Tennis. **$**

Alta

Full-Service Resort

★ ★ ★ **GRAND TARGHEE SKI AND SUMMER RESORT.** *3300 E Ski Hill Rd, Alta (83342). Phone 307/353-2300; toll-free 800/827-4433; fax 307/353-8148. www.grandtarghee.com.* Located at the main gateway to Grand Teton and Yellowstone national parks, this self-contained resort with panoramic views of three states offers a variety of outdoor activities. Skiing (both downhill and cross-country) is the main draw here, but summer brings opportunities to ride horses, mountain bike, hike, play Frisbee, golf on a designated 18-hole course, and more. Adventurers can challenge themselves on the climbing wall or on the ropes course and zip line, while scenic chairlift rides cater to those who prefer simply to enjoy the beautiful vistas. On-site shopping and dining options include the Targhee Steakhouse, the Trap Bar & Grill, and a general store that sells snacks and sundries. 90 rooms, 4 story. Closed late Apr-May and Oct-late Nov. Check-in 4 pm, check-out 11 am. Four restaurants, two bars. Children's activity center. Fitness room, fitness classes available, spa. Outdoor pool, whirlpool. Tennis. Ski in/ski out. Airport transportation available. **$$**

Buffalo (B-4)

See also Gillette, Sheridan

Founded 1884
Population 3,302
Elevation 4,640 ft
Area Code 307
Zip 82834
Information Chamber of Commerce, 55 N Main; phone 307/684-5544 or toll-free 800/227-5122
Web Site www.buffalowyo.com

Buffalo began as a trading center at the edge of Fort McKinney, one of the last of the old military posts. In 1892, trouble erupted here between big cattlemen and small ranchers with their allies, the nesters, in the Johnson County Cattle War. Several people were killed before Federal troops ended the conflict.

Located at the foot of the Big Horn Mountains, Buffalo attracts many tourists, hunters, and anglers; the economy is dependent on tourism, as well as lumber, minerals, and cattle. A Ranger District office of the Bighorn National Forest (see SHERIDAN) is located in Buffalo.

What to See and Do

Fort Phil Kearny Site. *13 miles N on Hwy 87. Phone 307/684-7629.* This cavalry post was the scene of a clash between Sioux, Arapahoe, Cheyenne, and US soldiers; site of Fetterman and Wagon Box battles; visitor center. (Mid-May-Sept, daily) **$**

Jim Gatchell Memorial Museum. *100 Fort St, Buffalo (82834). Adjacent to the courthouse. Phone 307/684-9331. www.jimgatchell.com.* Collection of Native American artifacts, local and regional history, and pioneer equipment; natural history display. (Mid-Apr-late Nov: Mon-Fri 9 am-4 pm; closed Thanksgiving) **$**

Special Event

Johnson County Fair and Rodeo. *Phone 307/684-7357.* Features working cowhands; parade. Rodeo held last three days of fair. Second week in Aug.

Limited-Service Hotel

★ **COMFORT INN.** *65 Hwy 16 E, Buffalo (82834). Phone 307/684-9564; toll-free 800/424-6423; fax 307/684-9564. www.choicehotels.com.* 42 rooms, 2 story. Pets accepted, some restrictions; fee. Complimentary continental breakfast. Check-in 2 pm, check-out 11 am. High-speed Internet access, wireless Internet access. Whirlpool. **$**

Specialty Lodging

PARADISE GUEST RANCH. *282 Hunter Creek Rd, Buffalo (82834). Phone 307/684-7876; fax 307/684-7380. www.paradiseranch.com.* This magnificent dude ranch is the West at its best. The beautiful log cabins have outdoor porches. At the French Creek Saloon, there are talent shows and square dancing. The ranch was the inspiration for *The Virginian.* 18 rooms. Closed Oct-May. Complimentary full breakfast. Check-in 3 pm, check-out 10 am. Bar. Children's activity center. Outdoor

pool, whirlpool. Airport transportation available. No credit cards accepted. **$$$$**

Casper (C-4)

See also Douglas

Founded 1888
Population 46,742
Elevation 5,140 ft
Area Code 307
Information Chamber of Commerce Visitor Center, 500 N Center St, PO Box 399, 82602; phone 307/234-5311 or toll-free 800/852-1889
Web Site www.casperwyoming.org

Before oil was discovered, Casper was a railroad terminus in the cattle-rich Wyoming hinterlands, where Native Americans and emigrants on the Oregon Trail had passed before. Casper was known as an oil town after the first strike in 1890 in the Salt Creek Field, site of the Teapot Dome naval oil reserve that caused a top-level government scandal in the 1920s. World War I brought a real boom and exciting prosperity. A half-million dollars in oil stocks was traded in hotel lobbies every day; land prices skyrocketed and rents inflated while oil flowed through some of the world's biggest refineries. The crash of 1929 ended the speculation, but oil continued to flow through feeder lines to Casper. Oil continues to contribute to the area's economy; also important are tourism, agriculture, light manufacturing, coal, bentonite, and uranium mining.

What to See and Do

Casper Mountain and Beartrap Meadow Parks. *10 miles S. Phone 307/235-9311.* Nordic ski trails (fee). Snowmobile trails (registration required), mountain bike trails. Picnicking, camping (fee), shelters (reservations required). (Daily) Located on the mountain is

> **Lee McCune Braille Trail.** Flora, fauna, and geology are the focus of this trail (1/3 mile) geared for both the sighted and the visually impaired. The self-guided loop trail has signs in both Braille and English at 36 interpretive stations. Safety ropes are provided for guidance. **FREE**

Casper Planetarium. *904 N Poplar St, Casper (82601). Phone 307/577-0310.* Three one-hour shows every evening. (Early June-early Sept and Thanksgiving-Dec 24, daily) **$$**

Devil's Gate. *63 miles S on Hwy 220. Phone 307/328-2953.* Pioneer landmark noted by emigrants moving west on the Oregon and Mormon Trails. Church of Jesus Christ of Latter-Day Saints interpretive center tells of the 1856 Martin's Cove disaster, in which as many as 145 people died when confronted by an early, severe winter. Hiking. (Daily; closed Dec 25) **FREE**

Edness K. Wilkins State Park. *8700 E Hwy 20/26, Evansville (82636). 4 miles E via I-25, Hat Six exit on Hwy 87. Phone 307/577-5150. wyoparks.state.wy.us/edness1.htm.* Approximately 300 acres on the Oregon Trail, bordered by the historic Platte River. Day-use park. Swimming pond, fishing; hiking paths, picnicking. **$**

⭐ **Fort Caspar Museum and Historic Site.** *4001 Fort Caspar Rd, Casper (82604). Phone 307/235-8462.* A US Army post in the 1860s, Fort Caspar served as a base for soldiers who first sought to protect pioneers, telegraph linemen, and mail carriers and later fought Lakota warriors in a series of increasingly violent battles. Abandoned in 1867 after the railroad became the focal point of cross-country travel, Fort Caspar now features a number of replica buildings built in 1936 to depict the fort as it was in 1865. Also on-site is a museum stocked with artifacts of regional historic importance. (Mid-May-mid-Sept, daily; rest of year, Mon-Fri, Sun)

Hogadon Ski Area. *1800 E K St, Casper (82601). 11 miles S via Hwy 251. Phone 307/235-8499.* Two double chairlifts, Pomalift; patrol, school, rentals; snowmaking; cafeteria. Longest run 3/4 mile; vertical drop 600 feet. (Late Nov-mid-Apr, Wed-Sun, holidays; closed Dec 25) **$$$$**

Independence Rock. *45 miles SW on Hwy 220. Phone toll-free 800/645-6233.* "Register of the Desert," 193 feet high. Inscribed with more than 50,000 pioneer names, some dating back more than 100 years. Many names are obscured by lichen or worn away.

National Historic Trails Interpretive Center. *1501 N Poplar St, Casper (82601). Phone 307/261-7700. www.wy.blm. gov/nhtic.* Casper sits on numerous historic trails, including the Oregon, California, Mormon, Pioneer, and Pony Express trails, all prime westerly routes of the mid-19th century. To commemorate the regions rich trail legacy, the Bureau of Land Management opened the National Historic Trails Interpretive Center in 2002, with exhibits covering everything from packing for a cross-country journey in a covered wagon to negotiating such a wagon across a raging river. The historic trail route is now marked and runs directly through the centers property. (Apr-late Oct: daily 8 am-7 pm; Nov-late Mar: Tues-Sat 9 am-4:30 pm; closed holidays) **$$**

Nicolaysen Art Museum & Discovery Center. *400 E Collins Dr, Casper (82601). Phone 307/235-5247.* Changing and permanent exhibits. (Tues-Sun; closed holidays) **FREE**

Special Event

Central Wyoming Fair and Rodeo. *Fairgrounds, 1700 Fairgrounds Rd, Casper (82601). Phone 307/235-5775.* Carnival, PRCA rodeo, cattle show, and drill teams competition are some of the activities at the annual fair. Mid-July.

Limited-Service Hotels

★ **COMFORT INN.** *480 Lathrop Rd, Evansville (82636). Phone 307/235-3038; toll-free 800/424-6423; fax 307/235-3038. www.comfortinn.com.* 56 rooms, 2 story. Pets accepted, some restrictions. Complimentary continental breakfast. Check-in 2 pm, check-out 11 am. Indoor pool, whirlpool. **$**
🔲 🛏

★ **HAMPTON INN.** *400 West F St, Casper (82601). Phone 307/235-6668; toll-free 800/426-7866; fax 307/235-2027. www.hamptoninn.com.* 121 rooms, 2 story. Complimentary continental breakfast. Check-in 2 pm, check-out 11 am. High-speed Internet access. Fitness room. Indoor pool, whirlpool. Airport transportation available. Business center. **$**
🏃 🛏 🏃

★ ★ **HOLIDAY INN.** *300 West F St, Casper (82601). Phone 307/235-2531; toll-free 877/576-8636; fax 307/473-3111. www.casperhi.com.* 200 rooms, 2 story. Pets accepted. Check-in 3 pm, check-out noon. Restaurant, bar. Fitness room. Indoor pool, whirlpool. Airport transportation available. Business center. **$**
🔲 🏃 🛏 🏃

★ **SHILO INN.** *I-25 and Curtis Rd, Casper (82636). Phone 307/237-1335; toll-free 800/222-2244; fax 307/577-7429.* 101 rooms. Pets accepted. Complimentary continental breakfast. Check-in 3 pm, check-out noon. Indoor pool, whirlpool. **$**
🔲 🔲 🛏

Restaurants

★ ★ **PAISLEY SHAWL.** *416 W Birch St, Glenrock (82637). Phone 307/436-9212; toll-free 800/458-0144; fax 307/436-9213. www.hotelhiggins.com.* This quaint, continental restaurant is housed in the Hotel Higgins (1916), a National Register bed-and-breakfast filled with period antiques. American menu. Lunch, dinner. Closed Sun- Mon; holidays. Bar. Children's menu. Outdoor seating. **$$**

★ ★ **SILVER FOX RESTAURANT AND LOUNGE.** *3422 S Energy Ln, Casper (82604). Phone 307/235-3000; fax 307/234-5324. www.armorssilverfox. com.* American menu. Lunch, dinner. Closed Sun; holidays. Bar. Children's menu. Casual attire. **$$$**

Cheyenne (E-5)

See also Laramie, Wheatland

Founded 1867
Population 50,008
Elevation 6,098 ft
Area Code 307
Zip 82001
Information Cheyenne Convention & Visitors Bureau, 121 W 15th St; phone 307/778-3133 or toll-free 800/426-5009
Web Site www.cheyenne.org

Cheyenne was named for an Algonquian tribe that roamed this area. When the Union Pacific Railroad reached what is now the capital and largest city of Wyoming on November 13, 1867, there was already a

A Good 'Ol Frontier Town

Cheyenne grew up with the arrival of the railroad in 1867–going from a population of zero to three thousand in five months. By 1880, 10,000 people made their home here. This rapid growth produced an unusual unity of architectural design. Cheyenne has one of the best-preserved frontier town centers in Wyoming.

Begin a walking tour at the Wyoming Transportation Museum, 15th Street and Capitol Avenue. Formerly the depot for the Union Pacific Railway, this massive structure of stone and brick surmounted by a bell tower, was built in 1886. The building now serves as a railway museum.

Walk north to 16th Street, the city's main street during the frontier era. Many of the handsome redbrick storefronts from the 1880s are still in use. Stop by the Old Town Square, a pedestrian-friendly, two-block area with boutique shopping and reenactments of Old West activities, including a nightly shoot-out with gunslingers in period garb. The Cheyenne Visitors and Convention Bureau is adjacent to the square at 309 West 16th Street.

At the corner of 16th Street and Central Avenue is the Historic Plains Hotel (1600 Central Ave). Built in 1910, this grand old hotel has a wonderfully atmo-

spheric lobby and one of the oldest restaurants and bars in the state. The Plains is a favorite watering hole for Wyoming's political movers and shakers.

Walk up Capitol Avenue, past opulent, late-Victorian state office buildings and storefronts, with the state capitol building looming in the distance. Turn on 17th Street, and walk east to Lexies Café (216 E 17th), a Cheyenne dining institution. This period restaurant is located in the city's oldest structure, the luxurious 1880s home of Erasmus Nagle. In summer, there's al fresco dining against the backdrop of the town's historic district.

Continue north along House Street, past more historic homes, to the Historic Governor's Mansion (200 E 21st St). Built in 1904, this beautifully preserved sandstone structure was the home of Wyoming's governors until 1977. Today, free tours of the building focus on period furnishings and artifacts.

Head west on 23rd Avenue. The Wyoming State Museum (2301 Central Ave), is the states foremost history museum, telling Wyoming's story from the era of the dinosaurs to the present, with especially good exhibits on the state's Native American and early settlement history. The museum also houses the states art collection, rich in late 19th-century Western art.

Continue one block west to Capitol Avenue and turn north. The Wyoming Arts Council Gallery (2320 Capitol Ave) is housed in an 1880s carriage house and is dedicated to mounting the works of contemporary Wyoming artists.

The Wyoming State Capitol Building, at 24th and Capitol Avenue, with its gleaming 24-karat gold leaf dome and feints toward French Renaissance architectural style, has dominated Cheyenne's skyline since 1888. The interior is equally grandiose, with marble floors, mahogany woodwork, and banks of stained glass. Free tours lead through the legislative chambers, or visitors can explore the building's art, historical displays, and huge stuffed buffalo (the states symbol) on their own.

From there, continue south along Capitol Avenue, turning west at 18th Street. The Nelson Museum of the West (1714 Carey Ave), offers 11,000 square feet of exhibits focusing on Native America and the Old West. One block farther south, at Carey and 16th, is Cheyenne's farmers' market, where local growers sell produce on Saturday mornings.

Cheyenne Frontier Days

The rodeo equivalent of the Super Bowl, Cheyenne Frontier Days is not just a sporting event; it's also a rollicking street party, a family-friendly country fair, and an annual celebration of the Wyoming capitol city's cowboy heritage. Nicknamed "The Daddy of 'Em All"—the "em all" referring to the rest of the countrys rodeos—the event lives up to its name.

Frontier Days began in 1897 at the behest of an agent from the Union Pacific Railroad. In an effort to increase leisure traffic, the company encouraged the cities on its lines to organize annual festivals and fairs. Cheyenne's entry took off quickly: The second Frontier Days (1898) saw a performance by "Buffalo Bill" Cody's Wild West Show. In 1903, President Teddy Roosevelt paid a visit, putting Frontier Days on the national stage.

By and large a volunteer effort, Frontier Days grew and grew (and got rowdier and rowdier, until the city buckled down on drinking and roughhousing), becoming one of the best-attended annual events in the West. Today, it attracts about 400,000 people every year, especially impressive in relation to Cheyenne's population of 50,000.

Held over the course of ten days in late July and early August, Frontier Days kicks off with a "Grand Parade" through historic downtown Cheyenne that features innumerable horses, even more cowboys, and a small faction of rodeo clowns. Most of the ensuing events take place at Frontier Park's Cheyenne Frontier Days Rodeo Arena, but all of Cheyenne bustles with activity for the duration.

The meat of the schedule is made up of nine rodeos, which run Saturday through the next weekends Sunday, all of them sanctioned by the Professional Rodeo Cowboys Association. Top cowboys compete in such staple events as bull riding, calf roping, barrel racing, and steer wrestling at the CFD Rodeo Arena.

The Frontier Days's pancake breakfasts, held three times over the course of the event, are also legendary. About 30,000 attendees gobble up 100,000 free flapjacks, which are poured on the griddle and flipped by the local Kiwanis club. (Legend has it that the batter is mixed up in a cement truck.) Chuck wagon cook-offs, also free, are another culinary highlight.

Beyond sport and food, music is another big source of entertainment at Frontier Days. Nightly concerts feature big Nashville names like George Strait and Kenny Chesney, as well as rockers like ZZ Top. Concert tickets are sold separately from the rodeo events. There are also free performances almost every day at Frontier Park.

Organizers invited members of Wyoming's native Shoshone tribe to perform at the second Frontier Days in 1898; the tradition continues to this day. Native American dancers, storytellers, and musicians perform regularly at the Indian Village, and vendors from various area tribes sell jewelry, food, and crafts.

A carnival midway, aerial show, and a re-created Old West town are among the other diversions.

Tickets for the rodeos and concerts are available by phone (toll-free 800/227-6336) or online (www. cfdrodeo.com). Reserve early and be prepared to

pay a premium for accommodations during the eventmost Cheyenne hotels charge 50 to 100 percent more for a double room during Frontier Days. The same goes for commercial campgrounds and RV parks.

town. Between July of that year and the day the tracks were actually laid, 4,000 people had set up living quarters and land values soared. Professional gunmen, soldiers, promoters, trainmen, gamblers, and confidence men enjoying quick money and cheap liquor gave the town the reputation of being "hell on wheels." Two railways and three transcontinental highways made it a wholesale and commodity jobbing point, the retail and banking center of a vast region. Cheyenne is the seat of state and county government. Agriculture, light manufacturing, retail trade, and tourism support the economy of the area.

What to See and Do

Cheyenne Botanic Gardens. *710 S Lions Park Dr, Cheyenne (82001). Phone 307/637-6458.* Wildflower, rose gardens, lily pond, community garden. (Mon-Fri; weekends, holidays, afternoons) **DONATION**

Cheyenne Frontier Days Old West Museum. *4610 N Carey Ave, Cheyenne (82001). Phone 307/778-7290.* Includes collections of clothing, weapons, carriages, Western art. Gift shop. (Daily; closed holidays) (See SPECIAL EVENTS) **$$**

⭐ **Cheyenne Street Railway Trolley.** *Convention & Visitors Bureau, 309 W Lincolnway, Cheyenne (82001). Phone 307/778-3133.* Two-hour historic tour of major attractions. (Mid-May-mid Sept, daily) **$$$**

Curt Gowdy State Park. *1319 Hynds Lodge Rd, Cheyenne (82009). 26 miles W on Happy Jack Rd (Hwy 210). Phone 307/632-7946.* The foothills of a mountain range separating Cheyenne and Laramie create the park formation. Two reservoirs provide trout fishing (no swimming); boating (ramps). Hiking. Picnicking. Camping (standard fees). **$$**

Historic Governors' Mansion. *300 E 21st St, Cheyenne (82001). Phone 307/777-7878.* (1904) The residence of Wyoming's governors from 1905 to 1976, this was the first governors' mansion in the nation to be occupied

by a woman, Nellie Tayloe Ross (1925-1927). (Tues-Sat; closed holidays) **FREE**

State Capitol. *24th St and Capitol Ave, Cheyenne (82001). Head of Capitol Ave. Phone 307/777-7220.* (1887) Beaux Arts building with murals in Senate and House chambers by Allen T. True. Ceiling of each chamber is of stained glass. Guided tours (Mon-Fri; closed holidays). **FREE**

Warren AFB. *7405 Marine Loop, Cheyenne (82005). W on Randall Ave. Phone 307/773-2980.* Museum traces history of base from 1867-present (Mon-Fri; also by appointment). (See SPECIAL EVENTS) **FREE**

Special Events

Cheyenne Frontier Days. *Frontier Park Arena, 4610 Carey Ave, Cheyenne (82001). Phone toll-free 800/227-6336. www.cfdrodeo.com.* One of the country's most famous rodeos; originated in 1897. Parades, carnivals; USAF *Thunderbirds* flying team; pancake breakfast; entertainment, square dancing nightly. Last full week in July.

Laramie County Fair. *Frontier Park. Cheyenne (82001). Phone 307/633-4534.* Includes livestock and farm exhibits. Early Aug.

Old-fashioned Melodrama. *Atlas Theater, 211 E 16th St, Cheyenne (82001). Phone 307/638-6543.* Cheer for the hero, support the damsel and foil the villian at the interactive play. July-mid-Aug.

Limited-Service Hotels

★ ★ **BEST WESTERN HITCHING POST INN RESORT & CONFERENCE CENTER.** *1700 W Lincolnway, Cheyenne (82001). Phone 307/638-3301; toll-free 800/221-0125; fax 307/778-7194. www.hitchingpostinn.com.* 166 rooms, 2 story. Pets accepted; fee. Check-in 3 pm, check-out noon. High-speed Internet access, wireless Internet access. Two restaurants, bar. Fitness room. Indoor pool, outdoor pool, whirlpool.

Airport transportation available. Business center. **$**
🅳 🔧 🧍 🛏 🏃

★ **COMFORT INN.** *2245 Etchepare Dr, Cheyenne (82007). Phone 307/638-720; toll-free 888/777-7218; fax 307/635-8560. www.comfortinn.com.* 77 rooms, 2 story. Pets accepted; fee. Complimentary continental breakfast. Check-in 3 pm, check-out noon. Fitness room. Outdoor pool. **$**
🔧 🧍 🛏

★ **FAIRFIELD INN.** *1415 Stillwater Ave, Cheyenne (82001). Phone 307/637-4070; Phone toll-free 800/228-9290; fax 307/637-4070. www.fairfieldinn.com.* 62 rooms, 3 story. Complimentary continental breakfast. Check-in 3 pm, check-out noon. High-speed Internet access, wireless Internet access. Indoor pool, whirlpool. **$**
🛏

★ ★ **LITTLE AMERICA HOTEL - CHEYENNE.** *2800 W Lincolnway, Cheyenne (82009). Phone 307/775-8400; toll-free 800/445-6995; fax 307/775-8425. www. littleamerica.com.* 188 rooms, 2 story. Check-in 2 pm, check-out noon. Two restaurants, bar. Fitness room. Outdoor pool. Golf, 9 holes. Airport transportation available. Business center. **$**
🧍 🛏 🍴 🏃

Restaurant

★ **POOR RICHARD'S.**
2233 E Lincolnway, Cheyenne (82001). Phone 307/635-5114. American menu. Lunch, dinner. Closed Sun. Bar. Children's menu. Casual attire. **$$**

Cody (A-2)

See also Yellowstone National Park; also see Cooke City, MT and Red Lodge, MT

Founded 1896
Population 7,897
Elevation 5,002 ft
Area Code 307
Zip 82414
Information Cody Country Chamber of Commerce, 836 Sheridan Ave; phone 307/587-2777
Web Site www.codychamber.org

Buffalo Bill Cody founded this town, gave it his name, and devoted time and money to its development. He built a hotel and named it after his daughter Irma,

arranged for a railroad spur from Montana and, with the help of his friend Theodore Roosevelt, had what was then the world's tallest dam constructed just west of town.

Cody is located 52 miles east of Yellowstone National Park (see); everyone entering Yellowstone from the east must pass through here, making tourism an important industry. A Ranger District office of the Shoshone National Forest is located here.

What to See and Do

⭐ **Buffalo Bill Historical Center.** *720 Sheridan Ave, Cody (82414). Phone 307/587-4771.* Five-museum complex; gift shops. (Apr-Oct, daily; Nov-Mar, Tues-Sun) (See SPECIAL EVENTS) **$$$$** Admission includes

Buffalo Bill Museum. *720 Sheridan Ave, Cody (82414). Phone 307/587-4771.* Personal and historical memorabilia of the great showman and scout includes guns, saddles, clothing, trophies, gifts, and posters.

Cody Firearms Museum. *720 Sheridan Ave, Cody (82414). Phone 307/587-4771.* More than 5,000 projectile arms on display. Comprehensive collection begun in 1860 by Oliver Winchester.

Plains Indian Museum. *720 Sheridan Ave, Cody (82414). Phone 307/587-4771.* Extensive displays of memorabilia and artifacts representing the people of the Plains tribes and their artistic expressions; clothing, weapons, tools, and ceremonial items.

Whitney Gallery of Western Art. *720 Sheridan Ave, Cody (82414). Phone 307/857-4771.* Paintings, sculpture; major collection and comprehensive display of Western art by artists from the early 1800s through today. **$$$$**

Buffalo Bill State Park. *47 Lakeside Rd, Cody (82414). 13 miles W on Hwy 14, 16, 20, on Buffalo Bill Reservoir. Phone 307/587-9227.* Wildlife is abundant in this area. Fishing; boating (ramps, docks). Picnicking. Primitive camping. **$$** Also here is

Buffalo Bill Dam and Visitor Center. *47 Lakeside Rd, Cody (82414). E end of reservoir. Phone 307/527-6076.* (1910) A 350-foot dam, originally called the Shoshone Dam. The name was changed in 1946 to honor Buffalo Bill, who helped raise money for its construction. The visitor center has a natural history museum, dam overlook, gift shop. (May-Sept, daily) FREE

River Runners. *1491 Sheridan Ave, Cody (82414). Phone 307/527-7238; toll-free 800/535-7238.* Whitewater trips; 90-minute to half-day trips. (June-Labor Day, daily) **$$$$**

Shoshone National Forest. *808 Meadow Ln, Cody (82414). Phone 307/527-6241. www.fs.fed.us/r2/shoshone.* This 2,466,586-acre area is one of the largest in the national forest system. It includes a magnificent approach route (Buffalo Bill Cody's Scenic Byway) to the east gate of Yellowstone National Park (see) along the north fork of the Shoshone River. The Fitzpatrick, Popo Agie, North Absaroka, Washakie, and a portion of the Absaroka-Beartooth wilderness areas all lie within its boundaries. It includes outstanding lakes, streams, big-game herds, mountains, and some of the largest glaciers in the continental United States. Fishing; hunting. Camping.

Sleeping Giant Ski Area. *349 Yellowstone Hwy, Cody (82414). 46 miles W on Hwy 14, 16, 20. Phone 307/587-4044. www.skisleepinggiant.com.* Chairlift, T-bar; patrol, school, rentals; snack bar. Longest run 3/4 mile; vertical drop 600 feet. (Dec-mid-Apr, Fri-Sun, holidays; closed Dec 25) Cross-country trails, snowmobiling. **$$$$**

Trail Town & the Museum of the Old West. *2 miles W on Yellowstone Hwy. Phone 307/587-5302.* Twenty-four reconstructed buildings dating from 1879 to 1899 and a cemetery on the site of Old Cody City along the original wagon trails. The buildings include a cabin used as a rendezvous for Butch Cassidy and the Sundance Kid and the cabin of Crow Scout Curley, the only one of General Custer's troops who escaped from the Battle of Little Bighorn. The cemetery includes the remains of Jeremiah "Liver-Eating" Johnson. (Mid-May-mid-Sept, daily) **$$**

Wyoming River Trips. *233 Yellowstone, Cody (82414). Phone 307/587-6661; toll-free 800/586-6661.* Ninety-minute-half-day trips. (Mid-May-late Sept, daily) **$$$$**

Wyoming Vietnam Veteran's Memorial. *Off Hwy 16/20 W of the airport. Phone 307/587-2297.* Black granite memorial lists names of state residents who died or are missing in action in Vietnam.

Special Events

Cody Nite Rodeo. *Stampede Park, 421 W Yellowstone Ave, Cody (82414). Phone 307/587-2777.* Cody is known as The Rodeo Capital of the World, and with good reason. Since the 1940s, the city has been the site of the Cody Nite Rodeo, the only nightly rodeo in the country. All summer long, patrons are treated to such staple events as calf roping, steer wrestling, barrel racing, andthe big eventbull riding. The upstart competitors hail from all over the globe, making Cody Nite Rodeo something of a minor league for the pro rodeo circuit. Geared toward families, the event also features a number of kid-oriented sidelights, most notably the audience participation of the Calf Scramble, when kids in attendance race to snatch a ribbon off an unsuspecting calf. The rodeo clowns are the unofficial hosts, serving up comedy skits when theyre not doing their real duty: keeping angry bulls from stomping dispatched riders. Nightly, June-last Sat in Aug.

Cody Stampede. *519 W Yellowstone, Cody (82414). Phone 307/587-2777. www.codystampederodeo.com.* Rodeo events include bareback riding, steer wrestling, tie down roping, saddle bronc riding, bull riding, barrel racing, and team roping. Early July.

Cowboy Songs and Range Ballads. *Buffalo Bill Historical Center, 720 Sheridan Ave, Cody (82414). Phone 307/578-4028.* The Cowboy Songs and Range Ballads program salutes the cowboy songwriters and poets who have captured the spirit, beauty, humor, and stories of the West in their poems and songs. More than just cowboy music, it's a Western weekend that's entertaining, educational, and fun. Early Apr.

Frontier Festival. *Buffalo Bill Historical Center, 720 Sheridan Ave, Cody (82414). Phone 307/587-4771.* Demonstrations of pioneer skills, cooking crafts; musical entertainment. Mid-July.

Yellowstone Jazz Festival. *Elks Club lawn, Cody (82414). Phone 307/754-6307. www.yellowstonejazz.com.* Each year the Yellowstone Jazz Festival attracts top jazz performers and musicians to the Yellowstone National Park area to participate in numerous jazz concerts. Mid-July.

Limited-Service Hotels

★ **COMFORT INN.** *1601 Sheridan Ave, Cody (82414). Phone 307/587-5556; toll-free 800/527-5544; fax 307/587-8727. www.blairhotels.com.* 75 rooms, 2 story. Check-in 2 pm, check-out noon. Airport transportation available.**$$**

★ ★ **HOLIDAY INN.** *1701 Sheridan Ave, Cody (82414). Phone 307/587-5555; toll-free 800/527-5544; fax 130/777-57. www.blairhotels.com.* 189 rooms, 2 story. Check-in 3 pm, check-out 11 am. High-speed Internet access, wireless Internet access. Restaurant, bar. Fitness room. Outdoor pool. Airport transportation available. Business center. **$**

🧍 🛏 🚶

Specialty Lodgings

MAYOR'S INN B&B. *1413 Rumsey, Cody (82414). Phone 307/587-0887; toll-free 888/217-3001. www. mayorsinn.com.* 5 rooms. Complimentary full breakfast. Check-in 3 pm, check-out 11 am. **$$**

RIMROCK RANCH. *2728 Northfork Hwy, Cody (82414). Phone 307/587-3970; toll-free 800/208-7468; fax 307/527-5014. www.rimrockranch.com.* 9 rooms. Closed Oct-Apr. Complimentary full breakfast. Check-in Sun 3 pm, check-out Sun 11 am. Outdoor pool, whirlpool. Airport transportation available. **$$$$**

🛏

SEVEN D RANCH. *774 County Rd, Cody (82414). Phone 307/587-9885; toll-free 888/587-9885; fax 307/587-9885. www.7dranch.com.* On creek in Shoshone National Forest.11 rooms. Closed mid-Sept-mid-June. Complimentary full breakfast. Check-in 3 pm, check-out 10 am. Restaurant. Children's activity center. Airport transportation available. **$$$$**

🅿

UXU RANCH. *1710 Yellowstone Hwy, Cody (82450). Phone 307/587-2143; toll-free 800/373-9027; fax 307/587-8307. www.uxuranch.com.* Rustic former logging camp in forest setting. 10 rooms. Closed Oct-May. Check-in 3 pm, check-out 11 am. Restaurant, bar. Children's activity center. Whirlpool. **$$$$**

Restaurant

★ ★ **MAXWELL'S.** *937 Sheridan Ave, Cody (82414). Phone 307/527-7749; fax 307/527-4697.* American menu. Dinner. Closed Sun; holidays. Children's menu. Casual attire. Outdoor seating. **$$**

Devils Tower National Monument (A-5)

Web Site www.npw.gov/deto

The nation's first national monument, Devils Tower was set aside for the American people by President Theodore Roosevelt in 1906. Located on 1,347 acres approximately 5 miles west of the Black Hills National Forest, this gigantic landmark rises from the prairie like a giant tree stump. Sixty million years ago volcanic activity pushed molten rock toward the earth's surface. As it cooled Devils Tower was formed. Towering 1,267 feet above the prairie floor and Ponderosa pine forest, the flat-topped formation appears to change hue with the hour of the day and glows during sunsets and in moonlight.

The visitor center at the base of the tower offers information about the area, a museum, and a bookstore (Apr-Oct, daily). A self-guided trail winds around the tower for nature and scenery lovers. There are picnicking and camping facilities with tables, fireplaces, water, and restrooms (Apr-Oct). Contact Superintendent, PO Box 10, Devils Tower 82714; phone 307/467-5283.

Douglas (C-5)

See also Casper, Lusk

Founded 1886
Population 5,076
Elevation 4,842 ft
Area Code 307
Zip 82633
Information Douglas Area Chamber of Commerce, 121 Brownfield Rd; phone 307/358-2950
Web Site www.jackalope.org

Cattlemen were attracted here by plentiful water and good grass. Homesteaders gradually took over, and agriculture became dominant. The town was named for Stephen Douglas, Lincoln's celebrated debating opponent. A Ranger District office for the Medicine Bow National Forest (see LARAMIE) is located in Douglas.

What to See and Do

Fort Fetterman State Historic Site. *752 Hwy 93, Douglas (82633).* 10 miles NW on Hwy 93. Phone 307/684-7629. wyoparks.state.wy.us/fetter.htm. Established in 1867 on a plateau above the North Platte River, Fort Fetterman served as a supply base for the wars against native tribes for 15 years. Now mostly in ruins, the fort offers a snapshot into the Douglas areas history, with a pair of restored buildings showcasing historic displays. The facilities include campsites, picnic areas, and an interpretive trail. (Daily sunrise-sunset; closed in winter; museum: daily 9 am-5 pm Memorial Day-Labor Day) **$** On grounds is

> **Fort Fetterman State Museum.** *752 Hwy 93, Douglas (82633).* Phone 307/358-2864. Located on a plateau above the valleys of LaPrele Creek and the North Platte River. Museum in restored officers' quarters; additional exhibits in ordinance warehouse. Picnic area. (Memorial Day-Labor Day, daily)

Medicine Bow National Forest. *S of town on Hwy 91 or Hwy 94 (see LARAMIE).*

Thunder Basin National Grassland. *N on Hwy 59.* Phone 307/358-4690. Approximately 572,000 acres; accessible grasslands, sagebrush, and some ponderosa pine areas. Bozeman and Texas trails cross parts of the grasslands. Large herds of antelope, mule deer; sage grouse. Hunting.

Wyoming Pioneer Memorial Museum. *State Fairgrounds, 400 W Center St, Douglas (82633).* Phone 307/358-9288. Large collection of pioneer and Native American artifacts; guns; antiques. (June-Sept, Mon-Sat; rest of year, Mon-Fri; closed winter holidays) **FREE**

Special Events

High Plains Old Time Country Music Show & Contest. *Douglas High School Auditorium, 1701 Hamilton, Douglas (82633).* Phone 307/358-2950. Late Apr.

Jackalope Days. *Hwy 120 and I-25, Douglas (82633).* Phone 307/358-2950. Carnival, entertainment, and exhibitors. Usually the third weekend in June.

Wyoming State Fair and Rodeo. *State Fairgrounds, 400 W Center St, Douglas (82633).* Phone 307/358-2398. Includes rodeo events, horse shows, exhibits. Aug.

Limited-Service Hotel

★ ★ **BEST WESTERN DOUGLAS INN AND CONFERENCE CENTER.** *1450 Riverbend Dr, Douglas (82633).* Phone 307/358-9790; toll-free 800/344-2113; fax 307/358-6251. www.bestwestern.com. 117 rooms, 2 story. Pets accepted; fee. Complimentary continental breakfast. Check-in 3 pm, check-out 11 am. High-speed Internet access, wireless Internet access. Restaurant, bar. Fitness room. Indoor pool, whirlpool. **$**

Dubois (B-2)

See also Grand Teton National Park

Founded 1886
Population 895
Elevation 6,940 ft
Area Code 307
Zip 82513
Information Chamber of Commerce, 616 W Ramshorn St, PO Box 632; phone 307/455-2556
Web Site www.duboiswyoming.org

On the Wind River, 56 miles from Grand Teton National Park (see), Dubois is surrounded on three sides by the Shoshone National Forest. The Wind River Reservation (Shoshone and Arapahoe) is a few miles east of town. Dubois, in ranching and dude ranching country, is a good vacation headquarters. There are plentiful rockhounding resources, and a large herd of Bighorn sheep roam within 5 miles of town. A Ranger District office of the Shoshone National Forest (see CODY) is located here.

What to See and Do

Big-game hunting. For elk, deer, moose, bear, and mountain sheep.

National Bighorn Sheep Interpretive Center. *907 Ramshorn, Dubois (82513).* Off Hwy 26, 287. Phone 307/455-3429. Major exhibit, "Sheep Mountain," features full-size bighorns and the plants and animals that live around them. Other exhibits promote education, research, and conservation of the sheep and their habitats. (Memorial Day-Labor Day, daily; winter hours vary) **$**

Wind River Historical Center. *909 W Ramshorn, Dubois (82513).* W on Hwy 26, 287. Phone 307/455-2284.

Exhibits and displays depicting natural and social history of the Wind River Valley; includes Native American, wildlife, and archaeological displays; also Scandinavian tie-hack industries. (Mid-May-mid-Sept, daily; rest of year, by appointment) **DONATION**

Limited-Service Hotel

★ **SUPER 8.** *1414 Warm Springs Dr, Dubois (82513). Phone 307/455-3694; toll-free 800/800-8000; fax 307/455-3640. www.super8.com.* 34 rooms, 2 story. Pets accepted, some restrictions; fee. Check-in 3 pm, check-out 11 am. Whirlpool. **$**

Specialty Lodging

BROOKS LAKE LODGE. *458 Brooks Lake Rd, Dubois (82513). Phone 307/455-2121; fax 307/455-2221. www.brookslake.com.* Built as an inn for Yellowstone travelers in 1922, this historic property offers guests accommodations in the spirit of the early West in beautiful surroundings. 14 rooms. Closed mid-Apr-mid-June and mid-Sept-early Oct. Complimentary full breakfast. Check-in noon, check-out 11 am. Restaurant, bar. Fitness room, spa. Whirlpool. Airport transportation available. Business center. **$$$**

Evanston (E-1)

See also Green River, Kemmerer

Settled 1869
Population 10,903
Elevation 6,748 ft
Area Code 307
Zip 82930
Information Chamber of Commerce, 36 10th St, PO Box 365, 82931-0365; phone 307/783-0370 or toll-free 800/328-9708
Web Site www.evanstonwy.org

Coal from the mines at Almy, 6 miles north of Evanston, supplied trains of the Union Pacific Railroad, which operated a roundhouse and machine shop in Evanston beginning in 1871. By 1872, the mines employed 600 men.

While cattle and sheep ranching remain important industries, the discovery of gas and oil has triggered a new "frontier" era for the town. Evanston is also a trading center and tourist stopping point.

What to See and Do

Fort Bridger State Museum. *30 miles E on I-80, at Fort Bridger State Historic Site. Phone 307/782-3842.* Museum in barracks of partially restored fort named for Jim Bridger, scout and explorer. Pioneer history and craft demonstrations during summer; restored original buildings. (May-Sept, daily; rest of year, weekends; closed mid-Dec-Feb) Picnicking. (See SPECIAL EVENTS) **$**

Special Events

Cowboy Days. *236 9th St, Evanston (82930). Phone toll-free 800/328-9708.* PRCA rodeo with carnival, entertainment, parade, exhibits, booths, cookouts. Labor Day weekend.

Horseracing. Wyoming Downs. *10180 Hwy 89 N, Evanston (82931). 12 miles N on Hwy 89. Phone 307/789-0511.* Thoroughbred and quarter horse racing. Pari-mutuel wagering. Weekends and holidays. Memorial Day-Labor Day.

Mountain Man Rendezvous. *Fort Bridger State Museum, I-80 E, Evanston (82933). Phone 307/789-3613.* Black powder gun shoot, Native American dancing, exhibits, food. Labor Day weekend.

Uinta County Fair. *Fairgrounds, 122 Bear River Dr, Evanston (82930). Phone 307/783-0313. www.uinta-countyfair.com.* 4-H, FFA exhibits, carnival, food are just some of the activities at this county fair. First full week in Aug.

Limited-Service Hotel

★ ★ **BEST WESTERN DUNMAR INN.** *PO Box 768, Evanston (82930). Phone 307/789-3770; toll-free 800/654-6509; fax 307/789-3758. www.bestwestern.com/dunmarinn.* 165 rooms. Check-in 2 pm, check-out noon. High-speed Internet access, wireless Internet access. Restaurant, bar. Fitness room. Outdoor pool, whirlpool. **$**

Fort Laramie National Historic Site (D-5)

See also Torrington

Web Site www.nps.gov/fola

20 miles NW on Hwy 26, then W on Hwy 160; 3 miles SW of town of Fort Laramie.

Fort Laramie played an important role in much of the history of the Old West. It was one of the principal fur-trading forts in the Rocky Mountain region from 1834-1849 and one of the most important army posts on the Northern plains from 1849-1890. The first stockade built here, owned at one time by Jim Bridger and his fur-trapping partners, was Fort William, located on the strategic route to the mountains later to become the Oregon, California, and Mormon trails. In 1841, the decaying Fort William was replaced with an adobe-walled structure called Fort John on the Laramie River.

Gillette (B-5)

See also Buffalo, Devils Tower National Monument

Population 17,635
Elevation 4,608 ft
Area Code 307
Information Convention & Visitors Bureau, 1810 S Douglas Hwy #A, 82718; phone 307/686-0040 or toll-free 800/544-6136
Web Site www.visitgillette.net

What to See and Do

Keyhole State Park. *352 McKean Rd, Moorcroft (82721). 45 miles E via I-90, then 6 miles N on Pine Ridge Rd. Phone 307/756-3596.* Within sight of Devils Tower (see). Surrounding mountains form the western boundary of the Black Hills. Antelope, deer, and wild turkeys are common to this area. Reservoir is excellent for water sports. Swimming, fishing, boating (ramps, marina); picnicking, lodging, camping, tent and trailer sites (standard fees). **$$**

Tours of coal mines. *1810 S Douglas Hwy, Gillette (82718). Phone 307/686-0040; toll-free 800/544-6136.*

Reservations recommended. (Memorial Day-Labor Day, daily) **FREE**

Limited-Service Hotel

★ ★ **CLARION HOTEL.** *2009 S Douglas Hwy, Gillette (82718). Phone 307/686-3000; toll-free 800/686-3368; fax 307/686-4018. www.westernplaza.com.* 159 rooms, 3 story. Pets accepted; fee. Complimentary continental breakfast. Check-in 2 pm, check-out 11 am. Restaurant, bar. Fitness room. Indoor pool, whirlpool. Airport transportation available. Business center.**$**

Grand Teton National Park (B-1)

See also Dubois, Jackson, Teton Village, Yellowstone National Park

Web Site www.nps.gov/grte/

These rugged, block-faulted mountains began to rise about 9 million years ago, making them some of the youngest on the continent. Geologic and glacial forces combined to buckle and sculpt the landscape into a dramatic setting of canyons, cirques, and craggy peaks that cast their reflections across numerous clear alpine lakes. The Snake River winds gracefully through Jackson Hole ("hole" being the old fur trapper's term for a high-altitude valley surrounded by mountains).

John Colter passed through the area during 1807-1808. French-Canadian trappers in the region thought the peaks resembled breasts and applied the French word *teton* to them.

Entering from the north, from Yellowstone National Park (see), Highway 89/191/287 skirts the eastern shore of Jackson Lake to Colter Bay, continuing to Jackson Lake Junction, where it turns eastward to the entrance at Moran Junction (at Hwy 26). The Teton Park Road begins at Jackson Lake Junction and borders the mountains to Jenny Lake, and then continues to park headquarters at Moose. Highway 89/191/26 parallels Teton Park Road on the east side of the Snake River to the south entrance from Moran Junction. All highways have a continuous view of the Teton Range, which runs from north to south. Highway 26/89/191 is open year-round from Jackson to Flagg Ranch, 2 miles south of

Yellowstone National Park's South Gate, as is Highway 26/287 to Dubois. Secondary roads and Teton Park Road are open from May through October.

The park is open year-round (limited in winter), with food and lodging available in the park from mid-May through September and in Jackson (see). There are three visitor centers with interpretive displays: Moose Visitor Center (daily; closed Dec 25), Colter Bay Visitor Center & Indian Arts Museum (mid-May-late Sept, daily), and Jenny Lake Visitor Center (June-Labor Day). Ranger-led hikes are available (mid-June-mid-Sept, daily; inquire for schedule), and self-guided trails are marked. A 24-hour recorded message gives information about weather; phone 307/739-3611.

The park can be explored by various means. There is hiking on more than 200 miles of trails. Corrals at Jackson Lake Lodge and Colter Bay have strings of horses accustomed to rocky trails; pack trips can be arranged. Boaters and anglers can enjoy placid lakes or wild streams; the Colter Bay, Signal Mountain, and Leek's marinas have ramps, guides, facilities, and rentals. Climbers can tackle summits via routes of varying difficulty; the more ambitious may take advantage of Exum School of Mountaineering and Jackson Hole Mountain Guides classes that range from a beginner's course to an attempt at conquering the 13,770-foot Grand Teton, considered a major North American climbing peak.

Horses, boats, and other equipment can be rented. Bus tours, an airport, auto rentals, general stores, and guide services are available. Five National Park Service campgrounds are maintained: Colter Bay, Signal Mountain, Jenny Lake, Lizard Creek, and Gros Ventre (fee). Slide-illustrated talks on the park and its features are held each night (mid-June-Labor Day) at the amphitheaters at Colter Bay, Signal Mountain, and Gros Ventre.

Many river and lake trips are offered. Five-, 10-, and 20-mile trips on rubber rafts float the Snake River. Visitors can choose an adventure to suit their individual tastes (see JACKSON). A self-guided trail tells the story of Menor's Ferry (1894) and the Maude Noble Cabin. Jenny Lake has boat trips and boat rentals. Jackson Lake cruises are available, some reaching island hideaways for breakfast cookouts. Boat rentals also are available at Jackson Lake. The Grand Teton Lodge Company offers a full-day guided bus and boat trip covering major points of interest in the park (June-mid-Sept); phone 307/543-2811.

A tram with a vertical lift of 4,600 feet operates at Teton Village, rising from the valley floor to the top of Rendezvous Peak, just outside the park's southern boundary (see JACKSON).

The Chapel of the Transfiguration, located in Moose, is a log chapel with a large picture window over the altar framing the mountains (daily; services held late May-Sept).

The park is home to abundant wildlife, including pronghorn antelopes, bighorn sheep, mule deer, elk, moose, grizzly and black bears, coyotes, beavers, marmots, bald eagles, and trumpeter swans. Never approach or feed any wild animal. Do not pick wildflowers.

A park boat permit is required. A Wyoming fishing license is required for any fishing and may be obtained at several locations in the park. Camping permits are required for backcountry camping.

Grand Teton and Yellowstone national parks admission is $20 per car. Contact the Superintendent, PO Drawer 170, Moose 83012; phone 307/739-3399 or 307/739-3600 (recording).

CCInc Auto Tape Tours. This 90-minute cassette offers a mile-by-mile self-guided tour of the park. Written by informed guides, it provides information on history, points of interest, and flora and fauna of the park. Tapes may be purchased directly from CCInc, PO Box 227, 2 Elbrook Dr, Allendale, NJ 07401; phone 201/236-1666 or from the Grand Teton Lodge Company, phone 307/543-2811. $10-$15.

Limited-Service Hotel

★ ★ **TOGWOTEE MOUNTAIN LODGE.** *Hwy 26/287, Moran (83013). Phone 307/543-2847; toll-free 800/962-4988. www.cowboyvillage.com.* 89 rooms, 3 story. Check-out 11 am. Restaurant, bar. **$**

Full-Service Resorts

★ ★ ★ **JACKSON LAKE LODGE.** *N Hwy 89 and 1191, Moran (83013). Phone 307/543-3100; fax 307/543-3143. www.gtlc.com.* This lodge is a full-service property located in Grand Teton National Park. It offers a view across Jackson Lake. Grand lobby has two fireplaces, 60-foot picture window. Views of Mount Moran and the Grand Tetons. 385 rooms, 3 story. Closed early Oct-mid-May. Check-in 4 pm, check-out 11 am. Two restaurants, bar. Outdoor pool. Airport transportation available. **$$**
🅱 🖼

★ ★ ★ **JENNY LAKE LODGE.** *Inner Loop Rd-Box 240, Moose (83012). Phone 307/733-4647; fax 307/543-3358. www.gtlc.com.* Nestled at the base of the Tetons in Grand Teton National Park, this rustic, all-inclusive retreat is actually a cluster of western-style cabins outfitted with down comforters and handmade quilts. The pine-shaded property welcomes visitors from June through October for elegantly rustic accommodations and back-to-nature recreation including Jackson Hole Golf & Tennis Club, numerous hiking trails, and three lakes. 37 rooms. Closed early Oct-late May. Complimentary full breakfast. Check-in 4 pm, check-out 11 am. Restaurant. **$$$$**

Specialty Lodgings

GROS VENTRE RIVER RANCH. *18 Gros Ventre Rd, Moose (83011). Phone 307/733-4138; fax 307/733-4272. www.grosventreriverranch.com.* Guests stay in a log cabin or lodge, each with a magnificent view of the Teton Mountains. On 160 acres. 8 rooms. Closed Oct-mid-May. Complimentary full breakfast. Check-in 3 pm, check-out 10 am. High-speed Internet access. Restaurant. Fitness room. Airport transportation available. No credit cards accepted. **$$$$**
🔲 🏊

LOST CREEK RANCH. *Box 95KRW, Moose (83012). Phone 307/733-3435; fax 307/733-1954. www.lostcreek.com.* It's difficult to imagine a place more awe-inspiring than Lost Creek Ranch, where majestic snow-capped mountain peaks tower over a pristine wilderness of gurgling streams and flourishing wildlife. This guest ranch occupies a spectacular location, bordered by Grand Teton National Park and Bridger Teton National Forest and just 20 miles south of the resort town of Jackson Hole. One- and two-bedroom log cabins provide comfortable accommodations, and the authentic Western décor puts a smile on visitors' faces. Recreational activities include horseback riding, tennis, hiking, auto tours to nearby Yellowstone National Park, and float trips down the Snake River. The spa presents a more sybaritic experience, offering mineral wraps, sea salt body scrubs, and Dead Sea Fango mud massages. Guests forge new friendships over the family-style meals and traditional cookouts, and in the evenings, they revisit the Old West with swing dancing, cowboy poetry, and cowboy serenades. 30 rooms. Closed Oct-late May. Complimentary full breakfast. Check-in 3 pm, check-out 10 am. High-speed Internet access, wireless Internet access. Restaurant, bar. Children's activity center. Fitness room,

fitness classes available, spa. Outdoor pool, whirlpool. Tennis. Airport transportation available. **$$$$**
🚶 🏊 ⛷

Restaurants

★ **DORNAN'S CHUCK WAGON.** *10 Moose Jct, Moose (83012). Phone 307/733-2415 fax 307/733-3544. www.dornans.com.* American menu. Breakfast, lunch, dinner. Closed mid-Sept-mid-June. Bar. Outdoor seating. **$**

★ ★ ★ **JENNY LAKE LODGE DINING ROOM.** *Inner Loop Rd-Box 240, Moose (83012). Phone 307/543-2811; fax 307/543-3029. www.gtlc.com.* Dining in restored cabin. American menu. Breakfast, dinner. Closed early Oct-May. Jacket required. Reservations recommended. **$$$$**

Green River (E-2)

See also Evanston, Kemmerer, Rock Springs

Settled 1862
Population 12,711
Elevation 6,109 ft
Area Code 307
Zip 82935
Information Chamber of Commerce, 541 E Flaming Gorge Way, Suite E; phone 307/875-5711
Web Site www.grchamber.com

Green River, seat of Sweetwater County, is known as the trona (sodium sesquicarbonate) capital of the world. As early as 1852, Jim Bridger guided Captain Howard Stansbury on a Native American trail through the area. By 1862, a settlement here consisted mainly of the overland stage station, located on the east bank of the Green River. In 1868, Major John Wesley Powell started from here on his expedition of the Green and Colorado rivers. This point of departure is now known as Expedition Island. The Green River, one of Wyoming's largest, is the northern gateway to the Flaming Gorge National Recreation Area.

What to See and Do

Flaming Gorge National Recreation Area. *District Ranger, Box 279, Manila (84046). S on Hwy 530 or Hwy 191. Phone 435/784-3445. www.utah.com/nationalsites/flaming_gorge.htm.* This area, administered by the US Forest Service, surrounds Flaming Gorge

Reservoir in Wyoming (see ROCK SPRINGS) and Utah. Firehole campground and Upper Marsh Creek boat ramp are on the east shore of the reservoir; two other sites, Buckboard Crossing and Squaw Hollow, are on the west shore. Lucerne, Buckboard Crossing, Firehole, and Antelope Flats have camping and boat-launching ramps. Upper Marsh Creek and Squaw Hollow are boat ramp sites only. (Check road conditions locally before traveling during winter or wet periods.) There is usually ice fishing January-March. The Flaming Gorge Dam, administered by the US Bureau of Reclamation, the headquarters, three visitor centers, and several other recreation sites are located along the southern half of the loop in Utah. Campground fees; reservations required for group sites.

Sweetwater County Historical Museum. *Courthouse, 3 E Flaming Gorge Way, Green River (82935). Phone 307/872-6435.* Historical exhibits on southwestern Wyoming; Native American, Chinese, and pioneer artifacts; photographic collection. (July-Aug, Mon-Sat; rest of year, Mon-Fri; closed holidays) **FREE**

Limited-Service Hotel

★ ★ **LITTLE AMERICA HOTEL.** *I-80 exit 68, Little America (82929). Phone 307/875-2400; toll-free 800/634-2401; fax 307/872-2666. www.littleamerica. com.* A modest hotel providing a personal touch, guests will enjoy convenient guest room amenities, including a big-screen television. 140 rooms, 2 story. Check-in 3 pm, check-out noon. Restaurant, bar. Fitness room. Outdoor pool. **$**

🏃 🌊

Greybull (A-3)

See also Lovell

Population 1,789
Elevation 3,788 ft
Area Code 307
Zip 82426
Information Chamber of Commerce, 521 Greybull Ave; phone 307/765-2100
Web Site www.greybull.com

Just north of town are the rich geological sites Sheep Mountain and Devil's Kitchen. Sheep Mountain looks like a natural fortress surrounded by flatland when seen from the Big Horn Mountains. A Ranger District office of the Bighorn National Forest (see SHERIDAN) is located here.

What to See and Do

Greybull Museum. *325 Greybull Ave, Greybull. Phone 307/765-2444.* History and fossil displays; Native American artifacts. (June-Labor Day, Mon-Sat; Apr-May and Sept-Oct, Mon-Fri afternoons; rest of year, Mon, Wed, and Fri afternoons; closed Jan 1, Thanksgiving, Dec 25) **FREE**

Special Event

Days of '49 Celebration. *325 Greybull Ave, Greybull (82426). Phone 307/765-9619.* Parades, rodeo, running races, demolition derby. Concert, dances. Second weekend in June.

Jackson (B-1)

See also Alpine, Grand Teton National Park

Pinedale, Teton Village,

Population 4,472
Elevation 6,234 ft
Area Code 307
Zip 83001
Information Jackson Hole Area Chamber of Commerce, 990 W Broadway, PO Box 550; phone 307/733-3316
Web Site www.jacksonholechamber.com

Jackson, uninhibitedly western, is the key town for the mountain-rimmed, 600-square-mile valley of Jackson Hole, which is surrounded by mountain scenery, dude ranches, national parks, big game, and other vacation attractions. Jackson Hole is one of the most famous ski resort areas in the country, known for its spectacular views and its abundant ski slopes. It has three Alpine ski areas, five Nordic ski areas, and miles of groomed snowmobile trails. Annual snowfall usually exceeds 38 feet, and winter temperatures average around 21 F. The Jackson Hole area, which includes Grand Teton National Park, the town of Jackson, and much of the Bridger-Teton National Forest, has all the facilities and luxuries necessary to accommodate both the winter and summer visitor. Jackson Hole offers winter sports, boating, chuck wagon dinner shows, live theater productions, symphony concerts, art galleries, rodeos, horseback riding, mountain climbing, fishing, and several whitewater and scenic float trips. Two Ranger District offices of the Bridger-Teton National Forest are located in Jackson.

What to See and Do

Aerial Tramway. *Phone 307/733-2291.* Makes 2 1/2-mi ride to top of Rendezvous Mountain for spectacular views. Free guided nature hike. (Late May-early Oct) **$$$$**

Barker-Ewing Float Trips. *Grand Teton National Park Rd, Moose (83012). Phone 307/733-1800; toll-free 800/365-1800.* Ten-mile scenic trips on the Snake River, within Grand Teton National Park. Reservations necessary. **$$$$**

Bridger-Teton National Forest. *Phone 307/739-5500.* With more than 3.3 million acres, the forest literally surrounds the town of Jackson. Bridger-Teton was the site of one of the largest earth slides in US history, the Gros Ventre Slide (1925), which dammed the Gros Ventre River (to a height of 225 feet and a width of nearly 1/2 mile), forming Slide Lake, which is approximately 3 miles long. There are scenic drives along the Hoback River Canyon, the Snake River Canyon, and in Star Valley. Unspoiled backcountry includes parts of Gros Ventre, Teton, and Wind River ranges along the Continental Divide and the Wyoming Range. Teton Wilderness (557,311 acres) and Gros Wilderness (247,000 acres) are accessible on foot or horseback. Swimming, fishing, rafting; hiking, mountain biking, winter sports areas, camping (fee). Also in the forest is Bridger Wilderness. Fishing, boating; big-game hunting. For further information contact Forest Supervisor, 340 N Cache, PO Box 1888.

Gray Line bus tours. *1580 W Matrin Ln, Jackson (83001). Phone 307/733-4325 toll-free 800/443-6133* Tours in Jackson, Grand Teton, and Yellowstone national parks.

Jackson Hole Historical Society & Museum. *105 Mercill Ave, Jackson (83001). Phone 307/733-9605.* Fur trade exhibit. Research library. (Daily) **FREE**

Jackson Hole Museum. *105 N Glenwood, Jackson (83001). Phone 307/733-9605.* Regional museum of early West, local history, and archaeology. (Late May-Sept, daily) **$$**

Lewis and Clark Expeditions. *335 N Cache Dr, Jackson (83001). Phone 307/733-4022; toll-free 800/824-5375.* Scenic 3 1/2- and 6-hour whitewater float trips through Grand Canyon of Snake River. (June-mid-Sept, daily) **$$$$**

Mad River Boat Trips, Inc. *1255 S Hwy 89, Jackson (83001). Phone 307/733-6203; toll-free 800/458-7238.* Three-hour whitewater Snake River Canyon trips (daily). Also combination scenic/whitewater trips, lunch/dinner trips. Reservations suggested. **$$$$**

National Elk Refuge. *2 miles N of town. Phone 307/733-9212.* This 25,000-acre refuge is the winter home of thousands of elk and many waterfowl. Visitor center with slide show, exhibits, and horse-drawn sleigh rides (mid-Dec-Mar, daily).

National Museum of Wildlife Art. *2820 Rungius Rd, Jackson (83001). N of town. Phone 307/733-5771; toll-free 800/313-9553. www.wildlifeart.org.* Nearly blending into the hillside across from the National Elk Refuge, this organic-looking structure (made of red sandstone from Arizona) houses an impressive collection of wildlife art: more than 2,000 works dating from 2000 BC, the 21st century, and just about every artistic era in between. The museum is the largest arts facility dedicated to the theme of wildlife, and includes galleries dedicated to the American bison and legendary wildlife impressionist Carl Rungius. Among the other artists represented here are bird specialist John James Audubon, Dutch master Rembrandt, and cowboy artist Charles M. Russell. The kids program is excellent, with many interactive exhibits and a strong educational component; there is a restaurant and a gift shop on-site. In winter, sleigh tours of the National Elk Refuge originate here, and combination admission/sleigh tour packages are available. (Daily 9 am-5 pm; Sun from 1 pm in the spring and fall) **$$**

Snow King Ski Resort. *400 E Snow King Ave, Jackson (83001). Six blocks S of Town Square. Phone toll-free 800/522-5464. www.snowkind.com.* Triple, two double chairlifts, surface tow; school, rental/repair shop; snack bar, resort facilities. Longest run nearly 1 mile; vertical drop 1,571 feet. (Nov-Mar, daily) **$$$$**

Solitude Float Trips. *110 E Karns Ave, Jackson (83001). Phone 307/733-2871.* Offers 10-mile scenic trips within Grand Teton National Park. Reservations required.

Teton Mountain Bike Tours. *Phone toll-free 800/733-0788.* Guided mountain bike tours for all ability levels. Mountain bike, helmet, transportation, and local guides. Day, multiday, and customized group tours available.

Teton Wagon Train & Horse Adventure. *820 Cache*

Creek Rd, Jackson (83001). Phone 307/734-6101. Four-day guided covered wagon trip between Yellowstone and Grand Teton national parks (see). Activities include hiking, horseback riding, swimming, and canoeing. Meals, tents, and sleeping bags included. (Mid-June-late Aug) **$$$$** Also available is

> **Covered Wagon Cookout & Wild West Show.** *Phone 307/733-5386.* Ride covered wagons to outdoor dining area; eating area covered in case of rain. Western entertainment. Departs from Bar-T-Five Corral (late May-mid-Sept, Mon-Sat).

Triangle X Float Trips. *2 Triangle X Ranch Rd, Moose (83012). On the Snake River in Grand Teton National Park. Phone 307/733-5500.* Trips include 10-mile floats; sunrise and evening wildlife floats; also cookout supper floats. Most trips originate at Triangle X Ranch. (May-Oct) **$$$$**

Wagons West. *Phone toll-free 800/447-4711.* Covered wagon treks through the foothills of the Tetons. Gentle riding horses, chuck-wagon meals, campfire entertainment. Special guided horseback treks and hiking trips into surrounding mountains. Two-, four-, and six-day furnished trips. (June-Labor Day, Mon-Sat) Reservations necessary. Depart from motels in Jackson. **$$$$**

Special Events

Grand Teton Music Festival. *4015 W Lake Creek Dr, Jackson (83001). Phone 307/733-3050.* 12 miles NW in Teton Village. Symphony and chamber music concerts. Virtuoso orchestra of top professional musicians from around the world. Many different programs of chamber music and orchestral concerts. Early July-late Aug.

Jackson Hole Fall Arts Festival. *Phone 307/733-3316.* Three-week celebration of the arts featuring special exhibits in more than 30 galleries, demonstrations, special activities. Also dance, theater, mountain film festival, Native American arts, and culinary arts. Mid-Sept-early Oct.

Jackson Hole Rodeo. *447 W Snow King Dr, Jackson (83001). Phone 307/733-2805.* Jackson Hole Rodeo offers events like: barrel racing, calf roping, bull riding, saddle bronc riding, bareback bronc riding, and a calf scramble for kids. Memorial Day weekend-late Aug.

The Shootout. *Town Square, Jackson (83001). Phone 307/733-3316.* Real-life Western melodrama. Mon-Sat evenings, Memorial Day weekend-Labor Day.

Limited-Service Hotels

★ **BEST WESTERN THE LODGE AT JACKSON HOLE.** *PO Box 7478, Jackson (83002). Phone 307/739-9703; toll-free 800/458-3866; fax 307/739-9168. www.lodgeatjh.com.* 153 rooms, 3 story. Complimentary continental breakfast. Check-in 4 pm, check-out 11 am. Indoor, outdoor pool; whirlpool. **$$**
🏊

★ **QUALITY INN 49'ER INNS & SUITES.** *330 W Pearl St, Jackson (83001). Phone 307/733-7550; toll-free 800/451-2980; fax 307/733-2002. www.townsquareinns.com.* 150 rooms, 3 story. Pets accepted, some restrictions. Complimentary continental breakfast. Check-in 3 pm, check-out 11 am. Fitness room. Whirlpool. **$**
🐾 🏃

★★★ **RUSTY PARROT LODGE.** *175 N Jackson St, Jackson (83001). Phone 307/733-2000; toll-free 800/458-2004; fax 307/733-5566. www.info@rustyparrot.com.* Just minutes from Grand Teton and Yellowstone national parks and Jackson Hole, the lodge is also just three blocks from Town Square. Rustic rooms are filled with mountain-style touches: antler chandeliers, hand-made furniture, and goose-down comforters. A hearty breakfast is included in the rates. To rejuvenate the body and the spirit after a day on the slopes, try one of the many treatments available at The Body Sage, the on-site day spa. 31 rooms, 3 story. Complimentary full breakfast. Check-in 4 pm, check-out 11 am. Restaurant, bar. Spa. Whirlpool. **$$$**
🖄

★ **WYOMING INN.** *930 W Broadway, Jackson (83002). Phone 307/734-0035; toll-free 800/844-0035; fax 307/734-0037. www.wyoming-inn.com.* 73 rooms, 3 story. Complimentary continental breakfast. Check-in 3 pm, check-out 11 am. Airport transportation available. Business center. **$$**
🏃

Full-Service Hotel

★★★ **THE WORT HOTEL.** *50 N Glenwood St, Jackson (83001). Phone 307/733-2190; toll-free 800/322-2727; fax 307/733-2067. www.worthotel.com.* Reflecting the history and culture of Jackson Hole, this popular country inn is decorated with fabrics and furnishings of the Old West. 60 rooms, 2 story. Check-in 4 pm, check-out 11 am. Two restaurants, bar. Fitness room. Whirlpool. Airport transportation available. **$$$**
🏃

Full-Service Resorts

★ ★ ★ **SPRING CREEK RANCH.** *1800 Spirit Dance Rd, Jackson (83001). Phone 307/733-8833; toll-free 800/443-6139; fax 307/733-1964. www.springcreekranch. com.* Offering a great view of the Teton Mountain Range, surrounded by two national parks and tons of wildlife, this resort features great accommodations. The resort is located near many attractions. 122 rooms. Check-in 4 pm, check-out 11 am. High-speed Internet access, wireless Internet access. Restaurant, bar. Fitness room, spa. Outdoor pool, two whirlpools. Tennis. Airport transportation available. **$$$**

Specialty Lodging

THE ALPINE HOUSE COUNTRY INN & SPA. *285 N Glenwood St, Jackson (83001). Phone 307/739-1570; toll-free 800/753-1421. www.alpinehouse.com.* 22 rooms. Closed Apr and Nov. Check-in 3 pm, check-out 11 am. Ski in/ski out. **$$**

GRAND VICTORIAN LODGE.*85 Perry Ave, Jackson (83001). Phone 307/739-2294; toll-free 800/584-0532; fax 307/739-2196. www.grandvictorianlodge.com.* Victorian décor. 11 rooms, 3 story. Complimentary full breakfast. Check-in 3 pm, check-out 11 am. Whirlpool. **$$**

THE HUFF HOUSE INN BED & BREAKFAST. *240 E Deloney, Jackson (83001). Phone 307/733-4164; fax 307/739-9091. www.huffhouse.com.* Victorian house built in 1917. Each room is decked out with lovely appointments that help provide a warm and relaxing atmosphere. 6 rooms, 2 story. Children over 13 years only. Complimentary full breakfast. Check-in 3 pm, check-out 10 am. Whirlpool. **$$**

INN ON THE CREEK. *295 N Millward, Jackson (83001). Phone 307/739-1565. www.innonthecreek.com.* *9 rooms.* Closed three weeks in Apr. Complimentary full breakfast. Check-in 4-6 pm, check-out 11 am. **$$**

THE PAINTED PORCH. *3755 Moose-Wilson Rd, Wilson (83014). Phone 307/733-1981. www.jackson-holebedandbreakfast.com.* 3 rooms. Complimentary full breakfast. Check-in 3 pm, check-out 11 am. **$**

PARKWAY INN.*125 N Jackson St, Jackson (83001). Phone 307/733-3143; toll-free 800/247-8390; fax 307/733-0955. www.parkwayinn.com.* 49 rooms. Complimentary continental breakfast. Check-in 3 pm, check-out 11 am. Fitness room. Indoor pool, whirlpool. Ski in/ski out. No credit cards accepted. **$$**

THE WILDFLOWER INN. *3725 N Teton Village Rd, Jackson (83002). Phone 307/733-4710 fax 307/739-0914. www.jacksonholewildflower.com.* This 3-acre log bed-and-breakfast is located just outside of town and only five minutes from the Jackson Hole Mountain ski area. 5 rooms, 2 story. Complimentary full breakfast. Check-in 4-6 pm, check-out 11 am. Whirlpool. **$$$**

Restaurants

★ ★ **ANTHONY'S.** *62 S Glenwood St, Jackson (83001). Phone 307/733-3717.* Italian menu. Dinner. Children's menu. Casual attire. Reservations recommended. **$$**

★ ★ ★ **BLUE LION.** *160 N Millward St, Jackson (83001). Phone 307/733-3912; fax 307/733-3915. www.bluelionrestaurant.com.* Housed in a charming old home, this restaurant offers creative preparations of many dishes. American menu. Dinner. Bar. Children's menu. Casual attire. Reservations recommended. Outdoor seating. **$$$**

★ ★ ★ **CADILLAC GRILLE.** *55 N Cache Dr, Jackson (83001). Phone 307/733-3279; fax 307/739-0110. www.cadillac-grille.com.* Aglow with neon lights, this energetic restaurant is on the town square's west side and has been open since 1983. The creative dishes are served in a fun, casual atmosphere. American menu. Lunch, dinner. Closed Dec 25; also Nov. Bar. Casual attire. Reservations recommended. Outdoor seating. **$$$**

★ ★ **CALICO.** *2650 Teton Village Rd, Jackson (83025). Phone 307/733-2460; fax 307/734-0451. www.calicorestaurant.com.* Italian menu. Dinner. Closed Thanksgiving. Bar. Children's menu. Casual attire. Outdoor seating. **$$**

★ **JEDEDIAH'S.** *135 E Broadway, Jackson (83001). Phone 307/733-5671.* American menu. Dinner. Closed Thanksgiving, Dec 25; also Super Bowl Sun. Children's menu. Casual attire. Outdoor seating. **$$**

★ ★ **MILLION DOLLAR COWBOY STEAK HOUSE.** *25 N Cache St, Jackson (83001). Phone 307/733-4790.www.milliondollarcowboybar.com.* Steak menu. Dinner. Closed Apr and early Nov-early Dec. Bar. Children's menu. Casual attire. Reservations recommended. **$$$**

★ ★ **OFF BROADWAY.** *30 S King St, Jackson (83001). Phone 307/733-9777.* American menu. Dinner. Closed Thanksgiving, Dec 25. Children's menu. Casual attire. Reservations recommended. Outdoor seating. **$$**
🅳

★ ★ ★ **SNAKE RIVER GRILL.** *84 E Broadway, Jackson (83001). Phone 307/733-0557; fax 307/733-5767. www.snakerivergrill.com.* With hardwood floors and a cozy stone fireplace set in the center of this rustic restaurant, diners will appreciate the charm of the Northwest. American menu. Dinner. Closed Dec 25; also Apr and Nov. Bar. Casual attire. Reservations recommended. Outdoor seating. **$$$**
🅳

★ ★ **STRUTTING GROUSE.** *5000 N Spring Gulch Rd, Jackson (83001). Phone 307/733-7788; fax 307/733-8473. www.jhgtc.com.* Just outside the southern border of Grand Teton National Park, this restaurant and lounge is part of the Jackson Hole Golf and Tennis Club. The dining room overlooks the golf course and mountains. American menu. Lunch. Closed mid-Oct-mid-May. Bar. Children's menu. Casual attire. Outdoor seating. **$$**

★ ★ ★ **SWEETWATER.** *85 S King St, Jackson (83001). Phone 307/733-3553; toll-free 800/222-4700; fax 307/739-4580.* Housed in an 1890s log cabin, this restaurant is located about two blocks from the Jackson town square and offers views of nearby mountains and hills. American menu. Dinner. Closed first two weeks in Apr. Children's menu. Casual attire. Reservations recommended. Outdoor seating. **$$$**

★ ★ **TETON PINES.** *3450 N Clubhouse Dr, Wilson (83014). Phone 307/733-1005; toll-free 800/238-2223; fax 307/733-2860. www.tetonpines.com.* American menu. Lunch, dinner. Bar. Children's menu. Casual attire. Reservations recommended. Outdoor seating. **$$**

★ ★ **VISTA GRANDE.** *2550 Teton Village Rd, Jackson (83001). Phone 307/733-6964.* Mexican menu.

Dinner. Closed Apr and Nov. Bar. Children's menu. Casual attire. Outdoor seating. **$$**

Jackson Hole(B-1)

Limited-Service Hotel

★ ★ **JACKSON HOLE LODGE.** *420 W Broadway, Jackson Hole (83001). Phone 307/733-2992; toll-free 800/556-4638; fax 307/739-2144. www.skijacksonhole.com.* 59 rooms. Check-in 4 pm, check-out 11 am. Ski in/ski out. **$**
🏊

Full-Service Resorts

★ ★ ★ ★ **AMANGANI.** *1535 NE Butte Rd, Jackson Hole (83001). Phone 307/734-7333; toll-free 877/734-7333; fax 307/734-7332. www.amanresorts.com.* East meets West at Jackson Hole's Amangani Resort. Sanskrit for "peaceful home," this American outpost of the internationally recognized Aman Resorts wins raves for its Asian-influenced design and blissful quietude in the heart of America's West. The sanctuarylike accommodations welcome world-weary city slickers with their perfect balance of Zen and contemporary luxury. Situated at the edge of East Gros Ventre Butte, this stylish resort mesmerizes guests with its majestic mountain views, and its location near Yellowstone and Grand Teton national parks makes it a favorite of jet-setting outdoor enthusiasts. Year-round, it is a perfect base for enjoying Jackson Hole's renowned skiing, ice climbing, fly fishing, and river rafting, though the dominant mood here is one of relaxation and renewal. The "anti-resort," Amangani's well-stocked library, full-service spa, and scenic infinity pool with inspiring views appeal to independent-minded travelers seeking a serene setting for introspection. 40 rooms, 2 story. Check-in 3 pm, check-out noon. High-speed Internet access. Restaurant, bar. Fitness room, spa. Outdoor pool, whirlpool. Business center. **$$$$**
🎿 🚶 🏊

★ ★ ★ ★ **FOUR SEASONS RESORT JACKSON HOLE.** *7680 Granite Loop Rd, Teton Village (83025). Phone 307/732-5000; toll-free 800/295-5281; fax 307/732-5001. www.fourseasons.com.* Only the Four Seasons could take a breathtaking setting in the Teton Mountains and make it seem even more magical. This award winning chain brings its service-oriented style to Wyoming at the sublime Four

Seasons Resort Jackson Hole. The resort's décor captures the spirit of America's West while adding sophistication and panache. The smallest details are the big picture here, where service is tops. The resort even boasts a ski concierge who handles lift tickets, advises skiers on trails, and assists with equipment selections. Ski-in/ski-out access is a big hit with alpine enthusiasts, while some visitors prefer fly fishing, mountain biking, and other outdoor pursuits. Guests reward themselves after an active day with a tasty meal at the cozy Westbank Grill, where meat, fish, and game are highlighted. 124 rooms. Pets accepted; some restrictions. Check-in 4 pm, check-out noon. High-speed Internet access, wireless Internet access. Three restaurants, two bars. Children's activity center. Fitness room, fitness classes available, spa. Outdoor pool, whirlpool. Ski in/ski out. Airport transportation available. Business center. **$$$$**

Specialty Lodgings

BENTWOOD INN BED & BREAKFAST. *4250 Raven Haven Rd, Jackson Hole (83001). Phone 307/739-1411. www.bentwoodinn.com.* 5 rooms. Complimentary full breakfast. Check-in 3 pm, check-out 11 am. **$$$**

THE SASSY MOOSE INN. *3859 Miles Rd, Jackson Hole (83014). Phone 307/733-1277; toll-free 800/356-1277; fax 307/739-0793. www.sassymoose.com.* 5 rooms. Complimentary full breakfast. Check-in 3 pm, check-out 11 am. Ski in/ski out. **$**

Spa

★ ★ ★ ★ **THE SPA AT FOUR SEASONS RESORT JACKSON HOLE.** *7680 Granite Loop Rd, Teton Village (83025) .www.fourseasons.com.* The Spa at the Four Seasons Resort Jackson Hole triumphantly marries the rugged style of the West with the elegance, service, and style associated with the prestigious Four Seasons brand. From the bountiful fresh fruit to the gently burning fire, this spa pampers its clients from the moment they enter this tranquil space. Après-ski massages and high altitude hydration facials and body treatments are among the most popular options, while signature therapies, such as the alpine berry body ritual and the hawthorn and mallow body glow, showcase local ingredients. The massage menu is well rounded, offering everything from aromatherapy and deep

tissue treatments to moonlight massages and native stone therapies. All visitors receive a warm welcome at this spa, which also offers specific selections for male clients. Hair and nail care is available in the adjacent salon, while the comprehensive fitness center and pool complete the well-rounded experience here.

Restaurant

★ ★ ★ **THE WESTBANK GRILL AT THE FOUR SEASONS RESORT.** *7680 Granite Loop Rd, Teton Village (83025). Phone 307/734-5040; fax 307/732-5001. www.fourseasons.com.* American menu. Breakfast, lunch, dinner. Bar. Children's menu. Business casual attire. Reservations recommended. Outdoor seating. **$$$**

Kemmerer (D-1)

See also Evanston, Green River

Population 3,020
Elevation 6,959 ft
Area Code 307
Zip 83101
Information Chamber of Commerce, 800 Pine Ave; phone 307/877-9761
Web Site www.kemmerer.org

A Ranger District office of the Bridger-Teton National Forest (see JACKSON) is located here.

What to See and Do

Fossil Butte National Monument. *11 miles W on Hwy 30 N. Phone 307/877-4455.* This ancient, now-dry lakebed, bordered by a pine- and aspen-clad butte, is one of the top fossil sites in the world, its limestone a biological time capsule that goes back 2 million years. The fossil record here is so complete that it has allowed researchers to reconstruct climate changes and the resulting effect on life in the area. Hiking is the best way to explore the 8,198-acre monument; the 1.5-mile Fossil Lake Trail loops around the old lakebed, and the Historic Quarry Trail, 2.5 miles long, gains 600 feet as it climbs the face of the butte to the original fossil quarry. While the area below was once covered in water, it is now a high desert, speckled with sagebrush and supporting a population of pronghorn antelope, mule deer, and the occasional moose. (Daily)

Lander (C-2)

See also Rawlins, Riverton

Settled 1875
Population 7,023
Elevation 5,360 ft
Area Code 307
Zip 82520
Information Chamber of Commerce, 160 N 1st St; phone 307/332-3892 or toll-free 800/433-0662
Web Site www.landerchamber.org

Lander was once called the place where the rails end and the trails begin. Wind River Range, surrounding the town, offers hunting and fishing, mountain climbing, and rock hunting. The annual One-Shot Antelope Hunt opens the antelope season and draws celebrities and sports enthusiasts from all over the country. Sacajawea Cemetery (burial place of Lewis and Clark's Shoshone guide) is located in Fort Washakie, 15 miles northwest on Highway 287. A Ranger District office of the Shoshone National Forest (see CODY) is located in Lander.

What to See and Do

Fremont County Pioneer Museum. *1440 Main*, Lander (82520). *Phone 307/332-4137.* Seven exhibit rooms and outdoor exhibit area document the pioneer, ranching, Native American, and business history of the area. (Mon-Fri, also Sat afternoons)

Sinks Canyon State Park. *3079 Sinks Canyon Rd, Lander (82520). 7 miles SW on Hwy 131. Phone 307/332-6333.* In a spectacular canyon, amid unspoiled Rocky Mountain beauty, lies the middle fork of the Popo Agie River, which disappears into a cavern and rises again several hundred yards below in a crystal-clear, trout-filled spring pool. Abundant wildlife in certain seasons. Visitor center; observation points. Fishing (except in the Rise of the Sinks). Hiking, nature trails. Groomed cross-country ski and snowmobile trails nearby. Limited tent and trailer sites (standard fees); other sites nearby.

South Pass City. *125 S Pass Main, South Pass City (82520). 33 miles S on Hwy 28, then 3 miles W. Phone 307/332-3684.* An example of a once-flourishing gold mining town. During the gold rush of 1868-1872, 1,200 people lived here. Women were first given equal suffrage by a territorial act introduced from South Pass City and passed in Cheyenne on December 10, 1869. The town is currently being restored and has more than 20 historic buildings on display (mid-May-Sept, daily). **$**

Limited-Service Hotel

★ ★ **BUDGET HOST INN.** *150 E Main St, Lander (82520). Phone 307/332-3940; toll-free 800/283-4678 fax 307/332-2651. www.wyoming.com/pronghornlodge. com.* 56 rooms, 2 story. Pets accepted; fee. Complimentary continental breakfast. Check-in 2 pm, checkout 11 am. Fitness room. Whirlpool. **$**
⬛🏃

Laramie (E-5)

See also Cheyenne

Founded 1868
Population 26,687
Elevation 7,165 ft
Area Code 307
Zip 82070
Information Albany County Tourism Board, 210 Custer; phone 307/745-4195
Web Site www.laramie-tourism.org

Laramie had a rugged beginning as a lawless leftover of the westward-rushing Union Pacific. The early settlement was populated by hunters, saloonkeepers, and brawlers. When the tracks pushed on, Laramie stabilized somewhat, but for six months vigilantes were the only law enforcement available against desperate characters who operated from town. Reasonable folk finally prevailed; schools and businesses sprang up, and improved cattle breeds brought prosperity. A Ranger District office of the Medicine Bow National Forest is located here.

What to See and Do

Laramie Plains Museum. *603 Ivinson Ave*, Laramie (82070). *Phone 307/742-4448.* Victorian mansion (1892); each room finished in a different wood; collections include antique furniture, toys, china, ranching memorabilia, Western artifacts. Special seasonal displays. (Tues-Sat) **$$**

Lincoln Monument. *8 miles SE on I-80.* World's largest bronze head (12 1/2 feet high, 3 1/2 tons), by Robert Russin of the University of Wyoming.

Medicine Bow National Forest. *W on Hwy 130, SW on Hwy 230, E on I-80 or N via Hwy 30, Hwy 34, I-25, local roads. For further information, contact the Forest*

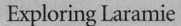

Exploring Laramie

Laramie has an oddly bifurcated nature: born of the railroad boom that followed the nations first transcontinental railway, the town preserves the rough-around-the-edges feel of an Old West frontier town. Since 1887, Laramie has also been the home of the University of Wyoming, for many years the states only center of higher education, which gives the town a patina of sophistication lacking in other Wyoming towns of this size. Laramie's well-preserved Victorian architecture and a comparative wealth of art and museums make it an excellent town to explore on foot.

Start a walking tour of Laramie on the steps of the towns city hall (406 Ivinson St). Just to the north is St. Matthews Cathedral (104 S 4th St), an imposing Neo-Gothic Episcopal church with an attached English-style garden. The church was constructed with funds donated by Edward Ivinson, one of the towns original settlers, who made his fortune on real estate and banking. Two of the churchs impressive stained-glass windows memorialize the lives of Mr. and Mrs. Ivinson.

The Ivinsons 1892 home is also among the towns landmarks. Now operated as the Laramie Plains Museum (603 Ivinson), this Queen Anne Victorian home was slated to be demolished (and the land used for a parking lot) before citizens raised money to turn it into a museum. The Ivinson mansion houses a valuable collection of household items from Laramie's pioneer days. Also on the spacious landscaped grounds are a carriage house and a one-room log schoolhouse.

Continue east on Ivinson Street to the campus of the University of Wyoming, beginning at 9th Street. This oasis of well-tended lawns and huge spruce trees contains a number of worthwhile museums and handsome university buildings, many constructed of the local yellow sandstone. At the corner of Ivinson and 10th Street is Old Main, the university's original structure from 1887. An imposing building fronted by columns and capped by a bell tower, Old Main is now office to the university president.

Head north on 10th Street past classroom buildings to the university's Geology Museum, near 10th and Clark streets. The museum has a major collection of Wyoming rocks and minerals, as well as some impressive fossils. Highlights include a mounted Apatasaurus (Brontosaurus) skeleton (one of only five in the world) and "Big Al", the most complete Allosaurus fossil ever found. A life-sized, copper-clad statue of Tyrannosaurus rex marks the museums entrance.

Walk a block east to Prexy's Pasture, the heart of the University of Wyoming campus. This large, grassy area was originally a pasture where the university's first president kept his personal herd of cattle. Today, it's the place to hang out in the sun, kick around a hacky sack, and toss Frisbees.

Continue southeast on the campus to the Anthropology Museum, near the corner of Ivinson and 14th streets. The museum has an excellent set of exhibits on the history and prehistory of Wyoming's Native Americans.

Walk north one block to University Street, where across a meadow of manicured lawn, the schools sororities and fraternities face each other. Head east, past the Fine Arts Center, then north to the Centennial Complex. This imposing structure, fashioned to resemble a six-story teepee, houses both the American Heritage Center, one of the finest museums in the state, and the University Art Museum. Unlike many large collections of art in the American West, this museum focuses on 20th-century and contemporary art.

Supervisor, 2468 Jackson St. Phone 307/745-2300. *www. fs.fed.us/r2/mbr.* The more than 1 million acres of this forest include the Snowy Range Scenic Byway; one 30-mile stretch on Highway 130, west from Centennial, is particularly scenic, with elevations as high as 10,800 feet at Snowy Range Pass. Winter sports areas, picnic grounds, camping (fee), and commercial lodges.

Snowy Range Ski Area. *6416 Mountain Mist Ct, Laramie (82070). 32 miles W on Hwy 130 (Snowy Range*

Rd). *Phone 307/745-5750. www.snowyrange.com.* Triple, three double chairlifts, T-bar; 25 runs; school, rentals, snowmaking; guided snowmobile tours; cafeteria, bar. Vertical drop 1,000 feet; longest run 2 miles. Cross-country trails nearby. (Mid-Nov-mid-Apr, daily) **$$$$**

University of Wyoming. *Between 9th and 30th Sts, 1 block N of Hwy 30 (Grand Ave). Phone 307/766-4075. www.uwyo.edu.* (1886) (11,057 students) The state's only four-year university. Its campus has the highest elevation of any in the United States. The UW Visitor Information Center, 1408 Ivinson Avenue, has displays, community and campus literature. On campus are

> **American Heritage Center & Art Museum.** *2111 Willet Dr, Laramie (82072). Phone 307/766-6622.* Nine galleries feature display of paintings, graphics, and sculpture from the 16th century to the present. Manuscripts, rare books, artifacts relating to Wyoming and the West. Research facilities. (Tues-Sun; closed holidays)

> **Geological Museum.** *S. K. Knight Geology Building,, Laramie (82070). Phone 307/766-4218.* Houses rocks, minerals, vertebrate, invertebrate, mammal, and plant fossils, including one of five brontosaurus skeletons in the world. (Mon-Fri) **FREE**

Wyoming Territorial Prison and Old West Park. *975 Snowy Range Rd, Laramie (82070). Just off I-80. Phone 307/745-6161; toll-free 800/845-2287.* Western heritage park with living history programs. Frontier town, Territorial Prison, US Marshals' Museum (fee), dinner theater (fee), playground, gift shop. (May-Sept, daily) **$**

Vedauwoo. *2468 Jackson St, Laramie (82070). 21 miles SE of Laramie. Phone 307/745-2300; toll-free 800/280-2267.* Sightseeing, camping, and climbing amid rock formations on the Medicine Bow National Forest. (Daily) Fee for camping. **FREE**

Limited-Service Hotel

★ ★ **RAMADA CENTER HOTEL.** *2313 Soldier Springs Rd, Laramie (82070). Phone 307/742-6611; toll-free 800/272-6232; fax 307/745-8371. www.ramada. com.* 100 rooms, 2 story. Pets accepted; fee. Check-in 3 pm, check-out noon. Restaurant, bar. Fitness room. Indoor pool, whirlpool. **$**

Lovell (A-3)

See also Greybull

Population 2,131
Elevation 3,837 ft
Area Code 307
Zip 82431
Information Lovell Area Chamber of Commerce, 287 E Main, PO Box 295; phone 307/548-7552
Web Site www.lovellchamber.com

A Ranger District office of the Bighorn National Forest (see SHERIDAN) is located here.

What to See and Do

Bighorn Canyon National Recreation Area. *South entrance 2 miles E on Hwy 14A, then 8 miles N on Hwy 37. For further information, contact Bighorn Canyon Visitor Center, Hwy 14A E. Phone 307/548-2251.* The focus of the area is 71-mile-long Bighorn Lake, created by the Yellowtail Dam in Fort Smith, Montana. Boats may travel through Bighorn Canyon, which cuts across the northern end of the Bighorn Mountains in north-central Wyoming and south-central Montana. The solar-powered Bighorn Canyon Visitor Center is in Lovell on Highway 14A (open daily). The Fort Smith Visitor Contact Station is in Fort Smith, Montana (open daily). Both centers are closed January 1, Thanksgiving, and December 25. Recreational and interpretive activities are available at both ends of the area, as are fishing, boating, picnicking, and camping. Adjacent and accessible from town is

> **Pryor Mountain Wild Horse Range.** *Phone 307/548-2251.* This 32,000-acre refuge, established in 1968, provides a sanctuary for wild horses descended from Native American ponies and escaped farm and ranch horses. Administered jointly by the National Park Service and the Bureau of Land Management.

Special Event

Mustang Days. *Lovell. Phone 307/548-7552.* Parade, rodeo, exhibits, entertainment, dancing, barbecue, and 7-mile run. Late June.

Restaurant

★ **INGENITO'S CANYON RESTAURANT.** *605 E Main St, Lovell (82431). Phone 307/548-6811; fax 309/548-6849.* American, Italian menu. Breakfast, lunch, dinner. Closed Thanksgiving, Dec 25. Children's menu. Casual attire. Outdoor seating. **$$**

Lusk (C-5)

See also Douglas

Founded 1886
Population 1,504
Elevation 5,015 ft
Area Code 307
Zip 82225
Information Chamber of Commerce, PO Box 457; phone 307/334-2950 or toll-free 800/223-5875
Web Site www.luskwyoming.com

Raising livestock has always been important in Lusk; fine herds of Simmental, Angus, and sheep are the local pride. Hunting is excellent for deer and antelope.

What to See and Do

Stagecoach Museum. *322 S Main, Lusk (82225). Phone 307/334-3444.* Relics of pioneer days, Native American artifacts; stagecoach. (Mon-Sat) **$**

Special Events

Legend of Rawhide. *342 S Main St,* Lusk (82225). *Phone 307/334-2950.* Live show performed since 1946. Concert, dances, trade show, golf tournament, gun show, parade, pancake breakfast. Second weekend in July.

Senior Pro Rodeo. *Phone 307/334-2950.* Labor Day weekend.

Limited-Service Hotel

★ BEST VALUE INN COVERED WAGON MOTEL. *730 S Main St, Lusk (82225). Phone 307/334-2836; toll-free 888/315-2378; fax 307/334-2977. www.coveredwagonmotel.com.* 51 rooms. Complimentary continental breakfast. Check-in 1 pm, check-out 11 am. High-speed Internet access, wireless Internet access. Fitness room. Indoor pool. **$**

Newcastle (B-6)

See also Rawlins, Riverton

Founded 1889
Population 3,003

Elevation 4,317 ft
Area Code 307
Zip 82701
Information Newcastle Area Chamber of Commerce, 1323 Washington, PO Box 68; phone 307/746-2739 or toll-free 800/835-0157

Web Site www.newcastlewyo.com/index.html

Originally, a coal mining town, Newcastle is now an oil field center with its own refinery. It is also a tourist center, with fishing, hunting, and recreational facitities nearby. A Ranger District office of the Black Hills National Forest is located here.

What to See and Do

Anna Miller Museum. *401 Delaware Ave, Newcastle (82701). Delaware and Washington Park. Phone 307/746-4188.* Museum of Northeastern Wyoming, housed in stone cavalry barn. Log cabin from Jenney Stockade, oldest building in the Black Hills, and an early rural schoolhouse. More than 100 exhibits. (Mon-Fri, Sat by appointment) **FREE**

Beaver Creek Loop Tour. *Washington Ave, Newcastle (82701). Phone 307/746-2739.* Self-guided driving tour designed to provide the opportunity to explore a diverse and beautiful country. It is a 45-mile tour covering 23 marked sites. **FREE**

Pinedale (C-2)

See also Jackson

Settled 1878
Population 1,181
Elevation 7,175 ft
Area Code 307
Zip 82941
Information Chamber of Commerce, 32 E Pine, PO Box 176; phone 307/367-2242
Web Site www.pinedaleinfo.com

Pinedale is a place where genuine cowboys can still be found, and cattle drives still occur. Mountains, conifer and aspen forests, and lakes and rivers combine to make this a beautiful vacation area. There are fossil beds in the area, and rockhounding is popular. Cattle and sheep are raised on nearby ranches. A Ranger District office of the Bridger-Teton National Forest (see JACKSON) is located in Pinedale.

What to See and Do

Bridger-Teton National Forest. Lies along the Wind River Range, east, north, and west of town. Fishing; hunting, hiking, camping (fee). In forest is

Bridger Wilderness. *5 Magnolia St, Pinedale (82941).* Approximately 400,000 acres of mountainous terrain entered only by foot or horseback. Trout fishing in snow-fed streams and more than 1,300 mountain lakes; hunting for big game. Backpacking. Permits required for some activities. Pack trips arranged by area outfitters.

Hunting. In-season hunting for elk, moose, deer, bear, antelope, mountain bighorn sheep, birds, and small game in surrounding mountains and mesas.

Museum of the Mountain Man. *700 E Hennick St, Pinedale (82941). Hennick St, exit 191, Fremont Lake Rd. Phone 307/367-4101.* Houses exhibits on fur trade, Western exploration, early history. (May-Oct, daily) **$$**

Scenic Drives. Skyline. Up into the mountains 14 miles the fauna changes from sagebrush to an alpine setting. Lakes, conifers, beautiful mountain scenery; wildlife often seen. **Green River Lakes.** North via Highway 352 to the lakes with Square Top Mountain in the background; popular with photographers. Wooded campground, trails, backpacking.

Water sports. Fishing for grayling, rainbow, mackinaw, brown trout, golden, and other trout in most lakes and rivers; ice-fishing, mostly located north of town. Swimming, water-skiing, boating, sailing regattas, float trips on New Fork and Green rivers.

Winter recreation. Cross-country skiing, groomed snowmobile trails, ice-fishing, skating.

Special Event

Green River Rendezvous. *Freemont Lake Rd and Canal St and Hwy 191, Pinedale (82941). Phone 307/367-2242.* Rodeo grounds, Sublette County. Noted historical pageant commemorating the meeting of fur trappers, mountain men, and Native Americans with the Trading Company's wagon trains at Fort Bonneville. Mid-July.

Limited-Service Hotel

★ **BEST WESTERN PINEDALE INN.** *850 W Pine St, Pinedale (82941). Phone 307/367-6869; toll-free 800/937-8376; fax 307/367-6897. www.bestwestern.com.* 59 rooms, 2 story. Pets accepted, some restrictions. Complimentary continental breakfast. Check-in 3 pm, check-out 11 am. Indoor pool, whirlpool.**$**

Rawlins (D-3)

See also Lander, Thermopolis

Founded 1867
Population 9,380
Elevation 6,755 ft
Area Code 307
Zip 82301
Information Rawlins-Carbon County Chamber of Commerce, 519 W Cedar, PO Box 1331; phone 307/324-4111 or toll-free 800/228-3547
Web Site www.wyomingcarboncounty.com

Rawlins, a division point of the Union Pacific Railroad, is located 20 miles east of the Continental Divide. In 1867, General John A. Rawlins, Chief of Staff of the US Army, wished for a drink of cool, clear water. Upon finding the spring near the base of the hills and tasting it, he said, "If anything is ever named after me, I hope it will be a spring of water." The little oasis was named Rawlins Springs, as was the community that grew up beside it. The city name was later shortened to Rawlins.

What to See and Do

Carbon County Museum. *904 W Walnut St, Rawlins (82301). 9th and Walnut sts. Phone 307/328-2740.* Houses artifacts of mining and ranching ventures. (Schedule varies)

Seminoe State Park. *6 miles E on I-80 to Sinclair, then 35 miles N on County Rd 351. Phone 307/320-3043.* Seminoe Dam impounds a 27-mile-long reservoir surrounded by giant white sand dunes and sagebrush. Pronghorn antelope and sage grouse inhabit area. Swimming, fishing (trout, walleye), boating (ramps); hiking, picnicking, tent and trailer sites (standard fee).

Wyoming Frontier Prison. *500 W Walnut St, Rawlins (82301). 5th and Walnut. Phone 307/324-4422.* Located on 49 acres, construction was begun in 1888. The prison operated from 1901-1981. Tours (fee). (Memorial Day-Labor Day, daily; rest of year, by appointment) **$$**

Special Event

Carbon County Fair and Rodeo. *Fairgrounds, Spruce, Rodeo, and Harshman sts, Rawlins (82301). Phone 307/324-6866.* Rodeo Park off Spruce St. Includes parades, exhibits, livestock, contests, demolition derby, old-timer rodeo. Second full week in Aug.

Limited-Service Hotel

★ ★ **DAYS INN.** *2222 E Cedar St, Rawlins (82301). Phone 307/324-6615; toll-free 800/329-7466; fax 307/324-7171. www.daysinn.com.* 118 rooms, 2 story. Pets accepted. Complimentary continental breakfast. Check-in 2 pm, check-out noon. Restaurant, bar. Outdoor pool. **$**

Riverton (C-3)

See also Lander, Thermopolis

Founded 1906
Population 9,202
Elevation 4,964 ft
Area Code 307
Zip 82501
Information Chamber of Commerce, 213 Main St; phone 307/856-4801 or toll-free 800/325-2732
Web Site www.rivertonchamber.org

Riverton is the largest city in Fremont County. Resources extracted from the region include natural gas, oil, iron ore, timber, and phosphate. Irrigation from the Wind River Range has placed 130,000 acres under cultivation, on which barley, alfalfa hay, beans, sunflowers, and grain are grown. The town is surrounded by the Wind River Reservation, where Arapaho and Shoshone live.

What to See and Do

Riverton Museum. *700 E Park St, Riverton (82501). Phone 307/856-2665.* Shoshone and Arapaho displays; mountain man display. General store, drugstore, post office, saloon, homesteader's cabin, church, bank, dentist's office, parlor, school, beauty shop. Clothing, quilts, cutters, buggies. **FREE**

Special Events

1838 Mountain Man Rendezvous. *Phone 307/856-7306* Council fire, primitive shoots, hawk and knife throw, games, food. Camping available. Early July.

Fremont County Fair & Rodeo. *Phone toll-free 800/325-2732.* The Fremont County Fair and Rodeo's activities include a parade, demolition derby, PRCA rodeos, hypnotists, music, and carnival rides. First full week in Aug.

Powwows. *Hwy 20 and Hwy 16, Riverton (82501). Phone 307/856-4801.* Shoshone and Arapaho tribal powwows are held throughout the summer.

State Championship Old-time Fiddle Contest. *Hwy 26 and Hwy 789, Riverton (82501). Phone 307/856-4801.* 21 miles NE via Hwy 26, 789 in Shoshoni. Divisional competition. Late May.

Wild West Winter Carnival. *Depot Building, 1838 Rendezvous Site, Riverton (82501). Phone 307/856-4801.* The Wild West Winter Carnival makes February a fun filled month of festivities. Crowning of royalty, ice sculpting, casino nights, ATV races, and tethered balloon rides are just a few of the events provided for your enjoyment. Early Feb.

Limited-Service Hotel

★ ★ **HOLIDAY INN.** *900 E Sunset Dr, Riverton (82501). Phone 307/856-8100; toll-free 877/857-4734; fax 307/856-0266. www.holiday-inn.com.* 122 rooms, 2 story. Pets accepted; fee. Check-in 3 pm, check-out noon. Restaurant, bar. Fitness room. Indoor pool. Airport transportation available. Business center. **$**

Rock Springs (E-2)

See also Green River

Population 19,050
Elevation 6,271 ft
Area Code 307
Zip 82901
Information Rock Springs Chamber of Commerce, 1897 Dewar Dr, PO Box 398, 82902; phone 307/362-3771 or toll-free 800/463-8637
Web Site www.rockspringswyoming.net

Rock Springs traces its roots to a spring, which offered an ideal camping site along a Native American trail and, later, a welcome station on the Overland Stage route. Later still, Rock Springs became a supply station that provided millions of tons of coal to the Union Pacific Railroad. Noted for its multiethnic heritage, the town's first inhabitants were primarily Welsh and English immigrants brought in by the railroad and coal companies. West of town are large deposits of trona (sodium sesquicarbonate), used in the manufacture of glass, phosphates, silicates, soaps, and baking soda.

What to See and Do

Flaming Gorge Reservoir. *SW via I-80.* This man-made lake, fed by the Green River, is 90 miles long with approximately 375 miles of shoreline, which ranges from low flats to cliffs more than 1,500 feet high. Surrounded by a national recreation area (see GREEN RIVER), the reservoir offers excellent fishing.

Special Events

Desert Balloon Rally. *Phone 307/362-3771.* Early July.

Red Desert Round-Up. *Yellowstone Rd and Hoskins Ln, Phone 307/352-6789.* One of the largest rodeos in the Rocky Mountains region. Late July.

Sweetwater County fair. *3320 Yellowstone Rd, Rock Springs (82901).* *Phone 307/362-3771.* Late July-early Aug.

Limited-Service Hotel

★ ★ **HOLIDAY INN.** *1675 Sunset Dr, Rock Springs (82901). Phone 307/382-9200; toll-free 800/465-4329; fax 307/362-1064. www.holiday-inn.com.* 170 rooms, 4 story. Pets accepted; fee. Check-in 2 pm, check-out noon. Restaurant, bar. Fitness room. Indoor pool, whirlpool. Airport transportation available. Business center. **$**

🐾 🏋 � 🏋 ✈

Sheridan (A-4)

See also Buffalo

Founded 1882
Population 13,900
Elevation 3,745 ft
Area Code 307
Zip 82801
Information Convention and Visitors Bureau, PO Box 707; phone 307/672-2485 or toll-free 800/453-3650
Web Site www.sheridanwyoming.org

Sheridan, named for General Philip Sheridan, was not settled until the Cheyenne, Sioux, and Crow were subdued after a series of wars in the region. While the land, rich with grass, was ideal for grazing livestock,

ranchers only moved in their herds after the tribes were driven onto reservations. For years, the town had a reputation for trouble because of rustling and boundary disputes. Nevertheless, the first dude ranch in history was established near Sheridan in 1904.

Today, the town is a tourist center with dude ranches, hotels and motels, and sporting facilities. The nearby Big Horn Range, once a favored hunting ground of Native Americans, is rich in big game and fishing. A Ranger District office of the Bighorn National Forest is located in Sheridan.

What to See and Do

Bighorn National Forest. *More than 1,100,000 acres W and S of town, traversed by three scenic byways: Hwy 14 (Bighorn Scenic Byway), Hwy 14A (Medicine Wheel Passage), and Hwy 16 (Cloud Peak Skyway). For further information, contact the Forest Supervisor, 2013 Eastside 2nd St. Phone 307/674-2600.* The Big Horn Mountains rise abruptly from the arid basins below to elevations of more than 13,000 feet. Fallen City, a jumble of huge rock blocks, can be viewed from Highway 14, as can Sibley Lake and Shell Canyon and Falls. From Burgess Junction, Highway 14A passes by Medicine Mountain, the site of the "medicine wheel," an ancient circular structure. Highway 16 features Meadowlark Lake and panoramic views of Tensleep Canyon and the 189,000-acre Cloud Peak Wilderness. The forest has resorts and campgrounds (fee); backpacking and horseback trails; skiing at Antelope Butte Ski Area (60 miles W on Hwy 14) and High Park Ski Area (40 miles E of Worland). Fishing; hunting, cross-country skiing, and snowmobiling.

Bradford Brinton Memorial. *239 Brinton Rd, Sheridan (82801). 7 miles S on Hwy 87, then 5 miles SW on Hwy 335. Phone 307/672-3173.* Historic ranch house built in 1892; purchased in 1923 by Bradford Brinton and enlarged to its present 20 rooms. Contains collections and furnishings that make this a memorial to the art and history of the West. More than 600 oils, watercolors, and sketches by American artists include Russell and Remington. Also bronzes, prints, rare books, ranch equipment, saddles, and Native American artifacts. (Mid-May-Labor Day, daily; also early Dec-Dec 24) **$**

King's Saddlery Museum. *184 N Main St, Sheridan (82801). Behind store. Phone 307/672-2702.* Collection of saddles; also Western memorabilia, Native American artifacts, old photographs, carriages. (Mon-Sat; closed holidays) **FREE**

Main Street Historic District. *39 N Scott St, Sheridan (82801). Phone 307/672-8881.* Take a walking tour of Sheridan, which boasts the largest collection of original late-1800s and early-1900s buildings in the state. **FREE**

Sheridan Inn. *856 Broadway St, Sheridan (82801). Phone 307/674-5440. www.sheridaninn.com.* The Sheridan Inn opened in 1893 with a bang: William Buffalo Bill Cody led a Wild West parade right into the dining room! (He later watched over auditions for his traveling show from the front porch.) The three-story hotel was immediately marketed as the finest hotel between Chicago and San Francisco, and is now on the National Register of Historic Places. Nearly demolished in the 1960s, the hotel was lovingly restored in the 1990s to house a restaurant and a museum. **$**

Trail End Historic Center. *400 Clarendon Ave, Sheridan (82801). Adjacent to Kendrick Park. Phone 307/674-4589.* Home of John B. Kendrick, Governor of Wyoming (1915-1917), later US Senator (1917-1933). Historical and family memorabilia. Mansion of Flemish-Revival architecture; beautifully carved and burnished woodwork is outstanding. Botanical specimens on landscaped grounds. (Apr-mid-Dec, daily; closed Veterans' Day, Thanksgiving) **$**

Special Events

Sheridan County Rodeo. *Phone 307/672-2079.* Second weekend in Aug.

Sheridan-Wyo PRCA Rodeo. *Phone 307/672-9084.* Carnival and parade. Mid-July.

Limited-Service Hotels

★ **DAYS INN.** *1104 E Brundage Ln, Sheridan (82801). Phone 307/672-2888; toll-free 800/329-7466; fax 307/672-2888. www.daysinn.com.* 47 rooms, 2 story. Complimentary continental breakfast. Check-in 2 pm, check-out 11 am. Indoor pool, whirlpool. **$**
⛱

★ ★ **HOLIDAY INN.** *1809 Sugarland Dr, Sheridan (82801). Phone 307/672-8931; toll-free 877/672-4011; fax 307/672-6388. www.holiday-inn.com.* 212 rooms, 5 story. Pets accepted, some restrictions. Check-in 3 pm, check-out noon. High-speed Internet access, wireless Internet access. Restaurant, bar. Fitness room. Indoor pool, whirlpool. Airport transportation available. Business center. **$**
🐾 🏃 ⛱ 🚶 ⛷

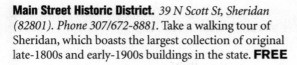

Teton Village (B-1)

See also Grand Teton National Park, Jackson

What to See and Do

Jackson Hole Mountain Resort. *3395 McCollister Dr, Teton Village (83025). 12 miles NW. Phone 307/733-2292; toll-free 800/333-7766. www.jacksonhole.com.* Easily Wyoming's highest-profile ski resort, Jackson Hole Mountain Resort is set on the eastern flank of the Teton Range, south of Grand Teton National Park and northwest of Jackson itself. Spread across two mountains (Apres Vous and Rendezvous), the resorts ski terrain features the longest continuous rise in the United States--4,139 feet--and 2,500 acres geared toward the skilled skier (10 percent beginner/40 percent intermediate/50 percent expert). There is also a superpipe and a terrain park for the snowboarding set, as well as a Nordic Center for cross-country enthusiasts. Among the 11 lifts are an aerial tram (which also runs in summer) and an eight-person gondola. The booming base village is abuzz with activity, with a number of new hotels and time-share complexes, as well as restaurants, stores, and a ski school. While not as well known for warm weather recreation, the resort also is a good base for hiking, golf, and horseback riding. (Dec-mid-Apr, daily) **$$$$**

Limited-Service Hotel

★ ★ **BEST WESTERN INN AT JACKSON HOLE.** *3345 W Village Dr, Teton Village (83025). Phone 307/733-2311; toll-free 800/842-7666; fax 307/733-0844. www.innatjh.com.* In the Teton Village part of the Jackson Hole ski area, about 12 miles from Jackson, this rustic lodge is located near Grand Teton National Park, Jackson Hole, and Yellowstone National Park. 83 rooms, 4 story. Check-in 4 pm, check-out 11 am. Two restaurants, bar. Outdoor pool, whirlpool. Ski in/ski out. Business center. **$$**
⛱ ⛷ 🚶

Full-Service Resorts

★ ★ **ALPENHOF LODGE.** *3255 W Village Dr, Teton Village (83025). Phone 307/733-3242; toll-free 800/732-3244; fax 307/739-1516. www.alpenhoflodge.com.* This Bavarian-style lodge is located at the base of Jackson Hole's ski hill. 42 rooms, 3 story. Closed Nov. Complimentary continental breakfast. Check-in 3 pm, check-out 11 am. Two restaurants, bar. Outdoor pool, whirlpool. Ski in/ski out. **$$**

★ ★ ★ **TETON MOUNTAIN LODGE.** *3385 W Village Dr, Teton Village (83025). Phone 307/734-7111; toll-free 800/801-6615; fax 307/734-7999. www.tetonlodge.com.* 129 rooms. Check-in 3 pm, check-out noon. High-speed Internet access. Restaurant, bar. Fitness room. Indoor pool, outdoor pool, children's pool, whirlpool. Ski in/ski out. **$$$**

Restaurant

★ ★ ★ **THE ALPENROSE IN THE ALPEN-HOF LODGE.** *3255 W Village Dr, Teton Village (83025). Phone 307/733-3242; toll-free 800/732-3244; fax 307/739-1516. www.alpenhoflodge.com.* At the base of the Jackson Hole ski area, the restaurant at this Bavarian-style lodge is the most well-regarded dining room in the area. Here the emphasis is on hearty dishes of Western-influenced continental cuisine. Variations on classic themes include the tableside preparation of caribou steak Diane or a great bananas Foster. The property's upstairs bistro offers more casual fare. American menu. Dinner. Closed Sun-Mon; also Nov. Bar. Casual attire. **$$$**

Thermopolis. (B-3)

See also Rawlins, Riverton

Founded 1897
Population 3,247
Elevation 4,326 ft
Area Code 307
Zip 82443
Information Chamber of Commerce, 119 S 6th St, PO Box 768; phone 307/864-3192 or toll-free 800/786-6772
Web Site www.thermopolis.com

The world's largest mineral hot spring is at Thermopolis, which lies in a beautiful section of Big Horn Basin where canyons, tunnels, and buttes abound. The town is surrounded by rich irrigated farm and grazing land.

What to See and Do

Boysen State Park. *827 Brannon Rd, Shoshoni (82649). 20 miles S on Hwy 20. Phone 307/876-2772.* Surrounded by the Wind River Reservation. Boysen Reservoir is 18 miles long and 3 miles wide. Beach on eastern shore, water-skiing, fishing for trout and walleye (all year), boating (ramp, marina); picnicking, restaurant, lodging, tent and trailer sites (standard fees).

Hot Springs County Museum and Cultural Center. *Canyon Hills Rd, Thermopolis (82443). 7th and Broadway. Phone 307/864-5183.* Home of "Hole-in-the-Wall" bar. Displays of arrowheads, minerals, gems; petroleum industry; country schoolhouse; agricultural building; railroad caboose; also period rooms and costumes. (Memorial Day-Labor Day, daily; rest of year, Mon-Sat; closed Jan 1, Thanksgiving, Dec 25) **$$**

Hot Springs State Park. *220 Park St, Thermopolis (82443). Across the Big Horn River, 1 mile N on Hwy 20. Phone 307/864-2176.* The second-most-visited tourist attraction in Wyoming after Yellowstone National Park, Hot Springs State Park in Thermopolis is the result of one of the largest mineral hot springs in the world. The springs created the magnificent Mineral Terracea colorful formation that is the result of eons of mineral deposits--and provide water for three facilities: the free State Bath House and a pair of commercial facilities with pools and water slides. There is also a free-ranging herd of bison, a pair of hotels, and a number of flower gardens that bloom brightly each summer. The Bighorn River runs right through the park, and a boat ramp allows floaters and anglers access to its waters. About 30 miles outside of Thermopolis is the Legend Rock Petroglyph Site, a sandstone cliff wall engraved with art that dates back 2,000 years; access must be arranged through an attendant at the State Bath House.

Wind River Canyon. *S on Hwy 20.* Formations visible in canyon walls range from early to recent geologic ages. Whitewater rafting (fee).

Wyoming Dinosaur Center. *110 Carter Ranch Rd, Thermopolis (82443). Phone 307/864-2997.* Exhibits mounted dinosaurs and dioramas, fossils, guided tours of excavation sites. (Daily) **$$$**

Special Events

Currier & Ives Winter Festival. *Hwys 173 and 120, Thermopolis (82443). Phone toll-free 800/786-6772.* Downtown. Town is decorated in 19th-century holiday style. Christmas choir, sleigh rides. Beard contest; cookie contest. Nov-Dec.

Gift of the Waters Pageant. *Hot Springs State Park, 220 Park St, Thermopolis (82443). Phone toll-free 800/786-6772.* Commemorates the deeding of the world's largest mineral hot springs from the Shoshone and Arapahoe to the people of Wyoming in 1896. Pageant features Native American dances, parade, buffalo barbecue. First weekend in Aug.

Limited-Service Hotels

★ **COMFORT INN.** *100 N Rd 11, Worland (82401). Phone 307/347-9898; fax 307/347-6734. www. comfortinn.com.* 50 rooms, 2 story. Complimentary continental breakfast. Check-in 1 pm, check-out 11 am. Fitness room. Indoor pool, whirlpool. Airport transportation available. **$**

★ **SUPER 8.** *Ln 5 Hwy 20 S, Thermopolis (82443). Phone 307/864-5515; toll-free 800/800-8000; fax 307/864-5447. www.super8.com.* 52 rooms, 2 story. Pets accepted; fee. Complimentary full breakfast. Check-in 2 pm, check-out 11 am. High-speed Internet access, wireless Internet access. Indoor pool, whirlpool. **$**

Torrington (D-6)

See also Wheatland, Fort Laramie National Historic Site

Population 5,651
Elevation 4,098 ft
Area Code 307
Zip 82240
Information Goshen County Chamber of Commerce, 350 W 21st Ave; phone 307/532-3879 or toll-free 800/577-3555
Web Site www.goshencountry.org

The town was a way station for the Oregon Trail, the Texas Trail, the Mormon Trail, and the Pony Express. It is now a livestock marketing center.

What to See and Do

Homesteader's Museum. *495 Main St, Torrington (82240). Phone 307/532-5612.* Items from the area's homesteading, ranching and settlement period (1830-1940). Ranch collection, furnished homestead shack; artifacts, photographs, archaeological materials. Changing exhibits. (Summer, daily; winter, Mon-Fri; closed holidays) **DONATION**

Western History Center. *5 miles W of Hwy 26. Phone 307/837-3052.* Exhibits on prehistory, archaeology, paleontology. Tours to dig sites (fee). (Tues-Sun, also by appointment) **DONATION**

Special Events

Goshen County Fair & Rodeo. *Phone 307/532-2525.* Mid-Aug.

Septemberfest. *Phone 307/532-3879.* Early Sept.

Wheatland (D-5)

See also Cheyenne, Torrington

Population 3,271
Elevation 4,748 ft
Area Code 307
Zip 82201
Information Platte County Chamber of Commerce, 65 16th St, PO Box 427; phone 307/322-2322
Web Site www.wheatlandwy.com

The southern edge of Medicine Bow National Forest (see LARAMIE) is 20 miles west.

What to See and Do

Glendo State Park. *397 Glendo Pk Rd, Glendo (82213). N on I-25. Phone 307/735-4433.* Rising out of Glendo Reservoir's east side at Sandy Beach are a series of sand dunes, some reaching from the Great Divide Basin to the sand hills in Nebraska. Chips, scrapers, and arrowheads dating back 8,000 years are sometimes found. Abundant wildlife. Near historic crossings. Swimming, water-skiing, fishing, boating (marina, ramp, rentals); hunting, picnicking, restaurant, grocery, lodging, tent and trailer sites (standard fees).

Guernsey State Park. *Hwy 317, Guernsey (82214). 12 miles N on I-25, then 12 miles E on Hwy 26, then N on Hwy 317. Phone 307/836-2334.* On the shores of Guernsey Reservoir; high bluffs surround the park with Laramie Peak on the west. Surrounding area is rich in historical interest including the Oregon Trail. Museum (mid-May-Labor Day, daily; free) has exhibits on early settlers, the Oregon Trail, geology. Park offers swimming, water-skiing; camping (standard fees). Some facilities may be closed Nov-Apr. **$$**

Special Events

Chugwater Chili Cookoff. *Chugwater town park, Chugwater. Phone 307/422-3564; toll-free 800/972-4454.*

Music, dancing, food. Family activities. Second Sat in June.

Platte County Fair and Rodeo. *59 Antelope Gap Rd, Wheatland (82201). Phone 307/322-9504.* Includes parade, livestock sale, barbecue, pig wrestling. Early Aug.

Limited-Service Hotel

★ **BEST WESTERN TORCHLITE MOTOR INN.** *1809 N 16th St, Wheatland (82201). Phone 307/322-4070; toll-free 800/662-3968; fax 307/322-4072. www. bestwestern.com.* 50 rooms, 2 story. Pets accepted; fee. Check-in 3 pm, check-out 11 am. High-speed Internet access. Outdoor pool. **$**

Yellowstone National Park (A-1)

see also Cody, Grand Teton National Park

See also Cody, Grand Teton National Park
Web Site www.nps.gov/yell/

In 1872, the US Congress set aside more than 3,000 square miles of wilderness in the Wyoming Territory, establishing the world's first national park. More than a century later, Yellowstone boasts a marvelous list of sights, attractions, and facilities: a large freshwater lake, the highest in the nation (7,733 feet); a waterfall almost twice as high as Niagara; a dramatic, 1,200-foot-deep river canyon; and the world's most famous geyser, Old Faithful.

Most of the park has been left in its natural state, preserving the area's beauty and delicate ecological balance. The widespread fires at Yellowstone in 1988 were the greatest ecological event in the more than 100-year history of the park. Although large areas of forest land were affected, park facilities and attractions remained generally undamaged. Yellowstone is one of the world's most successful wildlife sanctuaries. Within its boundaries live a variety of species, including grizzly and black bears, elk, deer, pronghorn, and bison. Although it is not unusual to encounter animals along park roads, they are more commonly seen along backcountry trails and in more remote areas. Never approach, feed, or otherwise disturb any wild animal. Stay in your car with the windows up

if you're approached by wildlife. Animals may look friendly but are unpredictable.

The Grand Loop Road, a main accessway within the park, winds approximately 140 miles past many major points of interest. Five miles south of the North Entrance is Mammoth Hot Springs, the park headquarters and museum (open year-round). The visitor center provides a general overview of the history of the park. High terraces with water spilling from natural springs are nearby. Naturalist-guided walks are conducted on boardwalks over the terraces (summer).

The Norris Geyser Basin is 21 miles south of Mammoth Hot Springs. The hottest thermal basin in the world provides a multitude of displays; springs, geysers, mud pots, and steam vents hiss, bubble, and erupt in a showcase of thermal forces at work. The visitor center has self-explanatory exhibits and dioramas (June-Labor Day, daily). A self-guided trail (2 1/2 miles) offers views of the Porcelain and Back basins from boardwalks (mid-June-Labor Day). The Museum of the National Park Ranger is also nearby.

At Madison, 14 miles southwest of Norris, the West Entrance Road (Hwy 20/91 outside the park) joins the Grand Loop Road. Heading south of Madison, it is a 16-mile trip to Old Faithful. Along the route are four thermal spring areas; numerous geysers, mud pots, and pools provide an appropriate prologue to the spectacle ahead. Old Faithful has not missed a performance in the more than 100 years since eruptions were first recorded. Eruptions occur on the average of every 75 minutes, although intervals have varied from 30 to 120 minutes. A nearby visitor center provides information, exhibits, and a film and slide program (May-Oct, mid-Dec-mid-March, daily).

From Old Faithful it is 17 miles east to West Thumb. Yellowstone Lake, the highest natural freshwater lake in the United States, is here. Early explorers thought that the shape of the lake resembled a hand, with the westernmost bay forming its thumb. A variety of rare species of waterfowl make their home along its 110 miles of shoreline. The 22-mile road from the South Entrance on the John D. Rockefeller Jr., Memorial Parkway (Hwy 29/287 outside the park) meets the Grand Loop Road here.

Northeast of West Thumb, about 19 miles up the western shore of Yellowstone Lake, the road leads to Lake Village and then to Fishing Bridge. Although fishing is not permitted at Fishing Bridge (extending 1 mile downstream, to the north, and 1/4 mile upstream, to the south of Fishing Bridge), the numerous lakes and rivers in the park make Yellowstone an angler's paradise. At Fishing Bridge the road splits; 27 miles east is the East Entrance from Highway 14/16/20, and 16 miles north is Canyon Village. Canyon Village is near Upper Falls (a 109-foot drop) and the spectacular Lower Falls (a 308-foot drop). The colorful and awesome Grand Canyon of the Yellowstone River can be viewed from several points; there are self-guided trails along the rim and naturalist-led walks (summer). Groomed cross-country ski trails are open in winter. Museum (mid-May-late Sept, daily).

Sixteen miles north of Canyon Village is Tower. Just south of Tower Junction is the 132-foot Tower Fall, which can best be observed from a platform at the end of the path leading from the parking lot. The Northeast Entrance on Highway 212 is 29 miles east of Tower; Mammoth Hot Springs is 18 miles west.

The rest of the park is wilderness, with more than 1,100 miles of marked foot trails. Some areas may be closed for resource management purposes; inquire at one of the visitor centers in the area before hiking in backcountry. Guided tours of the wilderness can be made on horseback; horse rentals are available at Mammoth Hot Springs, Roosevelt, and Canyon Village.

Do not pick wildflowers or collect any natural objects. Read all regulations established by the National Park Service and comply with them—they are for the protection of all visitors as well as for the protection of park resources.

Recreational vehicle campsites are available by reservation at Fishing Bridge RV Park (contact TW Recreational Services, Inc, at 307/344-7901 for general information or phone 307/344-7311 for reservations). During July and August, demand often exceeds supply and many sites are occupied by mid-morning. Overnight vehicle camping or stopping outside designated campgrounds is not permitted. Reservations are required for Bridge Bay, Canyon, Madison, Grant Village, as well as Fishing Bridge RV Park. There are seven additional National Park Service campgrounds at Yellowstone; these are operated on a first-come, first-served basis, so arrive early to secure the site of your choice. Campfires are prohibited except in designated areas or by special permit obtained at ranger stations. Backcountry camping is available by permit only, no more than 48 hours in advance, in person, at ranger stations. Backcountry sites can be reserved for a $15 fee.

Fishing in Yellowstone National Park requires a permit. Anglers 16 years and older require a $10/ten-day or $20/season permit. Rowboats, powerboats, and tackle may be rented at Bridge Bay Marina. Permits are also required for all vessels (seven-day permit: motorized, $10; nonmotorized, $5) and must be obtained in person at any of the following locations: South Entrance, Bridge Bay Marina, Mammoth Visitor Center, Grant Village Visitor Center, Lake Ranger Station, and Lewis Lake Campground. Information centers near Yellowstone Lake are located at Fishing Bridge and Grant Village (both Memorial Day-Labor Day, daily).

At several locations there are visitor centers, general stores for provisions, photo shops, service stations, tent and trailer sites, hotels, and lodges. Bus tours run through the park from mid-June to Labor Day (contact Xanterra Parks and Resorts at 307/344-7311). Cars can be rented in some of the gateway communities.

CCInc Auto Tape Tours offers two 90-minute cassettes that feature a mile-by-mile self-guided tour of the park. Written in cooperation with the National Park Service, it provides information about geology, history, points of interest, and flora and fauna. Tapes can be obtained at gift shops throughout the park. Tapes also may be purchased directly from CCInc, PO Box 227, 2 Elbrook Dr, Allendale, NJ 07401; phone 201/236-1666. $10-$15.

TourGuide Self-Guided Car Audio Tours, are produced in cooperation with the National Park Service. This system uses the random-access capability of CD technology to instantly select narration on topics like wildlife, ecology, safety, history, and folklore. Visitors rent a self-contained player (about the size of a paperback book) that plugs into a car's cigarette lighter and broadcasts an FM signal to its radio. A screen on the unit displays menus of chapters and topics, which may be played in any order for an individualized, narrated auto tour (total running time approximately five hours). Rent a player by contacting Xanterra Parks and Resorts at 301/344-7311. For further information, contact TIS, Inc, 1018 Burlington Ave, Suite 101, Missoula, MT 59801; phone 406/549-3800 or toll-free 800/247-1213. Per day. Over $15.

The official park season is May 1-October 31. However, Highway 212 from Red Lodge, Montana, to Cooke City, Montana (outside the northeast entrance), is not open to automobiles until about May 30 and closes about October 1. In winter, roads from Gardiner to Mammoth Hot Springs and to Cooke

Snowmobiling in and around Yellowstone

Once synonymous with winter in Yellowstone, snowmobiling in the park has recently become the focal point of continually evolving environmental policies. For years, use of the machines has been a controversial, divisive issue in the park and the gateway communities.

A study in the late 1990s concluded that the pollution from the snowmobiles—both in terms of carbon monoxide and noise—were negatively impacting the parks wildlife.

Regardless of the park's snowmobile policy, Yellowstone is a fantastic, frigid wonderland in the wintertime. As most roads, hotels, and campgrounds are closed, traffic is lighter, and cold and snow drive wildlife to lower elevations, making them easier to spot. The steaming thermal features are especially impressive in this icy landscape. And snowcoach tours and ski outings are attractive alternatives to straddling a noisy snowmobile.

The only roads that are open to cars during winter run from Gardiner, Montana, south to Mammoth Hot Springs and east to Cooke City, Montana; lodging is only available in Mammoth and Old Faithful. However, all paved roads are open to over-snow vehicles—snowmobiles (for now) and snowcoaches—from mid-December into March.

The current guidelines call for a daily quota of snowmobiles at each entrance and a licensed guide to lead all snowmobile expeditions. A list of licensed guides, as well as cross-country ski and snowcoach operations, is available at the Yellowstone Web site (www.nps.gov/yell).

While snowmobiles are likely on their way out in Yellowstone, the surrounding forests are an attractive alternative. In particular, the Gallatin National Forest (phone 406/522-2520) is crisscrossed by miles of snowmobile trails, and it will likely become the areas prime snowmobiling destination in the event of an outright ban in the park. West Yellowstone, Montana, has the highest concentration of rental operations and excellent access to trails into both Yellowstone and the Gallatin National Forest.

To the south, in and around Grand Teton National Park, the groomed Continental Divide Snowmobile Trail connects the Togwotee Pass area with Yellowstone, but the trails in-park stretch could well be closed to snowmobiles in coming winters. However, since the trail starts to the southeast of the park, the area will undoubtedly remain a snowmobiling destination. There are hundreds of miles of trails in the Bridger-Teton National Forest and especially near the towns of Lander, Pinedale, and Dubois.

Yellowstone Association Institute

With its steaming geysers, healing forests, and abundant wildlife, the country's first national park begs for a bit of interpretation. In response, the Yellowstone Association Institute presents a predominately adult-oriented curriculum that runs the gamut from wolf-watching to fly-fishing, educating more than 1,000 students annually. Courses are held in both winter and summer with a heavy emphasis on the 'Leave No Trace' philosophy.

The annual course catalog includes more than 400 classes, including courses on wildlife biology, geology, history, arts, and recreation. A few of them are one-day classes, but serious adventurers can embark with instructors on multi-day backcountry

adventures that delve into the ecology of wolves or bears. The Web site (www.yellowstoneassociation. org/institute) features an online catalog.

While Yellowstone's 2.4 million acres serve as a nifty extension, the Institutes main campus, nicknamed "The Serengeti of North America" for its diversity of wildlife, is at the Lamar Buffalo Ranch in the Lamar Valley. After bullets and exotic diseases decimated the iconic beasts in the 19th century, the National Park Service domesticated 28 of the park's few remaining bison at the ranch in 1907. Yellowstones buffalo prospered under the sponsorship of Homo sapiens: The original 28 boomed into a self-sustaining population by the time the ranch hands left the picture in 1952. Today, about 4,000 bison roam the park, a living legacy of the old ranch.

In 1979, the non-profit Yellowstone Association adopted the ranch as a campus for its field studies program, now known as the Yellowstone Association Institute. The cynical image of a modern Yellowstone vacation includes animal-induced traffic jams, throngs of tourists at Old Faithful, and mad dashes from overlook to overlook, but the old Lamar ranch is a hubbub-free zone and a window into the park considerably clearer than a bug-splattered windshield.

The institute's tuition fees are very democratic: about $70 per day. A cot in a cabin runs about $25 a night, and students and staff share a well-equipped kitchen in the bunkhouse. There are 16 basic guest cabins at the ranch, with three cots to a cabin. The bunkhouse houses two classrooms, a common kitchen, and three bathrooms (with showers).

There is a definite sense of community at the old buffalo ranch, and the kitchen is its social hub. Meals are serve-yourself; guests supply their own food, which they are able to store in the fridge (one bin and one shelf per guest).

The Lamar ranch is also a study in sustainable living. It has its own well and septic system. A system comprised of two banks of solar panels and a pair of propane generators provides the electricity. Aside from a phone line, the campus is entirely off the grid.

Several institute courses are done in conjunction with Xanterra, Yellowstone's primary concessionaire. Guests spend nights at the park's historic lodges and hotels while taking an instructor-led class during the days. (See www.travelyellowstone.com or call 307/344-7311 for more information.) Custom outings are also available. For additional information, contact the Yellowstone Association Institute (PO Box 117, Yellowstone National Park, WY 82190, phone 307/344-2294).

Cheyenne grew up with the arrival of the railroad in 1867—going from a population of zero to three thousand in five months. By 1880, 10,000 people made their home here. This rapid growth produced an unusual unity of architectural design. Cheyenne has one of the best-preserved frontier town centers in Wyoming.

Begin a walking tour at the Wyoming Transportation Museum, 15th Street and Capitol Avenue. Formerly the depot for the Union Pacific Railway, this massive structure of stone and brick surmounted by a bell tower, was built in 1886. The building now serves as a railway museum.

Walk north to 16th Street, the city's main street during the frontier era. Many of the handsome redbrick storefronts from the 1880s are still in use. Stop by the Old Town Square, a pedestrian-friendly, two-block area with boutique shopping and reenactments of Old West activities, including a nightly shoot-out with gunslingers in period garb. The Cheyenne Visitors and Convention Bureau is adjacent to the square at 309 West 16th Street.

At the corner of 16th Street and Central Avenue is the Historic Plains Hotel (1600 Central Ave). Built in 1910, this grand old hotel has a wonderfully atmospheric lobby and one of the oldest restaurants and bars in the state. The Plains is a favorite watering hole for Wyoming's political movers and shakers.

Walk up Capitol Avenue, past opulent, late-Victorian state office buildings and storefronts, with the state capitol building looming in the distance. Turn on 17th Street, and walk east to Lexies Café (216 E 17th), a Cheyenne dining institution. This period restaurant is located in the city's oldest structure, the luxurious 1880s home of Erasmus Nagle. In summer, there's al fresco dining against the backdrop of the town's historic district.

Continue north along House Street, past more historic homes, to the Historic Governor's Mansion (200 E 21st St). Built in 1904, this beautifully preserved sandstone structure was the home of Wyoming's governors until 1977. Today, free tours of the building focus on period furnishings and artifacts.

Head west on 23rd Avenue. The Wyoming State Museum (2301 Central Ave), is the states foremost history museum, telling Wyoming's story from the era of the dinosaurs to the present, with especially good exhibits on the state's Native American and early settlement history. The museum also houses

City, Montana, are kept open, but the road from Red Lodge is closed; travelers must return to Gardiner to leave the park. The West, East, and South Entrances are closed to automobiles from November 1 to about May 1, but are open to oversnow vehicles from mid-December to mid-March. Dates are subject to change. For current road conditions and other information, phone park headquarters at 307/344-7381. Entrance permit, $20 per vehicle per visit, good for seven days to Yellowstone and Grand Teton.

Note: Weather conditions or conservation measures may dictate the closing of certain roads and recreational facilities. In winter, inquire before attempting to enter the park.

Limited-Service Hotels

★ ★ **GRANT VILLAGE.** *Phone 307/344-7311; fax 307/344-7456. www.travelyellowstone.com.* 300 rooms. Check-in 4 pm, check-out 11 am. Two restaurants, bar. **$**

★ ★ **LAKE YELLOWSTONE HOTEL.** *Yellowstone National Park (82190). Phone 307/344-7311; fax 307/242-3707. www.travelyellowstone.com.* Overlooks Yellowstone Lake. This beautiful lakeside retreat, with cozy guest rooms, was built in 1891. 158 rooms. Closed mid-Oct-late May. Check-in 3 pm, check-out 11 am. Restaurant, bar. **$$**

★ ★ **OLD FAITHFUL INN.** *Phone 307/344-7311; fax 307/344-7456. www.travelyellowstone.com.* Some rooms have views of Old Faithful. Historic log structure built in 1904. 325 rooms, 4 story. Closed mid-Oct-early May. Check-out 11 am. Restaurants, bar. **$$**
🖻

★ ★ **OLD FAITHFUL SNOW LODGE.** *Phone 307/344-7311; fax 307/344-7456. www.travelyellowstone.com.* 95 rooms. Closed mid-Oct-mid-Dec and mid-Mar-early May. Check-out 11 am. Two restaurants, bar. **$$**
🖻

Restaurant

★ ★ **LAKE YELLOWSTONE DINING ROOM.** *Hwy 89, Yellowstone National Park (82190). Phone 307/344-7311. www.ynp-lodges.com.* American, seafood menu. Breakfast, lunch, dinner. Closed Oct-May. Bar. Children's menu. **$$**

Index

Chain Restaurants

Montana

Billings

Golden Corral, 570 S 24th St W, Billings, MT, 59102, (406) 655-4453, 11 am- 9 pm

Godfather's Pizza, 503 24th St W, Billings, MT, 59102, (406) 652-3150

Godfather's Pizza, 905 Main St, Billings, MT, 59105, (406) 252-0865

Cracker Barrel, 5620 S Frontage Rd, Billings, MT, 59101, (406) 254-9403, 6 am- 10 pm

Fuddruckers, Homestead Business Park 2011 Overland Ave, Billings, MT, 59106, 11 am- 9 pm

Fuddruckers, 300 S 24th St West, Billings , MT, 59102, 11 am- 9 pm

Fuddruckers, 875 Main St, Billings, MT, 59105, 11 am- 9 pm

Bozeman

Fuddruckers, 2905 W Main St, Bozeman, MT, 59718, 11 am- 9 pm

Great Falls

Tony Roma's, 1400 Market Pl Dr, Great Falls, MT, 59404, (406) 727-7427, 11 am- 10 pm

Golden Corral, 1624 Market Pl Dr, Great Falls, MT, 59404, (406) 453-3500, 11 am- 9 pm

Godfather's Pizza, 1300 10th Ave S, Great Falls, MT, 59405, (406) 761-7722

Fuddruckers, 3315 10th Ave South, Great Falls, MT, 59405, 11 am- 9 pm

Helena

Golden Corral, 2910 Prospect Ave, Helena, MT, 59601, (406) 442-8725, 11 am- 9 pm

Godfather's Pizza, 2216 N Montana Ave, Helena, MT, 59601, (406) 443-7050,

Kalispell

Sizzler, 1250 Hwy 2 W, Kalispell, MT, 59901, (406) 257-9555, 11 am- 10 pm

Missoula

Fuddruckers, 2805 N Reserve, Missoula, MT, 59808, 11 am- 9 pm

Fuddruckers, Southgate Mall, 2901 Brooks, Missoula, MT, 59803, 11 am- 9 pm

Cracker Barrel, 2929 Expo Pkwy, Missoula, MT, 59808, (406) 721-9820, 6 am- 10 pm

North Dakota

Bismarck

The Ground Round, 526 S 3rd, Bismarck, ND, 58504, (701) 223-0000, 11 am- 11 pm

Cracker Barrel, 1685 N Grandview Ln, Bismarck, ND, 58501, (701) 223-2785, 6 am- 10 pm

Big Boy, 413 Shirley St, Bismarck, ND, 58504, (701) 258-4125, 6:30 am- 10 pm

Fargo

Village Inn, 3140 25th St S, Fargo, ND, 58103, (701) 232-9233, 11 am- 10 pm

The Ground Round, 2902 13th Ave S, Fargo, ND, 58103, (701) 280-2288, 11 am- 11 pm

Hooters, 1649 38th St S, Fargo, ND, 58107, (701) 281-8302, 11 am- midnight

Godfather's Pizza, 4340 13th Ave SW, Ste A, Fargo, ND, 58103, (701) 277-1666

Chili's, 4000 13th Ave SW, Fargo, ND, 58103, (701) 282-2669, 11 am- 10 pm

Grand Forks

Village Inn, 3951 32nd Ave S, Grand Forks, ND, 58201, (701) 772-7241, 7 am- midnight

The Ground Round, 2800 32nd Ave S, Grand Forks, ND, 58201, (701) 775-4646, 11 am- 11 pm

Minot

The Ground Round, 2110 Burdick Exp, Minot, ND, 58701, (701) 838-3500, 11 am- 11 pm

Wahpeton

Godfather's Pizza, 809 Dakota Ave, Wahpeton, ND, 58075, (701) 642-6242

West Fargo

Uno Chicago Grill, 1660 13th Ave East, West Fargo, ND, 58078, (701) 478-8667, 11 am- 12:30 am

South Dakota

Brookings

Godfather's Pizza, 610 Medary Ave, Brookings, SD, 57006, (605) 692-9700

Harrisburg

Godfather's Pizza, 315 Willow St, Harrisburg, SD, 57032, (605) 767-1527

Huron

Godfather's Pizza, 195 21st St SW, Huron, SD, 57350, (605) 352-6925

Mitchell

Godfather's Pizza, 1109 N Main, Mitchell, SD, 57301, (605) 996-2300

Parker

Godfather's Pizza, 27600 S Dakota Hwy 19, Parker, SD, 57053, (605) 297-2297

Rapid City

Golden Corral, 1180 N Lacrosse St, Rapid City, SD, 57701, (605) 399-2195, 11 am- 9 pm

Godfather's Pizza, 110 Campbell St, Rapid City, SD, 57701, (605) 342-0212

Fuddruckers, 2200 N Maple, Rapid City, SD, 57701, 11 am- 9 pm

Chili's, 2125 Haines Ave, Rapid City, SD, 57701, (605) 388-8100, 11 am- 10 pm

Sioux Falls

The Ground Round, 1301 W 41st St, Sioux Falls, SD, 57105, (605) 334-8995, 11 am- 11 pm

Godfather's Pizza, 5107 W 41st St, Sioux Falls, SD, 57106, (605) 361-8029

Godfather's Pizza, 200 S Kiwanis Ave, Sioux Falls, SD, 57104, (605) 334-5050

Godfather's Pizza, 2331 E 10th St, Sioux Falls, SD, 57103, (605) 338-5225

Fuddruckers, 3101 W 41st St, Sioux Falls, SD, 57105, 11 am- 9 pm

Cracker Barrel, 2409 S Shirley Ave, Sioux Falls, SD, 57106, (605) 362-9395, 6 am- 10 pm

CiCi's Pizza, 5007 S Louise Ave, Sioux Falls, SD, 57103, (605) 362-9900, 11 am- 9 pm

Chili's, 3720 W 41st St, Sioux Falls, SD, 57106, (605) 361-3900, 11 am- 10 pm

Chevy's, 2801 S Louise Ave, Sioux Falls, SD, 57106, (605) 362-2610, 11 am- 10 pm

Watertown

Godfather's Pizza, Watertown Mall, Watertown, SD, 57201, (605) 882-1232

Yankton

Godfather's Pizza, 2101 BRdway, Yankton, SD, 57078, (605) 665-2525

Wyoming

Casper

Village Inn, 325 So Durbin St, Casper, WY, 82601, (307) 234-1614, 7 am- midnight

Village Inn, 350 SE Wyoming Blvd, Casper, WY, 82609, (307) 234-1485, 7 am- midnight

Hometown Buffet, 601 Wyoming Blvd, Casper, WY, 82609, (307) 577-5953, 11 am- 8:30 pm

Godfather's Pizza, 2877 E 2nd St, Casper, WY, 82609, (307) 265-1221

Cheyenne

Village Inn, 411 E 16th St, Cheyenne, WY, 82001, (307) 638-3107, 7 am- midnight

Village Inn, 2414 W Lincoln Way, Cheyenne, WY, 82001, (307) 637-0414, 7 am- midnight

Old Country Buffet, Frontier Mall, 1400 Dell Range Rd, Cheyenne, WY, 82009, (307) 637-5906, 11 am- 9 pm

Godfather's Pizza, 5719 Yellowstone Rd, Cheyenne, WY, 82009, (307) 634-5222

Chili's, 1320 Del Range Blvd, Cheyenne, WY, 82009, (307) 635-1224, 11 am- 10 pm

Douglas

Village Inn, 1840 Richards, Douglas, WY, 82633, (307) 358-5600, 7 am- midnight

Gillette

Village Inn, 806 E Second St, Gillette, WY, 82716, (307) 682-8823, 7 am- midnight

Golden Corral, 2700 S Douglas Hwy, Gillette, WY, 82718, (307) 682-9130, 11 am- 9 pm

Godfather's Pizza, 501 W Lakeway, Gillette, WY, 82718, (307) 686-7777

Jackson

Village Inn, 100 S Flat Creek Dr (Box 4831), Jackson, WY, 83001, (307) 733-2171, 7 am- midnight

Laramie

Village Inn, 3225 Grand Ave, Laramie, WY, 82070, (307) 745-5311, 7 am- midnight

Godfather's Pizza, 3236 Grand Ave, Laramie, WY, 82070, (307) 742-8293

Riverton

Golden Corral, 400 N Federal Blvd, Riverton, WY, 82501, (307) 856-1152, 11 am- 9 pm

Rock Springs

Village Inn, 2028 Dewar Dr, Rock Springs, WY, 82901, (307) 362-1205, 7 am- midnight

Golden Corral, 1990 Dewar Dr, Rock Springs, WY, 82901, (307) 362-7234, 11 am- 9 pm

Notes

Notes

Notes

Notes

Notes

Notes

Notes